US AGAINST THEM

CHICAGO STUDIES IN AMERICAN POLITICS

A series edited by Benjamin I. Page, Susan Herbst, Lawrence R. Jacobs, and James Druckman

Also in the series:

In Time of War: Understanding American Public Opinion from World War II to Iraq
by Adam J. Berinsky

The Partisan Sort: How Liberals Became Democrats and Conservatives Became Republicans
by Matthew Levendusky

Democracy at Risk: How Terrorist Threats Affect the Public
by Jennifer L. Merolla and Elizabeth J. Zechmeister

Agendas and Instability in American Politics, Second Edition
by Frank R. Baumgartner and Bryan D. Jones

The Private Abuse of the Public Interest
by Lawrence D. Brown and Lawrence R. Jacobs

The Party Decides: Presidential Nominations Before and After Reform
by Marty Cohen, David Karol, Hans Noel, and John Zaller

Same Sex, Different Politics: Success and Failure in the Struggles over Gay Rights
by Gary Mucciaroni

US against THEM

Ethnocentric Foundations of American Opinion

DONALD R. KINDER & CINDY D. KAM

THE UNIVERSITY OF CHICAGO PRESS   Chicago and London

DONALD R. KINDER is the Philip E. Converse Collegiate Professor in the Department of Political Science at the University of Michigan, as well as a professor of psychology and a research professor in the Center for Political Studies of the Institute for Social Research. His previous books include *News That Matters: Television and American Opinion* (with Shanto Iyengar) and *Divided by Color: Racial Politics and Democratic Ideals* (with Lynn Sanders), both published by the University of Chicago Press.

CINDY D. KAM is associate professor of political science at Vanderbilt University. She is the author, with Robert J. Franzese Jr., of *Modeling and Interpreting Interactive Hypotheses in Regression Analysis.*

The University of Chicago Press, Chicago 60637
The University of Chicago Press, Ltd., London
© 2009 by The University of Chicago
All rights reserved. Published 2009
Printed in the United States of America

18 17 16 15 14 13 12 11 10 09   1 2 3 4 5

ISBN-13: 978-0-226-43570-1 (cloth)
ISBN-13: 978-0-226-43571-8 (paper)
ISBN-10: 0-226-43570-9 (cloth)
ISBN-10: 0-226-43571-7 (paper)

Library of Congress Cataloging-in-Publication Data
Kinder, Donald R.
    Us against them : ethnocentric foundations of American opinion / Donald R. Kinder & Cindy D. Kam.
        p. cm.—(Chicago studies in American politics)
    Includes bibliographical references and index.
    ISBN-13: 978-0-226-43570-1 (hardcover : alk. paper)
    ISBN-13: 978-0-226-43571-8 (pbk. : alk. paper)
    ISBN-10: 0-226-43571-9 (hardcover : alk. paper)
    ISBN-10: 0-226-43571-7 (pbk. : alk. paper) 1. Ethnocentrism—United States. 2. Public opinion—United States. 3. Social values—United States. 4. Americans—Attitudes. 5. Social psychology—United States. 6. United States—Public opinion. 7. United States—Social life and customs. I. Kam, Cindy D., 1975– II. Title. III. Series: Chicago studies in American politics.
    GN560.U6K56 2009
    305.800973—dc22

                                                        2009026115

♾ The paper used in this publication meets the minimum requirements of the American National Standard for Information Sciences—Permanence of Paper for Printed Library Materials, ANSI Z39.48-1992.

Contents

Preface   vii

Introduction: Sumner's Conjecture   1

I   THE NATURE OF ETHNOCENTRISM   5
1   Four Theories in Search of Ethnocentrism   7
2   Ethnocentrism Reconceived   31
3   American Ethnocentrism Today   42

II   EMPIRICAL CASES   71
4   Enemies Abroad   73
5   America First   105
6   Strangers in the Land   125
7   Straight versus Gay   151
8   Women's Place   172
9   Us versus Them in the American Welfare State   182
10   Ethnocentrism in Black and White   200

Conclusion: Ethnocentrism and Political Life   219

Appendix   237
Notes   245
References   315
Index   345

Preface

This book began, as perhaps many books do, in dereliction of duty. Kinder was spending the academic year 1994–95 on leave at Stanford University. Freed from administrative and teaching responsibilities at the University of Michigan, Kinder's one assignment for the year was to complete a chapter for the fourth edition of *The Handbook of Social Psychology*. He did not. (Eventually he did—very eventually; Kinder thanks, one more time, Daniel Gilbert, Susan Fiske, and Gardner Lindzey, the editors of the *Handbook*, for their patience.) Instead, Kinder spent the fall rummaging through Stanford's libraries, reading up on the subject of ethnocentrism.

The subject was of interest, at least to Kinder, because of a puzzling result he was about to report with Lynn Sanders in their book, *Divided by Color* (1996). The puzzling result was this: the resentment some white Americans feel toward black Americans figures heavily into their views, not just on affirmative action or school desegregation, but on welfare reform, capital punishment, urban unrest, family leave, sexual harassment, gay rights, immigration, spending on defense, and more. In assessing resentments directed specifically at black Americans, Kinder and Sanders seem to have tapped into a broader hostility, one that might be called ethnocentric.

And so Kinder spent the fall of 1994 reading: William Graham Sumner, who introduced the term *ethnocentrism* in the early years of the twentieth century in his famous book on folkways, T. W. Adorno and his colleagues' epic study of the authoritarian personality and the immense and sprawling literature it inspired, Henri Tajfel and the European perspective on identity and conflict, and much more besides. He then spent the winter (insofar as Palo Alto can be said to have a winter) writing. He returned to Ann Arbor with preliminary drafts of the first four chapters of what would become *Us Against Them*—an argument without evidence, one could say.

The argument was an effort to rehabilitate the concept of ethnocentrism, to suggest that something like ethnocentrism—a deep human predisposition to reduce all of social life to in-groups and out-groups—was an important (if unacknowledged) engine of contemporary American politics. The plan (let's pretend there was a plan) was to see if there was any merit to this argument by taking up empirical cases, one by one. Back in Ann Arbor, Kinder was working with a group of enormously talented graduate students: Lisa D'Ambrosio, Claudia Deane, Kim Gross, Tali Mendelberg, and Karin Tamerius. The group discussed, expanded on, and criticized what Kinder had written. The group began to produce conference papers that applied the argument to particular cases. Production was slow but steady. Well, it was slow. Slow but intellectually rewarding: ethnocentrism did indeed seem to be playing an important role in American public opinion across a set of distinct cases.

As others went on with their lives—dissertations, families, and careers— Kinder plowed ahead and was joined on the project by Kam in 1998. We thought seriously about the measurement and origins of ethnocentrism. We wrote three more conference papers, one on welfare reform, a second on the war on terrorism, and a third on morality politics. We combed through existing datasets to find additional test cases and to replicate our analyses wherever possible. We added a key piece to our argument, attempting to specify the conditions under which ethnocentrism would be more or less important in politics. In time, we found ourselves with both a compelling argument *and* a generous supply of evidence. We now felt confident that we had the materials for a book. But then disaster struck: Kinder became chair of his department, and Kam found herself awash in the responsibilities that rain down on an assistant professor. Somehow or another, eventually we prevailed.

*   *   *

Collaborations are almost never easy, and rarely are they fun. Ours was different. Easy, fun, and productive, all three. We like each other more now than when we started. We hope to find something else to work on together. First of all, we thank each other.

We are grateful as well to the aforementioned Lisa D'Ambrosio, Claudia Deane, Kim Gross, Tali Mendelberg, and Karin Tamerius for their advice and assistance in the early stages. Others helped in various ways: Katherine Drake at Michigan, and Carl Palmer and Sara Price at the University of California at Davis. Generous support came from the National Science Foundation (in the form of a Graduate Research Fellowship for Kam) and from UC Davis and Vanderbilt University. Over the life of the project, we gave papers and seminars at the American Political Science Association, the Midwest Political Science Association, UC Davis, the University of Michigan, and Stanford University. We had productive conversations with Nancy Burns, Philip Converse, Richard Hall, Hazel Markus, Lee Ross, Lance

Sandelands, David Sloan Wilson, Abby Stewart, and David Winter. We benefited enormously from close readings provided by Nancy Burns and Janet Weiss, as well as by the reviewers for the University of Chicago Press, who raised hard questions and offered us bracing advice, much of which we took. At the Press we thank Ben Page, series editor, and John Tryneski, editor supremo, for their patience and careful stewarding of our manuscript.

The book is dedicated to Benjamin (Jordan Weiss Kinder), Samuel (David Kinder Weiss), and Jacob (Russell Weiss Kinder), from whom Kinder has learned so much, and to Rob and Charlotte Mikos.

Sumner's Conjecture

Ethnocentrism is an ancient phenomenon but it is a modern word, invented at the opening of the twentieth century by William Graham Sumner, an eminent professor of political and social science at Yale. Sumner believed in the possibility of a comprehensive science of society—and was sure he was the one to supply it. He started in on his audacious project with what was intended to be an introductory essay on social norms. When, however, the chapter exceeded six hundred pages, Sumner surrendered to the advice of friends and permitted it to be published separately. *Folkways (A Study of the Sociological Importance of Usages, Manners, Customs, Mores, and Morals)* appeared in 1906 and shortly became, as it should have, a famous book.[1]

Sumner regarded "folkways" to be the "most fundamental, and most important operations by which the interests of men in groups are served" ([1906] 2002, p. 34). The very life of society consists, Sumner wrote, "in making folkways and applying them" ([1906] 2002, p. 34). Handed down from one generation to the next, embedded in practice and in belief, folkways covered virtually all aspects of social life. As Sumner put it,

> all the life of human beings, in all ages and stages of culture, is primarily controlled by a vast mass of folkways handed down from the earliest existence of the race. . . . There is a right way to catch game, to win a wife, to make one's self appear, to cure disease, to honor ghosts, to treat comrades or strangers, to behave when a child is born, on the warpath, in council, and so on in all cases which can arise. ([1906] 2002, pp. 4, 28)

Such "right ways" might differ enormously from one group to the next. Sumner's bold conjecture was that in every instance, for every folkway, members of a group were certain that their way of doing things—their folkways—were superior to the way things were done by others. *Ethnocentrism*, Sumner called it: the "technical name for this view of things in which one's own group is the center of everything" ([1906] 2002, p. 13):

Each group nourishes its own pride and vanity, boasts itself superior, ex-
alts its own divinities, and looks with contempt on outsiders. Each group
thinks its own folkways the only right ones, and if it observes that other
groups have other folkways, these excite its scorn. Opprobrious epithets
are derived from these differences. "Pig-eater," "cow-eater," "uncir-
cumcised," "jabberers," are epithets of contempt and abomination. . . .
[E]thnocentrism leads a people to exaggerate and intensify everything in
their own folkways which is peculiar and which differentiates them from
others. ([1906] 2002, p. 13)

Sumner was convinced that ethnocentrism was a universal feature of
human society. For proof, he cited Euripides, "common knowledge," and a
dozen or so ethnographies supplied by the anthropology of the day. From
Sumner, we learn that the indigenous people of Greenland believed that
Europeans had appeared on their homeland to be taught the good manners that they so conspicuously lacked; that the Mbayas of South America
presumed that the taking of wives and property from their neighbors was
divinely authorized; that people of true distinction arise only from the
grand and glorious Middle Kingdom, according to the Chinese; and so on.
More recent and systematic surveys generally support Sumner's conjecture.
When referring to outsiders, human populations resort easily and readily to
terms of contempt and condescension. Around the world, ethnocentrism
prevails.[2]

But if ethnocentrism itself is ubiquitous—if, as John Higham ([1955]
1988, p. 3) declares, "no age or society seems wholly free from unfavorable
opinions on outsiders"—ethnocentrism as a concept in political analysis is,
strangely, all but invisible. With a few notable exceptions, ethnocentrism is
hard to find in contemporary social science theorizing, and it is especially
hard to find in empirical studies of American public opinion of the sort that
we are about to report on here.[3] We think this is a mistake, one we intend
to correct. Our primary purpose is to demonstrate that ethnocentrism plays
an important role in contemporary American public opinion. On the issues
that animate the politics of our time—peace and security, immigration and
citizenship, poverty and inequality, and more—American opinion cannot
be fully understood, we say, without bringing ethnocentrism into account.

But really: ethnocentrism in *American* society? Conflict and violence organized by ethnicity and religion have become a common occurrence in the
postcolonial world, and we would not have to go very far out on a limb to suppose that such strife draws in part on ethnocentric motives. Ethnocentrism
may have a role to play in the Balkans or in Darfur, but does it operate in the
United States, itself a nation of immigrants, and the richest, best-educated,
and most durable democracy in the world? We aim to show that it does.

We should say that our interest lies not so much in ethnocentrism per se but in ethnocentrism's political expression. Following Gordon Allport, we acknowledge that from "the point of view of social consequences, much 'polite prejudice' is harmless enough—being confined to idle chatter" (1954, p. 15). Our concern here is with matters of real social consequence. We seek to show how ethnocentrism affects public opinion; contributes to processes of public discussion and deliberation that Mill, Hamilton, and others placed at the center of democratic politics; and, ultimately, gives shape and direction to government action and public policy.

WHAT LIES AHEAD

We begin in chapter 1 by scrutinizing four theories that claim to speak to ethnocentrism. The first treats ethnocentrism as the consequence of inter-group conflict. The second locates ethnocentrism in the psychodynamic processes of repression, projection, and displacement. The third claims that ethnocentrism arises out of a universal yearning for self-regard. And the fourth sees ethnocentrism as a biological adaptation, an aspect of human nature. Each of the four, we conclude, provides a valuable but partial picture of our subject.

Building on this work, the business of chapter 2 is to construct a more satisfactory theoretical framework. In the process, we grapple with three essential questions: What is the nature of ethnocentrism? How does ethnocentrism arise? And when does ethnocentrism become important to American public opinion?

With our framework established, we then proceed in chapter 3 to introduce and defend a particular way of measuring ethnocentrism. We show that ethnocentrism is pervasive in American society today. We demonstrate that ethnocentrism is distinct from political predispositions that are standard fixtures in contemporary accounts of public opinion. And we explain why some Americans are more ethnocentric than others.

Then, in the heart of the book, we apply our theoretical framework to a series of diverse cases. The power of ethnocentrism lies in its wide reach. If, as we will argue, ethnocentrism is a general predisposition, we should be able to detect its effects across political disputes that are in other respects very different from one another. And we do. Ethnocentrism plays an important part in American opinion in distinctly different domains: the war on terrorism, humanitarian assistance to foreign lands, immigration and citizenship, the sanctity of marriage, Social Security and welfare reform, and school desegregation and affirmative action. Taken together, the evidence accumulated over these very different cases establishes the importance of ethnocentrism to American public opinion.

Ethnocentrism is a deep and perhaps even irresistible human habit. But this does not mean that ethnocentrism is an inevitable feature of political life. To the contrary, we argue that the part played by ethnocentrism in politics depends on circumstances: on the ability of issues to command the public's attention and on the resonance between the issues playing out on the center stage of politics, on the one hand, and ethnocentrism, on the other. We develop this argument in chapter 2, and then we test it, whenever possible, as we proceed through the empirical cases, from protecting the homeland in chapter 4 through race-conscious policies in chapter 10.

We draw all of these various results together and explore their implications in the book's conclusion. There we take up, in turn, the surprising relationship between ethnocentrism and knowledge; the issue of demarcating where ethnocentrism matters and where it does not; the prospects for cosmopolitanism considered as a counterweight to ethnocentrism; the likelihood of ethnocentrism operating politically in places other than the United States; and finally, the implications of ethnocentrism for the character and quality of democratic politics.

But this discussion lies a fair ways ahead. We begin our journey in chapter 1, by taking up ethnocentrism and examining it from four distinct points of view.

The Nature
of Ethnocentrism

CHAPTER 1

Four Theories in Search of Ethnocentrism

What is the nature of ethnocentrism? How does ethnocentrism arise? And when—under what conditions—does ethnocentrism become important to politics? An adequate theory of ethnocentrism must provide convincing answers to all three questions: nature, origins, and consequences.

With this obligation in mind, our principal business in this chapter is to work through the major theories that claim to speak directly to ethnocentrism. In the pages ahead, we examine ethnocentrism from four distinct theoretical perspectives:

- Ethnocentrism as a consequence of realistic group conflict
- Ethnocentrism as an outgrowth of the authoritarian personality
- Ethnocentrism as an expression of social identity
- Ethnocentrism as an outcome of natural selection

As we will see, no single theory supplies completely satisfying answers to all three questions. Each, however, offers valuable insights, lessons for us to carry forward. Grappling with these alternative points of view here will pave the way to a more adequate theoretical framework for ethnocentrism, which we develop in chapter 2. To arrive at this better understanding of ethnocentrism today, we turn to the past, to traditions of explanation associated with William Graham Sumner, Daniel Levinson, Henri Tajfel, and Edward O. Wilson.

ETHNOCENTRISM DEFINED

But first a few words about ethnocentrism itself. Without a clear conception of our object of study, we could find ourselves in the unfortunate position of the Javanese folktale figure "Stupid Boy," who, as Clifford Geertz tells the tale, "having been counseled by his mother to seek a quiet wife, returned with a corpse." A corpse makes a quiet wife, all right, but surely this was not what mother had in mind.[1] Let's try to do better. When we say that ethnocentrism plays an important role in American public opinion, just what is it that we are arguing for?

Ethnocentrism is a mental habit. It is a predisposition to divide the human world into in-groups and out-groups. It is a readiness to reduce society to us and them. Or rather, it is a readiness to reduce society to us *versus* them. This division of humankind into in-group and out-group is not innocuous. Members of in-groups (until they prove otherwise) are assumed to be virtuous: friendly, cooperative, trustworthy, safe, and more. Members of out-groups (until they prove otherwise) are assumed to be the opposite: unfriendly, uncooperative, unworthy of trust, dangerous, and more. Symbols and practices become objects of attachment and pride when they belong to the in-group and objects of condescension, disdain, and (in extreme cases) hatred when they belong to out-groups. Ethnocentrism constitutes a readiness to act in favor of in-groups and in opposition to out-groups; it charts a safe path through a social world that may seem uncomfortable, difficult, and, at times, perilous.[2]

People differ—reliably and stably—in the degree to which they see the social world this way. At least since Darwin, it has been axiomatic in the biological sciences to regard living organisms not as constant classes but as variable populations. This point applies to barnacles and to human beings alike. People vary from one another in all sorts of ways: height, color, sociability, intelligence, and more—including ethnocentrism.

People vary from one another *incrementally*. It would be a mistake to conceive of ethnocentrism as a type and to assume that people either are ethnocentric or that they are not. People are more or less ethnocentric. They vary in the degree to which they reduce the social world to in-groups and out-groups, to us and them. Ethnocentrism is a quantity, not a kind.[3]

Ethnocentrism should not be interpreted as irrational, the twisted expression of repressed hostilities and primeval fears. Ethnocentrism is not a sickness. We do not require a therapist's technique to reveal it or psychodynamic processes to explain it. Ethnocentrism is normal. It is, one might say, a "natural" way to look upon the social world.

Finally, ethnocentrism is a *general* predisposition. It is in this respect that ethnocentrism differs from prejudice. In contrast to prejudice, ethnocentrism "has to do not only with numerous groups toward which the individual has hostile opinions and attitudes but, equally important, with groups toward which he is positively disposed." Moreover, while prejudice is hostility directed at a specific group, ethnocentrism refers to a "relatively consistent frame of mind concerning 'aliens' generally." Thus when we turn from race prejudice or anti-Semitism or any other particular social animosity, on the one hand, to ethnocentrism, on the other, we come face to face with "prejudice, broadly conceived" (Adorno et al. 1950, p. 102).[4]

ETHNOCENTRISM AS A CONSEQUENCE
OF REALISTIC GROUP CONFLICT

Defined this way, how might ethnocentrism—prejudice, broadly conceived—arise? Looking for answers, let's turn first to William Graham Sumner. As we noted in the introduction, Sumner introduced the term *ethnocentrism* into the social science lexicon. But we turn to him here because he also had interesting things to say about ethnocentrism's origins.

In Sumner's view, ethnocentrism included both in-group solidarity and out-group hostility. The two were connected inextricably. Both, Sumner argued, arose out of conflict, inevitable in a Hobbesian world of scarce resources:

> The insiders in a we-group are in a relation of peace, order, law, government, and industry, to each other. Their relation to all outsiders, or others-groups, is one of war and plunder. . . . Sentiments are produced to correspond. Loyalty to the group, sacrifice for it, hatred and contempt for outsiders, brotherhood within, warlikeness without—all grow together, common products of the same situation. ([1906] 2002, pp. 12–13)

This is Sumner's principal claim—that in-group solidarity *and* out-group hostility grow out of intergroup competition—and it remains a central feature of contemporary versions of realistic group conflict theory. From this perspective, antagonism between groups is rooted in actual conflict. Groups have incompatible goals, and they compete for scarce resources. Conflict is most intense where competition is keenest, where contending groups have the most at stake. In a way that would no doubt earn Sumner's approval, contemporary realistic group conflict theory treats ethnic and racial groups as "vehicles for the pursuit of interest in modern pluralist societies . . . participants in ongoing competition for control of economic, political, and social structures" (Giles and Evans 1986, pp. 470, 471).[5]

Sumner provided abundant examples of ethnocentrism, first in *Folkways* (1906) and then later in *The Science of Society* (Sumner, Keller, and Davie 1927). Of course, establishing that ethnocentrism is commonplace (Sumner was sure that ethnocentrism was universal) is not the same thing as explaining its origins. Was Sumner right to propose that ethnocentrism arises from group conflict?

Let's start with in-group solidarity. Sumner was emphatic that in-group solidarity arises from conflict between groups over scarce resources. In one form or another, this proposition can be found in the writings of Simmel, Marx, Sorel, and Dahrendorf, among others. But is it, as Dahrendorf has written, really a "general law" (1964, p. 58)? No. In *The Functions of Social Conflict* (1956), Coser argued that conflict with outsiders often leads to in-group solidarity, but not invariably. Conflict can also lead to demoralization, and in extreme cases, disintegration. Empirical studies suggest that Coser was correct. Conflict generates in-group solidarity only under certain conditions: when in-group solidarity is above some threshold before threat materializes, when threat is seen as a menace to the entire group, and when authoritative leadership seeks to mobilize solidarity (M. Brewer and Campbell 1976; Sherif et al. 1961; Stein 1976).

What of Sumner's second proposition, that conflict is the primary cause of out-group animosity? It turns out that there is empirical support aplenty for this. Consider, as one example, the remarkable field experiments carried out by Muzafer Sherif. In the most famous of these, Sherif recruited two dozen eleven-year-old boys for what was advertised as a summer camp experience. The boys were carefully screened and were mutually unacquainted. Prior to the experiment, they were randomly assigned to one of two groups and then transported separately to Robbers Cave, a state park in Oklahoma. There each group set about various activities designed to build solidarity. The boys went on hikes together, pitched tents, made meals, and built a rope bridge. All of this took place under the gentle direction and watchful eye of experimental assistants posing as camp counselors, who spent their off hours surreptitiously recording detailed observations of the day's proceedings. During this first stage of the experiment, which lasted one week, the two groups of boys occupied different sites within the park and were kept largely unaware of each other's presence.

During stage two, the Rattlers and the Eagles, as the groups now called themselves, were brought into a relationship of conflict through a series of staged contests. Points were awarded for victories on the athletic field, for the best skit, and for the tidiest cabins. The Rattlers and the Eagles were informed that at the end of their stay, the winning group was to be awarded a trophy and each member of the winning group given a splendid prize. The two groups were now taking their meals together, and at the entrance to the common mess hall the results of the day's competition were ostentatiously displayed and added to the ongoing total.

In short order, the Rattlers and the Eagles began to compete fiercely with one another. They exchanged insults, referring to each other as "rotten pukes" and "dirty bastards." They carried out midnight raids to tear up each other's cabins. They celebrated their victories and rationalized their defeats. They wrestled and fought each other, to the point where counselors had to step in to prevent injury. Sherif had predicted that the experimental creation of conflict would generate out-group hostility, but we suspect that he got rather more than he had bargained for.[6]

Realistic group conflict theory is also supported by the most robust empirical finding in the entire American race relations literature: that of a strong connection between the threat that blacks seem to pose to whites, on the one hand, and the hostility of whites' response, on the other. In *Southern Politics in State and Nation*, V. O. Key showed in masterly detail that politics in the American South through the middle of the twentieth century was most reactionary in the so-called black belt: those regions of the South characterized by rich soil where the plantation economy had flourished and black people lived in concentrated numbers. It was in the black belt where, as Key put it (1949, p. 5), whites possessed "the deepest and most immediate concern with the maintenance of white supremacy." Accordingly, it was within the black belt where support for secession and war was most adamant, where the subsequent drive for black disfranchisement came with greatest force, and where defense of segregation in the 1950s and '60s was most ferocious.[7]

Acknowledging that realistic group conflict theory represents a valuable perspective on social conflict, a major obstacle stands in the way of its application here. Examined closely, realistic group conflict theory has little to say about *generalized* hostility. Why should there be ethnocentrism—prejudice, broadly conceived—in the first place? Hostility directed at a specific group, yes, but hostility in general? Virtually all the empirical support for group conflict theory comes from one group's reaction to the threat posed by one other. In the altogether typical case, realistic group conflict theory takes up pairs of opposing groups: the Rattlers and the Eagles at summer camp, whites and blacks in the American South, and so on. Insofar as ethnocentrism entails hostility directed not at a single out-group but at many out-groups, these applications of realistic group conflict theory, however successful they may be in explaining particular instances of conflict, simply do not speak to ethnocentrism as we conceive it. From the perspective of group conflict theory, generalized prejudice is possible only in the presence of multiple and simultaneous intergroup conflicts. But we are interested in ethnocentrism in precisely this sense. Ethnocentrism is generalized prejudice. If our question is why some people are ethnocentric while others are not, why some but not others are predisposed to take many kinds of difference as warrant for condescension or contempt, then group conflict theory cannot take us very far. More promising, as we are about to see, is the theory of authoritarianism.[8]

ETHNOCENTRISM AS AN OUTGROWTH OF THE AUTHORITARIAN PERSONALITY

Theodor Adorno, Else Frenkel-Brunswik, Daniel Levinson, and Nevitt Sanford, who together produced the monumental study of the authoritarian personality (1950), lived in a more precarious world than did William Graham Sumner. Their study was launched in the early 1940s in the United

States against a backdrop of horrific events: crushing economic depression, cataclysmic war, and the deliberate liquidation of the Jewish population of Europe. Frenkel-Brunswik, one of the principal architects of the study, fled Vienna shortly after Hitler's rise to power. She was Jewish and no doubt knew anti-Semitism well. Little wonder that Adorno and his associates initiated their investigation hoping to illuminate the nature and origins of anti-Semitism and its implications for democratic society. But what began as a study of anti-Semitism ended up as an investigation of the prejudiced personality.

Adorno, Frenkel-Brunswik, Levinson, and Sanford were psychologists by training, and they organized their project around a psychological question: why do some individuals but not others find antidemocratic ideas so appealing? Taking for granted that antidemocratic ideas would be available in any society, they defined their goal to be to identify those who were drawn to antidemocratic ideas, to identify those who were repelled by such ideas, and to explain the difference.[9]

To carry out their project, Adorno's team made use of the new techniques of attitude measurement, in-depth interviewing, and rudimentary statistical analysis—methods that were unavailable to Sumner but were coming to prominence in the social sciences of their day. For theoretical inspiration, they drew primarily on psychodynamic concepts. This meant that Adorno and his colleagues were inclined to see susceptibility to antidemocratic ideas as irrational, an expression of unconscious drives, wishes, and emotional impulses. To understand antidemocratic belief, they urged, look deep into personality; and for evidence, sift through clues offered up by "dreams, fantasies, and misinterpretations of the world" (Adorno et al. 1950, pp. 8–9).

Among various antidemocratic beliefs that they might have examined, the four researchers chose anti-Semitism for their primary exhibit. Levinson took the lead in this portion of the project, and he began by formulating a set of propositions intended to capture the core of contemporary anti-Semitism.[10] He then translated these propositions into plain speech, into statements that ordinary people would recognize and that some might agree with. In final form, the anti-Semitism scale includes such claims as these:

> There are too many Jews in the various federal agencies and bureaus in Washington, and they have too much control over our national policies.

> Persecution of the Jews would be largely eliminated if the Jews would make really sincere efforts to rid themselves of their harmful and offensive faults.

> The trouble with letting Jews into a nice neighborhood is that they gradually give it a typical Jewish atmosphere.

In composing these statements, Levinson tried to avoid extreme anti-Semitism, to soften and partially disguise animosity toward Jewish people and Jewish faith by adding qualifying phrases and an occasional gesture to democratic ideals. As Roger Brown (1965, p. 483) once put it, "Each question has a kind of fair-minded and reasonable veneer. It is sometimes rather difficult to find the sting."[11]

Levinson and his associates administered their scale of garden-variety anti-Semitism to samples of college students, nurses, psychiatric patients, Kiwanis club members, schoolteachers, veterans, union members, and prison inmates. The propositions that make up the scale raise a variety of conceivable objections to Jews, some of them mutually contradictory: for example, that Jews push their way into places they do not belong, that they (at the same time) keep too much to themselves, and that they (nevertheless) must be segregated. Levinson found that people responded to the questions with impressive consistency, as if the questions were about one thing and one thing only. Some people were consistently sympathetic, while others—the majority—were consistently hostile.[12]

Levinson and his colleagues next wondered whether anti-Semitism might be associated with other varieties of prejudice. In taking up this question, the project moved from a particular animosity—anti-Semitism—to a general predisposition—what they called *ethnocentrism*. Levinson and his colleagues, unlike Sumner, were keenly interested in the possibility that some people were more ethnocentric than others. This is our interest as well. People differ from one another in all sorts of ways: height, color, sociability, intelligence, and more—including, we say with Levinson, ethnocentrism.

To see if such a thing as ethnocentrism might exist, Levinson prepared a set of propositions pertaining to a wide array of possible targets: blacks, Japanese Americans, the mentally ill, Filipinos, criminals, European refugees, "foreign ideas," and more. As in the measurement of anti-Semitism, the propositions were written in everyday language, hostility was softened, and the various complaints were phrased in ways that seemed consistent with common sense and democratic values.[13]

Levinson found considerable consistency here as well. Those Americans who insisted that blacks be kept in their place were likely also to express contempt or condescension for criminals, Japanese Americans, conscientious objectors, immigrants, foreign ideas, and all the rest—including Jews. Responses to the anti-Semitism scale and the ethnocentrism scale, Levinson discovered, were highly correlated. He concluded that "it is the total ethnocentric ideology, rather than prejudice against any single group, which requires explanation" (Adorno et al. 1950, p. 122).[14]

If, as Adorno, Frenkel-Brunswik, Levinson, and Sanford say, it is ethnocentrism that requires explanation, how did they explain it? Their first move was to argue that the striking consistency in belief that is the hallmark of ethnocentrism could be accounted for only by some underlying organizing psychological structure. Ethnocentrism could not reflect actual experience, for actual experience is too messy, too variegated, to produce such an integrated, cohesive ideology as ethnocentrism. Anti-Semitism, racism, opposition to immigration, and all the rest must be expressions of a unified and deep psychological force. Underneath ethnocentric ideology, Adorno and his team hoped to prove, was the authoritarian personality.

They began this part of the project by conducting intensive interviews with people who had scored either very high or very low on the ethnocentrism scale. The interviews were both designed and subsequently analyzed from the perspective of psychodynamic theory, and they seemed to reveal psychological inclinations—none of them flattering—that typified the ethnocentric: rigid adherence to traditional values, moralistic condemnation of those who violate convention, readiness to capitulate to established authorities (parents, bosses, "great leaders"), preoccupation with strength and power, disdain for imagination and generosity, cynicism toward human nature, and a conviction that wild and dangerous things go on in the world.

The next step was to formulate propositions to measure each of these psychological inclinations, to capture in questionnaire form the insights of the clinical interviews. According to Levinson and colleagues, this proved simple and straightforward:

> Once a hypothesis had been formulated concerning the way in which some deep-lying trend in the personality might express itself in some opinion or attitude that was dynamically, though not logically, related to prejudice against out-groups, a preliminary sketch for an item was usually not far to seek: a phrase from the daily newspaper, an utterance by an interviewee, a fragment of ordinary conversation was usually ready at hand. (Adorno et al. 1950, p. 225)

Whether or not things went quite this smoothly, the team did succeed in assembling a reliable measure of authoritarianism—the famous F scale (F for fascism).[15] They then proceeded to show that authoritarians—that is, people who scored high on the F scale—were in fact very likely to be both anti-Semitic and ethnocentric. Dislike of Jews, prejudice against blacks, contempt for foreigners, and similar attitudes all seem to arise out of a particular personality type, the authoritarian.

From the perspective of psychodynamic theory, ethnocentrism serves the authoritarian well. Out-groups—Jews, criminals, Japanese Americans—become convenient and safe psychological targets. Through the psychological process of displacement, such groups absorb the hostilities originally provoked by the authoritarian's parents. Through projection, out-groups take on forbidden qualities—unbridled power, liberation from the demands of work, free and easy sex—those things that the authoritarian secretly wants but cannot have. Adorno and his colleagues concluded that "the political, economic, and social convictions of an individual often form a broad and coherent pattern, as if bound together by a 'mentality' or 'spirit,'" which is itself "an expression of deep-lying trends in personality."[16]

When *The Authoritarian Personality* was published, it was greeted with widespread acclaim, and then, in the space of a few years, buried under an avalanche of criticism.[17] Two complaints did most of the damage, and both are highly relevant for what we care about here: the existence of ethnocentrism and its foundations in personality. The first objection concerns sample bias. Because of limitations of funding, Adorno and colleagues were forced to rely on volunteers for their studies, and this they accomplished by working through formal organizations. The almost inevitable result was a sample that was disproportionately middle class and socially active—and therefore, perhaps, more likely to show the coherence of ideas about social groups and politics that was the study's central finding.

A second and more lethal criticism has to do with scale construction. It begins with the seemingly innocent observation that the questions that make up the anti-Semitism, ethnocentrism, and F scales are formatted in identical fashion. In each instance, study participants were presented with a proposition—such as "Obedience and respect for authority are the most important values that children can learn"—and asked how much they agreed or disagreed with it. This is the Likert method of opinion assessment, and in principle there is little wrong with it (Likert 1932). The lethal mistake came not in the application of the Likert procedure per se but in the writing of the specific propositions. All the propositions were written to run in the same direction. In every case, agreement indicated a propensity toward anti-Semitism or ethnocentrism or authoritarianism; in every case, disagreement indicated the opposing propensity. Writing in defense of the anti-Semitism scale in particular, Levinson argued that "since the scale attempts to measure receptivity to anti-Semitic ideology, it seemed reasonable to use only anti-Semitic statements in the scale" (Adorno et al. 1950, p. 59).

Reasonable as it may have seemed at the time, this decision fatally compromises *The Authoritarian Personality*'s results. It means that the impressive figures Adorno and colleagues report on the internal consistency of their scales and, more important, the striking correlations they report on the relationship *between* the scales are inflated, perhaps egregiously so. The correlations within and between scales are partly a product of a tendency for people to agree to reasonable-sounding propositions, irrespective of their content. This tendency, the acquiescence response set, is well documented now, as it was not at the time Levinson and company were designing their research, and its effects are surprisingly powerful.[18]

So, is there really such a thing as ethnocentrism? If there is, does it reflect antidemocratic tendencies rooted in the authoritarian personality? Though nearly a thousand pages long, strikingly ambitious in purpose and intermittently brilliant in analysis, *The Authoritarian Personality*, in the end, cannot say.

The critics of *The Authoritarian Personality* were right to point out the study's defects, and they were persuasive. But it is important to recognize that the critics thereby established that Adorno, Frenkel-Brunswik, Levinson, and Sanford failed to prove their conclusions, not that their conclusions were necessarily incorrect.[19]

According to *The Authoritarian Personality*, a primary characteristic of ethnocentrism is the generality and consistency of out-group rejection:

> It is as if the ethnocentric individual feels threatened by most of the groups to which he does not have a sense of belonging; if he cannot identify, he must oppose; if a group is not "acceptable," it is "alien."
>
> [The ethnocentric person] is prepared to reject groups with which he has never had contact; his approach to a new and strange person or culture is not one of curiosity, interest and receptivity but rather one of doubt and rejection. The feeling of difference is transformed into a sense of threat and an attitude of hostility. The new group easily becomes an out-group. (Adorno et al. 1950, p. 149)

The authors of *The Authoritarian Personality* presented these points as if they were established facts, and that they had established them. We know now that they were mistaken. But, over the last five decades, in a series of studies, with measures corrected against the contaminations of response set, and for samples taken both inside and outside the United States, the generality and consistency of out-group animosity is a common result. So, for example, Americans who regard the Japanese with condescension tend to think the same about Mexicans. Russians who blame Jews for their nation's troubles also blame capitalists, dissidents, and nonethnic Russians. And on it goes. Much as Levinson and colleagues claimed more than fifty years ago, hostility toward any one group appears to be part of a broader system of belief, "a relatively consistent frame of mind concerning 'aliens' generally" (Adorno et al. 1950, p. 102).[20]

And what of their claim that ethnocentrism is an outgrowth of authoritarianism? Perhaps they were right on this point too—though arriving at this conclusion requires a reimagining of authoritarianism itself.[21]

For this we turn to Karen Stenner's book, *The Authoritarian Dynamic* (2005). Building on her work with Stanley Feldman (Feldman and Stenner 1997; Feldman 2003), Stenner offers a new and appealing conceptualization of authoritarianism. She begins by severing the connection between authoritarianism and psychodynamic theory. Stenner invites us to think of authoritarianism as arising out of a basic human dilemma. Living alongside others is an inescapable feature of human society. This leads inevitably to tension between personal autonomy and social cohesion. The problem is how to strike a proper balance between group authority and uniformity, on the one side, and individual autonomy and diversity, on the other. Authoritarians choose the former over the latter: they are inclined to glorify, encourage, and reward uniformity, while disparaging, suppressing, and punishing difference. According to Stenner, the

> overriding objective of the authoritarian is always to enhance oneness and sameness; to minimize the diversity of people, beliefs, and behaviors with which one is confronted; and to institute and defend some collective order that makes all of this possible. (2005, p. 143)

To measure authoritarianism, Stenner relies on a disarmingly straightforward method. She simply asks people to choose values that children should be encouraged to learn at home. Those who select "good manners" and "obedience" as primary virtues for children are authoritarian; those who choose "imagination" and "independence" are not.[22]

Stenner finds that authoritarianism, measured in this way, is a consistent and sometimes powerful predictor of political intolerance. Intolerance, in her analysis, includes such things as keeping "undesirables" out of the neighborhood, prohibiting dissemination of pornography, and requiring prayer in school. Authoritarianism and intolerance are consistently connected not only in the United States, but in many other places besides: in Britain, Spain, Russia, the Czech Republic, and scores of other countries. The details differ from one place to the next—for British authoritarians it is immigrants from South Asia who must be curtailed, while Russian authoritarians worry about controlling the peoples of the Caucasus—but the general pattern is much the same. From such evidence Stenner concludes that "authoritarianism is the primary determinant of general intolerance of difference worldwide" (2005, p. 133).[23]

Ethnocentrism and intolerance are not the same, and Stenner's analysis is confined entirely to the latter. She never takes up the relationship between authoritarianism and ethnocentrism. However, she does find a consistent connection between authoritarianism and many specific instances of intolerance, involving many different groups. It seems reasonable to conclude that authoritarianism, as Stenner defines it, and ethnocentrism, as we think of it, are related.

And so, although it has taken a good long while, it seems that Adorno and colleagues may have been right all along. They were right, first of all, to presume that people differ from one another in their general outlook toward others. People are more or less ethnocentric: predisposed to react with more or less pride to their in-group and predisposed to react with more or less suspicion, condescension, and contempt to groups not their own. They were right to draw a sharp distinction between ethnocentric ideology, on the one hand, and authoritarian personality, on the other. And with Stenner's evidence in hand, perhaps they were right as well to conclude that ethnocentrism is an outgrowth, at least in part, of the authoritarian personality. These are important lessons to carry forward. At the same time, to reduce ethnocentrism *entirely* to personality would be a mistake. The personality approach misses important parts of the story of the origins of ethnocentrism, as we will see. And a preoccupation with personality is blind to the part that elites play in the mobilization of ethnocentrism.[24]

ETHNOCENTRISM AS AN EXPRESSION OF SOCIAL IDENTITY

Skipping forward a generation, we come next to Henri Tajfel and social identity theory.[25] Tajfel was a leading figure in what came to be known as the European perspective on social psychology. He founded a Society, edited an influential monograph series, and was a prominent lecturer in Leiden, Paris, and Bologna. His ardent interest in social conflict was a product of his own experience. He was born European and Jewish; his family perished in the Holocaust. Throughout his professional career, Tajfel carried with him "memories of a raging storm" (1981, p. 7).

Tajfel was a sharp critic of American social psychology, which had become, in his judgment, "a social science practiced in a social vacuum" (1981, p. 1). To Tajfel the American turn to laboratory investigation of psychological micro-processes was a terrible mistake. Social psychology, Tajfel insisted, must "include in its theoretical and research preoccupations a direct concern with the relationship between human psychological functioning and the large-scale social processes and events which shape this functioning and are shaped by it" (1981, p. 18).

Given this line of criticism, it is ironic that Tajfel is remembered best for an experimental result from which all of society and culture and history had been deliberately obliterated. This was the so-called minimal group experiment, which questioned whether conflicts of interest were necessary to produce ethnocentrism, as Sherif and other realistic group conflict theorists insisted. Tajfel was impressed with the results of Sherif's field experiments, but he wondered whether explicit and objective conflicts of interest were actually necessary conditions for the emergence of ethnocentrism. Tajfel's answer, supplied by the minimal group experiment, was a resounding no.

In the first stage of the experiment, participants are assigned to different groups on what must surely have appeared to them to be trivial grounds. For example, in the original experiment, Bristol teenage boys were shown a rapid sequence of slides and asked to estimate the number of dots displayed on each. Based on their answers, or so they were told, they were then were divided into two groups, those who consistently overestimated the number of dots and those who consistently underestimated them. Neither group was more accurate, they were informed, nor was the tendency to over- or underestimate revealing of any deeper truth. It was just a convenient way to divide them up.

This is a defining feature of the minimal group experiment: the triviality of group affiliation. In another version of the experiment, group assignments appeared to be made on the basis of whether participants, all of whom were in the dark about abstract art, preferred the paintings of Klee to those of Kandinsky. In still another, one that could be called the ultimate minimal group experiment, participants were explicitly assigned to one group or the other by a public and ostentatious toss of a coin.[26]

After assignment to one group or the other, each participant is isolated into an individual cubicle, takes part in a problem-solving activity, and then is asked to allocate rewards to other participants (never to themselves). In the original experiment, Bristol schoolboys allocated points that were redeemable for money at the end of the experiment. As part of the allocation task, participants learn that the recipients are members of their own (minimal) group or members of the other (minimal) group; they are otherwise anonymous.

These ostensibly innocuous conditions produce in-group favoritism. In Tajfel's original experiment, more than 70 percent of participants allocated rewards in way that favored their group. And in scores of variations on the basic minimal group experiment design, the results are the same. Group membership—minimal group membership—generates rewards: money, but also affection, trust, and cooperation.

Minimal seems a fitting term to apply to the social system created in these experiments. In-group affiliation is superficial. Group membership is anonymous. Conflict of interest between groups is removed. Self-interest is set aside since participants allocate rewards only to others. Groups are temporary fabrications, so there is no history of hostility and no shadow of the future. And yet, in this artificial social system, in the absence of conflict of interest or the perception of threat, and putting aside differences in culture, social standing, and economic or political power, in-group favoritism always emerges. It emerges again and again, in experiments conducted among Bristol schoolboys, soldiers in the West German army, Maori children in New Zealand, trade school students in Geneva, undergraduates in New York City, and more.[27]

The ethnocentrism expressed in the minimal group experiment takes a particular and illuminating form. Participants in these experiments are allowed to allocate rewards pretty much as they wish. They can choose to reward their own group, or express generosity to the other group, or ignore the group boundary entirely. What they often do is allocate rewards so as to enhance the difference between their group and the other group. They are not fanatics in this: their choices also reflect everyday conceptions of equity and fairness. Still, the tendency to put distance between their group and the other group—between "us" and "them"—is impressive. They choose this option even when doing so diminishes the rewards enjoyed by their own group.[28]

This result is both replicable and, to us and many others, remarkable. It certainly surprised Tajfel, who created the minimal group condition under the assumption that it would serve as a neutral starting point, a baseline condition. Subsequent experiments would then systematically add in one feature at a time until in-group favoritism finally made an appearance. As things turned out, additional features were unnecessary.

To explain this remarkable and unexpected result, Tajfel and his Bristol colleagues created social identity theory. The theory begins with an assumption about human nature. Tajfel assumes that people—everywhere, regardless of circumstance—are motivated to maintain a positive identity. Social identity theory takes this point as axiomatic: individuals are always striving "to maintain or enhance their self-esteem" (Tajfel and Turner 1979, p. 40).[29]

People derive their sense of self, according to social identity theory, in large part from their membership in social groups. In this sense it could be said that not only are individuals in social groups, but also social groups are "in" individuals. Identity is largely a reflection of where and how people locate themselves in their society. In Tajfel's view, "the individual realizes himself in society—that is, he recognizes his identity in socially defined terms, and these definitions become reality as he lives in society."[30]

Identity is a psychological matter. It is determined not by objective membership but by the perception of belonging. The transformation of mere membership into a sense of identity takes place through a process of social categorization. Social categorization parses the social world into a manageable set of basic categories. Through social categorization, individuals define who they are and who others are. Such classifications are

cognitive tools that segment, classify, and order the social environment, and thus enable the individual to undertake many forms of social action.

But they do not merely systematize the social world; they also provide a system of orientation for self-reference: they create and define the individual's place in society. Social groups, understood in this sense, provide their members with an identification of themselves in social terms. (Tajfel and Turner 1979, p. 40)

One consequence of social categorization is accentuation: people accentuate similarities between themselves and their in-group, and accentuate differences between themselves and their various out-groups. Identity takes on an "us versus them" mentality. Individuals, one might say, are transformed into groups.[31]

The creation of social identity theory was motivated by the puzzle presented by the minimal group experiment result. It cannot be much of an achievement that the theory explains this one result, but it is worth recounting how the theory does so. Here is a lightly paraphrased account, from Hogg and Abrams, two of the theory's principal advocates:

The minimal group experiments demonstrate that mere social categorization—the discontinuous classification of individuals into two distinct groups—is sufficient to generate ethnocentrism and conflict.

Individuals in these studies are categorizing themselves in terms of the minimal category provided by the experiment. This process of categorization—of self and others—accentuates group differences on the only dimension readily available: the allocation of rewards. The accentuation of difference favors the ingroup because individuals are deriving their social identity in part from the category created in the experiment. The involvement of the self in the categorization process activates the need to maintain or enhance self-esteem, and this can be accomplished by favoring the ingroup—and hence the self—over the outgroup. (1988, p. 51)

In-group favoritism is a well-established result, but it is of course just a tendency, one that, as we noted earlier, is moderated by a sense of fairness. Furthermore, in studies that permit the distinction to be detected, ethnocentrism in the minimal group experiment appears to be more in-group favoritism than out-group hostility.[32] One might say that the in-group/out-group differentiation under examination in the minimal group experiments is a reflection of the merging of self and in-group, rather than the distancing of self from out-groups. This observation provides the point of departure for Marilynn Brewer's theory of social identity, the most interesting and important variation on Tajfel's original thinking.[33]

Taking a page out of Gordon Allport's classic 1954 book on prejudice, Brewer first stipulates that in-groups take psychological primacy over out-groups. Familiarity, loyalty, and preference for one's in-group all precede awareness of and attitudes toward out-groups. In the minimal group experiment, participants readily reward in-group members, but they are reluctant to punish out-group members. In-group bias is largely due to in-group favoritism, not out-group derogation. According to Brewer, "once the self has become attached to a social group or category, positive affect and evaluations associated with the self-concept are automatically transferred to the group as a whole" (2007, p. 732).[34]

Brewer argues that in-group favoritism has its origins in evolutionary processes; that it is a reflection, in the final analysis, of "the profoundly social nature of human beings as a species" (2007, p. 730). Group living is part of our ancestral history; it is, Brewer says, "the fundamental survival strategy that characterizes the human species." Over the course of evolutionary history, we have evolved to "rely on cooperation rather than strength, and on social learning rather than instinct" (1999, p. 433). Contemporary human nature, Brewer maintains, is characterized by "obligatory interdependence."

From this perspective, in-groups become a site for altruism. Within the group, norms facilitate reciprocal exchange. Expectations of cooperation and security promote mutual trust. Reciprocal attraction motivates compliance. Symbols and rituals emerge that differentiate the in-group from local out-groups, which reduce the risk that in-group benefits will be inadvertently extended to out-group members, and assure that in-group members will recognize their own entitlement to group benefits (M. Brewer 1999, pp. 433–34). In short, in-groups become "bounded communities of mutual cooperation and trust" (2007, p. 732). Brewer concludes that in-group favoritism arises not, as Tajfel would have it, out of a universal striving for self-esteem, but rather out of the fundamental human need for security.[35]

Finally, and this time drawing a distinction with Sumner, Brewer argues that there is no theoretical basis for expecting a close connection between in-group loyalty and out-group hostility. In-group loyalty may be a necessary condition for out-group hostility, but it is not sufficient. Put another way, strong attachment to the in-group is compatible with a wide range of sentiments toward out-groups: admiration, sympathy, indifference, as well as disdain and hatred. This seems to be so. Sometimes strong in-group loyalty is accompanied by strong out-group animosity (Gibson and Gouws 2000; Perreault and Bourhis 1999); sometimes not (M. Brewer and Campbell 1976; De Figueiredo and Elkins 2003; Feshbach 1994). In-group solidarity and out-group hostility appear to be bundled together less tightly than Sumner originally believed.[36]

The basic finding of in-group favoritism has stood up well to replications and challenges, and it remains provocative today. Like Solomon Asch's (1951) famous experiments on conformity or Stanley Milgram's (1974) unsettling studies on obedience to authority, Tajfel's minimal group experiment teaches us something about social life that we did not know before. In particular, the minimal group experiment suggests how ready we are to impose social categories and how far-reaching the consequences may be. It implies, contrary to realistic group conflict theory, that ethnocentrism does not require conflict of interest.[37] It also suggests, contrary to Levinson and *The Authoritarian Personality*, that ethnocentrism need not be interpreted as a dark and irrational expression of repressed hostilities and primeval fears. Ethnocentrism is a commonplace consequence of the human striving for self-regard and personal security.

Against these valuable contributions is the standard worry about generalizing from experimental results. What can in-group favoritism created in the laboratory tell us about ethnocentrism in the world?

Quite a lot, according to Donald Horowitz. In his excellent review and analysis of ethnic group conflict, Horowitz (1985) readily acknowledges that the minimal group experimental setup faced by Bristol schoolboys is quite different from the deadly serious and ongoing circumstance confronting rival ethnic groups. Nevertheless, Horowitz commends the minimal group experiment for isolating several vital features of actual group conflict: the "powerful pull of group loyalty, the quest for relative in-group advantage, and the willingness to incur costs to maximize intergroup differentials" (Horowitz 1985, p. 146). He then proceeds to take Tajfel's result as casting doubt on theories of ethnic conflict that assign primacy to competition over material interests.

Maybe so. Tajfel was himself quite modest on this point. His intention was not to deny objective conflicts of interest their place in an explanation of intergroup conflict. As he put it, social identity theory "cannot replace the economic and social analysis, but must be used to supplement it" (Tajfel 1981, p. 223). "It would be no less than ridiculous," Tajfel wrote, "to assert that objective rewards (in terms of money, standards of living, consumption of goods and services, etc.) are not the most important determinants" of contemporary group conflict.

Social identity theory attempts to identify the environmental conditions that give rise to ethnocentrism (or more precisely, to in-group favoritism). In this enterprise, Tajfel, Brewer, and others in this theoretical tradition display little interest in differences among individuals. All of us strive for self-esteem or for security. Placed in the right conditions, all of us are likely to express in-group favoritism.

This is a valuable perspective to bring to ethnocentrism—but it is not ours. Like Daniel Levinson and his colleagues, we are interested first and foremost in differences among individuals. We treat ethnocentrism as a predisposition, a form of individual readiness that guides perception, thought, and action. We argue that people differ from one another—reliably and durably—in degree of ethnocentrism: that some people are very ethnocentric; many are mildly ethnocentric; and a few are not ethnocentric at all. And we claim (and plan to convincingly show) that such differences in ethnocentrism can take us some distance in explaining the opinions Americans take on pressing issues of contemporary politics.

ETHNOCENTRISM AS AN OUTCOME OF NATURAL SELECTION

A century and a half after Charles Darwin completed *On the Origin of Species by Means of Natural Selection*, the evidence for evolution through natural selection is overwhelming. It is less a theory than a fact, as Ernst Mayr has put it (2001). Biologists have observed evolution in natural populations of plants and animals, and have reproduced evolution experimentally, in the laboratory and in the field. Intricate adaptations of organisms to their environment have been massively documented. The fossil record, while incomplete, follows predicted chronologies exactly. The scope of empirical confirmation is stunning: on the one hand, the generation and inheritance of genetic variation is understood down to the molecular level, and on the other, the geographic distribution of whole species—"biogeography"—is accounted for as well. Evolution through natural selection is the unifying theory of biology. "Nothing in biology makes sense, except in the light of evolution."[38]

This is an inspiring story of scientific achievement—but what does it have to do with our project? Quite a bit, according to the Harvard entomologist Edward O. Wilson. Surveying biological science from Darwin to the present day, Wilson singles out natural selection as "the essential first hypothesis for any serious consideration of the human condition" (1978, pp. 1–2). Until political science, psychology, economics, and the other social sciences absorb the lessons of evolution and natural selection, they will remain, according to Wilson, theoretically incapacitated, limited to mere description of the surface regularity of human behavior.[39]

Taking his own advice seriously, Wilson has made it his project to build a bridge from natural selection to human society. In *Sociobiology: The New Synthesis* (1975), Wilson summarized vast amounts of research on vertebrate social behavior. Drawing on ethology, ecology, and genetics, Wilson attempted to formulate general principles concerning the biological properties of whole societies, including, in the book's final and controversial chapter, human society. His subsequent writing—especially *On Human Nature* (1978), *Genes, Mind, and Culture* (with Charles Lumsden, 1981), and *Consilience* (1998)—has continued this work.[40]

According to Wilson, certain human social traits—for example, bodily adornment or funeral rites—are unique to the human species, occur in all cultures, and are as true to the human type as "wing tessellation is to a fritillary butterfly or a complicated spring melody to a wood thrush" (1978, p. 21). Wilson concludes that the accumulated evidence for a "large hereditary component" to human social behavior is "decisive" (1978, p. 19).

The key question for us is whether Wilson's conclusion holds in the particular case of ethnocentrism. Is ethnocentrism part of "human nature"?[41]

Perhaps it is. Social life surely enjoys huge comparative advantages over solitary life: in the sharing of knowledge, the division of labor, and the economies of mutual defense. This implies that evolutionary pressures would have favored motivational dispositions furthering group life. As a consequence, over the long haul, mutations furthering the capacity for in-group loyalty and out-group hostility might have spread through the population (e.g., D. Campbell 1965, 1975).[42]

However, if ethnocentrism entails both hostility to out-groups and attachment to in-groups, and if the latter rises to the level of altruistic sacrifice, then how could such a disposition evolve? This is the "central theoretical problem of sociobiology" (E. O. Wilson 1975, p. 3). Fallen heroes leave behind no offspring. If self-sacrifice results in fewer descendents, the genes that encourage heroic altruism can be expected to gradually disappear. Yet at the same time, there appear to be indisputable instances of altruism in the world, where one person increases the fitness of another at the expense of her own—as in surrendering needed food or shelter, or deferring in the choice of a mate, or placing one's self in between danger and another. How can these two points be reconciled?

Darwin suggested that altruism might be explained by natural selection acting on *groups*, as it does on individuals. In a famous passage from *The Descent of Man*, published some twenty years after *Origin of Species*, Darwin wrote:

> It must not be forgotten that although a high standard of morality gives but a slight or no advantage to each individual man and his children over other men of the same tribe, yet that an increase in the number of well-endowed men and advancement in the standard of morality will certainly give an immense advantage to one tribe over another. There can be no doubt that a tribe including many members who, from possessing in a high degree the spirit of patriotism, fidelity, obedience, courage, and sympathy, were always ready to aid one another, and to sacrifice themselves for the common good, would be victorious over most other tribes; *and this would be natural selection*. At all times throughout the world tribes have

supplanted other tribes; and as morality is one important element in their success, the standard of morality and the number of well-endowed men will thus everywhere tend to rise and increase. (Darwin 1871, pp. 159–60, italics added)

Darwin did not develop this idea, however, and for the better part of one hundred years, group selection played virtually no role in the standard theory of evolution.[43]

But in recent years, a modern theory of group selection has arisen. Under this account, altruism can evolve when there exists a multiplicity of groups, which vary in the proportion of altruistic types. Groups with more altruists must be more fit—they must produce more offspring. And the differential fitness of groups (favoring altruists) must be strong enough to counter the differential fitness of individuals within groups (favoring the selfish). Because altruism is maladaptive with respect to individual selection but adaptive with respect to group selection, it can evolve only if the process of group selection is sufficiently strong. According to Sober and Wilson (1998), evidence in support of group selection is now overwhelming.[44]

Suppose we accept the proposition that natural selection operates on groups as well as individuals, and that this is especially true for humans. Does this mean that a new and rosy picture of human benevolence has been thereby established, that a romantic vision of universal generosity fulfilled? No. In the first place, group selection theory does not abandon the idea of competition that forms the core of the theory of natural selection; rather, it provides an additional setting in which competition can occur. Second of all, group selection does not replace individual selection, it supplements it. Group selection leaves ample room for individuals to seek personal advantage. Altruistic motives are mixed with the purely selfish. Ambivalence is the human condition, and ambivalence is more likely to be resolved with opportunistic selfishness than sacrificial altruism (D. Campbell 1975; E. O. Wilson 1975). Third and most important for our purposes, altruism rooted in natural selection is not universal altruism. It is altruism for the benefit of the in-group *and* to the detriment of the out-group. If group selection provides the mechanism by which helping behavior directed at members of one's own group can evolve, "it equally provides a context in which hurting individuals in other groups can be selectively advantageous. Group selection favors within-group niceness *and* between-group nastiness" (Sober and Wilson 1998, p. 9). And within-group niceness and between-group nastiness is, of course, just a colloquial way to say "ethnocentrism."

Group selection suggests that ethnocentrism can be conceived of as an adaptation, a part of "human nature." It rides on the general point that key features of human behavior evolved by natural selection and are today constrained throughout the entire species by particular sets of genes. It makes a case for ethnocentrism as a general predisposition.[45]

This is an important conclusion, but it leaves open whether *individual differences* in ethnocentrism have a genetic source. We take for granted— and will shortly show—that contemporary Americans differ from one another in the degree to which they display ethnocentrism. Is it reasonable to suppose that such differences can be traced, at least in part, to underlying differences in "genetic blueprints"?

We think the answer is yes, and we think so primarily because of the empirical results from the new interdisciplinary field of human behavioral genetics—the intersection of genetics and the behavioral sciences.[46] Wilson drew on the early returns from this literature to bolster his case about the inheritability of human behavior. The examples available to Wilson at the time were certainly powerful—research linking genetic mutations to a wide array of neurological disorders, impairments of intelligence, and disease— but they left unclear whether genetic variation might also play a role in social behavior in the normal range. As we will see in a moment, research over the last decade or so makes this case powerfully.

The primary goal of quantitative behavioral genetics is to partition the observed variation in human traits into genetic and environmental sources. Of course, in one respect the genotype and the environment are equally important, in that each is indispensable to human development. Any observed behavior—any phenotype—is the result of a continuous interaction between genes and environment. Still, a deep and important question remains: to what extent do the differences observed among people reflect differences in their genotypes and to what extent do they reflect differences in their environments?[47]

Mathematically, this question can be written:

$$V^P = V^G + V^{CE} + V^{UE} + \varepsilon,$$

where V^P is the variance of the phenotype, V^G is the variance of the genotype, V^{CE} is variance of the common (or shared) environment, V^{UE} is the variance of the unique environment, and ε is error. V^G/V^P is the trait's heritability, the fraction of the observed variance in a certain trait that is caused by differences in heredity (Lush 1940, 1949). Estimates of heritability provide the "backbone" of human behavioral genetics (E. O. Wilson 1998).

The theoretical foundation for behavioral genetics was laid down by the rediscovery of Mendel's laws of single-gene inheritance in the early part of the twentieth century and the extension of these laws to complex factorial traits by Fisher (1918), Haldane (1932), and S. Wright (1921). This trio of brilliant statisticians generalized Mendel's experimental findings to quantitative differences, to differences of degree rather than kind. Inheritance of traits that form a continuously graded series from one extreme to the other without falling into kinds or types—traits like skin color or height or, as we would say, ethnocentrism—is complicated. It is complicated in the first instance because whatever genetic influence might be operating is almost certainly polygenic: that is, traits are influenced by large ensembles of genes, distributed across different chromosomal sites, each with modest effect, acting together, sometimes in complex ways. It turns out, nevertheless, that the principles of genetic transmission that Mendel discovered—segregation and independent assortment—apply to these more complicated cases.

The most direct and straightforward empirical method for partitioning phenotypic variation into genetic and environmental sources is the experiment. Experimentation is widely used in studies of plant and animal breeding but is obviously out of bounds for human populations. Next best is the statistical analysis of "natural experiments." The classic natural experiment in human behavioral genetics capitalizes on the difference between monozygotic (MZ), or identical, twins (who share an identical genetic inheritance, genetic relatedness of approximately 1.0) and dizygotic (DZ), or fraternal, twins (who develop from two separate eggs, fertilized by two separate sperm, genetic relatedness of approximately 0.5). Insofar as identical twins are more similar than fraternal twins on a particular trait, to that degree the trait can be said to be due to genetic differences. Other designs bring in additional family relationships: for example, parents and biological offspring, parents and adopted offspring, children of one identical twin pair and the children of the other, and so forth. Because genetic resemblance among different kinds of biological relatives is understood and can be expressed in precise numerical terms (Falconer 1961), all these designs offer the opportunity of estimating, under more or less reasonable assumptions, the heritability of virtually any (measurable) human trait.

Research in human behavioral genetics began with a focus on illness and achieved notable successes. In a relatively brief period, scores of debilitating diseases such as cystic fibrosis, hemophilia, color blindness, and schizophrenia were traced, in part, to genetic sources. More recently, research in the field has expanded its focus, taking up the heritability of various personality traits and social attitudes. The best of this work is characterized by meticulous attention to measurement, sophisticated statistical analysis, and data provided by carefully maintained archives.[48]

Consider the evidence on the heritability of social attitudes. The subject itself may seem ridiculous. Attitudes are *learned*. Everybody says so (almost everybody). In his influential essay, Gordon Allport (1935) offered three conjectures about the origins of attitudes. First of all, attitudes might be built up through the gradual accretion of experience; second, they might reflect a single dramatic emotional experience, or trauma; and third, they might be adopted ready-made from parents, teachers, and friends. That's it: nothing here about inheritance or biology or genetics. Allport took for granted that attitudes are learned, and so, in overwhelming numbers, have those who have written about attitudes since. So widespread is this assumption that the early behavior genetic studies of personality would sometimes include measures of social attitudes as a kind of control, on the (mistaken) idea that attitudes would provide a heritability baseline of zero.[49]

The seminal paper in this line of research was published in 1986 in the *Proceedings of the National Academy of Sciences*.[50] N. G. Martin and his colleagues compared a large Australian sample of MZ and DZ twins on a measure of general conservatism. Their analysis suggested not just a genetic component to conservatism, but a *large* genetic component to conservatism. Under their statistical model, more than half of the observed variation in conservatism is attributed to genetic difference.[51]

This result may seem surprising, but it is no fluke. Other studies, employing different designs, different samples, and somewhat different statistical techniques, arrive at essentially the same conclusion (e.g., Alford, Funk, and Hibbing 2005; Bouchard et al. 1990; Eaves and Eysenck 1974; Eaves et al. 1999; Olson, Vernon, and Jang 2001). Conservatism, it would seem, arises in an important way from genetic endowments.[52]

E. O. Wilson calls heritability estimates of the sort we are discussing here—heritabilities of about 0.5—"midrange" effects. We suppose that heritabilities of about 0.5 are midrange when compared against the near perfect genetic effect for finger length (Lynch and Walsh 1998). But to social scientists working at the individual level, midrange effects look pretty big. They *are* big: the findings suggest that roughly half of the variation we observe in ethnocentrism may be due to variation in the underlying genetic program.

CONCLUSIONS

We began our review of the principal theories of ethnocentrism with the hope of finding good answers to three basic questions: What is the nature of ethnocentrism? How does ethnocentrism arise? When does ethnocentrism become important to politics? If now we have come to the end of the review without altogether complete and convincing answers, we have certainly learned a lot that is valuable. We are indebted to Sumner for noticing ethnocentrism in the first place, for naming it felicitously, for defining it sensibly, and for insisting that the study of ethnocentrism must take into account economic, social, and political conditions. We are indebted to Daniel Levinson and his colleagues for imagining that people in modern democratic societies will vary in how fully they subscribe to ethnocentrism, and to their persistent successors who eventually established that ethnocentrism defined this way does indeed exist. We are indebted to Henri Tajfel for his remarkable experiments showing how readily we indulge in partitioning the social world into in-groups and out-groups. And we are indebted to E. O. Wilson and scores of scientists working at the intersection of the biological and behavioral sciences for two revelatory ideas: that ethnocentrism is part of human nature and that humans are more or less ethnocentric due to genetic inheritance.

If these pieces are partial, they are important, and we will try in the next chapter to put them together in a theoretically satisfying way. But one piece so far is missing altogether. Not one of the four theories we have examined here speaks to this question: when does ethnocentrism take on political significance? An adequate theory of ethnocentrism must define its nature, account for its origins, *and* specify the conditions under which it is more and less consequential. This is the business of chapter 2.

CHAPTER 2

Ethnocentrism Reconceived

Having completed our review of the leading theories of ethnocentrism in the last chapter, we turn now to the task of developing a more comprehensive and satisfactory framework of our own. In part this is a matter of identifying what is most useful in the work of our predecessors; in part it is a matter of bringing lines of theoretical analysis to bear on the problem of ethnocentrism in new ways; and in largest part it is a matter of developing an argument that specifies when ethnocentrism takes on, and fails to take on, political significance. Our aim is to construct a theoretical framework that is at once abstract enough to provide understanding that reaches beyond mere summary of empirical regularities and precise enough to instruct analysis of particular cases that are shortly to come.

Our framework is presented in three connected parts, each corresponding to one of the three questions that a theory of ethnocentrism must address. First, what is the nature of ethnocentrism? Second, how does ethnocentrism arise? And third, the question of consequences: when does ethnocentrism become important to public opinion?

THE NATURE OF ETHNOCENTRISM

Our view, set out in the last chapter, is that ethnocentrism is a predisposition to divide human society into in-groups and out-groups. People vary from one another in their readiness to look upon the social world in this way: that is, they are more or less ethnocentric. To those given to ethnocentrism, in-groups are communities of virtue, trust, and cooperation, safe and superior havens. Out-groups, on the other hand, are not. To the ethnocentric, out-group members and their customs seem strange, discomforting, perhaps even dangerous.

If ethnocentrism is a readiness to divide the world into in-groups and out-groups, then the nature of ethnocentrism is revealed in part by what we take the nature of a group to be. In our analysis, a group does not require

institutional sponsors or formal membership or face-to-face interaction—
though it might have all three. The defining point, rather, is psychological. Any aggregation of individuals can be a group if the aggregation is seen
and experienced in that way. Criminals, Arabs, college professors: all "are
groups in so far as they are social categories or regions in an individual's
social outlook—objects of opinions, attitudes, affect, and striving" (Adorno
et al. 1950, p. 146).

This means that membership is not sufficient to establish an in-group,
just as the absence of membership is not sufficient to establish an out-
group. What is required is psychological striving: attraction and identification in the case of in-groups; condescension and opposition in the case
of out-groups. In Sherif's field experiments, young boys fought each other
so fiercely because competition transformed mere membership into something psychologically consequential. Under Sherif's effective direction,
the Rattlers and the Eagles became tribes, sources of personal identity and
strong emotion.[1]

If a group is "any set of people who constitute a psychological entity for
any individual" (Adorno et al. 1950, p. 146), then groups have extraordinary
range. Catholics are a group, but so is the neighborhood bridge club. True
enough, but because of our interest in national politics, we are drawn much
more to the former than to the latter. Politics on a national scale is organized in these terms. When control over the national government becomes
the prize of politics, group attachments and oppositions based in particularistic features like kin or local community are subordinated to attachments
rooted in broader categories such as class and ethnicity (Posner 2004). A
consideration of broad social groups of this kind is perhaps especially relevant for an analysis of politics in the United States, a nation of continental
size and extraordinary heterogeneity. According to Walter Dean Burnham
(1974), the most persistent and intractable of American political conflicts
derive from "ethnocultural antagonisms": oppositions rooted in race, ethnicity, class, religion, and region.[2]

THE ORIGINS OF ETHNOCENTRISM

Most of the empirical work that follows concentrates on the consequences
of ethnocentrism. Our primary object is to show that attempts to explain
and predict public opinion must take ethnocentrism into account. This will
keep us thoroughly occupied, but our focus on the effects of ethnocentrism
does not relieve us of the obligation to supply at least a rudimentary account
of the origins of ethnocentrism. We spell out that account here and test it,
insofar as we can, in the following chapter.

Early Readiness

Early on, children display an inclination to parse the social world into "natural kinds." They believe that race and sex and ethnicity belong to the living world, and that differences between races or sexes or ethnicities are rooted in biology, or blood, or some such underlying essence. Such differences encompass inner qualities—temperament, intellect, character—as well as outward, physical ones. Children come to these beliefs on their own. They do not need to be taught that race and sex and ethnicity are natural kinds; they know these things themselves. Children are ready, one might say, for ethnocentrism.[3]

If all children are ready for ethnocentrism, why do some end up more ethnocentric than others? We claim that people vary in the degree to which their beliefs and feelings about social life can be described as ethnocentric. If they do not vary, then our attempt to understand differences in the American public's views on such things as homeland security and welfare reform by invoking ethnocentrism is doomed from the outset. There *are* reliable and consequential differences in ethnocentrism, we will shortly show. The question, then, is this: how do such differences arise?

Genetic Transmission and Social Learning

In the last chapter we learned that political predispositions bearing a resemblance to ethnocentrism have a sizable genetic component. Roughly one-half of the variation we observe in important social attitudes appears to be due to variation in genotypes. Accordingly, we propose that parents influence their biological offspring's ethnocentric predisposition through the genetic blueprint they provide at conception. Part of the mystery of individual differences in ethnocentrism, we say, lies in our genes.[4]

Part, but not all. Social learning theory proceeds from the premise that "the complex repertoires of behavior displayed by members of society are to a large extent acquired with little or no direct tuition through observation of response patterns exemplified by various socialization agents" (Bandura 1969, p. 213). Children do not rely exclusively on parents as socialization agents, but they rely on parents more than on any other single source. A significant part of social learning takes place through children imitating, internalizing, and reproducing what their parents say and do. This implies that the correspondence we expect to find between the ethnocentrism of parents and the ethnocentrism of children is due not only to genetic transmission but to social learning. And from the point of view of social learning theory, the magnitude of correspondence should depend on conditions that facilitate the learning process: such things as the clarity and consistency of cues given by parents, the prominence of politics in family discussions, and the attachment felt by offspring for their parents.[5]

Personality

One aspect of personality, authoritarianism, emerges from a basic and recurrent human dilemma (Feldman 2003; Feldman and Stenner 1997; Stenner 2005). Living alongside others is an inescapable feature of human society, and it leads inevitably to tension between personal autonomy and social cohesion. Authoritarians habitually choose the latter over the former: they are inclined to glorify, encourage, and reward uniformity, while disparaging, suppressing, and punishing difference.[6] By valuing uniformity and authority over autonomy and diversity, authoritarians, we propose, should be drawn "naturally" to an ethnocentric point of view. Ethnocentrism has its origins, in part, in authoritarianism.

Education

Education is widely thought to bestow the values and resources that encourage a "sober second thought," providing individuals with the capacity to override prejudice. This argument is made perhaps most forcefully in the literature on political tolerance, where democratic regimes are said to be tested by their willingness to tolerate a full and frank exchange of views. Political tolerance is a difficult test; it "implies a willingness to 'put up with' those things that one rejects. Politically, it implies a willingness to permit the expression of those ideas or interests that one opposes." Tolerance cuts against the human grain, since people "distrust what they do not understand and cannot control" and need to "feel safe against the terrors of the unknown" (Marcus et al. 1995, p. 28; McClosky and Brill 1983, pp. 13–14).

If political tolerance is very much an acquired taste, then the evidence is overwhelming that many Americans fail to acquire it. For example, in Samuel Stouffer's famous study carried out in the 1950s as the McCarthy hearings were underway, relatively few Americans were prepared to grant constitutional rights of speech and assembly to communists. Stouffer's results shattered the assumption that Americans would apply democratic procedures and rights to all, and subsequent research has massively reinforced the point.[7]

Of course, some Americans *are* prepared to defend ideas and activities they find distasteful. Such people, it turns out, come very disproportionately from the ranks of the well educated. Beginning with Stouffer's results on communists on up to contemporary disputes over gay rights and racist speech, more education is always associated with more tolerance.[8] Evidently education imparts knowledge, values, and experiences that together act as a counterweight to the "natural" inclination toward intolerance. Americans are more or less ethnocentric, we suggest, because of differences in education.

Consolidation and Stability in Adulthood

We know that broad personality traits—like introversion-extraversion or general temperament—show substantial and increasing stability over the life span, reaching a high plateau by middle age.[9] Political predispositions show the same pattern: by the midthirties, consolidation and consistency begin to replace the "attitudinal fragmentation and disorder" of the young adult years.[10] We expect ethnocentrism to follow a similar path. By middle age, if not before, ethnocentrism should be fully formed, a stable and general predisposition ready to guide perception, thought, and action.

THE CONSEQUENCES OF ETHNOCENTRISM

The principal purpose of our project is to establish that ethnocentrism plays an important part in matters of political consequence; more specifically, that ethnocentrism is a significant force shaping public opinion. By public opinion we mean, following V. O. Key, "those opinions held by private citizens which governments find it prudent to heed" (1961, p. 14). Such opinions, according to John Zaller, arise out of "a marriage of information and predisposition: information to form a mental picture of the given issue, and predisposition to motivate some conclusion about it" (1992, p. 6). Zaller's pithy formulation is appealing because it focuses attention on the primary empirical task we face here: namely, to determine the strength of the connection between ethnocentrism, considered as a predisposition, on the one hand, and the public's opinion on matters of public policy, on the other.

Ethnocentrism is a deep habit and a stable predisposition, but its importance to public opinion on government policy, we argue, is variable. As we will see, in some cases, at some points in time, ethnocentrism is important; in other cases, in other points in time, much less so. In *Nuts and Bolts for the Social Sciences*, Jon Elster (1989) argues that social scientists have been quite successful in developing and testing explanations, but much less successful in specifying the conditions under which those explanations apply. They "can isolate tendencies, propensities, and mechanisms and show that they have implications for behavior that are often surprising and counterintuitive. What they are more rarely able to do is to state necessary and sufficient conditions under which the various mechanisms are switched on" (1989, p. 9). Mindful of Elster's complaint, our aim here is to suggest the conditions under which ethnocentrism is "switched on" in political judgment—or in language we prefer, the conditions under which ethnocentrism is *activated*.[11]

On the subject of activation, our principal predecessors offer surprisingly little guidance. William Graham Sumner regarded ethnocentrism as a universal predisposition, and by this he seemed to mean both that ethnocentrism is present in all societies and that ethnocentrism is *always* in play. No help there.

Nor do Daniel Levinson and his colleagues have much to say on the subject of activation. Their purpose in *The Authoritarian Personality* was to offer an understanding of why people are more or less susceptible to antidemocratic appeals. Ethnocentrism (like authoritarianism) is a predisposition, a readiness to act, but it is not action itself. To understand action, to understand the expression of ethnocentrism in judgment or behavior, would require, Levinson and friends write in a discouraging and most unhelpful passage, "an understanding of the total organization of society" (1950, p. 7).

The tradition of research inaugurated by Henri Tajfel does little better. Tajfel's major contribution to ethnocentrism, we argue in chapter 1, was to demonstrate that ethnocentrism can arise out of a minimal group experience. In a series of remarkable studies, Tajfel showed that the mere categorization of individuals into one grouping or another is sufficient to generate in-group favoritism. The many replications that followed fortify the original result but provide little help in specifying the conditions that govern when in-group favoritism enters into politics.

Fourth and finally, E. O. Wilson has a thing or two to say about activation, but at a level of abstraction too high to be of much use here. Wilson's approach to activation, from the perspective of evolutionary biology, is to specify the causal mechanisms of human development that connect the genome to behavior. We have not yet arrived at good answers yet, though there is broad agreement on a first principle: namely, human behavior reflects an interaction between genes and culture (Boyd and Richerson 1985, 2005; D. Campbell 1965, 1975; Lumsden and Wilson 1981; Richerson and Boyd 2005; E. Wilson 1975, 1998). Genes and culture are "inseverably linked" (Lumsden and E. O. Wilson, 1983, p. 117). This seems true, as far as it goes, but, for our immediate needs, it does not go very far.

We are, in short, more or less on our own.

One increasingly popular option for those attempting to provide a scientific account of politics these days is the theory of rational choice. In *An Economic Theory of Democracy* (1957), to take an altogether splendid example, Anthony Downs imagined that parties and citizens follow the dictates of rationality, approaching "every situation with one eye on the gains to be had, the other eye on costs, a delicate ability to balance them, and a strong desire to follow wherever rationality leads" (pp. 7–8). Rational choice theory is "one of the most impressive intellectual achievements of the first half of the twentieth century" and "an elegant machine for applying reason to problems of choice" (H. Simon 1983, p. 12).

Acknowledging this point, we turn for help in another direction, to psychology. Psychologists have generally greeted the assumptions of rational choice theory with skepticism, finding rationality both unrealistic and preemptive, a distraction from discovering what is really going on (e.g., Abelson 1976, 1995; Kahneman 2003a; Kahneman and Tversky 1979; H. Simon 1955). Our account of activation is informed by a general theory of human judgment, the cumulative and considerable achievement of the last half century of cognitive science, a development led most notably by Herbert Simon, Daniel Kahneman, and Amos Tversky.

When set against the model of rational choice that has reigned supreme over economics, the general model of reasoning offered up by psychology is, admittedly, something of a mess. But as Kinder and Weiss wrote some thirty years ago, just as the first waves of the new research on cognition were rolling in, "elegance ain't everything" (1978, p. 732). Putting the point rather more professionally, Daniel Kahneman began his Nobel Lecture by describing the contrast between economic and psychological approaches this way:

> Economists often criticize psychological research for its propensity to generate lists of errors and biases, and for its failure to offer a coherent alternative to the rational-agent model. This complaint is only partly justified: psychological theories of intuitive thinking cannot match the elegance and precision of formal normative models of belief and choice, but this is just another way of saying that rational models are psychologically unrealistic. Furthermore, the alternative to simple and precise models is not chaos. Psychology offers integrative concepts and mid-level generalizations which gain credibility from their ability to explain ostensibly different phenomena in diverse domains. (2003a, p. 1449)

The general theory we draw on here begins with the notion of bounded rationality, the assertion that "human thinking powers are very modest when compared with the complexities of the environments in which human beings live. Faced with complexity and uncertainty, lacking the wits to optimize, they must be content to suffice—to find 'good enough' solutions to their problems and 'good enough' courses of action" (H. Simon 1979, p. 3). Under bounded rationality, the human decision maker is represented as a person who is limited in computational capacity, and who searches very selectively through large realms of possibilities in order to discover what alternatives of action are available, and what the consequences of each of these alternatives are. The search is incomplete, often inadequate, based on uncertain information and partial ignorance, and usually terminated with the discovery of satisfactory, not optimal, courses of action. (H. Simon 1985, p. 295)

We argue that opinions on politics, like the decisions and judgments made in other domains of life, are governed by bounded rationality (Kahneman 2003a; Kahneman and Tversky 1979; Tversky and Kahneman 1974, 1981).[12] Two aspects of bounded rationality are especially relevant to the activation of ethnocentrism: sharp limitations of human attention and inevitable framing effects in human judgment. Ethnocentrism will be more or less important to public opinion on an issue depending on the ability of the issue to command the public's limited and fickle attention and on how the particular issue is framed.

Commanding Attention

The architecture of the human information processing system can be thought of as comprised of independent memories: a vast, virtually permanent memory store (long-term memory) and a small, temporary memory store, where information is consciously attended to and actively processed (working memory). Working memory has limited capacity, processes information serially, and encodes new information so that it can be "written" into long-term memory slowly. Attention is a scarce resource, and the command of attention is therefore crucial for "setting the agenda for human problem solving" (H. Simon 1983, p. 30).[13]

The capacity of politics to command attention should not be taken for granted. In a series of powerful essays written in the aftermath of World War I, Walter Lippmann argued that the trials and tribulations of daily life were compelling in a way that politics could rarely be. To expect ordinary people to become absorbed in the affairs of state would be to demand of them an appetite for political knowledge quite peculiar, if not actually pathological. We may be "concerned in public affairs," Lippmann wrote, but we are "immersed in our private ones" ([1922] 1997, p. 36).

Lippmann presented his argument without benefit of the kinds of systematic evidence we now require, but he was an unusually perceptive analyst, and on this point in particular he was surely right. Much as Lippmann suspected, Americans are "much more concerned with the business of buying and selling, earning and disposing of things, than they are with the 'idle' talk of politics" (Lane 1962, p. 25). While the vicissitudes of family, work, and health are central preoccupations, the events of political life remain, for the most part, peripheral curiosities. "Politics," as Robert Dahl once put it, "is a sideshow in the great circus of life" (1961, p. 305).[14]

A first precondition for the activation of ethnocentrism in the process of political judgment is that the issue in question command sufficient public attention. When for a significant fraction of the American public an issue becomes psychologically meaningful, then ethnocentrism may—*may*—come into play. Under these circumstances, when new information challenges a person's predisposition, an entire repertoire of defensive mental mechanisms swings into action. The person may engage in denial, bolstering, rationalization, differentiation, and more—all in the service of protecting and preserving the original predisposition. In this account, motivated reasoning, reasoning guided by predisposition, is impressively versatile— even if, as Abelson and Rosenberg once wrote, it would "mortify a logician" (1958, p. 5).[15]

But how do we fulfill that condition in politics? How do citizens "decide" to pay attention to one thing as against another? The simple answer is that this deciding is done, for the most part, for them. What the American public takes to be important in politics is a direct and immediate reflection of what the news media decide is important. How preoccupied Americans are with a problem depends in the first instance on the prominence of the problem in the news. Rising prices, unemployment, energy shortages, national defense: all these become high priority issues for the public after they first become high priority for newspapers and networks. News media are instruments of "agenda setting."[16]

Issues and problems come and go, and they typically come and go *rapidly* (Baumgartner and Jones 1993; Jones 1994).[17] Because some problems lend themselves to we-they thinking more than others do (see below), the importance of ethnocentrism as a predisposition guiding political judgment depends in part on the dynamics of agenda setting, the movement of problems onto and off of the national stage.

Framing the Issue

With the events of September 11, 2001, the war on terrorism moved dramatically onto the national stage. The attacks on New York and Washington commanded the American public's attention. The cluster of policies associated with terrorism thereby became eligible subjects for ethnocentric thinking. But the command of attention is a necessary condition, not a sufficient one. The activation of ethnocentrism requires something in addition: that the public understand the issue in a particular way—in a way that encourages them to see the issue in ethnocentric terms.

In a series of brilliant experiments, Daniel Kahneman and Amos Tversky showed that the judgments people reach and the decisions they make are subject to pervasive framing effects (Tversky and Kahneman 1981). Consider real patients confronting a choice between surgery and radiation. For one group of patients, the surgery option was described as associated with a 90 percent survival rate; for another group of patients, the same procedure was described as associated with a 10 percent mortality rate. The two descriptions—or frames—are formally identical. They differ only by what seems a superficial detail of presentation. It would be frivolous, from standard rational choice theory, for such a detail to matter. But in fact, patients presented with the survival frame were much more likely to choose surgery (McNeil et al. 1982). This result, and many more like it, leads to the conclusion that "framing effects are not a laboratory curiosity, but a ubiquitous reality" (Kahneman 2003a, p. 1459).[18]

Frames operate by altering the relative salience of different aspects of the problem. Different—but logically equivalent—frames highlight some features of the situation and mask others. Accessible features influence decisions; features of low accessibility are largely ignored. Framing is powerful because people generally passively accept the frame they are given.[19]

As Kahneman and Tversky discovered in decision making, so it should be in the judgments people form on matters of public policy. Perhaps even more so. For politics is "altogether too big, too complex, and too fleeting for direct acquaintance" (Lippmann [1922] 1997, p. 11). And so the public comes to depend on others for news about national and world affairs. Such affairs are inevitably complex, always subject to alternative interpretation. This gives elites the opportunity to impose their own particular interpretation of what is happening. Presidents, members of Congress, activists, policy analysts, candidates and officials, reporters, and editors are all engaged in a more or less continuous conversation over the meaning of current events. This conversation is formulated at least in part with the public in mind, and it becomes available to ordinary citizens in a multitude of ways: television news programs, newspaper editorials and syndicated columns, talk radio, blogs, direct mail, and Internet news services, among others. Through all these channels, citizens are bombarded with suggestions about how events should be understood—bombarded, we would say, with frames.

Elites spend as much time and money as they do crafting and disseminating frames because frames make a difference—good frames can command the attention of citizens and affect how they think.[20] This is relevant here because the activation of ethnocentrism is more likely insofar as there is resonance—"close correspondence" or "good fit"—between ethnocentrism, on the one hand, and what is taking place in politics that commands attention, on the other. Fit improves, and activation is more likely, when politics is portrayed as conflict among groups. All the better, from this perspective, if the conflict is framed as a struggle between just *two* groups—between, say, Palestinians and Israelis, or Sunni and Shia, or civilized nations and terrorist barbarians. Better still if such conflict can be framed in moral terms, as a struggle between good and evil. Conflict framed as a struggle between two groups—one side, malicious and brutal, bent on stealing or ruining; the other side, nobly determined to protect what is rightfully theirs—is just the sort of thing to set ethnocentrism to work.

ONWARD

Soon enough we will be swimming in details about American public opinion on particular topics: terrorism, foreign aid, immigration, gay marriage, welfare reform, affirmative action, and more. The details are important—they are indispensable if we are to create sensible models of public opinion from one topic to the next and therefore generate credible evidence that ethnocentrism actually adds to what we already know. At the same time, we run the risk of becoming captivated by detail, and distracted away from our main goal, which is to establish the importance of ethnocentrism in general, across many dissimilar issues. That is the main work of the framework spelled out in this chapter: to help us move back and forth between ethnocentrism as a general predisposition, on the one hand, and particular claims about concrete policy disputes, on the other.

We start in on the details in the next chapter. There we introduce and defend a particular way of measuring ethnocentrism (*two* ways, actually), describe the general shape of ethnocentrism in American society today, demonstrate that ethnocentrism is distinct from predispositions that are fixtures in standard accounts of public opinion, and show why some Americans are more ethnocentric than others.

CHAPTER 3

American Ethnocentrism Today

We have argued that ethnocentrism is an attitude that divides the world into two opposing camps. From an ethnocentric point of view, groups are either "friend" or they are "foe." Ethnocentrism is a general outlook on social difference; it is prejudice, broadly conceived.

Having developed this conception of ethnocentrism in the preceding chapters, here we introduce and explore measures of ethnocentrism set in the contemporary American scene. Our immediate purpose is to establish that our measures are worth taking seriously—and therefore so too are the tests of ethnocentrism's political significance that we present in the chapters to come.

We begin with a brief discussion of the surveys that supply the empirical testing ground for our project. Then we introduce and defend our measures of ethnocentrism: a primary measure based on stereotyping and a secondary measure based on sentiment. Next, in the core of the chapter, we employ these measures in order to test three basic claims about ethnocentrism in the contemporary United States. First, is in-group favoritism ubiquitous? Second, is animosity toward out-groups generalized? And third, are in-group favoritism and out-group animosity tightly bound to one another? Informed by these tests, we then create measures of ethnocentrism, examine their properties, and use them to investigate the relationship between ethnocentrism, on the one hand, and standard political predispositions, on the other. In the final section of the chapter, we take up the puzzle of individual differences in ethnocentrism. Why are some Americans more ethnocentric than others?

SOURCES OF EVIDENCE

Our test of the importance of ethnocentrism comes down to ascertaining ethnocentrism's impact on public opinion. To what degree, if at all, are Americans' views on the war on terrorism or affirmative action in college admissions a consequence of ethnocentrism? To answer such questions, we rely principally on recent sample surveys from two excellent sources: the General Social Surveys (GSS) carried out by the National Opinion Research Center at the University of Chicago; and the National Election Studies (NES) undertaken by the Center for Political Studies of the Institute for Social Research, located at the University of Michigan.[1]

We focus on these studies in the first instance because they carry the measures of group stereotypes that we believe should be the centerpiece of the empirical analysis of ethnocentrism. The stereotype measures were developed at the National Opinion Research Center and were included for the first time in the 1990 GSS. In slightly variant form, they were included on more recent editions of both the GSS and NES. The stereotype measures suit our purposes well: the battery of questions asks about the qualities of in-groups and out-groups (a necessary feature of ethnocentrism), about a multiplicity of qualities (multiple indicators are very valuable for measurement and analysis purposes), and about multiple out-groups (necessary as well since ethnocentrism entails generalized hostility). In short, GSS and NES supply just what we need. We will say more about the measures in the next section.

Moreover, both GSS and NES go to considerable—and expensive—lengths to attain representative samples. In each case, respondents are selected through a multistage area probability design. This ensures that every household in the continental United States has an equal probability of falling into the sample.

Of course, not all those designated by the sampling design are actually interviewed. Some cannot be located; some are never at home; and some, despite repeated urging, simply refuse. Still, more than seven in ten are successfully interviewed. The combination of probability sampling and high response rates implies that Americans interviewed by GSS and by NES should constitute a faithful sample of the nation as a whole—and for the most part, they do. On measures of income, education, marital status, and similar demographics, the samples we analyze resemble the national population quite closely.[2]

Another advantage is size. For example, in the fall of 1992, the NES carried out personal interviews with a sample of nearly 2500 Americans of voting age. Large samples are highly desirable for the kinds of analysis we undertake since, for some purposes, we need to partition the national population into subgroupings—defined by race or national heritage or gender or some other characteristic.

The surveys we analyze are large in another sense as well. They go on for quite a long while—in the view of some respondents, no doubt a *very* long while. The interviews are not brief snatches of conversation; they are lengthy discussions. For example, the average conversation between interviewer and respondent in the 1992 NES lasted for more than two and one-half hours (160 minutes, to be precise), divided roughly evenly into two separate conversations, one before the election and one right after. From our perspective, this is time well spent. The interviews cover a wide territory: in the domain of public policy, they range all the way from affirmative action and welfare reform to military aggression and foreign aid. Such diversity of cases is just what we need to test the claim of ethnocentrism. Moreover, the interviews devote considerable space to standard political predispositions as well as important aspects of social background: partisan identification, education, religion, and much more. Such assessments are vital to our project, for they allow us to estimate the impact of ethnocentrism on policy opinion while controlling for alternative explanations.

One final advantage of our reliance on GSS and NES is worth noting. Both GSS and NES are ongoing and long-running. GSS was launched in 1973; the first NES was carried out in 1948. Both are dedicated to ensuring comparability of analysis across time. Individual studies, of course, take place in different settings: before and after wars, in good times and bad, under Democratic and Republican administrations, in the midst of campaigns or in the quiet moments in between. The combination of comparable designs and measures in study after study, on the one hand, and dramatic variation in the political environment, on the other, enables us to treat such variation as "natural experiments." And as we will see, this gives us leverage over the question of the conditions under which ethnocentrism is activated.

MEASURING ETHNOCENTRISM

Ethnocentrism is commonly expressed through *stereotypes*. Stereotypes refer to the beliefs we possess about social groups—what we know or what we think we know about "poets, professors, professional wrestlers, and film stars" (Brown 1965, p. 188), among others.[3] Stereotypes capture the characteristics that define a social group, that set it apart from others. Most often, such characteristics have to do with underlying dispositions—temperament, intelligence, trustworthiness—the deep core of human nature. When we say that "Jews are pushy" or that "blacks are lazy," we are trafficking in stereotypes.[4]

Stereotyping is often held up for reprimand, but it is an inevitable aspect of human cognition. To negotiate and make sense of the world, we need stereotypes. "Life is so short," as Gordon Allport once put it, "and the demands upon us for practical adjustments so great, that we cannot let our ignorance detain us in our daily transactions. We have to decide whether objects are good or bad by classes. We cannot weigh each object in the world by itself. Rough and ready rubrics, however coarse and broad, have to suffice" (1954, p. 9).

If stereotypes are grounded in ordinary cognitive processes and if they reduce the social world to manageable size, they are, of course, very much a mixed blessing. For one thing, stereotypes exaggerate differences and sharpen boundaries: in-groups and out-groups appear more different from each other than they actually are (e.g., D. Campbell 1967; Taylor et al. 1978; Krueger, Rothbart, and Sriram 1989). For another, stereotypes tend to portray members of out-groups as though they were all the same: individual variation is flattened, anomalous cases are set aside (e.g., Kunda and Oleson 1995, 1997; Kinder and McConnaughy 2006; Park and Rothbart 1982). Third, stereotypes are permeated by affect. To say that "Jews are pushy" or that "blacks are lazy" is not only to make a judgment but also to express an emotion. And fourth, stereotypes are easily activated and, once activated, influence judgment and behavior in a variety of ways.[5]

To measure ethnocentrism expressed in terms of stereotypes, we draw on a battery of questions developed by the National Opinion Research Center at the University of Chicago and used for the first time in the 1990 installment of the GSS.[6] In these questions, survey respondents were presented with a series of paired antonyms—*hardworking* versus *lazy*, say—and asked to judge whether members of some designated group—whites, for example—are mostly hardworking, mostly lazy, or somewhere in between. Here is the question exactly as it appeared in the 2000 NES:

> Now I have some questions about different groups in our society. I'm going to show you a seven-point scale on which the characteristics of people in a group can be rated. In the first statement a score of 1 means that you think almost all of the people in that group are "hard-working." A score of 7 means that you think almost all of the people in the group are "lazy." A score of 4 means that you think the group is not towards one end or the other, and of course you may choose any number in between that comes closest to where you think people in the group stand.
>
> Where would you rate whites in general on this scale?

After being asked to judge whites on this score, respondents were asked to make the same judgment, this time about blacks, Asian Americans, and Hispanic Americans, in turn. The procedure was then repeated for two additional dimensions: "intelligent versus unintelligent" and "trustworthy versus untrustworthy."[7]

These questions suit our purposes well. Moral character and intellectual capacity are central features of stereotypes in general (e.g., Stangor and Lange 1994; Fiske 1998). Moreover, claims of in-group superiority are commonly expressed precisely in these terms: that in-groups are generally more trustworthy, more industrious, and so on than are out-groups (M. Brewer and Campbell 1976).[8] And on a more technical note, assessments of in-groups and out-groups along multiple dimensions—intelligence, trustworthiness, hard-working, and so on—mean that we can submit our overall measure of ethnocentrism to stringent empirical tests (as we will shortly see).

In the GSS and NES questions, social groups are defined by race: white, black, Asian American, and Hispanic American. This, of course, is not the only way to partition the social world, and so not the only way to define ethnocentrism. All societies are divided, and they are divided in a multitude of ways. Dispatch competent ethnographers to any country in the world, Daniel Posner suggests, and they will return with accounts of dozens of differences among the population they were sent to study: "the color of their skin, the religions they practice, the dialects they speak, the places from which they migrated, the foods they eat, and the marriage rituals they practice" (2005, p. 529). Acknowledging that human society can be partitioned in limitless variety, group boundaries specified by race in particular should serve us well in our effort to demonstrate the political significance of ethnocentrism.

We say this partly for historical reasons. From the very outset, American politics and society have been organized in important ways by conflict over race. Constitutional arguments over the meaning of citizenship; the debate over slavery and secession; the Civil War, Reconstruction, and Redemption; the rising of the civil rights movement; on up through contemporary arguments over affirmative action and fair representation: race has been and remains today a central theme of American political life (e.g., Burnham 1974; Myrdal 1944; Klinkner and Smith 1999).

And although race may be a specious concept—largely without support in modern biology—it remains a powerful idea in everyday life. Here we refer to the folk theory of race, race as popularly understood (Hirschfeld 1996). The folk theory of race begins with the axiom that human populations can be partitioned into distinct types or kinds on the basis of their concrete, physical differences. Race is transmitted and fixed at birth; it is inherited and immutable. Differences among races are natural: they derive from some underlying essence. And finally, this essence finds expression not only in physical appearance but in qualities of temperament, intellect, and character as well. Defined this way, the folk theory of race is widespread and deeply entrenched (e.g., Bargh 1999; Devine 1989; Hirschfeld 1996).[9]

Finally, notice that the stereotype questions are formatted so that people can express favoritism for their own group without flagrantly violating norms of fairness. Thus, for example, white Americans who believe that blacks are less intelligent than whites can say so indirectly, in a sequence of separated judgments, without ever having to subscribe explicitly to the invidious comparison. In addition to this practical advantage, measuring ethnocentrism through social comparison is also appropriate on theoretical grounds. Ethnocentrism entails assessments of in-groups and of out-groups, and this is just what the stereotype battery requires.[10]

The stereotype battery fits our conception of ethnocentrism well, but we should not make the mistake of thinking that the correspondence is perfect. Nor should we imagine that we have come across an immaculate measure of stereotyping: measurement is inevitably imperfect. For these reasons, it is always prudent to have a backup, if only to check on the robustness of results. Our second-best measure of ethnocentrism draws on the NES 0–100 point "feeling thermometer" scale. Designed to serve as a general-purpose measure of political evaluation, the thermometer scale was introduced into the NES series in 1964. It is presented to survey respondents this way:

> I'd like to get your feelings toward some of our political leaders and other people who are in the news these days. I will use something we call the feeling thermometer and here is how it works:
>
> I'll read the name of a person and I'd like you to rate that person using the feeling thermometer. Ratings between 50 degrees and 100 degrees mean that you feel favorable and warm toward the person. Ratings between 0 degrees and 50 degrees mean that you don't feel favorable toward the person and that you don't care too much for that person. You would rate the person at the 50-degree mark if you don't feel particularly warm or cold toward the person.

After evaluating a series of prominent political leaders, respondents are asked to apply the same thermometer scale to a succession of political and social groups. Counted among these groups are (almost always) whites, blacks, Asian Americans, and Hispanic Americans.

The thermometer scale offers a more direct look into the emotional aspect of ethnocentrism than does the stereotype battery, but the parallel in measurement between the two is otherwise close. As with the stereotype battery, when presented with the thermometer scale, people are asked to evaluate in-groups and out-groups in separate assessments, and they can express favoritism for their own group without conspicuously violating norms of fairness.

In a short while we will document that the two measures are correlated— as they should be since we think of them as alternative measures of the same underlying construct. We will also show that the two measures are distinct—a reflection at least in part of the difference between cognitive and affective systems.[11] This means that in the chapters ahead, we can use the one measure to check on the other. And it also means that we can take our investigation of ethnocentrism further back into the past than we otherwise could: while the stereotype battery is a relatively recent addition to the GSS and the NES, the thermometer scale has been appearing in national surveys for much longer.[12]

IN-GROUP FAVORITISM?

Sumner was convinced that ethnocentrism was a universal condition. First in *Folkways* and then more systematically in *The Science of Society*, he reviewed the anthropological evidence, concluding that around the world, ethnocentrism prevails.

Since Sumner's time, the single best test of the claim of ethnocentrism's universality comes from a most remarkable—and mostly overlooked—study organized by Robert LeVine and Donald Campbell in the early 1960s. LeVine and Campbell set out to test the universality of ethnocentrism by examining group perceptions and assessments in multiple cultural settings. Toward that end, they arranged for standardized interviews to be carried out in 1965 with 1,500 respondents distributed evenly across each of 30 ethnic groups scattered across Uganda, Kenya, and Tanzania. The groups selected constituted the "major peoples with compact territorial identity" in the region and represented a wide range of economic, linguistic, and cultural traditions. Those interviewed were asked (in the local language) about their own group as well as each of 9 out-groups in their own country. They were questioned about many things: their familiarity and contact with other groups, their willingness to take part in various social activities with members of other groups, and much more. But the primary business was to ask about stereotypes—both stereotypes that people applied to their own group and those they applied to others. That is, LeVine and Campbell decided that stereotyping was the place to look for evidence of ethnocentrism. We think they were wise to do so.

The results of this fascinating study, reported by Marilynn Brewer and Donald Campbell in 1976 in *Ethnocentrism and Intergroup Attitudes*, reveal pervasive in-group favoritism. All 30 groups rated their own group more favorably than they did the average out-group. On such central traits as honesty, friendliness, peacefulness, and generosity, in-groups regarded themselves as superior, on average, to out-groups. A more stringent test of in-group favoritism would consider not just the average out-group, but each out-group taken up individually. Did all groups rate their own group more favorably than they did *all* out-groups? Almost: 27 of 30 groups did so.[13]

TABLE 3.1. In-group favoritism expressed through stereotypes (lazy versus hard-working)

Assessments by:	Assessments of:			
	Whites	Blacks	Hispanics	Asians
Whites	0.32	−0.06	0.02	0.29
	(1627)	(1609)	(1538)	(1511)
Blacks	0.20	0.24	0.16	0.25
	(264)	(268)	(249)	(239)
Hispanics	0.33	−0.01	0.28	0.30
	(168)	(168)	(167)	(157)
Asians	0.38	−0.18	0.02	0.63
	(28)	(27)	(27)	(28)

Source: 1992 NES.

Note: Table entry is the average assessment of each group, among respondents in each racial/ethnic group, on the lazy versus hard-working trait question. The trait assessments are coded from −1 (Nearly all are lazy) to +1 (Nearly all are hard-working). Number of observations appears in parentheses.

Some traits show more evidence of ethnocentrism than others. In-group favoritism was most pronounced on characteristics that make for comfortable and smooth interpersonal relations. *We* are trustworthy, cooperative, peaceful, and honest; *those people over there* are untrustworthy, competitive, quarrelsome, and dishonest. Brewer and Campbell concluded that the fundamental distinction between in-group and out-group is captured by "feelings of trust, familiarity, and personal security." Following Enloe (1972), they suggest that the basic function of group life is to inform an individual "where he belongs and whom he can trust."[14]

Brewer and Campbell are convincing, but their evidence has nothing to say about ethnocentrism among groups in advanced industrial societies like the United States. How common is in-group favoritism in a fully modern setting? Do Americans attribute favorable characteristics more to their own group than they do to out-groups? Or, put the other way around, do they attribute undesirable characteristics less to their own group than they do to out-groups?

To answer these questions, consider table 3.1. There we have summarized results for a single characteristic (lazy versus hard-working) taken from a single survey (the 1992 NES). The columns of the table are defined by the group that is being rated. In the 1992 NES, the columns refer to ratings of whites, blacks, Hispanics, and Asians. The rows of the table are defined by the group that is providing the rating: ratings by whites, blacks, Hispanics, and Asians. The main elements of the table are mean scores on the trait, coded from −1 (almost all are lazy) to +1 (almost all are hard-working), with 0 representing the midpoint. A positive score indicates a favorable judgment, just as a negative score indicates an unfavorable judgment. The table also provides the number of cases (in parentheses) for each calculation. In some instances, this number is small (for Asian Americans, the number is perilously small).

Do whites, as predicted, attribute the characteristic of hard-working more to their own group than they do to blacks, Hispanics, and Asians? The first row of table 3.1 shows that they do. Asian Americans display in-group favoritism too, and even more conspicuously (fourth row of table 3.1). The results for blacks and Hispanics are different, however. Both blacks and Hispanics see their own group as generally hard-working—but they generally see other groups as hard-working too. As a result, in-group favoritism among black and Hispanic Americans is partial or limited. It shows up in just one respect. Black Americans believe blacks to be more hard-working than Hispanics, and Hispanics, returning the favor, believe that Hispanics are more hard-working than blacks.

The pattern of results shown in table 3.1 is entirely general. It is just what we see elsewhere, in other NES and GSS surveys, and on other characteristics: intelligence, patriotism, self-reliance, trustworthiness, propensity for violence, and more. Everywhere we look, we find general in-group favoritism among white and Asian Americans, and partial in-group favoritism among black and Hispanic Americans.[15]

Replication is reassuring, but the samples for Asian Americans in GSS and NES are so undersized that we cannot be sure that in-group favoritism really applies to them. To find a sizable and high-quality sample of Asian Americans, we turned to the Multi-City Study of Urban Inequality (MCSUI). Supported by the Russell Sage Foundation, MCSUI was carried out between 1992 and 1994 in four American cities: Atlanta, Boston, Detroit, and Los Angeles. In Los Angeles alone, where our analysis concentrates, more than 4000 adults were interviewed, divided more or less evenly among whites, blacks, Hispanics, and Asians (the last three groups were deliberately oversampled). Conveniently for our purposes, MCSUI included a stereotype measure. Each Los Angeles respondent was asked to offer judgments about the character of four racial groups—whites, blacks, Hispanic Americans, and Asian Americans—with respect to each of five characteristics: intelligence, friendliness, fairness, law-abiding, and self-supporting.[16]

It turns out that Asians living in Los Angeles regarded their group to be superior, on average, to *all* other groups on *every* characteristic. Asians are smarter, friendlier, fairer, more law-abiding, and more self-supporting than are whites, blacks, and Hispanics—all this according to Asians themselves. It would appear that the pattern we detected in GSS and NES surveys with small samples holds generally.[17]

Elsewhere in the Los Angeles study, we find what we found before. Whites display in-group favoritism generally. Blacks and Hispanics show in-group favoritism partially: they display in-group favoritism compared to each other, but not toward more advantaged groups. There is one interesting wrinkle here. Neither the GSS nor the NES form of the stereotype battery asks about friendliness. The Los Angeles study did. And when it comes to friendliness, the expected ethnocentric pattern shows up for *all* groups. Blacks and Hispanics, like whites and Asians, believe their group is easier to get along with than other groups are. This result is interesting in light of Brewer and Campbell's claim, based on surveys in East Africa, that in-groups constitute communities of trust and comfort.[18]

Sumner treated ethnocentrism as a universal condition, an inescapable consequence of inevitable conflict between rival groups. Our first round of results suggests that Sumner was wrong. In-group favoritism is common, but not universal. For African Americans and Hispanic Americans, ethnocentrism is partial—it shows up vis-à-vis some out-groups but not for others, and for some characteristics but not for all. Put another way, in the United States at the beginning of the twenty-first century, blacks and Hispanics have a comparatively difficult time asserting their own group's superiority. Ethnocentrism would seem to be, as Tajfel once put it, something of "a one-way street," appearing with consistency only in the views of dominant groups.[19]

An inkling of this was turned up by Brewer and Campbell in their results from East Africa. They found that traits having to do with achievement and status were less apt to show evidence of in-group favoritism. Judgments about a group's intelligence or wealth seemed to be conditioned on actual levels of resources and power. Group members might prefer to see themselves as capable and successful, but such judgments are constrained by real conditions. Likewise, in modern complex societies, low-status group members may evaluate high-status groups more positively on aspects tied directly to status differences. In effect, as Marilynn Brewer says, "they are simply acknowledging objective differences in status, power, or wealth and resources" (2007, p. 733).[20]

That is what we find for ethnocentrism expressed in terms of group stereotypes. What happens when we test for in-group favoritism making use of the thermometer scale?

Table 3.2 presents a representative sample of results, drawing again from the 1992 NES. The table is set up in just the same way as its predecessor, with the columns of the table defined by the group that is being evaluated and the rows of the table defined by the group that is providing the evaluation. This time the elements of the table are mean scores on the thermometer rating scale, ranging in principle from 0 (very cold) to 100 (very warm).

TABLE 3.2. In-group favoritism expressed through sentiment

Ratings by:	Ratings of:			
	Whites	Blacks	Hispanics	Asians
Whites	71.3	61.2	58.2	58.4
	(1645)	(1638)	(1592)	(1609)
Blacks	71.5	88.0	67.2	61.9
	(272)	(276)	(256)	(253)
Hispanics	71.7	69.4	79.4	62.9
	(170)	(170)	(174)	(165)
Asians	65.2	59.6	56.0	72.8
	(27)	(26)	(26)	(27)

Source: 1992 NES.

Note: Table entry is the average rating of each group, among respondents in each racial/ethnic group, using the feeling thermometer. Number of observations appears in parentheses. The ratings are coded from 0 (Coldest) to 100 (Warmest).

Table 3.2 reveals general support for in-group favoritism—*very general support*. Whites and Asians feel more warmly toward their own group than they do toward others. But so too do blacks and Hispanics. Moreover, this pattern of general in-group favoritism emerges in other surveys we have analyzed, again for all groups, and at least as strongly. Expressed in terms of sentiment, in-group favoritism is thriving.[21]

Taken all around, then, we find consistent—if not quite universal—support for in-group favoritism. And we find in-group favoritism not among artificial experimental groups or among ethnic groups of East Africa. Rather, we find it among whites and blacks and Hispanics and Asians in the world's oldest and richest democratic republic.

PREJUDICE, BROADLY CONCEIVED?

If ethnocentrism is really "prejudice, broadly conceived," then we should find two kinds of consistency in the beliefs and attitudes that Americans hold toward social groups. First of all is consistency among various beliefs about a particular group. Whites who regard blacks as lazy should also think of them as unintelligent and untrustworthy. It was consistency of this kind that Levinson and his colleagues (Adorno et al. 1950) took as evidence for anti-Semitism. Second, we also look for consistency among beliefs *across* groups. What is the relationship between, say, black Americans' view of Hispanics' intelligence and their assessment of the trustworthiness of Asian Americans? There is no logical connection between the two. But according to ethnocentrism, black Americans who are unimpressed with the intelligence of Hispanic Americans should also find Asian Americans untrustworthy.

A seemingly straightforward index of consistency is provided by the correlation coefficient. It is a simple matter to calculate the relevant coefficients, and when we do, we discover plenty of consistency of both kinds. Whites who regard blacks as lazy also think of them as unintelligent and untrustworthy, just as black Americans who appear unimpressed with the intelligence of Hispanic Americans also find Asian Americans untrustworthy. And on it goes.

These results are certainly compatible with the claim of prejudice broadly conceived, but for technical reasons, it is hard to know exactly what to make of them. On the one hand, the observed correlations are no doubt attenuated because of unreliability in the measures: the response categories are coarse, respondents misspeak, interviewers make mistakes, and so on. This means that the evidence for ethnocentrism might well be stronger than the raw correlations suggest. On the other hand, the correlations may be artificially enhanced due to systematic response error. The stereotype questions are designed to measure just one thing—beliefs about the characteristic attributes of groups—but because of their unusual format, they may also inadvertently measure something else as well: namely, the systematic way respondents make their way through the question series. Faced with the stereotype battery, respondents may proceed by relying on a judgment heuristic that Amos Tversky and Daniel Kahneman call "anchoring and adjustment" (Tversky and Kahneman 1974). The implication here is that the real evidence for ethnocentrism might be weaker than the raw correlations suggest.

Confirmatory factor analysis (CFA) is the proper remedy for problems of this sort. Using CFA, we can test the claim of generalized prejudice, while correcting for both kinds of error (Jöreskog 1969; Bollen 1989). A typical set of CFA results appears in table 3.3. This analysis is based on the responses of white Americans to the stereotype battery present in the 1992 NES. To test the claim of generalized prejudice, we factor analyzed the empirical structure of twelve indicators: four groups—blacks, Hispanics, Asians, and whites—rated on three attributes—intelligent, hard-working, and violent. (We included stereotypes about whites, the in-group, as well as stereotypes about the three out-groups, so we could test whether in-group solidarity and out-group prejudice are connected. We will get to those results shortly.) As we have noted, ethnocentrism requires consistency at two levels: both within group and across group. In the factor analysis model, group-specific factors cause assessments of particular attributes: that is, the latent variable "attitude toward Hispanics" causes judgments about intelligence among Hispanics, laziness among

TABLE 3.3. Prejudice broadly conceived? Maximum likelihood factor analysis of group stereotypes held by whites (estimates based on variance-covariance matrix)

| | Factor loadings | | | | |
	Whites	Asians	Hispanics	Blacks	Reliability
Whites—lazy	0.64				0.31
Whites—smart	−0.68				0.32
Whites—peaceful	−0.78				0.45
Asians—lazy		0.70			0.26
Asians—smart		−0.81			0.41
Asians—peaceful		−0.78			0.45
Hispanics—lazy			0.61		0.26
Hispanics—smart			−0.70		0.45
Hispanics—peaceful			−0.63		0.33
Blacks—lazy				0.76	0.44
Blacks—smart				−0.70	0.42
Blacks—peaceful				−0.72	0.37

Chi-square with 30 degrees of freedom = 133.90 ($p < 0.01$).

Adjusted goodness of fit = 0.961.

Root mean square residual = 0.051.

| Correlations between the latent factors | | | | |
	Whites	Asians	Hispanics	Blacks
Whites	1.00			
Asians	0.13	1.00		
Hispanics	0.03	0.56	1.00	
Blacks	−0.05	0.39	0.71	1.00

Source: 1992 NES.

Hispanics, and so forth. The model allows for these group-specific factors to be correlated: that is, the latent variable "attitude toward Hispanics" is correlated with the latent variable "attitude toward Asian Americans," and so on.[22]

The results appear in table 3.3. Notice first of all that the model fits the observed relationships quite well.[23] Second, particular stereotyped beliefs load sizably and quite uniformly on each of the four group factors. Thus, the requirement of consistency within group holds.[24] And third, the relationships between attitudes toward out-groups are also significant and substantial. They range from 0.39 (the correlation between attitude toward Asian Americans and attitude toward black Americans) to 0.71 (the correlation between attitude toward Hispanic Americans and attitude toward black Americans). That is, what whites think about one out-group is quite consistent with what they think about another, just as ethnocentrism requires.

The results presented in table 3.3 closely resemble what we turn up when we estimate comparable models in other surveys, for whites and for other racial groups as well. By these various tests, ethnocentrism does indeed seem to be prejudice, broadly conceived.[25]

IN-GROUP SOLIDARITY AND OUT-GROUP PREJUDICE?

As we learned in chapter 1, William Graham Sumner thought that in-group solidarity and out-group prejudice would always be found together: "Loyalty to the group, sacrifice for it, hatred and contempt for outsiders, brotherhood within, warlikeness without—all grow together, common products of the same situation" ([1906] 2002, p. 13).

This is not what we find. Table 3.3 contains the relevant results, and as shown there, the evidence runs against Sumner's expectation. The correlations between attitude toward the in-group (whites) and attitude toward various out-groups are miniscule: 0.13, 0.03, and −0.05. The latter two are essentially zero—neither differs from zero by standard statistical tests. And the former, though barely statistically significant, is trivial substantively and runs in a direction opposite to that predicted.

Nor do we turn up more favorable evidence elsewhere: in the 1990 GSS, or in the 1996 NES, or in the 2000 GSS. Alternative measures and specifications produce the same result. Contrary to the proposition that the more in-group favoritism, the more out-group animosity, the two seem quite unconnected.[26] This finding supports Marilynn Brewer's (2007) conclusion, based primarily on her review of experimental results. Strong attachment to the in-group appears to be compatible with a wide range of sentiments toward out-groups. In-group solidarity and out-group hostility are bundled together less tightly than Sumner originally believed.[27]

MEASURES OF ETHNOCENTRISM

For all the analysis that is to come, we need to build a general measure of ethnocentrism; two measures, really: a primary measure based on stereotypes; and a secondary measure, based on sentiment. The two scales are put together in parallel ways. Both hinge on comparison, on preferring in-groups to out-groups.

Here is the formula for building the primary measure of ethnocentrism (E):

$$E = \{(\text{Trait}_1 \text{ in-group score} - \text{Trait}_1 \text{ average out-group score})$$
$$+ (\text{Trait}_2 \text{ in-group score} - \text{Trait}_2 \text{ average out-group score})$$
$$+ (\text{Trait}_3 \text{ in-group score} - \text{Trait}_3 \text{ average out-group score})\}/3$$

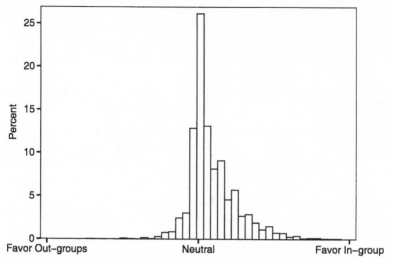

FIGURE 3.1. Distribution of ethnocentrism based on social stereotypes. Source: 1992, 1996, 2000, and 2004 NES.

Notice that by this formula each trait—hard-working or intelligent or trustworthy—carries equal weight. More complicated schemes are possible, of course, but the factor analysis results imply something very close to equal weighing. Our experience with more complicated weighting schemes is that they produce overall scores that are difficult to distinguish from that generated by equal weighting. And in any case, weighting traits equally generates a reliable overall scale (Cronbach's coefficient *alpha* for **E** = 0.77).[28]

E is scored to range from −1 to +1. A "perfect" score of +1 means that on each and every trait, "nearly all" members of the in-group are believed to be virtuous and "nearly all" members of all out-groups are believed to be virtue-less. A score of +1 is perfect in the sense that it represents an extreme form of ethnocentrism. A score of −1 is equally perfect, but in the opposite direction: −1 represents a topsy-turvy world in which out-groups are seen as virtuous and in-groups as utterly without virtue. An overall score of 0, finally, indicates an absence of ethnocentrism, that on average, in-group and out-groups are indistinguishable.

Figure 3.1 presents the distribution of scores on **E**. (The figure is based on pooling respondents from the 1992, 1996, 2000, and 2004 NES.) That the American public is ethnocentric on balance is revealed in figure 3.1 in two ways: first, the curve is displaced modestly away from the neutral point to the right, in the ethnocentric direction; and second, the curve is modestly asymmetric, sloping downward less precipitously to the right, toward the ethnocentric point of view.

Figure 3.1 reveals what might be called mild ethnocentrism. On the one hand, in-group favoritism is common. A clear majority of the American public—58.9 percent to be exact—scored above the neutral point (0), where in-groups and out-groups are thought to be equal.[29] On the other hand, in-group favoritism is restrained. No one claims categorical superiority: that members of one's own group are uniformly intelligent, hard-working, and trustworthy while members of all other groups are uniformly stupid, lazy, and unreliable. What we have here is a sense of perceptible but subtle superiority, widely shared.

To Levinson and his colleagues, ethnocentrism was something dark and dangerous. In their account, the "ethnocentric individual feels threatened by most of the groups to which he does not have a sense of belonging; if he cannot identify, he must oppose; if a group is not 'acceptable,' it is alien" (Adorno et al. 1950, p. 147). Likewise for Sumner: in his analysis, the typical manifestations of ethnocentrism included contempt, abomination, plunder, and war (Sumner [1906] 2002, pp. 12–13). No doubt ethnocentrism can take extreme form, but we do not insist on it; and in any case, it is not what we generally find.

Our second and secondary measure of ethnocentrism (call it E^*) is based on thermometer score ratings and is assembled by the same logic:

E^* = {feeling thermometer rating for in-group –
average feeling thermometer rating for out-groups}

Like E, E^* is scored to range from –1 to +1. Here a "perfect" score of +1 means that the in-group is rated very warmly (100 degrees) and all out-groups are rated very coldly (0 degrees). As before, a score of –1 is equally perfect in the opposite direction. An overall score of 0, finally, indicates an absence of ethnocentrism, that on average, in-group and out-groups elicit indistinguishable feelings. This formula generates a very reliable overall scale (Cronbach's coefficient *alpha* for E^* = 0.88).[30]

Figure 3.2 presents the distribution of scores on E^*. (As before, we pool respondents from the 1992, 1996, 2000, and 2004 NES.) In a society free of ethnocentrism, E^* scores should be distributed in a symmetric and narrow band around the neutral point, indicating that Americans feel no more warmly (or coolly) toward their own group than they do toward out-groups. In practice, as figure 3.2 shows, this is not what we find. The distribution of the ethnocentrism scale is not centered at neutrality. Instead, like scores on E but more decisively, scores on E^* are displaced to the right, in the ethnocentric direction. Nor is the distribution symmetric; rather, respondents thin out much more rapidly to the left of neutrality than they do to the right, in the region of ethnocentrism. As before, extreme ethnocentrism is rare, but in mild form, it is pervasive.[31]

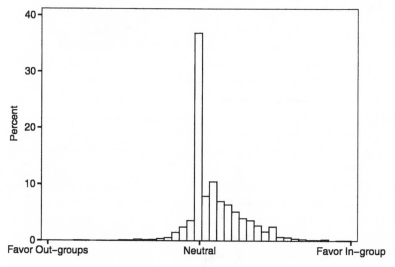

FIGURE 3.2. Distribution of ethnocentrism based on group sentiment. Source: 1992, 1996, 2000, and 2004 NES.

We have been proceeding under the assumption that that the two measures of ethnocentrism—E and E*—reflect the same underlying construct. That they are distributed in roughly equivalent ways is encouraging on this point, of course. But if they really are alternative (if inevitably imperfect) measures of ethnocentrism, they must be correlated with one another. And so they are: pooling respondents from the 1992, 1996, 2000, and 2004 NES, the Pearson correlation (r) is 0.42.

CORRELATES OF ETHNOCENTRISM

Next we examine ethnocentrism's place among a standard set of social and political predispositions. We have argued that ethnocentrism represents a distinctive way of looking at the world. From an ethnocentric point of view, groups are either "friend" or "foe." As such, ethnocentrism might be correlated with other political predispositions—with certain varieties of conservatism, say—but it cannot be interchangeable with them. If that turned out to be true, then we would have no reason to proceed, no warrant for arguing that the understanding of public opinion has been diminished by the failure, up until now, to take ethnocentrism seriously. To see how closely ethnocentrism is associated with standard political predispositions, we rely on our primary measure of ethnocentrism, the one based on stereotypes (E), though the results would be no different were we to use the alternative measure based on group sentiment (E*).

We start with partisanship, first among equals when it comes to political predispositions. Most Americans think of themselves as Democrats or as Republicans. Party identification is a standing decision, a "durable attachment, not readily disturbed by passing events and personalities" (Campbell et al. [1960] 1980, p. 151). And it is consequential: "To the average person, the affairs of government are remote and complex, and yet the average citizen is asked periodically to formulate opinions about these affairs. . . . In this dilemma, having the party symbol stamped on certain candidates, certain issue positions, certain interpretations of reality is of great psychological convenience" (Stokes 1966, pp. 126–27; also see Bartels 2000; Converse 1966; Green, Palmquist, and Schickler 2002). To the extent that the issues we take up in the chapters ahead—from the war on terrorism to affirmative action in college admissions—generate strong and durable disagreements between Democratic and Republican elites, we would expect Democrats and Republicans in the general public to disagree as well. Put differently, partisanship is likely to play an important part in our analysis of public opinion. True enough, but whatever part partisanship plays in opinion must be independent of the part ethnocentrism plays. As table 3.4 reveals, partisanship and ethnocentrism are virtually uncorrelated.[32]

What about the relationship between ethnocentrism and views on the size and scope of government authority? Compared to citizens of other developed democracies, Americans are, on average, "suspicious of government, skeptical about the benefits of government authority, and impressed with the virtue of limiting government" (Kingdon 1999, p. 29). Moreover, differences among Americans on broad questions of governmental authority

TABLE 3.4. The relationship between ethnocentrism and social and political predispositions

	Full sample	Whites	Blacks	Hispanics
Partisanship	−0.06	−0.00	0.02	0.03
	(4923)	(3931)	(598)	(394)
Limited government	−0.03	−0.09	−0.05	−0.02
	(4947)	(3951)	(604)	(392)
Egalitarianism	−0.19	−0.18	0.07	−0.02
	(4974)	(3964)	(609)	(401)
Ideological identification	−0.07	−0.07	0.02	0.03
	(4945)	(3951)	(599)	(395)
Social trust	−0.08	−0.17	−0.02	−0.07
	(4898)	(3901)	(602)	(395)

Source: 1992, 1996, 2000, and 2004 NES.

Note: Table entry is the Pearson correlation coefficient. Number of observations appears in parentheses.

generate corresponding differences on a wide range of specific policy questions. Limited government is an important idea—but as table 3.4 shows, it
has no association with ethnocentrism.[33]

Alongside the American taste for limited government, and to some degree in opposition to it, is a preference for egalitarianism—what Tocqueville
called the American "passion" for equality. Americans seem to take egalitarian beliefs—that everyone is fundamentally the same under the skin,
that everyone deserves the same chance in life—seriously, and such general
beliefs appear to influence what they think government should do (if anything) about poverty, health care, discrimination, and more. As might be
expected, and as table 3.4 shows, egalitarianism and ethnocentrism are negatively correlated. Ethnocentric Americans are inclined, slightly but consistently, to reject egalitarian principles.[34]

Next we consider ideological identification. It turns out that when
asked directly, many American are willing to describe themselves in ideological terms—as liberals or (more often) as conservatives—and these
descriptions appear to be, if not sophisticated or philosophical, politically meaningful. Self-identified liberals tend to favor redistributive policies and social change; self-identified conservatives tend to celebrate the
market and express misgivings about racial integration (Conover and Feldman 1981; Levitin and Miller 1979). Liberals and conservatives also differ
when it comes to ethnocentrism—Americans who think of themselves as
conservative are a bit more ethnocentric, on average, than are those who
think of themselves as liberal—though the difference is tiny, as shown in
table 3.4.[35]

This brings us to social trust. Renewing a claim first made by Alexis de
Tocqueville, Robert Putnam (1993, 1995, 2000) has argued that social trust
is essential to democratic society. Without trust, community withers and
cooperative projects unravel. The prospects for democracy in a society in
which people "do not get along well with one another, do not trust one another, and do not associate with one another" would seem, as Robert Lane
once put it, "unpromising"; life in such a place would be "solitary, poore,
nasty, brutish, and short" (1959, p. 163, citing Hobbes's *Leviathan*).

Survey questions intended to measure social trust have been included
in recent National Election Studies. By design, these questions are utterly
general. They do not refer to any particular people (neighbors, coworkers,
strangers on the street). Nor do they do specify what it is that is to be en-
trusted (secrets, material possessions, one's own physical safety). As Almond
and Verba put it, the standard questions would seem to require "sweeping
judgments of human nature" (1963, p. 267). As such, we would expect to
find a negative relationship between ethnocentrism and social trust. And, as
shown in table 3.4, we do.[36]

The relationship between ethnocentrism and social trust is surprisingly weak, however. We expected to see a stronger relationship because of the emphasis placed on trust in defining in-group relations. In-groups, as Marilynn Brewer argues, are "bounded communities of mutual cooperation and trust" (2007, p. 732). In Brewer's analysis of ethnocentrism, nothing distinguishes social relations carried on within the group with those carried on across group boundaries more than trust.[37]

In sum, partisanship, limited government, equality, ideological identification, and social trust are often treated as important ingredients in American public opinion. Our analysis of opinion will certainly take them into account. But the findings presented in table 3.4 make clear that we can put away the worry that ethnocentrism brings nothing new to political analysis—that ethnocentrism is just another word for conservatism or anti-egalitarianism or the like. Ethnocentrism represents a distinctive outlook on social life, one that, as we will shortly show, has a distinctive and independent impact on public opinion.

ORIGINS OF ETHNOCENTRISM

In chapter 2 we argue that children are ready for ethnocentrism, that they come equipped with a predisposition to partition the world into social groups, treated as natural kinds, and that they express rudimentary forms of ethnocentrism: strong attachment to national symbols; ardent belief that their country and customs are best; stereotyped understandings of race, class, and gender. In time, some become less ethnocentric than others, and it is variation in ethnocentrism that is our immediate subject here. Such variation arises, we suggest, from three principal sources: from instruction and genetic endowment provided by parents, from the emergence of personality, and from values and skills imparted by higher education.

Parents

We expect to find a correspondence between the ethnocentrism of parents and the ethnocentrism of children on two grounds. First is learning. According to social learning theory, "the complex repertoires of behavior displayed by members of society are to a large extent acquired with little or no direct tuition through observation of response patterns exemplified by various socialization agents" (Bandura 1969, p. 213). Children do not rely exclusively on parents as socialization agents, but they rely on parents more than on any other single source. A significant part of social learning takes place through children imitating, internalizing, and reproducing what their parents say and do.

A second mechanism implicating parents is genetic transmission. As E. O. Wilson (1978) and others claim, a sizable fraction of human behavioral variation is plausibly attributed to genetic differences. Recent findings suggest that political predispositions bearing a strong resemblance to ethnocentrism have a significant and sizable genetic component. Thus parents may influence their biological offspring as much through the "genetic blueprint" they provide at conception as through the modeling and instruction they supply later on.[38]

In short, either for reasons of social learning or for reasons of genetic inheritance, or both, we should find evidence of correspondence in ethnocentrism of parents and their offspring.

The best place to look to see if this is so is the extraordinary study of political socialization created by M. Kent Jennings. In the spring of 1965, under Jennings's direction, a national sample of high school seniors was interviewed on a wide range of political subjects. Simultaneously and independently, parents of the students were questioned as well, on many of the same subjects.[39] Fortunately for our purposes, the standard thermometer score battery appeared in both sets of interviews. Parents and offspring alike were asked to report their feelings toward a series of social groups— including groups defined by race. Not so fortunately, racial groups in 1965 meant white or black. Asian Americans and Hispanic Americans were not on the list, and in 1965, it probably would have seemed strange to the majority of the respondents to have included these two groups. In order to build a measure of ethnocentrism, however, we needed more than just ratings of blacks and whites. And so we supplemented racial evaluations with religious ones. In 1965, parents and offspring were asked to evaluate Catholics, Jews, and Protestants as well as blacks and whites. And from other questions included in the interview, we were able to ascertain the race and religious affiliation of both parents and offspring. Using information about race and religion, we then could place parents and offspring into one of three classes. If they displayed in-group favoritism on race and religion, they received a score of 1.0. If they displayed in-group favoritism neither on race nor on religion, they received a score of 0.0. And if they displayed in-group favoritism on one form of classification but not on the other, they received a score of 0.5.[40]

Is this measure good enough? One encouraging sign is that it suggests, as do our other measures, that the American public is inclined toward ethnocentrism: 48.0 percent of the offspring sample and 50.6 percent of the parents show in-group favoritism on both racial and religious grounds.[41] Another and perhaps more instructive test is to see if the abbreviated measure we have concocted out of the Jennings study correlates with the measures of ethnocentrism we prefer. To carry out this test, we returned to the 2000 NES and created a measure following the identical protocol to the one governing scale construction in the 1965 socialization study (that is, a measure of in-group favoritism based on race—black, white—and religion—Catholic, Jewish, Protestant). Happily for our purposes, this measure turns out to be positively and substantially correlated with E^*: Pearson $r =$ 0.55. It seems that the abbreviated measure is good enough and that we can proceed (cautiously) to analyze the origins of ethnocentrism measured in this way.[42]

Due either to social learning or to genetic inheritance, we expect to find correspondence between parent and offspring ethnocentrism. And we do find it. Parental ethnocentrism and offspring ethnocentrism are related. The relationship is significant and strong.[43] Converting the parameter estimates into predicted values, a "completely ethnocentric" parent (score of 1.0) would be expected to have an ethnocentric offspring with probability 0.54; the probability falls to 0.45 for a parent who is partially ethnocentric; it falls again to 0.37 for a parent who gives no sign of ethnocentrism.[44]

To what degree does this correspondence arise from social learning as against genetic inheritance? Under social learning theory, the magnitude of correspondence between parents and children should depend on conditions that facilitate the learning process.[45] Correspondence should increase under two conditions: when politics is prominent in family life (when parental instruction is more readily available) and when parents and children are close (when offspring will be more prepared to accept what their parents say and do). Is this so?

In a word, no. Parental influence does *not* increase when parents are politically active (the relationship goes in the opposite direction, though not significantly); parental influence does *not* increase when the family discusses politics; parental influence does *not* increase among offspring who are engaged in political life; parental influence does *not* increase among offspring who know a lot about politics; finally, parental influence does *not* increase when parents and their children are close (as claimed by the children). All this evidence runs against a social learning account of parental influence.[46]

Assume, instead, that the considerable correspondence we see between parents and their offspring is due to genetic transmission.[47] Under genetic transmission, mothers and fathers should have independent and equal effects on their offspring. We can test this by taking advantage of a special feature of the Jennings socialization study design. Interviews were carried out with the fathers of one-third of the seniors, the mothers of one-third, and *both* parents of the remaining third.[48] Among this last group, when we predict offspring's ethnocentrism from father's ethnocentrism and mother's ethnocentrism, we find each parent contributes independently and equally.[49]

In short, parents do seem to be protagonists in the story of ethnocentrism's origins. Children grow up and enter the world of politics more or less ethnocentric, and this is a reflection, in an important way, of the ethnocentrism of their parents. Although the evidence we have presented here is far from decisive, the transmission of ethnocentrism from one generation to the next would seem to have more to do with genetic inheritance than with social learning.

Personality

Daniel Levinson and his colleagues concluded that the origins of ethnocentrism are to be found in the authoritarian personality. Under intense scrutiny, the empirical case supporting their conclusion collapsed—but perhaps they were right nevertheless. According to Karen Stenner, in the United States and around the world, political, racial, and moral intolerance are "driven by the same engine, fueled by the same impulses" (2005, p. 269). The engine Stenner had in mind was, of course, authoritarianism, and this time around, the evidence is convincing (Feldman 2003; Feldman and Stenner 1997; Stenner 2005). And so, perhaps ethnocentrism arises, in part, from authoritarianism, a general and deep-seated characterological predisposition to choose conformity over autonomy.

Are authoritarianism and ethnocentrism related? We can see if this is so because recent installments of the NES have included four standard questions widely used (by Stenner and others) to provide a reliable measure of authoritarianism. The questions ask about the values most important for parents to emphasize in the raising of their children, with each posing a choice between the authority of parents and the autonomy of children.[50] Measured in this fashion, authoritarianism *is* related to ethnocentrism. Pooling recent NES surveys, the Pearson *r* between authoritarianism and ethnocentrism is 0.20.[51]

A more demanding test of the claim that ethnocentrism has its origins in authoritarianism can be carried out using the 1992–1996 NES Panel. Here the test is to predict ethnocentrism expressed in 1996 from authoritarianism measured in 1992, while controlling on the effects due to other plausible factors: education, race, gender, social isolation, and more.[52] Under these conditions, we find a statistically significant though modest effect of authoritarianism. This result is consistent with the claim that ethnocentrism arises in part—in rather small part—from authoritarianism.[53]

TABLE 3.5. Ethnocentrism and education

	[1]	[2]	[3]
Years of schooling	−0.20***	−0.15***	−0.05
	0.02	0.03	0.03
Any college		−0.02***	0.14***
		0.01	0.04
Any college*			−0.21***
Years of schooling			0.05
N	4767	4767	4767

Source: 1992, 1996, 2000, and 2004 NES.

Note: Table entry is the ordinary least-squares coefficient with standard error below. Years of schooling range from 0 (zero years) to 1 (17 years). Any college is a dummy for any postsecondary educational experiences. All models include year intercepts and measures of occupation, income, homeownership, age, sex, race, and ethnicity. Full results appear in the Web appendix.

***$p < 0.01$; **$p < 0.05$; *$p < 0.10$, two-tailed.

Education

Education, so the standard argument goes, provides values and skills that enable individuals to overcome prejudice. From Stouffer's (1955) results on communist subversion in the 1950s to contemporary disputes over gay rights and racist speech, education is almost always associated with greater tolerance. In the conventional view, education confers knowledge, principles, and experiences that together act as a counterweight to the "natural" inclination toward prejudice. Based on this literature, we expect that individual differences in ethnocentrism can be explained, in part, by differences in education.

Education does indeed predict ethnocentrism: as years of education increase, ethnocentrism declines. Education, of course, is correlated with other aspects of social background—occupation, income, age, and so on— that may themselves predict ethnocentrism. When we include a comprehensive set of such background measures in a regression model, the effect of education on ethnocentrism remains significant and sizable. This result appears in column 1 of table 3.5.

Further analysis suggests that the college experience in particular has a special role to play in ethnocentrism's decline. First of all, attending college has an effect on ethnocentrism over and above the effect due to years of education (column 2 of table 3.5). And second, each year of education spent in college has a greater effect on ethnocentrism than does each year of education spent outside of college (column 3).[54]

Based on these results, it would seem that education, and especially the experiences associated with higher education, build tolerance and erode ethnocentrism.[55]

ETHNOCENTRISM A STABLE PREDISPOSITION?

We expect that, like other core aspects of personality and political identity, ethnocentrism will display substantial and increasing stability in adulthood. Ascertaining whether this is so requires panel data—repeated observations of the same individuals over time. The best evidence comes once again from the Jennings socialization study. High school seniors were first interviewed in the spring of 1965, as graduation approached. The same group was questioned again in 1973, once more in 1982, and on one final occasion in 1997. As noted earlier, we are able to fashion a serviceable measure of ethnocentrism out of the 1965 survey materials, one based on race and on religion. The identical measure was available in 1973 and in 1997 as well (though, alas, not in 1982).

One simple way to gauge over-time continuity is provided by the Pearson correlation coefficient. The Pearson correlation represents the extent to which the relative ordering of individuals—in this case, from not at all ethnocentric to extremely ethnocentric—is the same on one occasion as it is on another. A score of 1.0 means that the relative ordering is identical on the two occasions; a score of −1.0 represent a complete reversal of the relative orderings; and a score of 0.0 means that there is no relationship at all between the two orderings. Regarding ethnocentrism, we find substantial but far from perfect continuity in the Jennings study materials: between 1965 and 1973, the Pearson $r = 0.25$; between 1973 and 1997, $r_r = 0.30$.

We can go a layer deeper into this question through a more refined processing of the raw correlation coefficients. "More refined" means partitioning the observed Pearson correlations into two components: a reliability component, reflecting the degree to which the measures are contaminated by error; and a stability component—"true stability"—reflecting the degree to which the two measures would be correlated if not for the attenuating presence of error. Remember that we are relying on an abridged measure of ethnocentrism in this analysis, so we can be sure that there is imprecision aplenty. To correct for error of this kind, we rely on the model developed by D. Wiley and J. Wiley (1970).[56]

The magnitude of stability coefficients is tied to the length of interval between observations. Under usual circumstances (in the absence of cyclical change), the coefficients will decline as the interval increases. With this contingency in mind, the coefficients estimated from the socialization study—based in the first instance on an interval of 8 years and in the sec-

TABLE 3.6. Stability of ethnocentrism

Period	Stability
1965–73	0.73
1973–97	0.80
1992–94	0.89
1994–96	0.99
2000–02	0.68
2002–04	0.72

Source: 1965–1997 Political Socialization Study Panel; 1992–1996 NES Panel; 2000–2004 NES Panel.

Note: Table entry is the Wiley-Wiley stability coefficient.

ond on an interval of 24 years—indicate very impressive stability (see table 3.6). The coefficients suggest, moreover, that ethnocentrism becomes increasingly stable in middle age, consistent with the evidence on personality consolidation over the life span.

As a check on these results, we carried out parallel analysis on two short-term panel studies: the 1992–1994–1996 NES and the 2000–2002–2004 NES Panels. Because the Wiley-Wiley model requires observations at three points in time, we are restricted to estimating the stability of ethnocentrism as measured by thermometer score ratings, since the thermometer score but not the stereotype battery was included in all three waves of these two NES Panel studies. These results are also presented in table 3.6. They show that once the unreliability of measurement is taken into account, ethnocentrism is very stable in the short-run in the early 1990s, but markedly less so in the first years of the twenty-first century.[57]

Ethnocentrism conforms less completely to the protocol of a stable predisposition between 2000 and 2004. Why? It is as if something intruded forcefully on American life, upsetting the normal order. The obvious candidate here, it seems to us, is the terrorist attacks on New York and Washington on September 11, 2001, and the urgent shift in policy and national purpose that immediately followed. We cannot be certain about this, but several pieces of evidence point in this direction.

For one thing, according to our standard measure, between 2000 and 2002 Americans became visibly *less* ethnocentric. That is, they were less likely to claim that their variety of American (white, black, whatever) was superior to other varieties of Americans. This is consistent with the idea that on September 11, it was the nation that was attacked; in the aftermath of September 11, Americans came together, united against a common external enemy.

Second, if the events of September 11 were in fact disconcerting for ethnocentrism, leading to the relative instability we see in table 3.6, they should have been especially disconcerting for young Americans, relatively new to politics, whose ethnocentric inclinations were not yet settled. This turns out to be true. When we reestimated the Wiley-Wiley model separately within three age groupings, we found that September 11 was especially discombobulating among the young. For the younger generation, the attacks on New York and Washington and the war on terrorism the attacks provoked seemed to force a rethinking of in-groups and out-groups, of who is with us and who is against us.[58]

CONCLUSIONS

We have offered this chapter as a gateway linking our theory of ethnocentrism, on the one side, with empirical applications of the theory to a diverse series of policy domains shortly to commence, on the other. We introduced and defended two independent but complementary measures of ethnocentrism: a primary one based on group stereotypes, and a secondary one based on group sentiments. Both presume the primacy of racial classifications in the distinction between in-group and out-group. The two measures of ethnocentrism are correlated, and both suggest that in the richest and oldest liberal democracy in the world, ethnocentrism is pervasive.

The evidence for in-group favoritism is stronger for sentiment than it is for stereotype. The stereotype measure turns up pervasive evidence of in-group favoritism only among whites and Asian Americans. Less advantaged groups—in the present case, blacks and Hispanic Americans—have a more difficult time asserting their own group's superiority. But the measure of ethnocentrism based on sentiment reveals universal in-group favoritism, much as Sumner would have expected. Perhaps stereotypes, in contrast to feelings, are encumbered by the weight of objective conditions and by the social construction of difference. Feelings are something else again—something more elemental—and they give direct expression to the elemental predisposition of ethnocentrism.

Next we show that our measures of ethnocentrism are for the most part unrelated to social and political predispositions that are standard fixtures in the analysis and understanding of American public opinion. Ethnocentrism is not remotely the same thing as partisanship, or limited government, or egalitarianism, or ideological identification, or social distrust. This disposes of the worry that ethnocentrism merely duplicates predispositions already used in political analysis.

Toward the end of the chapter, we turned our attention to the origins of ethnocentrism. We argued that people vary in the degree to which their beliefs and feelings about social life are governed by ethnocentrism, and we suggested that such variation arises primarily from biological diversity transmitted through genetic inheritance, from the emergence of authoritarian personality, and from experiences supplied by education. Ethnocentrism is generally stable in adulthood, increasingly so across the life span. Only a national catastrophe appears strong enough to alter ethnocentrism, and even then, principally among the young.

With these important points established, it is time to move on to our real business: to ascertain the role of ethnocentrism in contemporary public opinion. Should the United States supply economic assistance to countries struggling to establish democratic forms of government? Should the flow of people from Latin America and Asia to U.S. shores be turned back? Should the welfare system be reformed, the scope and range of benefits curtailed? On these and other topics, we will assess the claim of ethnocentrism: that political opinions derive in an important way from a general outlook that partitions the world into us against them.

: 2 :

Empirical Cases

Our primary purpose is to establish that ethnocentrism, as defined and measured in part 1 of the book, plays an important role in contemporary American public opinion. On the issues that animate the politics of our time—peace and security, immigration and citizenship, poverty and inequality, and more—American opinion cannot be fully understood, we intend to show, without taking ethnocentrism into account. With this purpose in mind, part 2 moves through a series of empirical cases, one to a chapter.

Each chapter, each case, takes up opinion within a specific domain of American public policy. We chose these domains to be broadly representative of the full policy space. This means that both foreign and domestic policies are represented. And it means that within the domestic sphere, both economic and cultural issues are examined. The breadth of the test of ethnocentrism implied by this broad sampling of policy domains is crucial to our enterprise. The charm of ethnocentrism as an explanation for public opinion lies in its supposed wide reach. If ethnocentrism really is a general predisposition, we must be able to detect its effects across multiple political disputes.

Put another way, one of ethnocentrism's distinctive features is its flexibility. By this we mean that depending on circumstances, the line between in-groups and out-groups can be supplied by a variety of differences: by alma mater, neighborhood, academic specialty, and many more. All of us belong to many tribes. Which of our tribal associations is salient depends on what is happening around us.

When it comes to politics and policy, nation is a particularly potent tribe. In a complicated and dangerous world, one's nation offers a kind of "refuge, a place to be at home with oneself and with one's own kind" (Eley and Suny 1996, p. 31; Anderson 1983; Anthony Smith 2001). Each nation has its own glorious homeland, its own flag, anthem, ceremonies, symbols, and heroes, music, literature and art—each, that is to say, has its own way of doing things. As such, nation supplies a powerful and seemingly natural way for people to define in-groups and out-groups, to distinguish Us from Them. The first three chapters of part 2 take up domains of policy in which national identity plays a central role: confronting enemies abroad (chapter 4), extending assistance to foreign lands and peoples (chapter 5), and defining citizenship and restricting immigration (chapter 6).

Nation may be a powerful way to define in-groups and out-groups, but it is certainly not the only way. The remainder of part 2 is devoted to domestic politics. Chapter 7 takes up a set of issues brought to national attention by the gay rights movement, where the main line of difference is supplied by sexual orientation. Chapter 8 does the same for policies pressed by the modern women's movement; in this case it is gender that defines in-group and out-group. In chapter 9 the subject is American welfare policy, where the lines are drawn by work and wealth. And chapter 10 considers policies in the domain of race, where tribes are defined and perhaps divided by color.

All things considered, the cases we are about to take up generally fulfill the conditions spelled out in chapter 2 for the activation of ethnocentrism. We therefore generally expect to find strong connections between ethnocentrism and public opinion as we make our way through the various chapters. For the most part we do find such connections—though along the way we run into some major surprises and much fascinating detail. We begin our journey in chapter 4 with threats to national security and defense of the homeland.

CHAPTER 4

Enemies Abroad

William Graham Sumner regarded conflict with outsiders to be the principal source of ethnocentrism. He argued that solidarity within in-groups and hostility for out-groups originate out of the same inescapable and recurrent condition: that of fierce conflict between groups over scarce resources:

> The insiders in a we-group are in a relation of peace, order, law, government, and industry, to each other. Their relation to all outsiders, or others-groups, is one of war and plunder. . . . Sentiments are produced to correspond. Loyalty to the group, sacrifice for it, hatred and contempt for outsiders, brotherhood within, warlikeness without—all grow together, common products of the same situation. ([1906] 2002, pp. 12–13)

As we learned in chapter 2, in-group solidarity and out-group hostility are bound together much less tightly than Sumner believed. But this correction does not mean that we should pass over the special role ethnocentrism might play in generating support for "war and plunder" against outsiders.

There certainly is a lot of it. In the twentieth century alone, millions of people—soldier and civilian, men, women, and children alike—have perished in warfare. The lives of millions more have been diminished or ruined.[1] Conflict is not only horrific and commonplace. It also fulfills the conditions for the activation of ethnocentrism just about perfectly. First of all, nothing attracts and holds the public's attention like warfare. And second, warfare is typically portrayed, understood, and justified (by all parties) as a noble and heroic struggle between good and evil, between innocence and barbarism. This chapter investigates whether, as we expect, ethnocentrism predisposes Americans to lend their support to policies of confrontation and violence against outside enemies.

We will begin by examining the current and ongoing war on terrorism, and we will linger here awhile. It is our first empirical case, and we want to make it thoroughly. And as it is our first case, it will serve as a prototype for much that follows: a thorough presentation now will save us time later.

After examining ethnocentrism and terrorism, the chapter will take up two additional examples: the cold war (the struggle against communism and the Soviet Union that marked the second half of the twentieth century); and then Desert Storm (the U.S.-led effort to expel Saddam Hussein's forces from Kuwait in 1991). Taken together, these three test cases provide strong evidence that ethnocentrism is a primary ingredient in the American public's support for forcefully confronting adversaries abroad. Toward the end of the chapter, having established this point, we turn to the question of activation. Ethnocentrism is a deep habit and a stable predisposition, but its importance to politics depends on circumstances. What can we learn from these cases about the conditions that are necessary for ethnocentrism's activation?

WAR WITHOUT END

Tuesday, September 11, 2001, dawned temperate and nearly cloudless in the eastern United States. Millions of men and women readied themselves for work. Some made their way to the Twin Towers, the signature structures of the World Trade Center complex in New York City. Others went to Arlington, Virginia, to the Pentagon. Across the Potomac River, the United States Congress was back in session. At the other end of Pennsylvania Avenue, people began to line up for a White House tour. In Sarasota, Florida, President George W. Bush went for an early morning run.

For those heading to an airport, weather conditions could not have been better for a safe and pleasant journey. (National Commission on Terrorist Attacks 2004, p. 1)

As things turned out, not so safe and not so pleasant. Early on the morning of September 11, Mohamed Atta and his companions commandeered four huge commercial aircraft, laden with passengers and fuel, and flew them into the World Trade Center, the Pentagon, and a grassy field in Pennsylvania. The Twin Towers collapsed. Thousands died. Ordinary life came to an abrupt halt. That evening, in a televised address from the White House, President Bush announced to the nation that the United States was at war. "We will make no distinction between the terrorists who committed these acts and those who harbor them" said the president. "No American will ever forget this day."

Priorities and polices shifted immediately. The president approved the creation of a new cabinet agency dedicated to homeland security. He directed Secretary of State Powell to deliver an ultimatum to the Taliban regime in Afghanistan: surrender Osama Bin Ladin and his chief lieutenants, close all terrorist camps, and reveal all knowledge of al Qaeda operations, or face extinction. Agents of the Immigration and Naturalization Service (INS), working in cooperation with the Federal Bureau of Investigation (FBI), began arresting individuals for immigration violations; eventually hundreds would be incarcerated as "special interest" detainees. The Patriot Act, a hugely complicated proposal to enhance the government's ability to gather intelligence within the United States and to encourage the sharing of such information between intelligence and law enforcement communities, was hastily assembled. By the end of October, it was the law of the land, having passed both houses of Congress by large majorities.

In the meantime, plans for military retaliation were going forward. On the twentieth of September, addressing a joint session of Congress and a national television audience, President Bush blamed al Qaeda for the terrorist attacks on New York and Washington. He also made public the demand that had already been conveyed through private diplomatic channels: "The Taliban must act, and act immediately. They will hand over the terrorists, or they will share their fate. . . . Every nation, in every region, now has a decision to make," the president declared. "Either you are with us, or you are with the terrorists." On October 7, the president authorized air strikes and Special Operations attacks on vital al Qaeda and Taliban targets. Ground attacks shortly followed. By the middle of November, the Taliban had fled Kabul, and by early December, all major Afghan cities had fallen to the U.S.-led coalition forces.

The Taliban regime was the first target, but very early in the Bush administration's response to 9/11, the determination was made that the United States must fight terrorism everywhere. It would be a global war. The aim would be to "eliminate all terrorist networks, dry up their financial support, and prevent them from acquiring weapons of mass destruction" (National Commission on Terrorist Attacks 2004, p. 334). In phase two of the war on terrorism, the Bush administration turned its attention to Iraq. In October 2002, the president pointed to the "gathering threat" posed to the United States by Hussein. "The attacks of September the 11th showed our country that vast oceans no longer protect us from danger. Before that tragic date, we had only hints of al Qaeda's plans and designs. Today in Iraq, we see a threat whose outlines are far more clearly defined, and whose consequences could be far more deadly."[2]

Our purpose here is to explain the American public's reaction to the Bush administration's plans and policies on terrorism, with special attention trained on whatever part may have been played by ethnocentrism. Going into this analysis, it seemed to us that terrorism would invite we-they thinking. To most Americans, the new adversaries they face in this conflict are unfamiliar. They come from faraway, exotic places. Their language, religion, customs, and sheer physical appearance: all of it is strange. As a consequence, Americans who are generally predisposed toward ethnocentrism—who as a matter of habit divide the world into in-groups and out-groups, into communities of trust and communities of suspicion—should be especially likely to lend their support to the new war on terrorism.

AMERICAN SUPPORT FOR THE WAR ON TERRORISM

To see if this is so, we analyze national survey data supplied by the 2000–2002 National Election Study (NES), conducted by the Center for Political Studies at the Institute for Social Research at the University of Michigan. The 2000–2002 NES Panel is beautifully designed for our purposes. Respondents comprising a representative national sample of Americans of voting age were interviewed before and immediately after the 2000 election and re-interviewed before and after the 2002 midterm elections.[3]

The 2000 NES, carried out before 9/11, includes a wide array of standard measures of political predispositions, including ethnocentrism. One might say that in our analysis, ethnocentrism is assessed at a moment of comparative innocence. In the fall of 2000, all that would shortly come—the horrifying collapse of the Twin Towers, the dark gash into the Pentagon, the transformation of U.S. policy, a new and indefinite war on terrorism—was unimagined.

The 2002 NES was carried out after 9/11 and in an entirely altered context. Domestic security alerts issued by the Department of Homeland Security were now routine. American-led forces had swept the Taliban regime out of power in Afghanistan. Planning for war with Iraq was underway. Naturally, the 2002 NES included an extensive set of questions relevant to this new world: questions on homeland security, the war against the Taliban, military involvement in Iraq, and more.

Together, then, the 2002 and the 2000 interviews provide just the kind of evidence our project requires. By analyzing the 2000–2002 NES Panel, we can see whether ethnocentrism, measured before 9/11, helps account for American attitudes toward the policies and events and authorities that have dominated national politics since.

For convenience, we classify measures of support for the war on terrorism present in the 2002 NES as falling into one of three categories. First are policies intended to make the country safe. All were included as part of a standard NES question battery on government spending. This battery presents a series of federal programs, asking respondents in each case whether, if they had a say in making up the federal budget, spending should be increased, decreased, or kept about the same. Included within a long series of government programs were four with high relevance for our project: (1) homeland security, (2) the war on terrorism, (3) tightening border security to prevent illegal immigration, and (4) national defense.

Americans favored all four initiatives. The least popular among them was national defense, yet nearly 60 percent of Americans wanted the government to spend more on defense and only about 7 percent wanted to spend less. And support goes up from there. Nearly two-thirds of Americans said spend more on homeland security; likewise for spending on the war on terrorism; and 70 percent wanted to spend more on border security. In short, when asked whether the government should do more to make the country safe, Americans said yes.[4]

A second aspect of support has to do with military action. In a speech to the nation shortly after 9/11, President Bush warned the world that "any nation that continues to harbor or support terrorism will be regarded by the United States as a hostile regime." The 2002 NES asked two questions on U.S. policy toward hostile nations. One looked to the past and asked whether the war against the Taliban regime in Afghanistan was worth the cost. Nearly 80 percent of Americans in the fall of 2002 said that they believed it was. The other question asked not for an assessment of the past but for advice about the future. After being reminded that President Bush and his top aides were discussing the possibility of taking military action against Iraq to remove Saddam Hussein from power, respondents were asked whether they favored or opposed military action against Iraq. On balance, Americans supported this move. Most—more than 80 percent—expressed an opinion, and of these, backers of the president's policy outnumbered opponents by better than two to one.[5]

Third and finally, we take up public support for the president. Perhaps it was inevitable that the war on terrorism would become the president's war. The reasons are partly historical: 9/11 happened on President Bush's watch. They are also practical: the command and control center of U.S. foreign policy resides within the White House. And they are also partly symbolic: the president is the single most visible and potent representation of the nation. In the immediate aftermath of 9/11, the public turned to the president for reassurance and consolation, and in the weeks and months that followed, for policies to insure the safety of the country. Several questions on presidential performance were included in the 2002 NES, and all indicated substantial support for the president. More than 80 percent of the public said they approved of President Bush's response to the terrorist attacks of September 11; more than 70 percent approved how he was handling the war on terrorism; and nearly 70 percent gave their stamp of approval to George W. Bush's overall performance as president.[6]

Taken all around, then, roughly one year after the terrorist attacks, the American public expressed considerable support for the war on terrorism. The war was more popular in some quarters, of course, than in others. Some Americans said that federal spending for fighting terrorism should be cut back, or that we were spending too much on border control, or that the war against the Taliban was a mistake, or that President Bush was making a mess of things. More thought the opposite. And many Americans took up positions in between. The question for us is what role, if any, does ethnocentrism play in explaining variation in support for the war on terrorism?

ESTIMATING THE EFFECT OF ETHNOCENTRISM

To estimate the effect of ethnocentrism, our analysis must take into account other relevant considerations. As we learned in chapter 3, ethnocentrism is correlated with other political predispositions. This means we must do what we can to make sure, in our analysis, that we are not assigning an effect to ethnocentrism that really belongs to some other causal force. We are interested in the independent effect of ethnocentrism, other relevant considerations held constant.

This is an altogether general problem, making trouble throughout the social sciences, not just in our project in particular. The solution is likewise general. The solution is multiple regression analysis—an analysis that takes into account other relevant considerations, other alternative explanations. As a matter of practice, in each chapter, for each domain of policy, we present a "standard model," a specification that captures the conventional wisdom about the primary ingredients that make up opinion in that domain. We really should say standard *models*. At this stage of development in public opinion research, there is no such thing, in any domain, as *the* standard model. What we have on offer instead is a family of plausible models. To each such model we add a measure of ethnocentrism. Properly estimated, these models can tell us what we need to know: namely, whether the survey data we observe are consistent with the claim that ethnocentrism influences Americans' support for the war on terrorism, and, if so, how large the effect of ethnocentrism is. This method is hardly foolproof—drawing causal inferences from nonexperimental data remains tricky business—but it is a highly useful tool, and using it deftly will move us much closer to where we want to be.

And so, as a practical matter, to make our empirical estimates of the impact of ethnocentrism credible, our analysis includes explanations of support for the war on terrorism in addition to ethnocentrism. Three such alternative explanations are especially plausible.

The first is *partisanship*. Most Americans think of themselves as Democrats or Republicans. This attachment to party is a standing commitment, a "persistent adherence," as the authors of *The American Voter* put it, one that profoundly influences how citizens see the world of politics:

> To the average person, the affairs of government are remote and complex, and yet the average citizen is asked periodically to formulate opinions about these affairs. . . . In this dilemma, having the party symbol stamped on certain candidates, certain issue positions, certain interpretations of reality is of great psychological convenience. (Stokes 1966, pp. 126–27)

The war on terrorism has largely been the work of a Republican president, supported disproportionately by Republicans in Congress and Republican elites around the country, and we should see clear consequences of this in the thinking of ordinary Americans (Mueller 1973; Holsti 1996; A. Campbell et al. [1960] 1980, p. 146).[7]

Second is *education*. In the previous chapter, we showed that education and ethnocentrism are negatively correlated. We also know that education is often a powerful predictor of political opinion. Hence we need to add education to our analysis here, for fear that we will otherwise attribute causal potency to ethnocentrism that really belongs to education.[8]

Third is *perception of threat*, on the prediction from realistic group conflict theory that support for waging war on anti-American terrorists should be proportionate to the severity of the threat that such terrorists appear to pose (e.g., Blumer 1958; Coser 1956; Sherif and Sherif [1953] 1966; Sumner [1906] 2002). We represent threat with a single question, asked as part of the 2002 NES. The question assesses Americans' estimation of the vulnerability of the United States to terrorist strikes:

> How likely do you think it is that the U.S. will suffer an attack as serious as the one in New York and Washington some time in the next 12 months? Would you say very likely, somewhat likely, somewhat unlikely, or very unlikely?

Three features of this question are worth noting. First of all, it asks about *imminent* threat—the likelihood of an attack taking place within the next twelve months. Second, it asks about a *serious* strike—comparable in magnitude to the attacks of 9/11. And third, it asks about threat to the *nation*— whether the United States would suffer an attack. Defined in this fashion, many Americans took the threat posed by terrorism seriously: 19.2 percent said that it was very likely and another 47.7 percent said that it was somewhat likely that the country would suffer a calamitous attack some time in

the next twelve months. We expect such people to be among the most ardent advocates of strong precautionary and preemptive action.[9]

Mathematically, the model can be written this way:

$$y^* = \mathbf{x}'\boldsymbol{\beta} + \varepsilon$$
$$= \beta_0 + \beta_1\text{Ethnocentrism} + \beta_2\text{Partisanship} + \beta_3\text{Education} + \beta_4\text{Threat} +$$
$$\ldots + \varepsilon$$
$$\Pr(y = m) = \Pr(\tau_{m-1} < y^* < \tau_m) = \Phi(\tau_m - \mathbf{x}'\boldsymbol{\beta}) - \Phi(\tau_{m-1} - \mathbf{x}'\boldsymbol{\beta})$$

In the expressions above, y refers to opinion on spending for homeland
security, border control, and other matters discussed above (in our analysis,
each issue is taken up separately). The term y^* represents the unobserved
latent variable in each case. That is, we assume that the opinion expressed
on any particular question arises from a latent, continuous attitude, and
that our survey questions segment this continuum as a series of ordered
thresholds (y^* falls into one of m categories). All of the opinion variables
are coded such that higher values indicate more support for the war on
terrorism.[10]

With one exception, the independent variables in the model are measured in the 2000 NES. (The exception is threat, which, of course, no one
thought to include in the 2000 survey.)[11] This means in particular that ethnocentrism is measured some two years before the opinions themselves
are. This makes for a fair but difficult test. We are asking whether ethnocentrism assessed in the fall of 2000 can explain support for policies—the
Patriot Act, war in Afghanistan, a Homeland Security Department—that
had not yet even been imagined. And it is a good test in that the panel design
relieves some of the headache that normally accompanies causal inference
from correlational data. Our analysis assumes that ethnocentrism causes support for the war on terrorism, not the other way around. Measuring ethnocentrism in 2000 and opinion in 2002 makes this assumption easier to
swallow.[12]

Finally, in this analysis, ethnocentrism is a measure of in-group favoritism over out-groups, based on responses to the battery of stereotypes present in the 2000 NES—or E, as we called it in chapter 3. To create the measure, we simply followed the protocol spelled out there. We scored E to
range from –1 to +1. A "perfect" score of +1 means that on each and every
trait, "nearly all" members of the in-group are believed to be virtuous and
"nearly all" members of all out-groups are believed to be virtue-less. A score
of +1 represents an extreme form of ethnocentrism. A score of –1 is equally
perfect, but in the opposite direction: –1 represents an upside-down world
in which out-groups are seen as virtuous and in-groups as utterly without
virtue. An overall score of 0, finally, indicates an absence of ethnocentrism:
that, on average, in-group and out-groups are indistinguishable.[13]

ETHNOCENTRISM AND SUPPORT FOR THE WAR
ON TERRORISM

We present our results in a series of three tables. Table 4.1 summarizes the findings for policies designed to protect the homeland, table 4.2 does the same for military intervention, and table 4.3 summarizes the findings regarding support for President Bush. Each table is organized as an array of columns, with each column representing a distinct opinion measure, from spending more on the war on terrorism (in table 4.1) to evaluations of President Bush (in table 4.3). Each table displays ordered-probit coefficients, with standard errors underneath.[14] Most important for our purposes is the first row of each table, which gives the coefficient associated with ethnocentrism. This coefficient reveals whether, as we predict, differences in ethnocentrism are systematically related to differences in support for the war on terrorism, while holding other considerations—party identification, threat, and so on—constant.

The tables reveal that this is so. Americans who believe their own group to be superior are also inclined to say that we should be spending more on the war, on keeping our borders impregnable, and on building a strong national defense (table 4.1). They favor war with Iraq (table 4.2). They think

TABLE 4.1. Ethnocentrism and support for the war on terrorism I: Protecting the homeland

| | | Government spends more on: | | |
	War on Terror	Homeland security	Border control	National defense
Ethnocentrism	1.38***	0.53	1.13***	0.95***
	0.46	0.46	0.35	0.31
Partisanship	−0.54***	−0.38**	−0.42***	−0.90***
	0.18	0.19	0.14	0.13
Education	−0.85***	0.34	−0.52***	−0.21
	0.26	0.28	0.19	0.18
Threat	0.73***	0.37	0.48***	0.36**
	0.22	0.22	0.16	0.15
N	440	396	844	839
Effect of **E**	0.54→0.86	0.66→0.79	0.66→0.89	0.50→0.75

Source: 2000–2002 NES Panel.

Note: Table entry is the ordered probit regression coefficient with standard errors below. Models also control for political awareness, sex, race, and ethnicity. Full results appear in the Web appendix. The bottom row of the table gives the effect associated with a shift in Ethnocentrism from Low (−0.1) to High (0.6) in the predicted probability of support for spending more on protecting the homeland (see text for details).

***$p < 0.01$; **$p < 0.05$; *$p < 0.10$, two-tailed.

TABLE 4.2. Ethnocentrism and support for the war on terrorism II: Going to war

	Afghanistan worth it	Support military action in Iraq
Ethnocentrism	0.00	0.65**
	0.37	0.28
Partisanship	−0.61***	−1.07***
	0.17	0.11
Education	0.57**	−0.58***
	0.23	0.16
Threat	−0.22	0.30**
	0.19	0.14
N	895	899
Effect of E	0.82→0.82	0.42→0.60

Source: 2000–2002 NES Panel.

Note: Table entry is the ordered probit regression coefficient with standard errors below. Models also control for political awareness, sex, race, and ethnicity. Full results appear in the Web appendix. The bottom row of the table gives the effect associated with a shift in Ethnocentrism from Low (−0.1) to High (0.6) in the predicted probability of support for the war on terrorism (see text for details).

***$p < 0.01$; **$p < 0.05$; *$p < 0.10$, two-tailed.

TABLE 4.3. Ethnocentrism and support for the war on terrorism III: Backing the president

	General performance	War on terror	Handling 9/11
Ethnocentrism	0.62**	0.76*	0.88**
	0.30	0.44	0.44
Partisanship	−1.80***	−0.83***	−0.96***
	0.13	0.18	0.20
Education	−0.18	0.02	−0.72***
	0.17	0.24	0.27
Threat	0.09	0.08	−0.03
	0.14	0.20	0.22
N	885	456	446
Effect of E	0.64→0.78	0.70→0.85	0.80→0.93

Source: 2000–2002 NES Panel.

Note: Table entry is the ordered probit regression coefficient with standard errors below. Models also control for political awareness, sex, race, ethnicity, and assessments of personal and national economic conditions. Full results appear in the Web appendix. The bottom row of the table gives the effect associated with a shift in Ethnocentrism from Low (−0.1) to High (0.6) in the predicted probability of approving of the president (see text for details).

***$p < 0.01$; **$p < 0.05$; *$p < 0.10$, two-tailed.

President Bush has been effective in responding to the terrorist attacks, and they give his presidency high marks in general (table 4.3).[15]

The coefficients on ethnocentrism and their respective standard errors tell us whether the effects of ethnocentrism are statistically distinguishable from zero, but they do not tell us anything about the magnitude of the effects. The values presented in the bottom row of tables 4.1 to 4.3 provide this information, by showing the effect of ethnocentrism, holding all else constant, on the probability of supporting various aspects of the war on terrorism. These values are based on comparisons between two hypothetical individuals, alike in all respects except for their scores on ethnocentrism. In one case, the hypothetical individual scores at the low end of the normal range of ethnocentrism found in the American public (−0.1 on the E scale). In the other case, the hypothetical individual scores at the upper end of the normal range (0.6 on the E scale).[16]

Here's an example of how to read these calculations. Table 4.1 indicates that when it comes to spending on the war on terrorism, a given individual with a low score on ethnocentrism has a predicted 0.54 probability of supporting increased spending on the war on terrorism. In contrast, the identical individual with a high score on ethnocentrism has a 0.86 predicted probability. The shift in ethnocentrism from low to high yields a corresponding 0.32 shift in the probability of support for a key element of the war on terrorism. As we can see throughout tables 4.1 to 4.3, the effect of ethnocentrism is not only statistically significant, but also substantively impressive.[17]

Across the three tables, the effect of ethnocentrism is significant and sizable in nearly all cases. The one exception has to do with the question of whether the war against the Taliban regime in Afghanistan was worth it, where ethnocentrism plays no role. Indeed, it fails utterly: the estimated effect is zero to nearly three decimal places ($b_1 = .001$). The reason for this one failure is unclear, at least to us. Perhaps it has to do with the overwhelming popularity of the policy. Perhaps the war against the Taliban played on ethnocentrism in countervailing ways, appealing to ethnocentric Americans for reasons having to do with dramatic military intervention and forceful protection of the homeland, while simultaneously appealing to Americans who reject ethnocentrism for reasons having to do with liberating the Afghanistan people from the oppressions practiced by the Taliban regime. Or perhaps ethnocentrism is called up more readily in judgments about the uncertain future than in assessments of the completed and fixed past. It is hard to say exactly why ethnocentrism fails to predict opinion on this one item.

However this case is to be understood, it is important to recognize that it is an anomaly. The first set of empirical tests run overwhelmingly in the expected direction. By this evidence, ethnocentrism plays a major role in motivating American support for the war on terrorism.

Ethnocentrism is not the whole story, of course, nor did we expect it to be. For example, Republicans and Democrats differ on virtually all aspects of the war on terrorism we examined, and the differences are often substantial. Republicans were more likely than Democrats to say that we should spend more on the war on terrorism, on tightening up the nation's borders, and on national defense. Republicans were more likely to see the war in Afghanistan as worth the cost and more likely to favor military intervention in Iraq. And they were—no surprise here—much more favorably impressed with George W. Bush's performance as president.[18]

The public appeared to take other considerations into account as well, albeit not so heavily nor so consistently. Better-educated Americans were more skeptical of policies designed to increase national security, more satisfied with the completed war against the Taliban, more wary of the pending war against Hussein, and more apt to be critical of the president's response to 9/11. And Americans who were most worried about the country's vulnerability favored forceful measures, both to protect the nation—by spending more on homeland security or by controlling immigration—and to eliminate the terrorist threat—by going into Iraq to remove Hussein from power.[19]

Taken all around, our results suggest that American support for the war on terrorism is a reflection of not one thing but several: partisanship, education, threat, and—especially—ethnocentrism.[20]

Ethnocentrism by Another Measure Works as Well

We have argued that the best way to measure ethnocentrism is through stereotypes. Claims of in-group superiority are commonly expressed through stereotypes: that in-groups are generally smarter, more industrious, more trustworthy, and so on than are out-groups (M. Brewer and Campbell 1976). Our principal measure of ethnocentrism, the one we have relied on so far in our analysis of public support for the war on terrorism, is accordingly based on Americans' beliefs about the characteristic traits of social groups—that is, on stereotypes.

As we argued in the previous chapter, an alternative and second-best measure of ethnocentrism can be fashioned out of the thermometer scale, which, as it happens, appears in the 2000 NES. There, Americans were asked to report their feelings toward a variety of social and political groups on a 0–100 point thermometer, from very cold to very warm. Among the groups rated in this fashion were whites, blacks, Hispanic Americans, and Asian Americans. From these thermometer scale ratings, it is a simple matter to construct a measure of ethnocentrism that is parallel in form to the stereotype measure we have been using (and that, on theoretical grounds, we prefer).[21]

When we replaced the stereotype-based measure of ethnocentrism with the measure created out of thermometer scores and reran the analysis summarized in tables 4.1 to 4.3, we found similar results. In particular, ethnocentrism, measured now by thermometer score ratings, retains its role as an important determinant of American support for the war on terrorism. The effect of ethnocentrism is a bit attenuated compared to what we see with our first-choice measure, but the pattern is identical and the overall story much the same.[22]

This result—close replication across the two measures—is important first of all because it means that our results do not depend on any particular and perhaps idiosyncratic method of assessing ethnocentrism. It is important in another way, too: replicated results here give us license to test ethnocentrism in settings where the stereotype measure is unavailable, where we must rely on thermometer score ratings alone (an opportunity we exploit later in this chapter).

Ethnocentrism as In-Group Pride and Out-Group Hostility

We have stressed the point that ethnocentrism is prejudice in general, that it has to do both with in-groups and out-groups. To the extreme ethnocentric, the world appears divided sharply into "us" and "them." Ethnocentrism entails favoritism toward in-groups and animosity toward out-groups. If this is so—if as Daniel Levinson and his colleagues put it, ethnocentrism is really "prejudice, broadly conceived" (Adorno et al. 1950, p. 102)—then the effects of ethnocentrism on American support for the war on terrorism that we have documented so far should reflect in some measure both components: *both* in-group favoritism *and* out-group hostility.

To test this idea, we repeated the analysis summarized in tables 4.1 to 4.3, but this time we broke the ethnocentrism scale into two components, the first having to do with the characteristics of the respondent's own group, the second having to do with the characteristics of out-groups. For simplicity's sake, only the coefficients of interest, for in-group pride and out-group hostility, appear in table 4.4.[23]

We expect to see positive coefficients on the in-group pride component of ethnocentrism. Positive coefficients tell us that Americans who regard their own group as especially virtuous support the war on terrorism—and indeed, positive coefficients abound. Moreover, if our story is about ethnocentrism and not just about nationalism or in-group pride, we expect to see negative coefficients on the out-group hostility component of ethnocentrism—meaning that Americans who regard other groups as especially

TABLE 4.4. In-group pride, out-group hostility, and support for the war on terrorism

	Spend more on war on terror	Spend more on homeland security	Spend more on border control	Spend more on national defense	Afghanistan worth it	Support military action in Iraq	Bush: General performance	Bush: War on terrorism	Bush: Handling 9/11
In-group pride	1.58***	0.64	1.24***	1.00***	−0.06	0.60**	0.73**	0.80*	1.00**
	0.49	0.48	0.36	0.33	0.38	0.29	0.31	0.45	0.46
Out-group hostility	−0.95*	−0.16	−0.82*	−0.83**	−0.15	−0.78**	−0.31	−0.64	−0.63
	0.57	0.59	0.43	0.39	0.47	0.34	0.37	0.55	0.54
N	440	396	844	839	895	899	885	456	446

Source: 2000–2002 NES Panel.

Note: Table entry is the ordered probit regression coefficient with standard errors below. Models also control for partisanship, education, political awareness, sex, race, ethnicity, and threat. Models predicting presidential approval also control for assessments of personal and national economic conditions. In-group pride is coded from 0 (positive) to 1 (negative assessments). Out-group hostility is coded from 0 (positive) to 1 (negative assessments). Full results appear in the Web appendix.

***p < 0.01; **p < 0.05; *p < 0.10, two-tailed.

deficient should support the war on terrorism. And negative coefficients appear as well. If anything, in-group favoritism seems a bit more important than out-group hostility, especially in support for the president. But more impressive is that both components play a role in American support for the war on terrorism. Moreover, since both variables are scaled from 0 to 1, the relative magnitude of the effects can be compared by examining the raw size of the coefficients—and in general, the effects are similarly sized. These results reinforce the idea that a key part of American support for the war on terrorism is ethnocentrism—not in-group pride alone, and not mere suspicion of out-groups—but prejudice, broadly conceived.

Ethnocentrism, Not Conservatism

Perhaps the effects we have attributed to ethnocentrism are actually due to forms of conservatism that are correlated with ethnocentrism but omitted from our standard model. As noted in chapter 3, ethnocentrism is correlated (albeit mildly) with several varieties of contemporary American conservatism, implying that the effects we have so far assigned to ethnocentrism might really belong, at least in part, to conservatism.

Perhaps. But when we add various tried-and-true measures of conservatism to the standard model—commitments to moral traditionalism and to limited government, opposition to equality, identification as a conservative—the effect of ethnocentrism on American support for the war on terrorism barely changes. To take a representative example, with measures of all four varieties of conservatism added to the standard model, the estimated effect of ethnocentrism on American support for greater spending on war on terrorism dips from 1.38 to 1.13. This is a decline all right, but a small one. Taking conservatism into account does nothing to alter our conclusion that American support for the war on terrorism arises importantly from ethnocentrism.[24]

Ethnocentrism, Not Authoritarianism

As we learned in chapter 1, Levinson and his colleagues argued that ethnocentrism must be an expression of a unified and deep psychological force—the authoritarian personality (Adorno et al. 1950). While their empirical conclusions have been largely discounted, we think their theoretical intuitions were right. By valuing uniformity and authority over autonomy and diversity, authoritarians may come "naturally" to ethnocentrism (Stenner 2005). We expect authoritarianism and ethnocentrism to be correlated. Moreover, there are good reasons to suppose that authoritarianism might be an important factor in American opinion on terrorism. Authoritarians are distinguished by their predisposition to submit to established authorities and to support violence against targets sanctioned by such authorities (Adorno et al. 1950; Altemeyer 1981, 1996; Feldman and Stenner 1997; Stenner 2005). If this is so, then authoritarians should be eager to enlist in the president's war on terrorism.

And so, we need to determine whether the story we are telling here about ethnocentrism should be recast as a story about authoritarianism. Fortunately for this purpose, the 2000 NES included four questions designed to measure authoritarianism. Following Stenner and Feldman, the questions ask about the values most important for parents to emphasize in the raising of their children, with each question posing a choice between the authority of parents and the autonomy of children. The virtue of these questions is that they capture the conceptual core of authoritarianism while avoiding the problems that crippled the original measure.[25]

As expected, authoritarianism and ethnocentrism are positively correlated (Pearson $r = 0.22$). This is consistent with the claim that authoritarian personalities find an ethnocentric worldview appealing, that ethnocentrism emerges, in part, from authoritarianism.

What happens, then, when this measure of authoritarianism is added to the standard model? It would hardly be surprising if it turned out that Americans who value authority and deference in family relationships are also inclined to close ranks behind their president. What would be surprising—and disastrous for the account we are developing here—is if the effects we have been attributing to ethnocentrism were to vanish once we take authoritarianism into account.

This is not what happens. On the one hand, authoritarianism does have a significant role to play in public support for the war on terrorism. Americans who claimed to prize obedience to authority in their homes were, as predicted, more enthusiastic about the war on terrorism: willing to spend more to keep the country safe; prepared to support military action against Hussein; and, in various ways, favorably inclined toward the president, the nation's most visible and commanding authority figure. Authoritarianism is an important part of the story, especially in building support for the president. But, on the other hand, adding authoritarianism diminishes the independent effect due to ethnocentrism only slightly. On *every* aspect of the effort against terrorism, the importance of ethnocentrism is maintained. Consider this altogether typical result: with authoritarianism added to the standard model, the estimated effect of ethnocentrism on American support for greater spending on national defense, given by b_1, is 0.83 (se = 0.32). This is down, but only slightly, from the original estimate with authoritarianism omitted ($b_1 = 0.95$, se = 0.31).[26]

More generally, this analysis indicates that ethnocentrism and authoritarianism contribute independently to American support for the war against terror, and that ethnocentrism is the more important of the two. The essential lesson here is that holding constant the effects due to authoritarianism (and partisanship and education and threat and a series of additional controls), American support for the war on terrorism arises significantly and substantially from ethnocentrism.

COLD WAR

Ethnocentrism seems to be a crucial source for the mobilization of popular support against the terrorist threat. This is an important result in and of itself, but we are after more. Does our account explain public support for confronting America's enemies in other settings? What about the cold war?

Shortly after World War II, the Soviet Union moved to consolidate its control over Eastern Europe, orchestrating a communist coup in Czechoslovakia and instituting an economic and military blockade of Berlin. In his famous "long telegram" in 1946 and a *Foreign Affairs* essay a year later, George Kennan articulated an intellectual rationale for how the United States should deal with this new world power. According to Kennan, domestic political considerations required that the Soviet Union find external adversaries. Under these circumstances, overtures of friendship from the United States would prove unavailing. Rather than cooperation, Kennan recommended "firm and vigilant containment of Russian expansive tendencies." For the next fifty years, the primary adversary of the United States would be the Soviet Union, and for much of this period, Kennan's advice of containment would be at the center of U.S. policy.

Enormous changes have taken place in U.S.-Soviet relations since Kennan wrote his telegram—not least, the dissolution of the Soviet empire. Nevertheless, we expect that American attitudes toward the Soviet Union in the latter stages of the twentieth century will arise, in part, from ethnocentrism, on three grounds. First, even if ethnocentrism does not require enemies, it does encourage the ready perception of enemies, the turning of difference into danger and threat. Second, intermittently over the decades, the Soviet Union has supplied plenty of reasons for Americans to worry about its intentions. And third, the cold war lends itself exquisitely to ethnocentric language and appeals, on both sides.

To see if ethnocentrism has a part to play in Americans' wariness toward the Soviet Union, we analyzed the 1988 NES, carried out during a thaw in U.S.-Soviet relations. After a chilly Reykjavik summit meeting in 1986,

TABLE 4.5. Ethnocentrism and opposition to the Soviet Union

	Prevent spread of communism	Tougher in dealings with Soviet Union	Disapprove of arms agreements
Ethnocentrism	0.72***	0.53***	0.36**
	0.14	0.14	0.16
Partisanship	−0.38***	−0.33***	−0.33***
	0.09	0.09	0.10
Education	−0.76***	−0.41***	−0.40***
	0.12	0.12	0.14
N	1472	1294	1436
Effect of **E**	0.63→0.79	0.23→0.35	0.08→0.13

Source: 1988 NES.

Note: Table entry is the ordered probit regression coefficient with standard errors below. Models also control for political awareness, sex, race, and ethnicity. Full results appear in the Web appendix. The bottom row of the table gives the effect associated with a shift in Ethnocentrism from Low (−0.1) to High (0.6) in the predicted probability of opposing the Soviet Union (see text for details).

***$p < 0.01$; **$p < 0.05$; *$p < 0.10$, two-tailed.

President Reagan and Premier Gorbachev continued, in a series of subsequent summits, to attempt to negotiate an agreement to limit each superpower's nuclear forces. Three questions included in the 1988 NES allow us to determine whether ethnocentrism dampens the American public's interest in détente. The first question deals directly with Kennan's doctrine of containment. In response to this question, more than two-thirds of Americans said that the United States should do everything in its power to prevent the spread of communism. A second question has to do with the proper approach the United States should take to the Soviet Union, distinguishing generally between accommodation and confrontation. In the fall of 1988, Americans were quite evenly divided between these two general options: 32 percent chose getting tougher; 42 percent preferred cooperation; with the rest distributed in between. And on the third question, an overwhelming majority of Americans said that they approved of recent agreements between the United States and the Soviet Union designed to reduce each country's stockpile of nuclear weapons.[27]

In this analysis, we assess ethnocentrism through thermometer score ratings (**E*** rather than **E**) since the stereotype battery was not included in the 1988 NES. In other respects, the analysis takes the usual form.[28] The results appear in table 4.5. The table is organized in the standard way, as an array of columns, with each column representing one of the three measures of opinion: preventing the spread of communism on the left, accommodation versus confrontation in the middle of the table, and disapproval of arms agreements with the Soviets on the right. The coefficient in the first row reveals whether, as we expect, ethnocentrism predicts opposition to the Soviet Union, holding constant whatever effects might be due to party identification, education, and other considerations.

As expected, ethnocentric Americans agree with the goal of preventing the spread of communism, they choose toughness over cooperation in U.S.-Soviet relations, and they are more likely to express skepticism toward arms control agreements reached between the United States and the Soviet Union. The effect of ethnocentrism is significant and sizable in each case, though it is especially sizable on containment.

In their intensive clinical investigations reported in *The Authoritarian Personality* (1950), Adorno and his colleagues found a core aspect of anti-Semitism to be the fear of being overwhelmed, that Jews should be, in effect, quarantined lest their immorality contaminate or infect those around them. Something like that might be going on here; the question on containment refers to the "spread" of communism, as if it were a plague. More generally, if ethnocentrism is not the only ingredient in American opinion on policy toward communism—partisanship and education are part of the mix as well—it is certainly an important one.[29]

DESERT STORM

Our third and final case returns us to the Middle East. On August 2, 1990, Iraqi troops poured across the border into Kuwait and quickly seized control of the country's vital centers. In less than a week, Hussein was able to announce to the world that Kuwait belonged, or in the formulation he preferred, had rightfully been returned, to Iraq. President George H. W. Bush denounced the invasion, referring to it as a form of "naked aggression," and pledged U.S. participation in an economic blockade of Iraq. He dispatched U.S. warships to the Persian Gulf and, several days later, announced that he was sending U.S. troops to Saudi Arabia to defend against potential Iraqi incursions there. Early in November, without clear evidence that the economic sanctions were working and apprehensive that the international coalition enforcing the economic blockade might unravel, Bush began to lay the groundwork for a military offensive. Following the midterm congressional elections, the president announced a substantial increase in the U.S. military presence in the Middle East. By the end of the month, Bush succeeded in persuading the United Nations Security Council to authorize force against Hussein's troops unless they withdrew from Kuwait by the fifteenth of January. On the home front, meanwhile, Bush's impatience with economic sanctions and his escalation of the military option provoked alarm and criticism from Democrats in Congress. Hearings began, followed by a

TABLE 4.6. Ethnocentrism and support for Desert Storm

	Emotional responses		Policy opinions			Evaluations of president	
	Pride	Anger	Military force over diplomacy	Sending troops was right	Should have kept fighting	Management of Gulf crisis	General performance
Ethnocentrism	0.86***	2.01***	1.30***	0.52	0.74***	0.83***	0.86***
	0.27	0.48	0.40	0.32	0.28	0.28	0.26
Partisanship	−0.63***	0.16	−1.08***	−0.73***	0.07	−0.79***	−1.25***
	0.13	0.18	0.17	0.16	0.13	0.14	0.13
Education	0.06	0.00	−0.80***	−0.10	−0.61***	−0.28	−0.29
	0.19	0.24	0.24	0.22	0.19	0.19	0.18
N	800	801	634	790	803	792	779
Effect of **E**	0.49→0.72	0.86→0.99	0.53→0.84	0.72→0.83	0.33→0.53	0.76→0.89	0.71→0.87

Source: 1990–1991–1992 NES Panel.

Note: Table entry is the ordered probit regression coefficient with standard errors below. Models also control for political awareness, sex, race, and ethnicity. Assessments of personal and national economic conditions are included in the last two models. Full results appear in the Web appendix. The bottom row of the table gives the effect associated with a shift in Ethnocentrism from Low (−0.1) to High (0.6) in the predicted probability of supporting Desert Storm (see text for details).

***$p < 0.01$; **$p < 0.05$; *$p < 0.10$, two-tailed.

contentious floor debate. As the January 15 deadline approached, Congress voted, largely along partisan lines, to authorize the use of force. Promising that victory would establish "a new world order," the president declared as the deadline expired that "the world could wait no longer." On January 16, with no sign of Iraqi withdrawal, U.S. forces entered the war, first through a devastating aerial bombardment and then, five weeks later, in a massive ground assault. Iraqi troops broke and ran. In short order, a cease-fire was announced, sovereignty restored to Kuwait, and victory declared.

From the point of view of most Americans, by the end of February the Persian Gulf War—or Desert Storm, as the U.S. military called it—passed quickly into history. But while it was taking place, the war caught and held the American public's attention. To what extent was the American public's reaction to Desert Storm grounded in ethnocentrism?

We can find out by drawing on the well-timed 1990–1991–1992 NES Panel. As part of NES's continuing study of congressional elections, personal interviews were completed with a national probability sample of 2000 American citizens of voting age immediately following the 1990 national midterm elections. Most were questioned after President Bush announced increases in troop strength in the Middle East and before the congressional debate over the authorization of force. Nearly 1400 of these same respondents were then reinterviewed in June and July 1991, as the dust of Desert Storm had begun to settle, and then again in the fall of 1992, both before and after the national elections.

As table 4.6 shows, ethnocentrically inclined Americans were more likely to report pride in the American triumph and much more likely to express anger toward Hussein.[30] Ethnocentrism affected Americans' views on policy as well (also shown in table 4.6). Ethnocentric Americans favored military intervention over diplomacy. They were more likely to say, after the fighting was over, that we did the right thing in sending in troops. And they were more apt to express the wish that the war had been carried on to Baghdad to remove Hussein from power.[31] Finally, when fighting began in the middle of January, public support for President Bush skyrocketed, and as the results in table 4.6 indicate, ethnocentrism was clearly implicated in the president's gaudy approval numbers. In the summer of 1991, amid welcome home parades and an outpouring of national pride, the president's support drew importantly on ethnocentrism—just as would be true for his son a decade later, in the aftermath of 9/11.[32]

RÉSUMÉ OF RESULTS

By the evidence presented here, ethnocentrism figures importantly in how Americans think about their nation's enemies. To grasp the magnitude of ethnocentrism's effect across these three cases, we translated the tabled coefficients presented so far into graphical form. Figure 4.1 does this for five representative cases: spending more on the war on terrorism; taking military action against Iraq; approval of George W. Bush's performance as president; confrontation rather than cooperation vis-à-vis the Soviet Union; and carrying the war to Baghdad in 1991 to remove Hussein from power. Each graph depicts the predicted support for each of these five aspects of support for confronting America's enemies as a consequence of variation in ethnocentrism, holding constant other considerations.[33]

Figure 4.1 shows precisely how support for taking on American enemies gathers strength with increasing ethnocentrism. Take, as a typical example, the prospect of going to war with Iraq in the fall of 2002. Figure 4.1 indicates

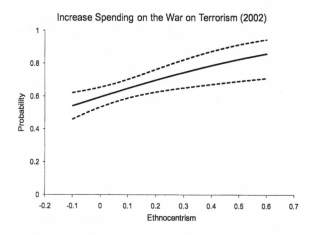

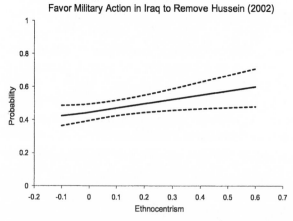

FIGURE 4.1. Ethnocentrism and America's enemies. Predicted probabilities with 95 percent confidence intervals. Estimates from tables 4.1–4.3, 4.5–4.6. Source: 1988 NES; 1990–1991–1992, 2000–2002 NES Panels.

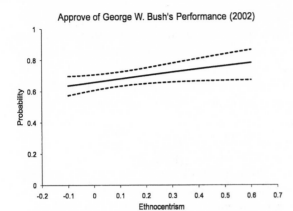

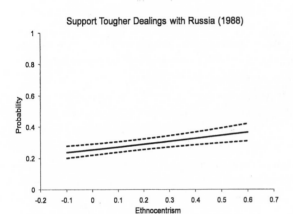

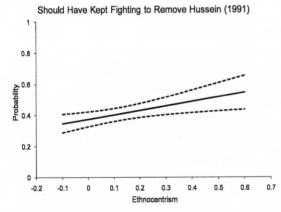

FIGURE 4.1. (*continued*)

that across the normal range of ethnocentrism found in the American public today (roughly speaking, from −0.1 to +0.6), the predicted probability of supporting military action against Iraq increases from 42 percent to over 60 percent. The other graphs presented in figure 4.1 tell essentially the same story. Ethnocentrism, it would seem, plays an important part in marshalling American support for confronting enemies around the world.

ACTIVATION OF ETHNOCENTRISM

Ethnocentrism is a deep, abiding, and perhaps irresistible human habit. But this does not mean that ethnocentrism is an inevitable and fixed feature of political life. The part played by ethnocentrism in politics is variable, contingent on circumstance.

As we argued in chapter 2, this is so in part because of the dynamic nature of politics. Issues and problems come and go, and they come and go rapidly. And while the range of topics that government might take up is unimaginably large, the carrying capacity of citizens (and institutions) is distinctly limited. At any single moment, only a few topics can become the center of a society's attention. Moreover, only some of the issues and problems that command public attention lend themselves to ethnocentric thinking. In part this has to do with the distinct features of particular issues, but it also has to do with how issues are formulated in public discussion. The issues and problems that animate politics are always complex and can always be understood in more than one way. Elites frame problems in particular ways, and such frames, insofar as they resonate with the public, may activate ethnocentrism or suppress it.

This account of activation may be plausible. It may be psychologically realistic. But is it (to a first approximation) true?

Our empirical tests of activation, here and in succeeding chapters, mainly take the form of opportunistic analysis of "natural experiments." In politics, as in other domains of life, things change. Sometimes things change abruptly, dramatically, suddenly. And sometimes such changes have predictable implications. And finally, sometimes these implications can be tested because of the planned or more often serendipitous availability of relevant data. In short, the analysis of natural experiments takes advantage of the co-occurrence of a sudden change with the collection of information that allows a reasonably sharp empirical test. In this chapter we take advantage of two natural experiments to probe our theory of activation: the terrorist attack on the United States on September 11, 2001, paired up with the 2000–2002 NES Panel; and the rapid mobilization and demobilization of public attention occasioned by Desert Storm, neatly bracketed by the 1990–1991–1992 NES Panel.

Before and after 9/11

If the importance of ethnocentrism to politics depends on circumstance, and circumstance has to do with how Americans apportion their attention and how they understand the issues of the day, then support for the war on terrorism in the immediate aftermath of 9/11 should serve as an exemplary case for the activation of ethnocentrism. First of all, the terrorist attacks on New York and Washington commanded and held public attention. This was no ordinary day. History was happening, and it was being broadcast live. Americans of different backgrounds and interests were all thinking about the same thing. September 11 served to concentrate the government's attention as well. Priorities and policies shifted dramatically. The war on terrorism became and, at least for the first several years of the George W. Bush administration, largely remained *the* story.

Second, the war on terrorism lends itself just about perfectly to ethnocentric thinking. The attack itself was carried out by a small number of radical foreign nationals, whose appearance, history, language, and religion were alien to most Americans. It was carried out on American soil (the homeland). Iconic representations of American power were destroyed. Thousands of innocent people perished. The attack was carefully, diabolically planned halfway around the world, and yet the motives behind it remained, for most Americans, mysterious. The natural temptation to see this new war in we-they terms was reinforced by the frames that elites offered up. Discussions of the war were saturated with language and symbols that emphasized a conflict between civilization and fanaticism. To the major networks, it was "America" that was under attack and a "Nation" that was responding with heroism and resolve (Jamieson and Waldman 2002). "Either you are with us," the president said to the nations of the world, "or you are with the terrorists."

For reasons having to do with attention and understanding, then, we expect that ethnocentrism would be more important in Americans' thinking about politics immediately following 9/11 than in the period running up to 9/11. We can test this claim in a relatively sharp way by analyzing the 2000–2002 NES Panel. Remember that this is a *panel* study: that is, the *same* people were interviewed in 2000 and in 2002. Thus, we can compare the potency of ethnocentrism on opinion on topics relevant to the war on terrorism that were asked *both* in the 2002 NES (after 9/11) *and* in the 2000 NES (before 9/11). Three topics appeared in both waves: tightening border security, strengthening national defense, and supporting President Bush. Not surprisingly, American opinion on all three matters shifted noticeably from the fall of 2000 to the fall of 2002. After 9/11, more Americans wanted to increase federal spending on border control to prevent illegal

TABLE 4.7. The effect of ethnocentrism on American support for the war on terrorism before and after 9/11

	Tighten borders		National defense		Feelings toward Bush	
	2000	2002	2000	2002	2000	2002
Ethnocentrism	0.87***	0.98***	0.17	0.70**	−0.11	0.53**
	0.32	0.36	0.30	0.31	0.26	0.26
Partisanship	−0.27**	−0.33**	−0.90***	−0.83***	−2.33***	−2.01***
	0.13	0.14	0.13	0.13	0.13	0.12
Education	−0.45**	−0.44**	−0.47**	−0.13	−0.17	−0.12
	0.19	0.21	0.18	0.19	0.16	0.16
Authoritarianism	0.75***	0.33*	0.27	0.31*	0.51***	0.46***
	0.17	0.19	0.17	0.17	0.14	0.15
Religiosity	−0.13	0.07	0.45***	0.27*	0.69***	0.53***
	0.14	0.16	0.14	0.15	0.12	0.12
National					0.02	1.03***
econ. eval.					0.16	0.18
Household					−0.13	0.59***
econ. eval.					0.17	0.16
N	812	812	820	820	848	848

Source: 2000–2002 NES Panel.

Note: Table entry is the ordered probit regression coefficient with standard errors below. Models also control for political awareness, sex, race, and ethnicity. Full results appear in the Web appendix.

***$p < 0.01$; **$p < 0.05$; *$p < 0.10$, two-tailed.

immigration (70.0 percent versus 54.5 percent). Likewise, they wanted to increase spending on national defense (59.2 percent versus 42.9 percent).[34] And they evaluated President Bush much more favorably (an average rating of 66 on the 0–100 point thermometer scale in the fall of 2002 compared to a rating of 57 two years before).[35]

Our expectation is that in the post–9/11 world, ethnocentrism will shape these opinions more powerfully than in the pre–9/11 world. To test this expectation, we estimated the effect of ethnocentrism on opinions measured in 2000 (before 9/11) and then again for opinions on the same matters measured in 2002 (after 9/11). To make the comparison exact, we restricted this analysis to respondents who participated in both waves of the NES Panel, and we estimated the identical model in each instance. The results are presented in table 4.7.

As predicted, the impact of ethnocentrism is greater in the fall of 2002 than it is in the fall of 2000—greater, that it is to say, immediately after 9/11 than shortly before. This is true in all three cases. Either ethnocentrism is unimportant in 2000 and becomes important in 2002 in the cases of defense spending and support for the president; or, in the case of securing U.S. borders, ethnocentrism is important in 2000 and becomes even more important in 2002.[36]

We predicted these results but were not at all sure we would find them. The test is hard. It requires that the relationship between ethnocentrism and opinion, measured two years apart, surpass the relationship between ethnocentrism and opinion, measured in the same interview. All other things equal, the prediction would, of course, run the other way. And indeed, table 4.7 shows that partisanship and authoritarianism show just this pattern: each generally does a better job predicting opinion measured in 2000 than in predicting opinion measured in 2002. When it comes to ethnocentrism, however, things look very different, a sign that the train of events that began on September 11 served to activate ethnocentrism among the American public.[37]

To illustrate the magnitude of activation, we calculated the probability of support for one case, increased defense spending, as a consequence of ethnocentrism, holding constant the effect due to other predispositions. We performed each calculation twice: first for opinion as measured in 2000 and then for opinion as measured in 2002. The results are presented in figure 4.2. The difference in the slopes between the two paired lines—one for 2000, the other for 2002—reflects the magnitude of activation provided by 9/11.[38]

Before, Right after, and Long after Desert Storm

Our second test of activation is provided by the overlap between the first Iraq war—Desert Storm, as it was often called—and the serendipitously timed 1990–1991–1992 NES Panel. Earlier in this chapter we reported that ethnocentrically inclined Americans generally supported Desert Storm: they were more likely to report pride in the apparent victory and much more likely to express anger toward Hussein; favored military intervention over diplomacy; were more likely to say, after the fighting was over, that we did the right thing in sending in troops but that the war should have been carried on to Baghdad to remove Hussein from power; and they were more likely to support President George H. W. Bush enthusiastically.

All well and good—and all as expected. For according to our account of activation, the summer of 1991 would have furnished a congenial set of circumstances for ethnocentrism. In the first place, when fighting broke out in January, Americans turned on their televisions, and, as John Mueller

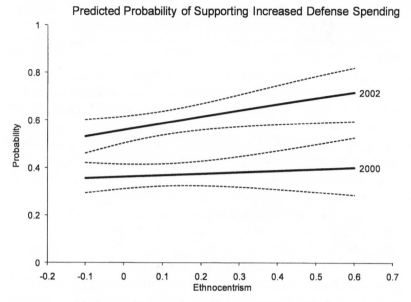

Predicted Probability of Supporting Increased Defense Spending

FIGURE 4.2. Activating ethnocentrism: the effect of ethnocentrism on American support for the increased defense spending, before and after 9/11. Predicted probabilities with 95 percent confidence intervals. Estimates from table 4.7. Source: 2000–2002 NES Panel.

(1994) has shown, they kept them on. Americans were captivated and consumed by the war. Second, as we suggested at the outset of the chapter, war lends itself readily to ethnocentric thinking. This habit was encouraged by U.S. leaders, including President Bush, who said on more than one occasion that Hussein was not merely an enemy but evil incarnate; Hussein was worse, the president declared, than Hitler. And it was encouraged as well by Hussein's dim-witted public relations performance. Shortly after the invasion of Kuwait, in an apparent effort to win over the American public and forestall U.S. intervention, Hussein staged a televised meeting with a group of Western hostages, whose evident and extreme discomfort was not relieved by Hussein referring to them as "guests." As a propaganda machine, things went from bad to worse. "Hussein's only adept accomplishment during the whole crisis period," according to Mueller, "was his consummate portrayal of the demon role" (1994, p. 41). For these reasons, the summer of 1991, in the immediate aftermath of Desert Storm's triumphant conclusion, should have produced, so to speak, an ethnocentric high point. A high point, though, compared to what?

Compared, on the one hand, to the fall of 1990, in the run-up to the war. In the 1990–1991–1992 NES Panel, those interviewed in the summer of 1991 were also questioned right after the 1990 national midterm elections. Most were interviewed after President Bush announced increases in troop strength in the Middle East but before the congressional debate over the authorization of force. All were interviewed before it became clear that military intervention was probable and well before the actual fighting had begun. Taken all around, the conditions prevailing at the time of the first interview were decidedly less congenial to the activation of ethnocentrism than what was shortly to come.

And—perhaps this is the more interesting point—a high point also compared to the fall of 1992, some eighteen months after the war's end. For by the fall of 1992, the war was not only over, it was largely forgotten. After the welcome home parades, the American public's attention turned away from the distant war to matters closer to home, especially to signs that the economy was faltering. As the presidential campaign got underway, President Bush did his best to remind voters of the glorious war—that Desert Storm had restored sovereignty to Kuwait, preempted Hussein's effort to develop nuclear weapons, and destroyed Iraq's ability to control oil prices. The message failed to take. The war belonged to history (J. Mueller 1994).

In short, between the fall of 1990 and the fall of 1992, we expect to see a spike in the power of ethnocentrism: modest before the fighting, high immediately after victory is declared, and subsiding as the war is forgotten. And that, by and large, is what we see.

These results are shown in table 4.8. They come from a panel study, remember, so we are examining the reactions of the *same* people assessed on three separate occasions: the fall of 1990, the summer of 1991, and the fall of 1992. We can test the hypothesis that the impact of ethnocentrism will increase between 1990 and 1991 with four distinct measures, and on each, as table 4.8 reveals, we find the effect of ethnocentrism is up, and up sharply. Activation holds on support for a military solution, sending the troops, strengthening defense, and approval of George Bush's performance as president. Roughly speaking, the effect of ethnocentrism doubles between 1990 and 1991.[39]

Table 4.8 also shows that effect of ethnocentrism diminishes between the summer of 1991 and the fall of 1992, as the war faded from memory. The decline coming out of Desert Storm is less dramatic than the increase going in, but it is still apparent on all four cases we can examine: sending troops to the Middle East, carrying the fight to Baghdad, strengthening defense, and supporting President George Bush.[40]

In addition to the strong support for our claim about the activation and deactivation of ethnocentrism, there is perhaps one other thing to take notice of in table 4.8. As the importance of ethnocentrism for presidential performance diminishes between 1991 and 1992, the importance of voters' assessments of national economic conditions sharply increases.[41] In these coefficients is written the tale of George Bush's legendary—indeed Churchillian—fall. In the summer of 1991, President Bush was hailed as a national hero; eighteen months later, he was thrown out of office, his reelection bid decisively rejected.

Of course, the big lesson of this analysis, from our point of view, has to do with the activation—and deactivation—of ethnocentrism. To see this lesson more clearly, we summarize the relevant results in graphical form in figure 4.3. The curves marking the effect of ethnocentrism are close to horizontal in 1990 and 1992, and tilt upward sharply in 1991, a reflection, in

TABLE 4.8. The effect of ethnocentrism on American support for Desert Storm before, right after, and well after the fighting

	Prefer military Solution			Sending troops the right thing			Should have carried the fighting to Baghdad		
	1990	1991	1992	1990	1991	1992	1990	1991	1992
Ethnocentrism	0.45	1.28***	N/A	−0.07	0.52†	0.09	N/A	0.74***	0.41
	0.34	0.41		0.30	0.35	0.33		0.28	0.27
Partisanship	−0.35**	−1.12***		−0.59***	−0.75***	−0.84***		0.07	0.23*
	0.17	0.18		0.15	0.18	0.18		0.13	0.13
Education	−0.11	−0.83***		0.25	−0.10	−0.08		−0.61***	−0.39**
	0.24	0.24		0.23	0.25	0.26		0.19	0.19
N	621	621		704	704	704		801	801

	Strengthen defense			Bush job approval		
	1990	1991	1992	1990	1991	1992
Ethnocentrism	0.37	0.67**	0.45	0.46*	0.99***	0.82***
	0.27	0.27	0.27	0.25	0.27	0.25
Partisanship	−0.77***	−0.71***	−0.73***	−1.28***	−1.35***	−1.32***
	0.13	0.13	0.13	0.13	0.14	0.13
Education	−0.55***	−0.47***	−0.60***	−0.03	−0.33*	0.00
	0.18	0.18	0.18	0.18	0.19	0.18
National econ. eval.				1.06***	1.03***	1.95***
				0.22	0.21	0.20
Household econ. eval.				0.23	0.56***	0.44***
				0.15	0.17	0.17
N	602	602	602	736	736	736

Source: 1990–1991–1992 NES Panel.

Note: Table entry is the ordered probit regression coefficient with standard errors below. Models also control for political awareness, sex, race, and ethnicity. Full results appear in the Web appendix. N/A indicates that the dependent variable was not available in that year of the survey.

***$p < 0.01$; **$p < 0.05$; *$p < 0.10$; † $p < 0.15$, two-tailed.

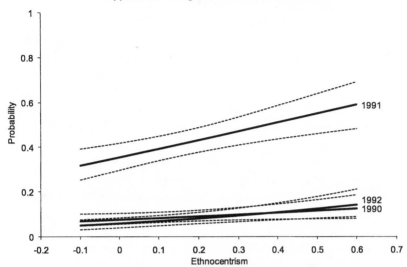

FIGURE 4.3. Activating ethnocentrism: the effect of ethnocentrism on presidential approval before, right after, and well after the fighting. Predicted probabilities with 95 percent confidence intervals. Estimates from table 4.8. Source: 1990–1991–1992 NES Panel.

our reading, of how rapidly public attention lurches from one preoccupation to the next.[42]

CONCLUSIONS AND IMPLICATIONS

As expected, on the international scene, ethnocentrism encourages American support for war and confrontation: for the contemporary fight against terrorism; for the long struggle between the United States and the Soviet Union; and, a decade before al Qaeda became part of the nation's vocabulary, for military intervention against Iraq and Saddam Hussein. The effects of ethnocentrism are sizable. They hold up in stringent tests and across alternative specifications. They cannot be accounted for by conservatism or by authoritarianism. And they are over and above the effects due to partisanship, education, and other significant considerations.

Is this really surprising? If ethnocentrism is distrust of strangers, then war, terrorism, and global communism would seem to be easy cases.

There is probably something to this. Among others, E. O. Wilson (1978) has suggested that ethnocentrism and aggression are intimately related. Wilson argues that aggression is an innate predisposition; that under certain specifiable conditions, humans are biologically prepared to fight; and that such aggression is facilitated by an exaggerated allegiance to kin and fellow tribesmen (see 1978, pp. 111, 119).

From another point of view, however, the results presented here *are* surprising. Keep in mind how we have measured ethnocentrism. We readily concede that it would be unsurprising and quite uninformative if Americans who thought *terrorists* dangerous lined up in support of President George W. Bush's war. That's not what we have shown here. We have shown, instead, that Americans who are unimpressed with the character and capacity of *their fellow Americans*—white, black, Hispanic, and Asian—are most enthusiastic about a war on terrorism. Again, it is those Americans who regard their own racial or ethnic group to be superior to other American racial and ethnic groups who favored confrontation over cooperation with the Soviet Union and who were especially angry at Hussein and especially prepared to carry the war to Baghdad. And so on. What is informative about these results is that support for war and confrontation arises not from an aversion to Arabs or to Islamic fundamentalists but from a general aversion; from prejudice, broadly conceived; and from not just out-group hostility, but also from in-group pride—in a word, from ethnocentrism.

Our purpose here has been to begin to make the case *both* that ethnocentrism is of general importance to understanding public opinion *and* that the magnitude of ethnocentrism's effect depends in a systematic and intelligible way on circumstances. Ethnocentrism generally predisposes Americans to favor war and confrontation over diplomacy and cooperation, but this effect becomes especially important under certain circumstances: at moments when the public's attention is concentrated, not scattered; and when the few issues that command public attention lend themselves to we-they thinking. So it was in the aftermath of 9/11; and so it was, for a brief time, after Desert Storm.

The promise of ethnocentrism as an explanation resides in its long reach. It could even be said that the claim of ethnocentrism *requires* explanatory power across cases. Onward, then, to additional cases. Next we take up humanitarian aspects of U.S. foreign policy. Just as ethnocentrism underpins American support for war and confrontation, so may it interfere with American concern for other nations and peoples.

CHAPTER 5

America First

In the spring and early summer of 1994, in the Republic of Rwanda, nearly a million people were massacred. Though carried out principally by machete, the Rwandan genocide represented the most efficient mass killing since Hiroshima and Nagasaki. To prevent these horrific events, the U.S. government did—nothing. Early warnings of imminent mass violence were ignored. Urgent requests from the Belgian peace-keeping contingent for reinforcements were denied. After the massacres began, no U.S. troops were sent to stop the slaughter. Indeed, not a single meeting of senior U.S. foreign policy advisers was even convened. In the meantime, one-tenth of the population of Rwanda was erased from the earth.[1]

Some years later, President Bill Clinton would refer to inaction in the face of the Rwandan genocide as his administration's worst mistake. On a visit to Rwanda in 1998, the president offered an apology of sorts:

> We in the United States and the world community did not do as much as we could have and should have done to try to limit what occurred. It may seem strange to you here, but all over the world there were people like me sitting in offices, day after day after day, who did not fully appreciate the depth and speed with which you were being engulfed by this unimaginable terror.[2]

In chapter 4 we learned that ethnocentrism plays an important part in generating American support for confronting U.S. adversaries around the world. Here we address a complementary proposition: that ethnocentrism plays an important part in generating American indifference to the troubles suffered by those who happen to live outside U.S. borders.

It could be said that our business here is to pursue a conjecture offered up by Adam Smith in *The Theory of Moral Sentiments*. Writing in the middle of the eighteenth century on the obligations of duty, Smith invites us to imagine the reaction of an educated and cultivated European to the news that the entire Chinese empire had been swallowed by a catastrophic earthquake:

> He would, I imagine, first of all, express very strongly his sorrow for the misfortune of that unhappy people, he would make many melancholy reflections upon the precariousness of human life, and the vanity of all the labours of man, which could thus be annihilated in a moment. . . . And when all this fine philosophy was over, when all these humane sentiments had been once fairly expressed, he would pursue his business or his pleasure, take his repose or his diversion, with the same ease and tranquility, as if no such accident had happened. The most frivolous disaster which could befal himself would occasion a more real disturbance. If he was to lose his little finger to-morrow, he would not sleep tonight; but, provided he never saw them, he will snore with the more profound security over a hundred million of his brethren, and the destruction of that immense multitude seems plainly an object less interesting to him, than this paltry misfortune of his own. ([1759] 1817, p. 215)

So it seemed to Smith in a very different time, and so it seems to us, by and large, today. To Smith's conjecture we add this: the proposition that in the face of great calamity taking place elsewhere, it is the relatively ethnocentric who sleep the soundest.

We will investigate the empirical merit of this hypothesis in several domains. First we will consider the part played by ethnocentrism in American attitudes toward foreign aid in general. Next we will take up three concrete instances of foreign assistance: technical and economic help to the countries of Eastern Europe struggling toward democracy after the demise of the Soviet Union, economic sanctions imposed on South Africa intended to lighten the oppressions of apartheid, and military assistance to the contras in Nicaragua in their effort to overthrow the Sandinista regime. Third, we will determine the extent to which ethnocentrism encourages indifference to the horrors of wars waged on foreign soil. Finally, we will conduct a test of activation, contrasting American opposition to foreign aid before and after 9/11.

FOREIGN AID IN GENERAL

Americans are philosophically conservative but programmatically liberal. They complain about government in the abstract, but they tend to support government programs in particular (Free and Cantril 1967). By overwhelming margins, Americans want government to do more on education, health, the environment, public safety, highways and bridges. On and on it goes.

Such programmatic liberalism is impressive in magnitude and range. But it does not extend to foreign aid.

For example, of the twenty-one government programs asked about in the 2002 National Election Study (NES), foreign aid attracted the least support of all. Just 10 percent of Americans said that government spending on foreign aid should be increased; nearly 50 percent recommended that spending be cut. There is, moreover, nothing new in this. Figure 5.1 shows that as far back as we can trace public opinion, American support for foreign aid has been feeble—both in absolute terms and in comparison to other government initiatives. Americans favor spending more on heath, education, and the environment, but such generosity evaporates when it comes to providing help to other nations. Opposition to foreign aid is substantial and tenacious. We expect this opposition derives, at least in part, from ethnocentrism.[3]

To determine if this is so, we estimate the effect of ethnocentrism on opinion on foreign aid, using the standard model we introduced in the last chapter. These results are presented in table 5.1. Here we are predicting opposition to foreign aid in general, as expressed in the fall of 2002, from ethnocentrism measured in 2000, holding constant other relevant

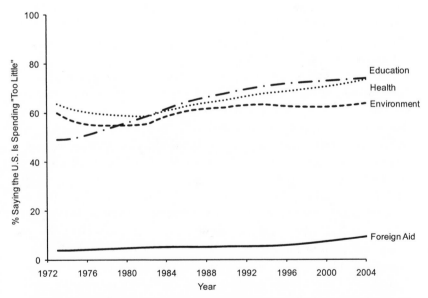

FIGURE 5.1. American support for government programs (health, education, environment) and foreign aid, 1973–2004. Lowess-smoothed values, based on weighted means. Source: 1972–2004 GSS.

TABLE 5.1. Ethnocentrism and American opposition to
foreign aid in general

	Foreign aid in general
Ethnocentrism	0.69**
	0.29
Partisanship	−0.29**
	0.12
Education	−0.38**
	0.17
N	847
Effect of **E**	0.37→0.57

Source: 2000–2002 NES Panel.

Note: Table entry is the ordered probit regression coefficient with standard errors below. Models also control for
political awareness, sex, race, and ethnicity. Full results
appear in the Web appendix. The bottom row of the table
gives the effect associated with a shift in Ethnocentrism
from Low (−0.1) to High (0.6) in the predicted probability of supporting decreased spending on foreign aid (see
text for details).

***$p < 0.01$; **$p < 0.05$; *$p < 0.10$, two-tailed.

considerations (partisanship, education, political awareness, sex, race, and
ethnicity).[4] We expected ethnocentrism to undermine support for foreign
aid, and it does.

The effect shown in table 5.1 withstands alternative model specifications.
For example, the effect of ethnocentrism on opposition to foreign aid is undiminished if we add a measure of belief in limited government to the standard model. Where government intrudes, waste and inefficiency are sure to
follow—or so many Americans believe. Those who think that limited government is best might be inclined to suspect that foreign aid rarely reaches
those who actually need it. Plausible enough, and when we add to our analysis a high-performing measure of limited government, this expectation is
born out: believing in limited government works against support for foreign
aid. It does so, however, without cutting into the effect due to ethnocentrism—indeed, if anything, the estimated effect of ethnocentrism increases
a bit when limited government is taken into account.

The powerful role ethnocentrism appears to play in undercutting support for foreign aid is likewise undiminished when we take into account beliefs about equality. One might expect that a commitment to egalitarianism
would encourage generosity in foreign aid. When we added a measure of
equality to our standard model, this expectation is confirmed, but whether

we take belief in equality into account in our analysis makes no difference to our finding that opposition to foreign aid stems in an important way from ethnocentrism.[5]

How important? One way to answer this question is to rely on the standard model to generate predicted probabilities of cutting foreign aid as a function of variation in ethnocentrism. Following this procedure (spelled out in more detail in the previous chapter), we find that Americans who score low on the ethnocentrism scale are expected to be quite unlikely to favor cutting foreign aid: their predicted probability of supporting decreased spending on foreign aid is about 0.37. By contrast, those scoring high on ethnocentrism are quite likely to favor cuts: their predicted probability is 0.57. Thus, with other considerations held constant, a shift in ethnocentrism across the natural range is associated with a 0.20 increase in the probability of support for reducing foreign aid—a substantial effect.[6]

FOREIGN AID IN THE PARTICULAR

What about foreign aid in the particular? Next we take up three distinct, important, and concrete cases of foreign aid: economic assistance to Eastern Europe, diplomatic and economic pressure on South Africa, and military help to the contras in Nicaragua.

Eastern Europe

A new policy question for the United States emerged from the astonishing run of events that brought an unanticipated and rapid end to the Soviet Union. Mikhail Gorbachev opened up Soviet society ("glasnost"), attempted to transform the USSR's economy ("perestroika"), and embarked on a series of summit meetings with President Ronald Reagan to reduce each superpower's stock of nuclear weapons. In late fall of 1989, the Berlin Wall came down. Shortly thereafter, the separate republics that had comprised the Soviet Union, led by Lithuania and other Baltic states, began to declare their independence from Moscow. On December 15, 1991, Gorbachev formally dissolved the Soviet Union.

The end of the Soviet empire gave rise to the new nations of Eastern Europe, struggling with varying conviction and success to establish democratic governments and market economies. And this development, in turn, gave rise to a new policy question: would the United States help?

For this purpose, the 1990–1991–1992 NES Panel is very nicely timed, and, conveniently for our purposes, the NES Panel carried a pair of relevant policy questions. The first question appeared in the 1991 interview and asked whether the United States should give economic assistance to those countries in Eastern Europe that had turned toward democracy. Put this way, foreign aid was actually quite popular. A majority of Americans—57.2 percent—supported a policy of providing economic assistance to Eastern European countries struggling toward democracy; just 42.8 percent opposed it. No doubt the reference to democratic aspirations in the survey question is responsible, at least in part, for this relatively warm reception. The second relevant question, which appeared on the 1992 interview, asked about U.S. assistance to the countries of the former Soviet Union. Presented this way, with no reference to democratization, foreign aid drew much less support: just 15.6 percent wanted to increase spending on countries of the former Soviet Union, 40.9 percent elected to keep spending the same, and a plurality—43.5 percent—said that the United States should cut spending.[7]

Can Americans' views on foreign aid to Eastern European be explained, at least in part, by ethnocentrism? Yes. As shown in figure 5.2, ethnocentric Americans are reluctant to help Eastern European countries move toward democracy, and they think the United States should give less to countries of the former Soviet Union.[8]

The effects are significant and sizable in both instances, though notice that the effect of ethnocentrism is more sizable in the latter case than the former (as shown by the sharper slope of the line). The latter refers to help for countries "of the former Soviet Union"; the former refers to help for countries that "have turned toward democracy." From an American point of view, the Soviet Union and democracy are powerful symbols. The question about countries of "the former Soviet Union" suggests difference and danger. The question about countries that have "turned toward democracy" implies sameness and virtue. Perhaps it should not surprise us that ethnocentrism is engaged more by one than by the other.

South Africa

Apartheid came to South Africa in 1948, with the electoral triumph of the Nationalist Party and its promise to protect the embattled white minority against the *svart gevaar*—the "black menace." After 1948, South Africa designed and implemented as comprehensive and thoroughgoing a racist regime as the world has seen. The population was partitioned into clear biological racial categories (white, colored, Indian, and African). Laws were passed that made marriage and sexual relations across racial lines illegal. Voting rights of colored and African people were eliminated. Segregation was widely and strictly enforced. Schools, buses, restaurants, hotels, universities, elevators: all were to be kept racially pure. Africans were herded into overcrowded and resource-poor territories; colored and Indian

Opposition to Foreign Aid to
Countries That Have Turned toward Democracy

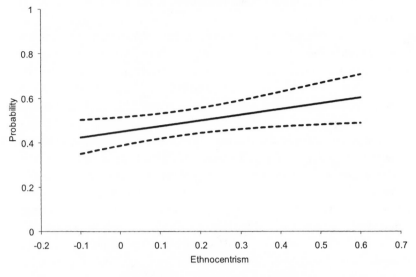

Countries of the Former USSR

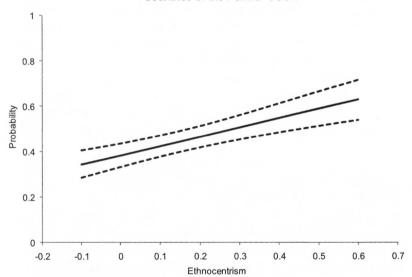

FIGURE 5.2. Ethnocentrism and American opposition to assistance for Eastern Europe. Predicted probabilities with 95 percent confidence intervals. Estimation results appear in the Web appendix. Source: 1990–1991–1992 NES Panel.

populations were pushed into segregated townships. Protest and challenge were met by a well-trained and heavily equipped police force and, when necessary, by the most powerful and disciplined military in all of sub-Saharan Africa.

The dismantling of this entrenched system of oppression required the rise of brave movements of liberation within South Africa. It also required transformations in the outside world. Instead of military assistance and economic aid, by the 1970s the South African regime began to attract moral condemnation and talk of sanctions. In the United States, protest against apartheid gained momentum. In the mid-1980s, thousands of Americans— clergy, trade unionists, students, civil rights leaders, and even, occasionally, members of Congress—were arrested while picketing South African consulates. American universities began to sell their investments in companies that did business with South Africa, and some large American corporations began to withdraw from their South African enterprises. Economic sanctions against South Africa to speed up reform of apartheid began to be discussed in the U.S. Congress. In the fall of 1986, as the South African government declared a national emergency and attempted to reestablish control over the homeland territories and townships, Congress passed, over President Reagan's veto, the Comprehensive Anti-Apartheid Act. The act banned new investments and bank loans, ended air links between South Africa and the United States, prohibited a range of South African imports, and threatened to cut off military assistance to allies suspected of breaching the international arms embargo then in place against South Africa.[9]

It is against this background of change and turmoil that we pick up the analysis of the relationship between ethnocentrism and apartheid. Did ethnocentrism, as we expect, impede support for imposing sanctions on South Africa?

To answer this question we examine opinion in response to a pair of policy questions. The first question, which appeared on the 1988 NES, asks whether the United States should apply economic sanctions to pressure the South African government to change its racial laws. Of those who claimed to have an opinion, most favored the application of sanctions—58.6 percent did so, and most of these strongly favored sanctions. The second question, present two years later in the 1990 NES, took notice of shifts in U.S. policy and changes within South Africa. It asked whether the United States should *increase* sanctions to pressure South Africa to make *further* changes. As before, the balance of opinion favored pressure on apartheid: 43.2 percent supported increasing sanctions; 27.6 percent said that sanctions should be reduced; the remainder, some 29.2 percent, supported the status quo.[10]

Two features of opinion on apartheid are noteworthy. First is the substantial number of refusals. Many Americans said, when asked for their opinion on sanctions against South Africa, that they had no opinion, that they had not thought enough about the issue. In 1988, 60.2 percent of the sample admitted that they had no opinion on sanctions; 34.1 percent did so in 1990.

In some ways this is just a reminder, if we needed it, of the normally subordinate place of politics in everyday life. This may be especially so for the affairs of distant lands. It is as Adam Smith imagined: when "educated and cultivated" people turn their mind to apartheid, they may well feel sorrow and sympathy. They see that it is a catastrophe—in this case, man-made. But then they turn their attention back to their own urgent affairs. As for what the United States should do about racial oppression in South Africa, they really could not say.

A second feature, perhaps even less surprising, is that among those who do have an opinion, very large racial differences emerge. While whites were evenly divided on the question of sanctions, blacks favored sanctions overwhelmingly. In 1988, 52.6 percent of whites who took a position favored imposing economic sanctions on the South African government; 35.0 percent favored increasing U.S. sanctions to press for further changes in South Africa in 1990. The corresponding percentages for black Americans were 89.7 percent and 76.6 percent, respectively. If not quite unanimous, black support for sanctions was nearly so.[11]

Our analysis must take both these features—many refusals, huge racial differences—into account. First of all, in recognition of the racial divide in opinion, we analyze blacks and nonblacks separately. Because we have relatively few black cases to analyze and because black Americans support sanctions overwhelmingly, we cannot take this part of the analysis very far. Indeed, for the most part, we must set black Americans to one side. Before we do so, however, we should say that in the rudimentary analysis we were able to carry out, there are strong hints that on the issue of racial apartheid, ethnocentrism operates very differently among black Americans compared to nonblacks.

The general proposition we are testing in this chapter is that ethnocentrism encourages the view of "America first." Ethnocentrism, we say, breeds skepticism if not outright hostility among Americans toward policies designed to help those in other lands. We have already presented empirical support for this proposition, and there is more still to come. But for black Americans contemplating assistance to those oppressed by apartheid, the relationship reverses. Ethnocentric African Americans *favor* sanctions. Black Americans who think their own racial group superior to others are more likely to say that the United States should press harder for progressive change in South Africa. This is the first case of what we might call ethnocentrism in the service of a liberal cause. It is unusual but not unique, as we will see in subsequent chapters.[12]

Setting these results to one side, how does the general proposition fare among the rest of the American population? We are actually interested here in two aspects of opinion: not just what people think about sanctions and South Africa, but also whether they express an opinion at all. As we have noted, on the question of increasing sanctions applied to South Africa, only about two-thirds of the public express an opinion. No doubt some of this is a straightforward expression of ignorance. Some people know little or nothing about life in South Africa, and some who do may be clueless about the meaning or efficacy of economic sanctions. But there also may be something happening here that has to do with ethnocentrism and with the nature of the issue under examination.

If ethnocentrism breeds an indifference to the suffering of others, then the relatively ethnocentric might be more likely to say they have no opinion in this case. The issue is not important enough, the suffering is not *our* suffering enough, to motivate the attention and rumination required to form an opinion. What we need, then, is a systematic analysis of who has an opinion on sanctions and who does not. The purpose here is to discover the extent to which no opinion on South Africa is simply and entirely a straightforward reflection of a more general withdrawal from political life, or whether ethnocentrism might also be involved.

It turns out that expressing a position on whether the United States should impose (or increase) sanctions on the South African government *is*, in large part, straightforward. Those who know more about politics, who are better educated, who talk about politics with their friends and family, and who know their way around ideological terminology are much more likely to report an opinion. But this is not the whole story. Our analysis also reveals significant effects of ethnocentrism on expressing an opinion, in both years, and in the predicted direction. Those who score high on the ethnocentrism scale are significantly more likely to say they have no opinion on sanctions than are those who score low. The results from the 1990 NES appear in figure 5.3. As predicted, ethnocentrism seems to breed indifference to the suffering of others.[13]

We are equally interested, of course, in the effect of ethnocentrism on the direction of American opinion on sanctions, among those who took a position. On both occasions we find a statistically significant, positive, and substantial relationship. In the fall of 1988, ethnocentric Americans are inclined against imposing economic sanctions on South Africa. In the fall of 1990, they are inclined against increasing sanctions (the 1990 findings are summarized in figure 5.3).[14]

In short, ethnocentrism affects opinion in this domain of policy in two ways: first, ethnocentrism works against knowing (or caring) enough about

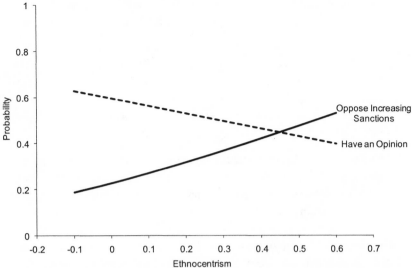

FIGURE 5.3. Ethnocentrism and American opposition to economic sanctions against South Africa, 1990. Predicted probabilities. Estimation results appear in the Web appendix. Source: 1990–1991–1992 NES Panel.

faraway troubles to form an opinion in the first place; and second, among those who do form an opinion, ethnocentrism works to marshal opposition against extending help.[15]

Central America

In 1979, in the small Central American country of Nicaragua, the dictatorship of Anastasio Somoza was overthrown by a Marxist-led movement, the Sandinistas. At first, the Carter administration provided assistance to the fledgling government, but when it was revealed that the Sandinista regime was supplying military aid to the Marxist guerillas fighting the American-supported government in El Salvador, Carter immediately suspended all assistance.

This attitude hardened considerably under the Reagan presidency. Reagan and his advisers were reluctant to commit U.S. troops in the effort, but in other respects threw their support to the Sandinista opposition, the contras, as they were called. In Reagan's view, the Nicaraguan contras were freedom fighters, noble peasants struggling against communist tyranny. They were, in Reagan's words, "the moral equivalent of our Founding Fathers and the brave men and women of the French Resistance." In a televised address to the nation in March 1984, the president argued strongly for their cause. He called the Sandinista regime "a communist reign of terror" and went on to assert:

> If the Soviet Union can aid and abet subversion in our hemisphere, then the United States has a legal right and moral duty to help resist it. This is not only in our strategic interests; it is morally right. It would be profoundly immoral to let peace-loving friends depending on our help be overwhelmed by brute force if we have any capacity to prevent it.[16]

Congress did not always agree. Support nevertheless continued to flow to the contras—covertly, by presidential authorization without congressional knowledge, and indirectly, by solicitation of assistance from other countries, notably Saudi Arabia.

This policy blew up in the president's face when it was revealed, in November 1986, that weapons had been sold to the Iranian government in the hope—unrealized, as things turned out—that Iran would be able to effect the release of American hostages held in Lebanon, and that some of the proceeds from this transaction—the Iranians had been overcharged for the weapons—had been diverted to the contras, in defiance of congressional legislation expressly forbidding assistance to the contras. The press had a field day. John Poindexter, the president's national security adviser, resigned; Oliver North, a member of Poindexter's staff and the chief operational officer behind these maneuvers, was fired; and the president's popularity plummeted. The Iran-contra affair, as it was called, became Reagan's gravest crisis. Although the Tower Commission eventually concluded that the president knew nothing of the diversion of funds to the contras, its report, released in the spring of 1987, did Reagan no favors, for it portrayed him, toward the end of his presidency, as confused, out of touch, and ineffective.

From the point of view of ethnocentrism, support for the contras is complicated. On the one hand, as we have seen in this chapter, ethnocentrism motivates opposition to foreign aid—in general and in concrete instances. On this ground alone, the relatively ethnocentric should *oppose* aid to the contras. On the other hand, as we saw in the preceding chapter, ethnocentrism also motivates support for fighting enemies—and no enemy loomed larger in the second half of the twentieth century to American eyes than the Soviet Union and communism. We learned in chapter 4 that ethnocentric Americans were disproportionately inclined to choose toughness over cooperation in U.S.-Soviet relations; more likely to express skepticism toward arms control agreements reached between the United States and the Soviet Union; and, especially relevant here, more apt to agree that the spread of communism must be stopped. On *this* ground alone, the relatively ethnocentric should *support* aid to the contras in their struggle against the Soviet-supported, avowedly Marxist Sandinista regime.

Americans predisposed to ethnocentrism may have been caught in a dilemma by the plight of the Nicaraguan contras. Do they say no to foreign aid? Or do they say yes to containing the communist menace? They cannot have it both ways.

We can explore this dilemma (and determine if it was, indeed, a dilemma) by analyzing the 1988 NES, which carried a question on the contras. Not surprisingly, in the fall of 1988, after the Iran-contra revelations and the damage done to the Reagan administration, aid to the contras was very unpopular: 60 percent of Americans interviewed in the 1988 NES said that assistance to the contras should be cut back or eliminated entirely; only 12 percent argued for an increase.[17]

When we apply our standard model to opinion on contra aid, we find no effect of ethnocentrism. The estimate is utterly zero ($b_1 = -0.02$, se $= 0.15$). This is as it should be. If ethnocentrism supplies compelling reasons to support the contras *and* to oppose them, then we should not have expected to find an effect of ethnocentrism.[18] We do expect that ethnocentrism will affect public opinion on aid to the contras—but not opinion *direction* (being for or against aid), but rather opinion *ambivalence* (cycling between favoring and opposing aid).

To test for ambivalence, we turned to the heteroscedastic probit model. Heteroscedastic probit enables us to estimate simultaneously the effect of ethnocentrism on the direction of opinion (which we expect to be zero) and on the variance of opinion (which we expect to be positive). Here variance is taken as a sign of ambivalence (Alvarez and Brehm 2002). As ethnocentrism increases, we expect ambivalence to increase correspondingly.

The results, presented in table 5.2, lend some support to this hypothesis. The table displays the results from three different specifications, and gives the findings both for direction of opinion (in the top panel) and for the variance of opinion (bottom panel). As the table shows, ethnocentrism fails completely to predict the direction of opinion on aid to the contras. This holds in all three specifications and confirms what we found with the standard model. Ethnocentrism *does* predict ambivalence, however. As we expected, ambivalence (variance) increases with ethnocentrism. This holds in all three specifications as well, though the relationship is decisively significant in just one. Taken all together, these results suggest that the prospect of supplying assistance to the Nicaraguan contras in their struggle against communism places Americans predisposed to ethnocentrism in a dilemma, caught between wanting to say no to foreign aid and yes to containing communism.[19]

TABLE 5.2. Ethnocentrism and ambivalence toward the contras

Direction of opinion	[1]	[2]	[3]
Ethnocentrism	0.07	−0.01	−0.04
	0.10	0.10	0.18
Partisanship	−0.56**	−0.47**	−0.62**
	0.22	0.23	0.27
Education	−0.14	−0.10	−0.16
	0.09	0.08	0.11
Awareness	0.46***	0.46***	0.42***
	0.14	0.17	0.15
Female	−0.16*	−0.14*	−0.18*
	0.08	0.08	0.09
Black	−0.02	0.04	−0.04
	0.15	0.16	0.15
Hispanic	0.09	0.12	0.12
	0.07	0.08	0.10
Egalitarianism		−0.33*	
		0.18	
Religious Conviction			0.22**
			0.10
Intercept	−0.02	0.11	−0.04
	0.10	0.14	0.12

Variance of opinion			
Ethnocentrism	0.32	0.34	1.04*
	0.44	0.42	0.61
Strength of partisanship	−1.72***	−1.74***	−1.70***
	0.51	0.48	0.52
Education	0.56**	0.50**	0.25
	0.26	0.24	0.29
Awareness	−0.50	−0.52*	−0.44
	0.31	0.30	0.33
Female	0.37*	0.36*	0.19
	0.21	0.20	0.21
Black	0.22	0.26	−0.00
	0.44	0.45	0.42
Hispanic	−0.26	−0.28	−0.11
	0.31	0.30	0.39
Egalitarianism		0.01	
		0.41	
Religiosity			0.51*
			0.27
$P > 0$ for χ^2 LR test: $ln\sigma^2 = 0$	0.00	0.00	0.00
lnL	−849.60	−839.02	−769.58
N	1386	1381	1255

Source: 1988 NES.

Note: Table entries are heteroscedastic probit coefficients with standard errors below. ***$p < 0.01$; **$p < 0.05$; *$p < 0.10$, two-tailed.

COLLATERAL DAMAGE

In chapter 4 we saw that ethnocentrism contributes to American support for military intervention and to support for Desert Storm in particular. Ethnocentric Americans were more likely to report that they felt pride during the war and anger at Saddam Hussein. They favored military intervention over diplomacy. They were more likely to say, after the fighting was over, that we did the right thing in sending in troops and that the war was worthwhile. They expressed the wish that the fighting had been carried to Baghdad to remove Hussein from power. And they gave George H. W. Bush high marks for his leadership in the Persian Gulf and for his overall performance as president. In all these ways, ethnocentrism seems to supply ready support for carrying out military interventions against enemies abroad.

But what of the costs of war—costs born by the places and peoples who happen to get in the way? We would expect ethnocentrism to breed an indifference to such ravages, to see collateral damage in faraway places as necessary and inevitable, to be relatively unmoved by foreign suffering.

We can explore this general proposition by returning to the 1990–1991–1992 NES Panel Study, which neatly brackets Desert Storm. The study began just prior to the congressional debate over the authorization of force in the Gulf; continued with interviews carried out in June and July 1991, after the fighting ceased and victory declared; and came to completion with a pair of interviews in the fall of 1992, just before and then just after the national elections.

The 1990–1991–1992 NES includes five questions especially relevant to our interest in ethnocentrism and indifference to the human costs of war. Three concern emotion. Roughly midway through the summer 1991 interview, respondents were asked to recollect their emotional reactions to the war. Had they felt upset? Had they experienced feelings of sympathy for the Iraqi people? Had they felt disgust at the killing?

All three emotions were commonplace in the American public's reaction to the Gulf War: 75.8 percent of Americans questioned in the 1991 NES reported that they had felt upset during the war; 74.3 percent said the same about sympathy for the Iraqi people, and even more—83.8 percent—reported that they had felt disgust at the killing. And in each case, most of these said that they had felt the emotion strongly. Emotional reactions to the war were common all right, but we expect such emotions to be *less* common among ethnocentric Americans.

The 1990–1991–1992 NES Panel also carried two policy questions pertinent to the hypothesis of indifference. The first asked whether the United States acted quickly enough in providing assistance to the Kurds. More than

TABLE 5.3. Ethnocentrism and indifference to the casualties of war

	Upset over war	Sympathy for Iraqi people	Disgusted at the killing	Help Kurds	Immoral to bomb near civilians
Ethnocentrism	−0.66**	−0.54**	−0.19	−0.49*	−0.23
	0.26	0.25	0.30	0.27	0.25
Partisanship	0.37***	0.34***	0.57***	0.19	0.44***
	0.13	0.12	0.15	0.13	0.12
Education	0.23	0.17	−0.03	0.06	0.12
	0.19	0.18	0.21	0.19	0.18
Female	0.80***	0.42***	0.79***	−0.09	0.47***
	0.09	0.08	0.10	0.09	0.09
N	801	802	795	794	800
Effect of E	0.81→0.66	0.60→0.45	0.88→0.85	0.57→0.43	0.37→0.32

Source: 1990–1991–1992 NES Panel.

Note: Table entry is the ordered probit regression coefficient with standard errors below. Models also control for political awareness, race, and ethnicity. Full results appear in the Web appendix. The bottom row of the table gives the effect associated with a shift in Ethnocentrism from Low (−0.1) to High (0.6) in the predicted probability of being concerned about the casualties of war (see text for details).

***$p < 0.01$; **$p < 0.05$; *$p < 0.10$, two-tailed.

one-third—some 36.9 percent—said that the United States should not have become involved in the Kurdish problem at all. The second question inquired into the necessity during wartime of bombing near civilians. Nearly half—47.0 percent—strongly agreed that such practice was necessary.

The results, presented in table 5.3, generally conform to expectation. Ethnocentric Americans were less likely to report that they had felt upset during the Gulf War; less likely to report that they had felt sympathy for the Iraqi people; and less likely to report that they had felt disgust over the killing. They were less likely to say that the United States should provide assistance to the Kurdish people, and less likely as well to say that dropping bombs near civilians was immoral.[20]

The effects here are as expected, but they are also quite modest. In two instances, we cannot be sure that there is an ethnocentrism effect. Factors other than ethnocentrism generally carried more weight. One is partisanship: from the public's point of view, the war clearly belonged to President Bush and the Republican Party. Another is sex: women were consistently more likely to report emotional experience than men, and they were also much more concerned about civilian casualties.[21] All things considered, ethnocentrism appears to be more potent in pushing Americans to support war than in suppressing concern over the innocent casualties of war.

ACTIVATION

Earlier in the chapter we found that opposition to foreign aid stems in an important way from ethnocentrism. We found this to be so, remember, for opinion as expressed in the fall of 2002, not long after the attacks on the Twin Towers and the Pentagon, and in the midst of a buildup of a global war on terrorism. For reasons spelled out in the previous chapter, we would expect the power of ethnocentrism to undermine foreign aid to be at a relatively high point at this moment in American history.

We can test this precisely by taking advantage of the 2000–2002 NES Panel, just as we did in the last chapter. As before, we estimated the standard model predicting opposition to foreign aid measured in 2000 (before 9/11) and compared this result to that generated by the standard model predicting opposition measured in 2002 (after 9/11). We restricted this analysis to respondents who participated in both waves of the NES Panel to make the comparison exact, and we estimated the identical model in each instance.

As predicted, the impact of ethnocentrism is greater in the fall of 2002 than it is in the fall of 2000—greater, that it is to say, immediately after 9/11 than shortly before. These results are presented in figure 5.4. As indicated there, ethnocentrism is unimportant in fueling opposition to foreign aid prior to 9/11 and quite important afterward. Among other things, the terrorist

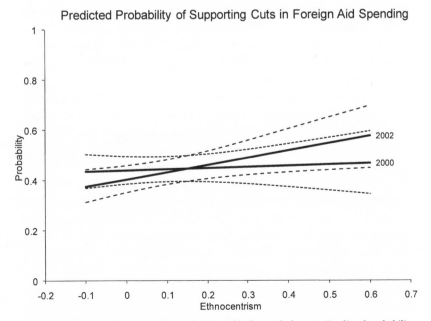

FIGURE 5.4. American opposition to foreign aid before and after 9/11. Predicted probabilities with 95 percent confidence intervals. Source: 2000–2002 NES Panel.

attacks on American soil seem to have had the consequence of bringing ethnocentrism more prominently into play in public opinion. In the previous chapter we saw a heightened effect of ethnocentrism on support for taking on U.S. enemies. Now we see a heightened effect of ethnocentrism on opposition to providing help to other nations. This provides more evidence that the part played by ethnocentrism in public opinion depends on circumstance.[22]

CONCLUSIONS AND IMPLICATIONS

By the results presented here, ethnocentrism undercuts American support for foreign aid—in general and in the particular. It works against support for technical and economic assistance to the countries of Eastern Europe struggling toward democracy after the collapse of the Soviet Union. Ethnocentrism reduces interest in and support for economic sanctions on South Africa intended to lighten racial oppression. Ethnocentrism generates ambivalence over military assistance to the contras in Nicaragua. And, to a more limited extent, ethnocentrism encourages indifference to the horrors of war waged on foreign soil.

Although it is hard to say for certain, it seems to us that we had fewer cases to analyze in this chapter than we did in the previous one. The American public appears to be preoccupied more with threats to Americans than with the needs of non-Americans. Providing for the national defense is the government's first priority, of course, but we think there is more to it than that. Consider this: in the scores and scores of questions on policy that have appeared over the last quarter century in the NES series, only one—whether the United States should impose sanctions on South Africa—has had anything to do with Africa. Famine, crippling debt, AIDS, the Rwandan genocide: none of these was deemed sufficiently important to warrant a single question on a NES interview. The questions that do appear on political surveys reflect governmental priorities and public concerns, and these seem rarely to focus on the sufferings of people elsewhere on the globe.

Does this mean that government assistance to those living outside the borders of the United States is always unpopular? No. A conspicuous example to the contrary is supplied by the Marshall Plan, named after George C. Marshall, army chief of staff during World War II and secretary of state thereafter. World War II had left Europe devastated—"a rubble-heap, a charnel house, a breeding ground of pestilence and hate" is the way Winston Churchill put it in the spring of 1947 (Patterson 1996, p. 130). Partly for humanitarian reasons, partly to build markets for U.S. goods, and partly to quell radical agitation, President Harry S. Truman and Secretary Marshall proposed a plan to provide Europe with massive assistance. The proposal was popular with the public and met little resistance in Congress. Between 1948 and 1952, the Marshall Plan funneled billions of dollars in aid to Western Europe.

In its original conception, the Marshall Plan included the Soviet Union and the eastern bloc nations, but this part of the enterprise quickly fell away. This made the plan much easier to sell, in the Congress and to the public. It meant that foreign aid could be defended on essentially ethnocentric grounds. The assistance was going to Western Europe—to "people like us"—and it was going to build an allied fortress against our looming adversary—the Soviet Union. Everett Dirksen, then a rising Republican member of Congress from Illinois, endorsed the Marshall Plan on the idea that it would help combat "this red tide" that was "like some vile creeping thing which is spreading its web westward." In November 1948 (after the Soviet Union was no longer in the picture), a Gallup poll found that the "*European Recovery Plan*" was supported by the American public by an overwhelming margin.[23]

Another way to describe what we have found in this chapter is that ethnocentrism discourages compassion for outsiders. According to Martha Nussbaum (2001), compassion is occasioned by the awareness of another person's undeserved misfortune. It requires the judgment that others are in a seriously bad way; that their predicament is no fault of their own; that they are in some fundamental way similar to us; and that their suffering is important to us, that such suffering becomes entangled in our own goals and projects (p. 55). These cognitive underpinnings of compassion suggest its limitations. Compassion begins, Nussbaum says, "from where we are, from the circle of our cares and concerns" (p. 16). Compassion for others different from us and far away from us is difficult to sustain: "there are so many things closer to home to distract us, and these things are likely to be so much more thoroughly woven into our scheme of goals" (p. 16). People must be convinced to widen their spheres of concern, so that compassion might "cross boundaries of race, or class, or religion, or even nationality" (p. 420). Although she does not use the word, it seems to us that a primary obstacle in the way of compassion, as Nussbaum describes it, is ethnocentrism.

We began this chapter by invoking the Rwandan genocide and pointing out that the United States did nothing to stop the slaughter that took place there in the spring and summer of 1994. Samantha Power (2002) argues that when faced with unambiguous evidence of genocide—the "problem from hell"—the United States typically does nothing. That is, the Rwandan experience is not the exception but the rule. Throughout the twentieth century, again and again, the United States has chosen to remain on the sidelines. Why? Not because we did not know. Not because we could not step in and diminish the horror. Power reads our failure to intervene as a failure of political will. "American leaders have been able to persist in turning away," Power concludes, "because genocide in distant lands has not captivated senators, congressional caucuses, Washington lobbyists, elite opinion shapers, grass-roots groups, or individual citizens" (2002, p. 509). Ethnocentrism quiets moral outrage and undermines demand for intervention. And in the absence of moral outrage and demand for action from the public, why would we expect leaders to risk their reputations and offices on uncertain humanitarian interventions abroad?

CHAPTER 6

Strangers in the Land

Most Americans can readily trace their family histories to some other place: Europe, the Middle East, Africa, Latin America, the Caribbean, the Indian subcontinent, Asia.[1] No other country has been settled by such a variety of peoples. To the impoverished and persecuted around the world, the United States has long been and perhaps remains today a "golden door," the opening to a prosperous, emancipated, and altogether better life.

Those in flight from grinding poverty or political violence have not always been invited in, of course. At the beginning of the twentieth century, millions sought refuge in the United States. They came from Russia, Turkey, Italy, and Romania; they flocked to the cities; and they triggered a nativistic reaction. In 1924, Congress passed the Immigration Restriction Act, which imposed sharp limits on immigration overall and deliberately favored those from Britain and northern Europe. The new law was, as the *Los Angeles Times* announced at the time with no irony intended, a "Nordic Victory."[2]

In politics, victories—even Nordic ones—are never permanent. The Immigration and Nationality Act Amendments, passed in 1965 at the high water mark of Lyndon Johnson's Great Society reforms, reversed forty years of restrictive regulation, and in 1980, refugee policy was liberalized. Immigration to the United States once again exploded (see figure 6.1). During the 1980s, 7.4 million people entered the country; even more, some 9.1 million, came during the following decade. By 2005, a majority of the states—twenty-nine in all—counted populations that were at least 5 percent foreign born. Immigration was back on the national agenda.[3]

The new immigration differed from previous waves in at least two important respects. First, the majority came not from Europe but from Latin America and Asia. As Ronald Takaki might put it, the new immigrants were "strangers from a different shore."[4] And second, large numbers entered the country illegally—about one thousand a day during the 1980s and '90s (see Edmonston and Passel 1994; Fix and Passel 1994).

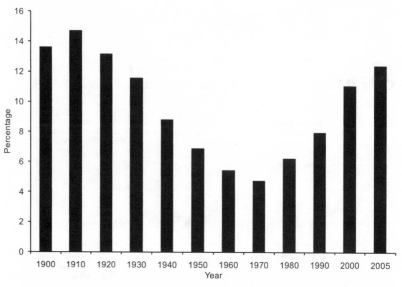

FIGURE 6.1. Immigrant share of U.S. population, 1900–2005. Source: U.S. Bureau of the Census.

Many Americans found this vast and apparently unstoppable tide of humanity alarming. As early as 1984, President Ronald Reagan warned that we had "lost control of our own borders" (M. Jones 1992, p. 287). In 1986, Congress passed the Immigration Reform and Control Act in an effort, largely unsuccessful, to stem the flow of illegal immigration. Outside the halls of Congress, meanwhile, citizens groups organized to protect, as they saw it, the country's mother tongue. Between 1980 and 2005, twenty-three states established English as the official state language. In several prominent cases—including California, Arizona, Colorado, and Florida—English language propositions, designed "to preserve, protect, and strengthen the English language, the common language of the United States," were placed on the ballot and adopted by popular vote (Citrin et al. 1990; Schildkraut 2005). In 1996, Congress passed the Illegal Immigration Reform and Immigrant Responsibility Act. The act facilitated the deportation of undocumented immigrants, strengthened control of the borders, and ramped up penalties for those engaged in the business of bringing people to the United States illegally.

As immigration continued unabated, alarms were sounded. We were told that the new immigration was threatening the white nation (Brimelow 1995); diluting the country's gene pool (Herrnstein and Murray 1994); and overwhelming government services (P. Wilson 1993). Continued immigration, it was said, would lead inevitably to "fragmentation, resegregation, and tribalization" (Schlesinger 1992, p. 23); it menaced not only American identity, but the nation itself: federation, succession, even extinction were conjured up as possible futures (Huntington 2004). Since the early 1980s, presidents, members of Congress, governors, candidates for high (and often rather low) public office have felt compelled to speak out on immigration. How many immigrants should come? Who should come? What does citizenship mean, and who may attain it?

We propose that at least some of the (often angry) opposition to immigration can be accounted for by ethnocentrism. Ethnocentrism predisposes people to react to difference with suspicion, contempt, or condescension, and the new immigrants present conspicuous differences. Language, color, dress, religion, and more: all these mark immigrants as different from the average American. Such differences, partly real, partly imagined, seem likely to trigger ethnocentrism. Moreover, the policy issues that arise around immigration—whether outsiders should be allowed in; whether borders should be strengthened or relaxed; whether outsiders, if allowed in, should be granted the same rights and privileges as insiders—lend themselves readily to ethnocentric appeals among elites and to ethnocentric thinking among the general public. Given all this, from the point of view of our project, anything less than large effects of ethnocentrism in the domain of immigration would be disconcerting.[5]

The argument we have just advanced applies to most of the American public, but not to all. In particular, it does not apply to those who are suspended between their identity as American and their attachment to their original home. This condition arises in Jones-Correa's (1998) ethnographic investigation of first-generation immigrants from Colombia, Ecuador, and the Dominican Republic living in New York in the early 1990s. Jones-Correa finds that many in this population come to the United States intending to stay only a short while. When they arrive fixed on the idea of return, they participate in politics accordingly. They work on problems connected to their homelands and they neglect problems they face in their new (and, they often assume, temporary) surroundings. They are, as Jones-Correa puts it, caught "between two nations."

Jones-Correa examines a particular case, but we take from his analysis a general lesson. We say that being suspended between two nations radically conditions how ethnocentrism works in the domain of immigration. For those "in between," we expect ethnocentrism to motivate *support* for immigration. Immigrants to the United States today come overwhelmingly from Latin America and Asia. Accordingly, among Hispanic and Asian Americans, on policies having to do with immigration, the usual effects of ethnocentrism should be reversed. Among Hispanics and Asians, ethnocentrism should lead to a more generous view on immigration.[6]

AMERICAN OPPOSITION TO IMMIGRATION

We begin with an analysis of the 1992 National Election Study because, among relatively recent surveys, it contains the richest battery of questions suited to our purpose. Following the standard NES design, a representative sample of voting-age Americans was interviewed just prior to the fall election and then again immediately after Election Day.[7]

In the fall of 1992, immigration was brewing as a political problem, but it did not become an important part of the national campaign. The presidential contest was first and foremost a referendum on the incumbent president's performance, and the economy was the pivotal issue. George H. W. Bush, the Republican incumbent, tried to steer the debate to some other subject: to the success of Desert Storm; to the character defects of Bill Clinton, his Democratic opponent; to Clinton's inexperience in foreign affairs; to the "do-nothing" Democratic Congress; or finally, and perhaps in desperation, to family values. To no avail: voters remained preoccupied with the slowdown in the national economy (partly real, partly imagined). At the close of the campaign, when asked to name the country's most pressing problems, voters mentioned the economy, taxes, the federal deficit, health care, education, abortion—but not immigration. On Election Day, with economic concerns paramount, Bush was sent home to Texas.[8]

The 1992 NES asked four questions on immigration policy: (1) whether immigration should be increased or cut back, (2) whether immigrants should be eligible for government benefits (Medicaid, food stamps, welfare) as soon as they arrive, (3) whether children of immigrants should be provided bilingual instruction in the public schools, and (4) whether English should be made the "official language" of the United States (that is, should government business be transacted in English alone).

On the whole, across these various questions, the public expressed considerable apprehension about immigration, if not downright hostility. First of all, Americans were much more likely to say that the number of immigrants permitted to enter the country should be diminished than to say the number should be increased (49.1 percent as against 7.9 percent). An overwhelming majority (79.7 percent) opposed the idea that legal immigrants should be eligible for government services as soon as they arrive. Only a relatively small fraction (some 17.3 percent) supported bilingual schools so that children of immigrants would be able to keep up their native language and culture if they wished. And a decisive majority (65.1 percent) lined up behind the idea of establishing English as the nation's official language.[9]

If on the whole these opinions seem ungenerous, there is really little new in this. As early as 1700, the Massachusetts Colony passed a law that denied entry to the sick or physically disabled. In January 1939, following Germany's annexation of Austria and invasion of Czechoslovakia, nearly three-quarters of Americans disapproved of opening U.S. borders to Jewish exiles seeking shelter from Hitler's regime. In 1975, as Saigon was about to fall, a clear majority of Americans opposed legislation that would have assisted the evacuation of South Vietnamese and their resettlement in the United States. In 1980, by roughly a two-to-one margin, Americans rejected the idea of conferring refugee status on Cubans fleeing their homeland. These examples could be multiplied without much effort. Whenever Americans have been asked about immigration, most have said, in one way or another, no.[10]

Of course, some Americans say yes: that the number of immigrants admitted to the country should be increased, that legal immigrants should have access to government services immediately upon their arrival, that public schools should support bilingual classrooms, and that establishing English as the official language of the United States is a terrible idea. We expect that differences in opinion on immigration can be traced back, in important part, to differences in ethnocentrism.

ETHNOCENTRISM AND PUBLIC OPINION ON IMMIGRATION

To make our empirical estimates of the impact of ethnocentrism credible, our analysis of immigration opinion takes into account several explanations in addition to ethnocentrism:

(1) *Displacement of personal troubles (scapegoating)*, whereby those Americans who have suffered travail in their private lives will be most inclined to restrict immigration and most inclined to deny recently arrived immigrants government benefits. Personal tribulations are assessed in three ways: through an index based on questions about family economic troubles over the past year[11]; a categorical variable that distinguishes between those who are currently laid off or unemployed or who had been so sometime in the past six months from the rest; and third, another categorical variable identifying those who are currently divorced.

(2) *Parochialism*, the notion that hostility directed at immigrants is partly a reflection of an unenlightened perspective on the wider world, measured by education and political knowledge.[12]

(3) *Threat*, the prediction from realistic group conflict theory that opposition to immigration is rooted in the perception of threat. We represent threat in three different ways: working in low-wage, low-skill occupations,

under the assumption that such workers are the most vulnerable to economic competition from today's immigrants;[13] living in states with large proportions of Hispanics and Asians, with the expectation that Americans' opinions on immigration will harden as the proportion of immigrants residing in their state increases;[14] and receiving federal assistance—specifically food stamps, Aid to Families with Dependent Children (AFDC), and Medicaid—anticipating that those most dependent on such programs may feel most threatened and so be most prepared to cut back on the numbers of immigrants permitted to enter and to withhold benefits from those already arrived.

(4) *Economic optimism*, on the idea that generous opinions on immigration are more likely among those who believe the American economy capable of taking in new arrivals.[15]

(5) *Moral traditionalism*, on the idea that immigration is likely to be opposed by those Americans who believe the society's moral values are collapsing.[16]

(6) *Political principles*, based on the assumption that Americans come to their opinions on immigration in least in part by deciding whether a particular policy matches or violates their principles, represented here by two core ideas in particular: equal opportunity and limited government.[17]

(7) *Partisanship*, based on the general importance of partisan cues for public opinion. In the case of immigration in particular, however, we are not sure what we will find. Immigration splits the Republican Party elite—cultural conservatives oppose immigration while free marketers favor it—and so partisan cues should prove less helpful here than they are ordinarily.

Finally, the standard model takes into account the expectation that the effects of ethnocentrism will differ between members of the public who think of themselves more or less completely as American, on the one side (whites and blacks for short), and those who may be suspended between their identity as American and their attachment to their original home nation, on the other (that is, Asians and Hispanics). Among Hispanic and Asian Americans, the effects of ethnocentrism should be reversed.[18]

In principle, this expectation is easy and straightforward to test. All we need to do is add two interaction terms to the standard model. The first picks up the possibility that on matters of immigration, ethnocentrism works differently among Hispanic Americans; the second picks up the parallel possibility that ethnocentrism works differently among Asian Americans. In practice, however, the 1992 NES interviewed so few Asian Americans that we are restricted here to testing just the first possibility—to looking for a reversal of the effect of ethnocentrism among Hispanic Americans.[19]

And so, mathematically:

$$y^* = \mathbf{x'\beta} + \varepsilon$$
$$= \beta_0 + \beta_1\text{Ethnocentrism} + \beta_2[\text{Ethnocentrism} \times \text{Hispanic}]$$
$$+ \beta_3\text{Household Economic Conditions} + \ldots + \varepsilon$$
$$\Pr(y = m) = \Pr(\tau_{m-1} < y^* < \tau_m) = \Phi(\tau_m - \mathbf{x'\beta}) - \Phi(\tau_{m-1} - \mathbf{x'\beta})$$

where y refers to the views Americans hold on the various aspects of immigration, each taken up separately. All of the opinion variables are coded such that higher values indicate a less generous view on immigration. β_1 gives the effect of ethnocentrism for non-Hispanic Americans; $\beta_1 + \beta_2$ gives the effect of ethnocentrism for Hispanic Americans; and β_2 tests whether the effect of ethnocentrism is different for the two populations.[20]

We coded variables and estimated parameters in the usual way. Ethnocentrism was coded from −1 to +1 (where +1 means that Americans regard out-groups to be inferior in every respect to their own group; −1 means that Americans regard out-groups to be superior in every respect to their own group; and 0 means that Americans regard out-groups and their own group to be on average indistinguishable). And given the form taken by the measures of immigration opinion, we relied again on ordered probit for statistical estimation.[21]

The results, summarized in table 6.1, show that views on immigration are a reflection of not one thing but several: parochialism, moral traditionalism, ambivalence about equal opportunity, skepticism about the capacity of the American economy, and last, but far from least, ethnocentrism. Ethnocentrism predisposes Americans (most Americans) to the view that immigration should be cut back; that immigrants should wait, perhaps indefinitely, for government benefits; that immigrant children should be required to learn English promptly; and that the United States should establish English as its official language. These effects are statistically significant and substantively sizable in every case.[22] Moreover, they appear, of course, over and above the effects due to all other factors.[23]

As expected, the effects of ethnocentrism run in the opposite direction among Hispanic Americans (row 2 of table 6.1). Hispanic Americans who regard their own group as superior are inclined to *favor* generous immigration policies: to support an increase in the number of people allowed to legally enter the United States, to provide government benefits to immigrants as soon as they arrive if they are otherwise eligible, to supply bilingual classes to immigrant children in the public schools, and to oppose the establishment of English as the nation's official language. If anything, as the bottom row of table 6.1 illustrates, the magnitude of the effects of ethnocentrism among Hispanic Americans on support for immigration is generally greater

TABLE 6.1. Ethnocentrism and opposition to immigration

	Decrease level of immigration	Require immigrants to wait for benefits	Require classes be held in English	Support English as official language
Ethnocentrism	0.92***	1.07***	0.67***	0.87***
	0.18	0.27	0.19	0.23
Ethnocentrism	−2.32***	−1.68*	−2.19***	−3.31***
× Hispanic	0.79	1.02	0.82	0.91
Education	−0.23*	−0.12	−0.02	−0.21
	0.13	0.17	0.13	0.16
Moral	0.78***	−0.32	0.33**	0.93***
traditionalism	0.15	0.21	0.16	0.18
Egalitarianism	−0.37**	−0.99***	−0.51***	−0.43**
	0.16	0.21	0.16	0.19
Limited	−0.04	0.17	0.23***	0.10
government	0.09	0.12	0.09	0.10
Partisanship	−0.02	−0.04	0.04	−0.16
	0.10	0.13	0.10	0.11
N	1662	1635	1682	1678
Effect of E among				
Non-Hispanics	0.40→0.66	0.80→0.94	0.25→0.42	0.54→0.77
Effect of E among				
Hispanics	0.53→0.19	0.86→0.75	0.46→0.12	0.52→0.05

Source: 1992 NES.

Note: Table entry is the ordered probit regression coefficient with standard errors below. Models also control for household economic conditions, unemployment, being divorced, education, political awareness, occupation, log of the proportion of Hispanic and Asian in state, dependence on government assistance, moral traditionalism, retrospective assessments of national economic conditions, egalitarianism, support for limited government, partisanship, race, ethnicity, and sex. Full results appear in the Web appendix. The bottom rows of the table give the effect associated with a shift in Ethnocentrism from Low (−0.1) to High (0.6) in the predicted probability of opposing immigration (see text for details).

$***p < 0.01$; $**p < 0.05$; $*p < 0.10$, two-tailed.

than the corresponding effects among black and white Americans on opposition to immigration.[24]

We can take this analysis a step further by examining an additional set of questions present in the 1992 NES. These questions ask about the consequences of immigration, as ordinary Americans make them out. One set of questions asks about what would likely happen in the United States should Hispanic immigration continue at its present pace—what would happen to culture, taxes, and employment. The second set poses the same questions about the consequences of Asian immigration. For the most part, Americans see more harm than good in these matters. On balance they deny that Hispanic or Asian immigrants have anything positive to add to American culture; they worry that increasing immigration will lead to more demand for public services, which in turn will drive up taxes; and they believe that increasing the numbers of Asian and Hispanic immigrants will take jobs away from Americans already here. Immigration from Asia provokes less alarm than immigration from Latin America, but only by a small amount.[25]

If we apply the same model to predict views on the putative consequences of immigration as we did to predict opinions on immigration policy, we find very much the same results. These findings are presented in table 6.2.

TABLE 6.2. Ethnocentrism and immigration's harm

	Hispanics immigrants' impact on			Asian immigrants' impact on		
	Culture	Taxes	Jobs	Culture	Taxes	Jobs
Ethnocentrism	1.39***	1.24***	1.20***	1.50***	1.21***	0.86***
	0.12	0.18	0.18	0.19	0.18	0.18
Ethnocentrism ×	-5.16***	-2.26***	-2.89***	-1.51*	-0.57	-1.94**
Hispanic	0.80	0.79	0.79	0.81	0.79	0.80
Education	-0.07	-0.08	-0.30**	-0.24*	-0.34***	-0.36***
	0.13	0.13	0.13	0.13	0.13	0.13
Moral	0.72***	0.95***	0.81***	0.35**	0.55***	0.76***
traditionalism	0.16	0.15	0.15	0.15	0.15	0.15
Egalitarianism	-0.61***	-0.37**	-0.29*	-0.39**	-0.25	-0.09
	0.16	0.16	0.16	0.16	0.16	0.15
Limited	-0.10	-0.03	-0.08	-0.04	-0.23***	-0.02
government	0.09	0.08	0.08	0.09	0.09	0.08
Partisanship	-0.05	-0.10	0.04	-0.04	-0.05	0.16*
	0.10	0.10	0.10	0.10	0.10	0.10
N	1688	1683	1686	1686	1681	1688
Effect of E among						
Non-Hispanics	0.83→0.97	0.44→0.76	0.37→0.69	0.72→0.95	0.28→0.61	0.46→0.69
Effect of E among						
Hispanics	0.77→0.03	0.61→0.33	0.43→0.09	0.71→0.70	0.43→0.61	0.45→0.19

Source: 1992 NES.

Note: Table entry is the ordered probit regression coefficient with standard errors below. Models also control for household economic conditions, unemployment, being divorced, education, political awareness, occupation, log of the proportion of Hispanic and Asian in state, dependence on government assistance, moral traditionalism, retrospective assessments of national economic conditions, egalitarianism, support for limited government, partisanship, race, ethnicity, and sex. Full results appear in the Web appendix. The bottom row of the table gives the effect associated with a shift in Ethnocentrism from Low (−0.1) to High (0.6) in the predicted probability of believing in immigration's harm (see text for details).

***$p < 0.01$; **$p < 0.05$; *$p < 0.10$, two-tailed.

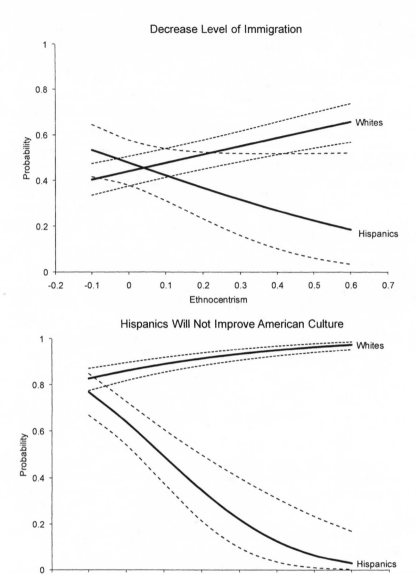

FIGURE 6.2. American opposition to immigration as a function of ethnocentrism. Predicted probabilities with 95 percent confidence intervals. Estimates from tables 6.1–6.2. Source: 1992 NES.

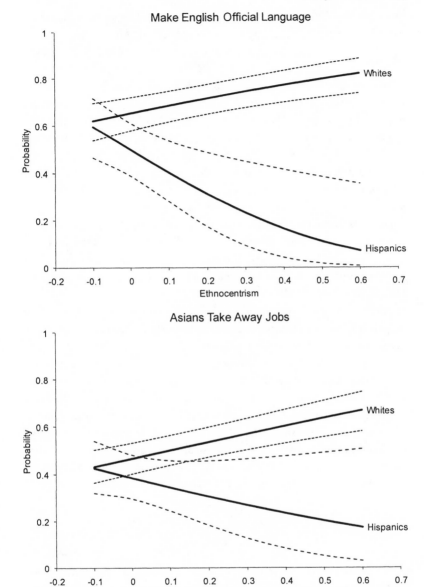

FIGURE 6.2. (*continued*)

As in the previous analysis, among black and white Americans, ethnocentrism has a powerful negative effect on opinion. Ethnocentrism is strongly associated with the view that immigrants have little to contribute to American culture; that by their demands for government services they are likely to push tax rates higher; and that they are likely to take away jobs from people already here—"stealing our jobs" in the vernacular (Nagourney 2007). And as before, we see the exact opposite among Hispanic Americans.

We summarize the effects of ethnocentrism in the domain of immigration in graphical form in figure 6.2. Figure 6.2 plots predicted opinion as a function of ethnocentrism, separately for whites and for Hispanics, on each of four issues: whether immigration should be increased or curtailed, whether English should be established as the official language of the United States, the consequences of Hispanic immigration on American culture, and the impact of Asian immigration on employment.[26]

The graphs show in a vivid way the importance of ethnocentrism for American opinion on immigration. The effects of ethnocentrism are substantial in all four instances: substantial and negative among white Americans; substantial and positive among Hispanic Americans. Take, as one example, whether the numbers of people allowed to enter the country legally should be increased or cut back. Across the normal range of ethnocentrism found in the American public today (from −0.1 to +0.6 on E, the ethnocentrism scale), the likelihood that an average white American would support cutting back on immigration increases from about 40 percent to 66 percent; in the meantime, over the same range, the likelihood that an average Hispanic American would support cutting back on immigration declines by more than half, from about 53 percent to about 19 percent.

The graphs also show that differences in opinion on immigration between Hispanic and white Americans are small among those who reject ethnocentrism (that is, who score low on the ethnocentrism scale). But the differences are *huge* among the ethnocentric (that is, those who score high on the ethnocentrism scale). In other words, if we could somehow eliminate ethnocentrism, differences of opinion on immigration between Hispanic and white Americans would vanish.

ETHNOCENTRISM AND IMMIGRATION AMONG BLACKS AND WHITES

Let's temporarily set Hispanic Americans to one side and dig a little deeper into the relationship between ethnocentrism and immigration among blacks and whites.

Here, There, Everywhere

Our results so far, based on the 1992 NES, indicate that American opposition to immigration arises in an important way from ethnocentrism. Ethnocentrism is not the only source of opposition, but it is an important one and perhaps the single most important of all. A first point we wish to add here is that this conclusion holds wherever we have looked. A strong effect of ethnocentrism on opposition to immigration shows up in all recent National Election Studies; under Democratic administrations and Republican ones; in good times and in bad. We don't mean to imply that the effect of ethnocentrism is uniform—as we will see later in the chapter, it is not. What we are saying is that in all these contexts, ethnocentrism contributes significantly and sizably to public disapproval of immigration.[27]

Ethnocentrism, Not Authoritarianism

Back in chapter 1, we drew attention to new work on authoritarianism. Karen Stenner and Stanley Feldman (Feldman 2003; Feldman and Stenner 1997; Stenner 2005) conceive of authoritarianism as a preference for social cohesion over personal autonomy. When thought about in this way, it would not be surprising to find authoritarians aligned against immigration. Keeping foreigners out would be an obvious way to protect uniformity and suppress difference. At the same time, we know from chapter 3 that authoritarianism and ethnocentrism are positively correlated. This means that to make sure that we have provided an unbiased estimate of the effect of ethnocentrism on opposition to immigration, we must simultaneously take into account the possible effect due to authoritarianism. What happens when we add a measure of authoritarianism to our standard model?[28]

We find, first of all, that authoritarianism independently predicts opposition to immigration (though in every case, the effect is small). More important, adding authoritarianism to the analysis takes *nothing* away from the role we have assigned to ethnocentrism. Holding constant the effects due to authoritarianism (and partisanship and education and all the rest), American resistance to immigration arises significantly and substantially from ethnocentrism.

"People Like Us"

The 2000 General Social Survey included the standard stereotype battery that we have argued constitutes the best available measure of ethnocentrism. It was conducted in early 2000, well before the general presidential election campaign got underway; it included an extensive collection of opinion measures in the domain of immigration; and, as usual for GSS and the National Opinion Research Center, it was carried out to exacting standards. For all these reasons, the 2000 GSS provides an especially valuable site for replication.

And replication is what we find. In the 2000 GSS, ethnocentrism is a powerful predictor of the view that immigration should be cut back; that immigration slows economic growth, increases crime, brings no new ideas, fractures national unity, and takes away jobs from (real) Americans; that English should be made the nation's official language; that bilingual programs in the public schools should be abolished; and that the government should feel no obligation to print ballots in any language other than English. The questions are slightly different than those we have been examining from the NES, but the results are entirely familiar.

One special feature of the 2000 GSS is that it asked four separate questions about whether immigration should be increased or scaled back. First came a general question, by and large indistinguishable from the one that appears in the NES that we have been analyzing so far. GSS respondents were asked whether "the number of immigrants from foreign countries who are permitted to come to the United States to live should be increased a lot, increased a little, left the same as it is now, decreased a little, or decreased a lot?" Respondents were then asked in consecutive questions about immigration from Latin America; about immigration from Asia; and finally, about immigration from Europe.

As we have come to expect, when asked the general question, Americans leaned heavily against immigration. Opinion was just as lopsidedly hostile when it came to immigration originating from Latin America or from Asia. Only in the case of immigration from European countries did this hard line soften somewhat, although even here, more Americans preferred cutting back to opening things up.[29]

When we apply the standard model to each of these four cases, we find, first of all, a statistically significant and substantively large effect of ethnocentrism on opposition to immigration in general, just as we did in our analysis of the NES. The effect of ethnocentrism is a bit larger on opposition to immigration from Latin American and on opposition to immigration from Asia, though in neither case is the difference significant. On immigration from Europe, by contrast, the effect of ethnocentrism is much smaller.[30]

These results are presented in figure 6.3. They make three points. First, the effect of ethnocentrism on immigration policy increases sharply as the immigrant population becomes, in the typical American's imagination anyway, stranger and less familiar. Second, Americans seem to have Asians and Hispanics primarily in mind when they are asked to think about immigration in general. And third, the figure clarifies the difference that ethnocentrism makes. Whether immigrants come from Asia or Latin American or Europe is utterly immaterial among Americans who have somehow overcome ethnocentrism. Among ethnocentrically predisposed Americans, however, the distinction is real and consequential. For those given to ethnocentric thinking, it matters a great deal whether applicants for mem-

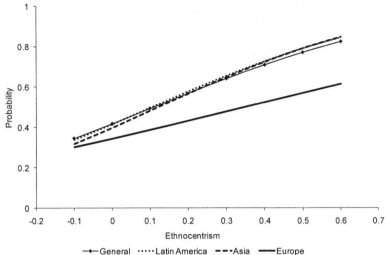

FIGURE 6.3. Ethnocentrism and opposition to immigration—immigration in general, from Latin America, Asia, or Europe. Predicted probabilities. Estimation results appear in the Web appendix. Source: 2000 GSS.

bership in the American nation originate from Europe, on the one hand, or from Asia or Latin America, on the other.

In-Group Pride and Out-Group Hostility

Taken all around, we have uncovered overwhelming support for the proposition that ethnocentrism is a key ingredient in public opinion on immigration. Indeed, in our analysis, ethnocentrism emerges as the single most important determinant of American opposition to immigration—across time and setting and for various aspects of immigration policy. But can we be confident that we have identified ethnocentrism at work? More precisely, can we be sure we are seeing ethnocentrism conceived as prejudice in general?

If, as Levinson and colleagues put it (Adorno et al. 1950), ethnocentrism is prejudice, broadly conceived, then the effects of ethnocentrism on immigration opinion that we have documented so far should reflect both attachment to in-group and disdain for out-groups. To find out if this is so, we repeated our earlier analysis, but first breaking the ethnocentrism scale into two separate components, one pertaining to the in-group and the other pertaining to out-groups.

These results, summarized in table 6.3, offer clear and consistent support for the conception of ethnocentrism as generalized prejudice. In

TABLE 6.3. In-group pride, out-group hostility, and opposition to immigration

	Decrease immigration	Wait for benefits	Classes in English	English official language	Hispanics' impact on			Asians' impact on		
					Culture	Taxes	Jobs	Culture	Taxes	Jobs
In-group pride	0.55***	0.90***	0.54**	0.91***	1.15***	0.80***	0.91***	1.10***	0.81***	0.57***
	0.21	0.30	0.22	0.26	0.22	0.21	0.21	0.22	0.21	0.21
Out-group hostility	1.52***	1.46***	0.80***	0.72**	1.82***	2.09***	1.75***	2.17***	1.84***	1.38***
	0.25	0.36	0.26	0.30	0.27	0.25	0.25	0.26	0.25	0.25
N	1524	1499	1542	1539	1548	1544	1547	1548	1543	1549

Source: 1992 NES.

Note: Table entry is the ordered probit regression coefficient. Standard errors appear below the coefficients. In-group pride is coded from 0 (negative) to 1 (positive assessments). Out-group hostility is coded from 0 (positive) to 1 (negative assessments). Models also control for household economic conditions, unemployment, being divorced, education, political awareness, occupation, log of the proportion of Hispanic and Asian in state, dependence on government assistance, moral traditionalism, retrospective assessments of national economic conditions, egalitarianism, support for limited government, partisanship, race, and sex. Analysis is restricted to whites and blacks. Full results appear in the Web appendix.

***p < 0.01; **p < 0.05; *p < 0.10, two-tailed.

TABLE 6.4. The effect of ethnocentrism on opposition to immigration, controlling on attitudes toward Hispanics and Asians

	Decrease immigration	Wait for benefits	Classes in English	English official language	Hispanics' impact on			Asians' impact on		
					Culture	Taxes	Jobs	Culture	Taxes	Jobs
[1] Ethnocentrism	0.90***	1.09***	0.64***	0.85***	1.38***	1.26***	1.21***	1.48***	1.18***	0.86***
	0.18	0.27	0.19	0.23	0.20	0.18	0.19	0.19	0.18	0.18
[2] Ethnocentrism controlling on attitude toward Hispanics	0.75***	0.98***	0.49**	0.76***	1.20***	1.12***	1.08***	1.36***	1.16***	0.79***
	0.19	0.28	0.20	0.24	0.21	0.19	0.19	0.20	0.19	0.19
[3] Ethnocentrism controlling on attitude toward Asians	0.78***	0.95***	0.52***	0.77***	1.29***	1.23***	1.15***	1.27***	1.04***	0.80***
	0.19	0.28	0.19	0.24	0.20	0.19	0.19	0.20	0.19	0.19

Source: 1992 NES.

Note: Table entry is the ordered probit regression coefficient with standard errors below. Each equation then adds, separately, hostility toward specific groups, measured with the feeling thermometer and rescaled from 0 (positive) to 1 (negative). Models also control for household economic conditions, unemployment, being divorced, education, political awareness, occupation, log of the proportion of Hispanic and Asian in state, dependence on government assistance, moral traditionalism, retrospective assessments of national economic conditions, egalitarianism, support for limited government, partisanship, race, and sex. Analysis is restricted to whites and blacks.

*** $p < 0.01$; ** $p < 0.05$; * $p < 0.10$, two-tailed.

particular, the results indicate that *both* in-group loyalty *and* out-group denigration make significant contributions to opinion, and on each and every aspect of immigration policy. Between the two, denigration of out-groups is consistently the more important. But the main story is that both attachment to in-group and disdain for out-groups figure importantly in opinion on immigration.[31]

So far so good for our conception of ethnocentrism. But it still might be that the hostility directed at out-groups that is contributing so consequentially to immigration opinion really only appears to be prejudice in general. Perhaps it is, in reality, prejudice toward a single group. More specifically, perhaps the real work is being done by sentiments directed at particular out-groups: at Asian Americans or especially at Hispanic Americans, the group that may exemplify the picture of today's immigrant in most Americans' imagination.

To see if this is so, we simply added to the standard model a measure of sentiments toward Hispanic Americans (given by the thermometer score rating), and then, in a separate analysis, a measure of sentiments toward Asian Americans (measured in the same way). Does the effect due to ethnocentrism decline when these particular group sentiments are added to the analysis?

Not really. The results appear in table 6.4. The first row of the table reproduces the estimated effect of ethnocentrism generated by the standard model. The second row gives the estimated effect of ethnocentrism controlling on whatever effect is due to sentiments toward Hispanic Americans. The third row then does the same, this time controlling on whatever effect is due to sentiments toward Asian Americans.

As table 6.4 reveals, adding in a particular group attitude makes only a small dent in the effect attributed to ethnocentrism (compare the coefficients arrayed in row 1 with those arrayed in rows 2 and 3). Attitudes toward Hispanic Americans and toward Asian Americans show a significant effect in nearly all instances, but their addition takes very little away from the effect due to ethnocentrism.[32] Ethnocentrism, as measured here, appears to be prejudice, generally conceived.

ETHNOCENTRISM AND IMMIGRATION
AMONG HISPANIC AMERICANS

So it goes for most Americans, those whose connection to the immigration experience is distant, the stuff of history books or of fading family memories. What about ethnocentrism and immigration policy among Hispanic Americans? Earlier we argued that some sizable fraction of Hispanic Americans find themselves "in between," neither completely away nor fully home on American soil. This might be especially true for Mexican Americans, who have settled in concentrated numbers in the American Southwest. Mexico is just across the way, and the border is porous. Because of this, we expected Hispanic Americans to look more favorably upon immigration and identify more completely with the plight of current immigrants—and that these tendencies would increase with increases in ethnocentrism. We saw this to be so in the analysis of the 1992 NES that led off the chapter. The more Hispanic Americans regarded their group to be superior, the more positive were their opinions on immigration.

These results, summarized in tables 6.1 and 6.2, are worth a closer look. On the question of whether immigration should be increased or decreased, on both aspects of language policy, and on the putative consequences of Hispanic immigration, the effect of ethnocentrism among Hispanics is equal to or greater than the (opposite-signed) effect among whites and blacks. But on the assessment of the consequences likely to follow from the continued influx of Asians into the United States, ethnocentrism among Hispanics fades into irrelevance. In other words, examined closely, the results for Hispanic Americans suggest not so much ethnocentrism in whole but rather ethnocentrism in part—in particular, the in-group pride component of ethnocentrism.

We can pursue this conjecture further by combining recent National Election Studies, thereby increasing the number of Hispanic Americans available for analysis. As it happens, the 1992, 1996, 2000, and 2004 installments of the National Election Studies include not only our standard measure of ethnocentrism, but also what is perhaps the most basic policy question in the domain of immigration—whether the number of people permitted to legally enter the United States should be increased or decreased. Three of the four studies also include a question on whether the government should spend more or less on protecting U.S. borders (1996, 2000, and 2004). And all four include key components of the standard model for opinion on immigration (partisanship, education, moral traditionalism, and equal opportunity).

In the pooled analysis, under the standard model, we find significant, strong, and positive effects of ethnocentrism, on both aspects of immigration policy. Hispanic Americans who score high on ethnocentrism are more favorable toward immigration: they want to increase the number of people allowed to come into the country and are not much interested in spending more on tightening up border security.[33]

These results replicate what we found in the 1992 NES, which is reassuring, but the real purpose of this analysis is to see whether, as we expect, the effects of ethnocentrism among Hispanic Americans are carried primarily by in-group attachment rather than out-group hostility. To see if this is so, we reestimated the standard model, first decomposing ethnocentrism into

TABLE 6.5. In-group pride, out-group hostility, and support for immigration among Hispanic Americans

	Increase immigration	Spend less on borders
In-group pride	1.62***	1.21**
	0.44	0.60
Out-group hostility	0.49	0.70
	0.54	0.72
N	387	236

Source: 1992, 1996, 2000, and 2004 NES.

Note: Table entry is the ordered probit regression coefficient with standard errors below. Dependent variables are coded such that higher values correspond with support for immigration. In-group pride is coded from 0 (negative) to 1 (positive assessments). Out-group hostility is coded from 0 (positive) to 1 (negative assessments). Models also control for partisanship, education, moral conservatism, and egalitarianism. Full results appear in the Web appendix.

***$p < 0.01$; **$p < 0.05$; *$p < 0.10$, two-tailed.

its two constituent parts: in-group pride and out-group hostility. These results appear in table 6.5.

The results indicate that most of the action in ethnocentrism among Hispanic Americans comes from in-group pride. Hispanic Americans who possess a strong sense of group pride are much more likely to favor increases in immigration and much less likely to support spending more on border control. At the same time, whether they regard their fellow Americans with sympathy, condescension, or outright hostility matters less—perhaps it matters not at all.[34]

ACTIVATION

In recent decades, millions of people have come to the United States. Most originated not from Europe but from Latin America and Asia, and many entered the country illegally. We have argued that the new immigrants, marked by differences of language, color, dress, religion, and more seemed likely to trigger an ethnocentric reaction, and indeed, we found ethnocentrism to be a powerful force behind opposition to immigration. But can we identify conditions under which ethnocentrism is more or less important?

Our empirical analysis so far has concentrated on the 1992 NES, taking advantage of the rich instrumentation relevant to immigration present in that year's questionnaire. Immigration was certainly on the national agenda in the fall of 1992, but it was a still more prominent part of the country's conversation heading into the 1996 campaign. As figure 6.4 shows, immigration was an important but second-tier story in the fall of 1992, but a dominating one in the fall of 1996.

Moreover, the discussion of immigration in the time leading up to the 1996 campaign was framed in such a way as to activate ethnocentrism. Consider Proposition 187 in California, a measure designed to deny public education and nonemergency medical benefits to illegal immigrants. In the fall of 1994, after a contentious and expensive campaign that featured television advertisements of Mexican nationals pouring over the border, California voters approved Prop 187 overwhelmingly. The primary provisions of the measure were quickly challenged and eventually set aside by court order, but the proposal had clearly struck a popular chord. Shortly after the California vote, 53 percent of respondents to a national survey said they would favor laws in their states that would eliminate education, health, and welfare benefits for illegal immigrants and their children (Times Mirror Center for the People and the Press 1995).

Immigration also became a focal point of Pat Buchanan's campaign for the 1996 Republican presidential nomination. For Buchanan, immigration posed a lethal threat to American culture. In response, he proposed a five-year ban on legal immigration and dramatically stricter border controls.

Meanwhile, immigration was becoming entangled in the increasingly visible debate on welfare reform. The bill that Congress passed and the president signed generally denied food stamps and Supplemental Security Income to legal immigrants until they had worked in the United States for a minimum of ten years or had become citizens. Congress also left to the states the option of refusing legal immigrants welfare and Medicaid funds.

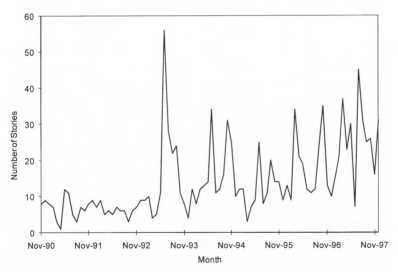

FIGURE 6.4. Prominence of immigration, 1990–97. Total number of immigration stories, per month. Source: 1990–97 *New York Times*.

TABLE 6.6. The effect of ethnocentrism on American opposition to immigration under conditions of low (1992) and high (1996) salience

	Decrease level of immigration		Require immigrants to wait for benefits	
	1992	1996	1992	1996
Ethnocentrism	1.31***	1.40***	0.76	1.58*
	0.42	0.43	0.64	0.84
N	366	366	360	360

Source: 1992–1996 NES Panel.

Note: Table entry is the ordered probit regression coefficient with standard errors below. Models also control for household economic conditions, unemployment, being divorced, education, political awareness, occupation, log of the proportion of Hispanic and Asian in state, dependence on government assistance, moral traditionalism, retrospective assessments of national economic conditions, egalitarianism, support for limited government, partisanship, race, and sex. Analysis confined to whites and blacks. Full results appear in the Web appendix.

***$p < 0.01$; **$p < 0.05$; *$p < 0.10$, two-tailed.

In addition, noncitizens who entered the United States after the law was in place would be subject to a five-year ban on most forms of means-tested federal aid.

Finally, before leaving Washington for the 1996 campaigns in their home states, members of the 104th Congress passed the Illegal Immigration Reform and Immigrant Responsibility Act. Among other things, the bill was designed to make deportation and exclusion easier, to strengthen border control, and to increase penalties for creating false documents or for smuggling people across the border.

Taken together, the nature and prominence of elite discussion about immigration implies that we should find ethnocentrism to be playing an even more important role in immigration opinion in 1996 than we found to be the case in 1992 (where it was already plenty important). Of great convenience for testing this hypothesis, the 1992 NES constituted the first wave of a panel, one that reached completion in the fall of 1996, and the 1996 interview repeated two of the immigration policy questions from the 1992 survey: whether immigration should be decreased and whether immigrants should have to wait for government aid. Our hypothesis is that ethnocentrism will shape these opinions more powerfully in 1996 than in 1992.

To test our claim, we estimated the standard model predicting opinions measured in 1992 and compared these results to those generated by the standard model predicting opinions measured in 1996, in the wake of a contentious and noisy national discussion. We restricted this analysis to persons who participated in both waves of the NES Panel in order to make the comparison exact. The results appear in table 6.6.

As predicted, the effect of ethnocentrism on opposition to immigration increases between 1992 and 1996. Both on restricting immigration and on withholding government benefits, the estimated effect of ethnocentrism is greater in 1996 than in 1992. However, neither increase is statistically significant.[35] The national conversation on immigration did grow more clamorous and contentious between 1992 and 1996, but we cannot be sure that this had any consequence for the importance of ethnocentrism. According to our analysis, ethnocentrism is a primary ingredient in public opposition to immigration—but this is nearly as true in 1992 as in 1996.

Immigration had already come onto the scene by 1992. Perhaps the threshold of attention and interest required for ethnocentrism's activation had already been breached. Or perhaps our test was insufficiently sensitive.

In the spring of 2007, in an early effort to drum up support for his presidential aspirations, Senator John McCain was blistered with questions about his "weak" stance on immigration. This inquisition took place not in California or Texas or in his home state of Arizona, but in Cedar Falls, Iowa. Furious opposition to immigration erupts in surprising places (Nagourney 2007).[36] Most places in the United States, of course, have recently experienced increases in immigrant populations. But there is huge variation in this. Between 1980 and 1990, some states actually lost foreign-born population, while others experienced especially sharp increases. We wondered whether recent increases in the foreign-born population make immigration a salient issue and a potent trigger for ethnocentrism.

To find out if this is so, we used the U.S. Census to calculate for each state the *change* in percentage of foreign-born residents from 1980 to 1990. We added this information to the 1992 NES, which has provided the centerpiece of our analysis in this chapter. Then we simply dropped two new variables into the standard model: growth in percentage foreign born and ethnocentrism × growth in percentage foreign born.

The results, presented in table 6.7, show that ethnocentrism generally matters more among Americans who live in states that have received comparatively large increases in immigration. Ethnocentrism matters more on whether immigration should be curtailed, whether new immigrants should be required to wait for government benefits, whether immigrant children should be required to learn English promptly, and whether the United States should establish English as its official language. The differences approach or pass conventional levels of statistical significance in three of four cases (all but the timing of government benefits).[37]

Figure 6.5 shows this triggering effect more clearly. The figure uses the coefficients presented in table 6.7 to estimate the effect of ethnocentrism in three hypothetical states that represent the natural range of change in

T A B L E   6 . 7 . The effect of ethnocentrism on American opposition to immigration
conditional on recent increase in state's foreign-born population

	Decrease level of immigration	Immigrants wait for benefits	Require classes in English	English as official language
Ethnocentrism (E)	0.80***	1.06***	0.47**	0.71***
	0.21	0.32	0.21	0.26
E × Growth in	0.74	0.20	1.27*	1.08
Foreign Born	0.71	1.04	0.73	0.90
N	1524	1499	1542	1539

Source: 1992 NES.

Note: Table entry is the ordered probit regression coefficient with standard error below. Models
also control for household economic conditions, unemployment, being divorced, education,
political awareness, occupation, log of the proportion of Hispanic and Asian in state, dependence on government assistance, moral traditionalism, retrospective assessments of national
economic conditions, egalitarianism, support for limited government, partisanship, race, and
sex. Analysis restricted to whites and blacks. Full results appear in the Web appendix.

***$p < 0.01$; **$p < 0.05$; *$p < 0.10$, two-tailed.

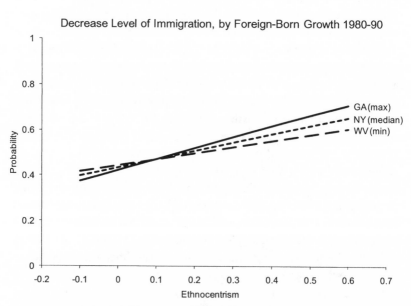

F I G U R E   6 . 5 . Activating ethnocentrism: the effect of ethnocentrism on American opposition
to immigration in three states that vary on recent change in foreign-born population. Predicted
probabilities. Estimates from table 6.7. Source: 1992 NES.

foreign-born population between 1980 and 1990: an 18 percent loss in foreign born between 1980 and 1990 (matching West Virginia at the bottom
of the natural range); a 16 percent increase in foreign born (New York,
right at the median); and a 58 percent increase in foreign born (Georgia,
at the top of the range). As figure 6.5 reveals, ethnocentrism is much more
important—more than twice as important—in fueling opposition to immigration for Americans living in a place like Georgia, which has experienced
sharp increases in immigrant population, than in a place like West Virginia,
which has not.[38]

CONCLUSIONS AND IMPLICATIONS

For most Americans today, as in times past, immigration is a problem. Most
think that the number of immigrants admitted to the country should be
decreased, that immigrants should wait for government services, that the
public schools should deny bilingual instruction to the children of immigrants, that English should be established as the country's official language,
and that immigration does more harm than good—to culture and to taxes
and to jobs. According to our analysis, such views have more than a single
source. Opinion on immigration reflects apprehension about change in society's moral standards, ignorance and parochialism, pessimism about the
national economy, ambivalence toward equality of opportunity, but most
of all, under a variety of alternative specifications and across different measures, ethnocentrism.

This is the main story, but there is another. Among Hispanic Americans,
whose experience of immigration is more intimate and whose identity may
be suspended between their nation of origin and their nation of residence,
ethnocentrism is also a powerful force, but moving in the opposite direction, in favor of immigration.[39]

Generally speaking, the effects of ethnocentrism we have uncovered
here reflect both in-group loyalty and out-group denigration—that is, they
reflect prejudice, generally conceived. Hispanic Americans again provide
the exception. Among Hispanic Americans, the impact of ethnocentrism
on immigration opinion is carried predominantly by in-group pride; out-
group hostility is much less important. This exception would seem to arise
from the special relationship between contemporary immigration and the
interests and experiences of Americans of Hispanic heritage.

Finally, we suggest that the effects of ethnocentrism reported in this
chapter are as large and as robust as they are because the issues provoked
by immigration lend themselves readily to ethnocentric framing and ethnocentric understanding. Should we allow them to come in? Should we tighten
our borders to keep them out? If we allow them in, should they be able to

enjoy the same rights and privileges as we do? By this argument, variation in the power of ethnocentrism in this domain of public opinion will depend primarily on how prominently and centrally immigration comes to occupy the American imagination. We have suggested here that when the national discussion about immigration grows sufficiently noisy, and especially when the issue becomes real as immigrants begin to settle nearby, ethnocentrism's role will expand.

Up until now, we have examined the part played by ethnocentrism in public opinion on issues that invoke the nation and that draw on national identity: the dangers of war and international confrontation in chapter 4; the squandering of the nation's treasury on foreign lands in chapter 5; and keeping strangers outside the national community here in chapter 6. In the chapters that follow we turn our attention to matters of domestic politics: to the role of ethnocentrism at home.

CHAPTER 7

Straight versus Gay

In June 1969, New York City police carried out a raid on the Stonewall Inn, a gay bar in Greenwich Village. At the time, such raids were routine. Discrimination against homosexuals was widespread—in opinion, custom, and law. Most American communities treated gay sex as a criminal offense. Homosexuals were prohibited by law from many forms of employment and were systematically excluded from military service. Same-sex marriage was unimaginable.

If the raid on Stonewall was routine, the response was not. Rather than being quietly carted off to jail, the patrons fought back. Scuffling spilled out into the streets; police officers were injured; violence spread through adjacent neighborhoods. Within the gay community, the "Stonewall Riots" were interpreted as a dramatic and exhilarating assertion of gay pride. A new militant movement arose. Grievances were expressed through unruly acts of public contention: sit-ins, marches, occupations, disruptions, and more. Gays and lesbians were encouraged to see a connection between their own personal struggles and the political critique that other social movements of the times—civil rights, antiwar, feminist—were directing at American society.

Confrontational forms of activism were supplemented by more conventional forms of political activity: litigation, quiet persuasion, organization, and community building. In 1973, gay activists succeeded in convincing the American Psychiatric Association to remove homosexuality from its list of mental disorders. And in 1975, the federal Civil Service Commission agreed to drop its blanket prohibition on gay employment.

With the 1980s came a new challenge, a lethal one. The AIDS virus spread among gay and bisexual men with alarming speed and often fatal consequence. The illness was devastating, and the weak response from government provided new energy and focus for the broader gay rights movement. Organizations were created to provide health care and social services, education and prevention campaigns were mobilized, and government was pressured to do more.

Others pressured government to do less. The political fight against the gay rights movement has been carried on principally by the Christian Right, itself a social movement, one concentrated among religious traditionalists (especially evangelical Protestants), and spearheaded by such organizations as the Christian Coalition and Focus on the Family. The professed aim of the Christian Right is to restore "traditional values" to public policy. It arose in the late 1970s in response to what the founders saw as widespread and flagrant "moral decay and spiritual decline." Among the moral catastrophes motivating the Christian Right to action were abortion, promiscuity, divorce, and feminism, but opposition to gay rights in particular has been a pillar of the Christian Right from the outset. Homosexuality, according to the Christian Right, is immoral, violates God's teachings, and is condemned by Holy Scripture.

The Christian Right has been effective in raising funds, recruiting activists, and then expanding the scope of conflict by taking the fight against gay rights to the ballot box or to the court of public opinion. School board elections, local ordinances designed to protect gays and lesbians from bias in housing or employment, President Bill Clinton's proposal to allow gays to serve openly in the military, state referenda on same-sex marriage: all these have served as sites for fierce conflict (Rimmerman, Wald, and Wilcox 2000). Debate is heated, differences in opinion are passionately felt, moral indignation and righteous hostility are de rigueur, opponents become enemies. "Few issues in American politics, sexual or not, inspire as much passion as the struggle over civil rights for gays and lesbians. . . . The rhetoric and tactics on both sides are often extreme, stretching and occasionally obliterating altogether the norms of civility in public discourse" (Wald 2000, p. 4).

As a general matter, ethnocentrism comes into play when political issues can be readily understood as struggles between "us" and "them"; better yet, as struggles between "us" and a sinister "them," a sinister "them" of the type we have encountered in previous chapters: terrorists, foreigners, illegal immigrants, and the like. For many straight-laced Americans, gays and lesbians fit this type well. Especially this should be so for ethnocentric Americans. On this reasoning, we expect opposition to the "homosexual agenda" to arise importantly from ethnocentrism—from an inclination, in extreme form, to divide the world into the righteous and the depraved.

RIGHTS

We will begin our test by examining public opinion on a cluster of issues dealing with civil rights: the right of gays and lesbians to marry, to adopt children, to serve in the military, and to be protected from employment discrimination. All four subjects were covered in the 2004 National Election Study, carried out as that year's presidential campaign reached its conclusion. Not surprisingly, the 2004 campaign was preoccupied primarily with the transformations in international relations and public policy set in motion by the terrorist attacks on New York and Washington on September 11, 2001. About gay rights, little was said.[1]

However, just below the presidential campaign, the issue of gay marriage was causing quite a commotion in the states and among conservative religious organizations like Focus on the Family, Alliance for Marriage, and the Family Research Council. The Christian Right began to pour money and organization into campaigns against same-sex marriage, arguing that a handful of liberal judges and activists were threatening the sacred and fundamental institution of marriage, the very foundation of Western civilization. Eleven states placed same-sex marriage on the November 2004 ballot, and in every case the prohibition side won by handsome majorities.

Consistent with this, in the fall of 2004, a clear majority of Americans interviewed by the NES—59.4 percent to be exact—opposed granting marriage licenses to same-sex couples.[2] A slightly smaller percentage, but still a majority (52.1 percent) would deny gay couples the right to adopt children.

The third question from the 2004 NES under examination here has to do with military service. Until quite recently, the U.S. military followed a systematic policy of exclusion: gay recruits or draftees were deemed unsuitable for service, and when members of the armed forces were suspected of homosexuality, they were discharged. This practice began to be challenged, first by service members who contested their discharges openly, and then through litigation in the courts. During his initial run for the presidency, Bill Clinton promised to do away with the practice altogether. Clinton's proposal met with ferocious resistance from the military and from certain segments of Congress, but by the summer of 1993 a compromise was struck and implemented soon thereafter. Under the new policy, recruits and military members can no longer be asked about their sexuality ("Don't Ask"), and those in the service must keep their sexual identity to themselves ("Don't Tell"). By the fall of 2004, some dozen years after the proposal was first floated, Americans in overwhelming numbers had come to accept the idea that homosexuals should be allowed to serve in the U.S. armed forces. In 2004, 53.4 percent strongly favored military service for gays; just 13.7 percent strongly opposed it.[3]

A fourth and final question takes us to the domain of work. In the 1970s, city governments began to pass local ordinances protecting gays from employment discrimination, first in university towns (Ann Arbor, Austin, Berkeley, Madison), and then spreading to larger cities with sizable and increasingly well-organized gay populations (Minneapolis, San Francisco,

Seattle). By 2000, eleven states had passed some form of statewide legislation prohibiting discrimination against gays (California, Hawaii, and most of New England); governors in eight other states issued executive orders banning discrimination on the basis of sexual orientation in state employment.

This movement to prohibit discrimination against gays and lesbians provoked a backlash, first and most famously in Dade County, Florida, where Anita Bryant argued that gay rights ordinances were an abomination. Bryant's success in repealing legal protection for gays inspired a variety of statewide efforts. Sponsors of these referenda argued "equal rights, not special rights," and their proposals to rescind legislation prohibiting discrimination on the grounds of sexual orientation were popular with voters and often succeeded at the ballot box. However, in 1996, the U.S. Supreme Court (*Romer v. Evans*) ruled that one such proposition—Amendment 2, passed by Colorado voters in 1992—was unconstitutional on grounds that it violated the equal protection clause of the Fourteenth Amendment. After *Romer*, enthusiasm for initiative-based efforts to rescind gay rights statutes noticeably diminished. Federal agencies have quietly added sexual orientation to their antidiscrimination policies. In the spring of 1998, President Clinton issued an executive order prohibiting discrimination based on sexual orientation in all federal agencies.[4]

Public opinion is generally consistent with current policy. In 2004, exactly half (50.0 percent) of Americans said that they strongly supported laws that would protect gays and lesbians from job discrimination, more than three times the number who said they were strongly opposed to such measures.[5]

Taken all around, then, the American public seems of two minds on gay rights. The "average American" seems quite willing to permit gays the freedom to pursue a livelihood and serve the nation, but is much less prepared to extend such rights into the intimate domains of marriage and family. As demands for equality penetrate deeper into private life, opposition rises. On all these questions, Americans take emphatic positions. They do not merely favor one side or the other; they favor one side or the other strongly.

To what degree are these strong differences in opinion due to ethnocentrism? To find out we estimated our standard model in the standard way. In the domain of gay rights, the standard model includes, in addition to ethnocentrism, religion, partisanship, education, authoritarianism, egalitarianism, as well as sex and race. We are especially interested here in the impact of religion, given the prominence of the Christian Right in organizing opposition to gay rights.[6]

The results, presented in table 7.1, reveal that ethnocentrism plays a principal role in energizing American opposition to gay rights. Ethnocentric

TABLE 7.1. Ethnocentrism and opposition to gay rights

	Marriage	Adoption	Military	Employment
Ethnocentrism	0.92**	1.11***	1.19***	0.60*
	0.37	0.37	0.32	0.31
Importance of religion	1.50***	1.17***	0.80***	0.63***
	0.18	0.19	0.16	0.16
Religious doctrine	0.70***	0.35**	0.33**	0.55***
	0.17	0.18	0.15	0.15
Partisanship	−0.87***	−0.86***	−0.58***	−0.48***
	0.15	0.16	0.14	0.13
Education	−0.48**	−0.67***	−0.26	−0.40**
	0.20	0.21	0.17	0.17
Authoritarianism	0.56***	0.64***	0.31*	0.35**
	0.18	0.20	0.17	0.16
Egalitarianism	−0.89***	−0.66**	−0.73***	−1.49***
	0.27	0.29	0.24	0.24
N	889	849	860	859
Effect of **E**	0.44→0.69	0.32→0.62	0.06→0.24	0.15→0.27

Source: 2004 NES.

Note: Table entry is the ordered probit regression coefficient with standard errors below. Models also control for religious denomination, race, ethnicity, and sex. Full results appear in the Web appendix. The bottom row of the table gives the effect associated with a shift in Ethnocentrism from Low (−0.1) to High (0.6) in the predicted probability of opposing gay rights (see text for details).

***$p < 0.01$; **$p < 0.05$; *$p < 0.10$, two-tailed.

Americans are significantly more likely to oppose gay marriage, to reject the claim that same-sex couples be allowed to adopt children, to voice disapproval of the notion that homosexuals be allowed to serve in the military, and to take issue with laws that would protect gays and lesbians from job discrimination. The effect of ethnocentrism is largest on adoption and smallest on employment discrimination, but it is statistically significant and substantively large in each of the four cases. Ethnocentrism is not the only factor shaping opinion on gay rights—table 7.1 also reveals sizable effects attributable to religion, as we expected, as well as to partisanship, education, egalitarianism, and authoritarianism. But taking all these effects into account, ethnocentrism makes a major contribution of its own.[7]

The difference ethnocentrism makes becomes apparent in the graphical presentation of predicted probabilities, shown in figure 7.1.[8] The effects of ethnocentrism are substantial, especially in the intimate realms of marriage and family. If ethnocentrism could somehow be removed from American society, we would be living in a visibly different place: a place where same-sex marriage and gay couple adoption enjoyed the support of a majority of Americans.[9]

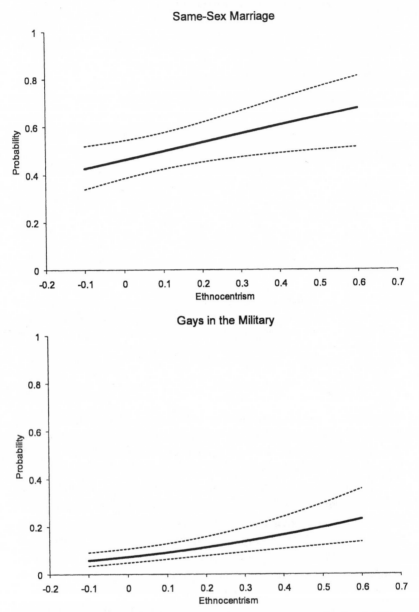

FIGURE 7.1. Ethnocentrism and American opposition to gay rights. Predicted probabilities with 95 percent confidence intervals. Estimates from table 7.1. Source: 2004 NES.

Adoption by Same-Sex Couples

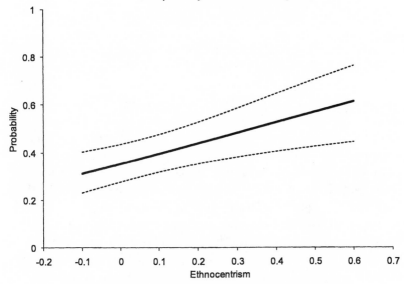

Antidiscrimination Job Laws for Homosexuals

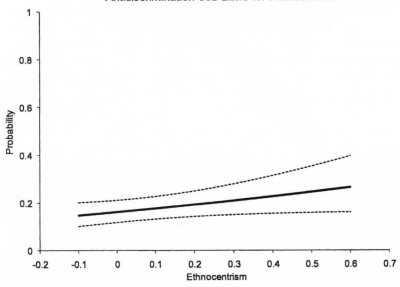

FIGURE 7.1. (*continued*)

AIDS

In its weekly newsletter published on June 5, 1981, the Centers for Disease Control and Prevention (CDC) in Atlanta reported that five previously healthy young men from Los Angeles had been diagnosed with a rare and serious pneumonia (*Pneumocystis carinii*). All five were described as "active homosexuals." Later on that summer, the *New York Times* carried a story about a mysterious illness afflicting gay men in New York and in San Francisco. In a few years' time, Americans came to learn that gay men—thousands of gay men—were dying from AIDS (acquired immune deficiency syndrome).

In the early stages of the AIDS epidemic, the federal government took little action. Health and Human Services funds to support research on AIDS were modest. Requests for incremental funding were sufficiently unpopular that they had to be hidden away, concealed in major appropriation bills. Ronald Reagan, president of the United States during this time, had nothing to say on the subject. Not until 1987 did the Food and Drug Administration (FDA) approve any drug treatment designed to combat HIV/AIDS, and by then, over 25,000 Americans had died.

The AIDS epidemic spread swiftly during the 1980s, peaking in 1992, when some 80,000 new cases were diagnosed. Faced with incontrovertible evidence of a horrific public health problem, federal funding for research increased sharply. New drug treatments were put on a fast track for approval at the FDA. In 1990, Congress passed its first major piece of legislation directed specifically and exclusively at AIDS. The legislation was named after Ryan White, a teenager from the American heartland, who was in fact white, and straight, and who had contracted HIV (human immunodeficiency virus) from a blood transfusion. The Ryan White Comprehensive AIDS Resources Emergency Act released several hundred million dollars to the states and to service organizations to increase the availability of medical care outside of hospitals for persons with AIDS. During the 1992 presidential campaign, Bill Clinton actively sought the support of gay and lesbian organizations. He promised to appoint a national AIDS policy director to coordinate initiatives from the White House. And he said that he would invest more resources into research and education on AIDS than had his Republican predecessors.[10]

These events form the immediate background for our analysis of the role ethnocentrism plays in the American public's political response to AIDS. We analyze two questions in particular, the first asked in late 1992 and the second in fall of 1993, at the very peak of the epidemic.[11]

The first of our questions has to do with whether the federal government should devote more resources on research to fight AIDS. As part of

TABLE 7.2. Ethnocentrism and AIDS

	Government spend less on AIDS	Worried about "catching" AIDS
Ethnocentrism	−0.06	1.25***
	0.21	0.35
Importance of religion	0.38***	0.39*
	0.13	0.21
Religious doctrine	0.02	0.28
	0.12	0.20
Partisanship	−0.23**	−0.37**
	0.10	0.17
Education	0.02	−0.67***
	0.14	0.21
Authoritarianism	−0.07	0.31
	0.12	0.19
Egalitarianism	−1.54***	−0.56**
	0.18	0.28
N	1529	584
Effect of **E**	0.38→0.37	0.04→0.21

Source: 1992 NES (column 1) and 1993 NES Pilot (column 2).

Note: Table entry is the ordered probit regression coefficient with standard errors below. Models also control for religious denomination, race, ethnicity, and sex. Full results appear in the Web appendix. The bottom row of the table gives the effect associated with a shift in Ethnocentrism from Low (−0.1) to High (0.6) in the predicted probability of supporting cuts in spending and being worried about "catching" AIDS.

***$p < 0.01$; **$p < 0.05$; *$p < 0.10$, two-tailed.

the standard NES government spending battery, the question asks whether federal spending on AIDS research should be increased, decreased, or kept about the same. For the most part, Americans said spend more: 62.0 percent said that federal spending on research on AIDS should be increased; just 7.9 percent said spending should be decreased; 30.1 percent said that spending should be kept the same.[12]

Results from applying the standard model to this opinion question appear in table 7.2. They indicate that ethnocentrism has nothing to do with opinion on how much the government should spend on AIDS. Other things matter—egalitarianism pushes opinion in the generous direction while religiosity pushes opinion in the opposite direction—but ethnocentrism pushes opinion in neither direction. The same conclusion holds if we re-estimate the standard model, replacing the stereotype-based measure of ethnocentrism with the version of ethnocentrism based on thermometer score ratings. Once again, ethnocentrism fails—utterly and completely—to distinguish those Americans who want to spend more on finding a cure for AIDS from those who want to spend less.

This is surprising. In the previous section we saw that ethnocentrism appears to be a major force behind American opposition to gay rights. Same-sex marriage, gay adoption, homosexuals serving in the armed forces, laws designed to protect gays from discrimination at work: opposition to each of these arises in an important way out of ethnocentrism. In the arena of rights, we found large and consistent effects. Here, we find no effect at all. Why?

Perhaps because from an ethnocentric point of view, there are good reasons both to spend more on AIDS and to spend less. Spending more on AIDS makes sense as protection against contamination. Investing in research and finding a cure are ways to make the epidemic go away, to reduce the chances that the rest of "us" will become infected. At the same time, spending less on AIDS also makes sense. Ethnocentric Americans might wonder why government resources should be squandered on those who do not deserve help, who are to blame for their own suffering, who, to put the point in biblical terms, are being punished by God for their earthly transgressions.[13]

Our second question on AIDS gives us some purchase on this puzzle in that it has to do with concerns about how the disease is transmitted. This question, taken from the 1993 NES Pilot Study, probed background beliefs about how one might "catch" AIDS. This is not itself a matter of policy, but it does have relevance for what kinds of policies might be required to protect public health in the face of the AIDS epidemic. Specifically, the question asks people how worried they would be about getting AIDS if they worked with a gay person. In contrast to the first AIDS question, here our prediction is straightforward: Americans of an ethnocentric inclination should be more worried about catching AIDS from a coworker.[14]

And so they are. This result is presented in the second column of table 7.2. Ethnocentric Americans are much more anxious about catching AIDS than are those who reject ethnocentrism. Education has a large negative effect, as we would expect. Religion, partisanship, and egalitarianism make a difference too. But on the question of illness and contamination, no single factor is as important as ethnocentrism.

SEX AND IMMORALITY

The ethnocentric agitation appears to be attached to homosexuality in particular and not to matters of sexuality in general. In the 2000 GSS, Americans were asked for their moral judgments on a wide variety of sexual practices: about sex education in the public schools, about whether contraception should be made available to teenagers, about the propriety of premarital sex, about sex between teenagers, about adultery, and finally about "sexual relations between two adults of the same sex."[15]

TABLE 7.3. Ethnocentrism and immorality of sexual practices

	Gay sex	Sex education	Contraception for teenagers	Premarital sex	Teenage sex	Extramarital sex
Ethnocentrism	1.22*	-0.94	0.18	0.54	1.64**	0.08
	0.68	0.77	0.49	0.53	0.64	0.74
Partisanship	-0.59**	-1.12***	-0.61***	-0.78***	-0.25	-0.34
	0.28	0.35	0.22	0.25	0.28	0.31
Education	-0.92**	-0.28	0.16	-0.45	-0.04	-0.54
	0.37	0.43	0.27	0.31	0.33	0.38
Authoritarianism	1.24***	1.43***	0.31	0.42	1.32***	1.12***
	0.38	0.47	0.29	0.32	0.37	0.43
Religious	1.39***	0.94***	0.93***	2.11***	1.01***	0.73**
attendance	0.28	0.33	0.21	0.24	0.27	0.30
Age	0.10	0.81*	1.29***	0.95***	1.44***	0.27
	0.39	0.47	0.31	0.33	0.40	0.42
N	241	299	300	296	301	256
Effect of **E**	0.55→0.84	0.08→0.02	0.31→0.35	0.24→0.37	0.89→0.99	0.95→0.96

Source: 2000 GSS.

Note: Table entry is the ordered probit regression coefficient with standard errors below. Models also control for egalitarianism, race, ethnicity, and sex. Full results appear in the Web appendix. The bottom row of the table gives the effect associated with a shift in Ethnocentrism from Low (−0.1) to High (0.6) in the predicted probability of viewing a behavior as "Always" or "Almost Always" wrong.

***$p < 0.01$; **$p < 0.05$; *$p < 0.10$, two-tailed.

In the year 2000, a decisive majority of the American public—58.7 percent to be precise—declared that gay sex was "always wrong." And as table
7.3 shows, this view was much more common among ethnocentric Americans. Controlling on party identification, authoritarianism, egalitarianism,
religion (and more), ethnocentrism powerfully predicts the judgment that
gay sex is immoral. The table also reveals that ethnocentrism is generally irrelevant to judgments made about other sexual practices. To the ethnocentric, there is something especially distressing about gay sex.[16]

HOMOSEXUALITY AS A NATURAL KIND

Ethnocentrism, we have argued, arises in part out of a tendency to see social
groups as natural kinds. Human groups are biological types, in possession
of an underlying essence. This ethnocentric tendency aligns in a surprising
way with the ongoing debate in science about the nature of homosexuality.
The current scientific view is to regard homosexuality as inborn and virtually impossible to alter. It is not a choice, a mere preference for one kind of
sexual life over another. And so here we expect ethnocentric Americans will

TABLE 7.4. Ethnocentrism and the nature of homosexuality

	Cannot be changed	Natural sexuality
Ethnocentrism	0.61*	0.74**
	0.37	0.37
Importance of religion	−0.53**	−1.02***
	0.21	0.22
Religious doctrine	−0.51**	−0.32
	0.20	0.20
Partisanship	0.37**	0.33*
	0.17	0.17
Education	0.28	0.41*
	0.22	0.21
Authoritarianism	−0.67***	−0.38*
	0.19	0.19
Egalitarianism	1.41***	1.41***
	0.30	0.29
N	537	582
Effect of **E**	0.58→0.74	0.57→0.75

Source: 1993 NES Pilot.

Note: Table entry is the ordered probit regression coefficient with standard errors below. Models also control for religious denomination, race, ethnicity, and sex. Full results appear in the
Web appendix. The bottom row of the table gives the effect associated with a shift in Ethnocentrism from Low (−0.1) to High (0.6) in the predicted probability of believing homosexuality cannot be changed or is natural.

***$p < 0.01$; **$p < 0.05$; *$p < 0.10$, two-tailed.

be more likely, not less, to endorse the scientific position on the nature of homosexuality (though not for scientific reasons).[17]

Two questions relevant to the current discussion were included in the 1993 NES Pilot Study. In both instances, about one-half of the public opted for the scientifically enlightened view: 52.3 percent said that people cannot choose their sexual orientation; 55.2 percent said that homosexuality is natural. And as table 7.4 makes clear, ethnocentrism is implicated in both. Those inclined toward ethnocentrism are more likely to say that homosexuality cannot be changed and that homosexuality is natural.[18]

Other things matter too, of course. In particular, education and egalitarianism are quite important, and they work as we would expect. This means that in this case they push opinion in the same direction that ethnocentrism does. More education, more equality, and more ethnocentrism imply the view that homosexuality is inborn and unalterable.

Authoritarianism is also important, but it moves opinion in the opposite direction. Authoritarianism implies the view that homosexuality is chosen and can be "fixed." In this case, as in several others we have encountered, ethnocentrism and authoritarianism work against each other.

ACTIVATION

In this chapter we have uncovered ample evidence of ethnocentrism's importance. Ethnocentrism is a powerful force behind American opposition to same-sex marriage, to adoption of children by gay couples, to gays serving in the military, and to laws designed to protect gays against discrimination on the job. Ethnocentric Americans are apprehensive about catching AIDS. They take exception to gay sex, and they think that homosexuality is inborn and impossible to alter. The results are strong, but they are not uniform. Ethnocentrism is more or less important, depending on circumstances.

The Color of AIDS

Our analysis turned up one glaring exception to the general pattern of strong effects. We found, to our surprise, no relationship between ethnocentrism and opinion toward government spending on AIDS. We suggested, without much confidence, that from an ethnocentric point of view, both increases in spending and cuts in spending might seem appealing. Spending more on AIDS research makes sense as protection against contamination. Spending less on AIDS research also makes sense: why squander government resources to help those who bring suffering on themselves?

This argument might work for the public as a whole, but it should not work for black Americans in particular. The original epidemiological work on AIDS located the illness in gay enclaves in major cities. At the beginning, AIDS was understood to be a gay man's disease, and insofar as AIDS attracted media attention, it was portrayed as such. With the discovery of HIV and a better understanding of how AIDS could be transmitted, the "face" of the disease began to change. Stories began to appear in major news outlets suggesting that black Americans were more likely than other groups to acquire AIDS. In November 1991, Earvin ("Magic") Johnson, an African American and one of the most celebrated athletes of his time, announced that he was retiring from professional basketball at the peak of his talent because he was infected with HIV. By the middle 1990s, HIV/AIDS had become a leading cause of death among black Americans.[19]

Insofar as black Americans have come to think of HIV/AIDS as a black problem, we would expect ethnocentrism to operate differently among them. Blacks should look at federal funding for AIDS research in much the same way that Hispanics look at immigration policies. As we learned in chapter 6, Hispanic Americans are more favorably disposed toward generous immigration policy than the rest of the population, and this is so especially among ethnocentric Hispanic Americans. We expect the same to be true for black Americans and AIDS.[20]

And it is. Among black Americans, ethnocentrism is associated with spending more on AIDS. This was so in 1992 and even more clearly so in 2000.[21] As summarized in figure 7.2, when it comes to government action on AIDS, ethnocentrism is utterly irrelevant for white Americans but highly relevant for African Americans. Among African Americans, ethnocentrism—in-group favoritism—leads to the view that government should spend more on finding a cure for AIDS. This makes sense in light of shifts within black communities in the understanding of AIDS—the growing appreciation, among black Americans, that HIV/AIDS is a special threat to their own kind.[22]

Gay Marriage and the Ballot

Same-sex marriage has come on the political scene quite recently. Conveniently for our project, it has come more prominently on the scene in some places than in others. This gives us an opportunity to test our account of activation.

The necessary back story begins in June 2003, when the Supreme Court, in a six-to-three decision, struck down the sodomy laws of thirteen states. In a scathing dissent, Justice Scalia slammed the Court for laying the groundwork for the legalization of same-sex marriage:

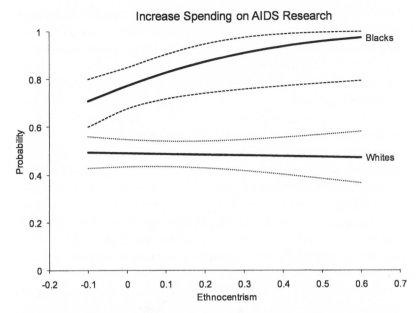

FIGURE 7.2. Ethnocentrism and support for spending more on AIDS research, separately by race. Predicted probabilities with 95 percent confidence intervals. Estimation results appear in the Web appendix. Source: 2000 NES.

Today's opinion dismantles the structure of constitutional law that has permitted a distinction to be made between heterosexual and homosexual unions, insofar as formal recognition in marriage is concerned. If moral disapprobation of homosexual conduct is "no legitimate state interest" for purposes of proscribing that conduct, and if, as the Court coos (casting aside all pretense of neutrality), "[w]hen sexuality finds overt expression in intimate conduct with another person, the conduct can be but one element in a personal bond that is more enduring," what justification could there possibly be for denying the benefits of marriage to homosexual couples exercising "[t]he liberty protected by the Constitution"? Surely not the encouragement of procreation, since the sterile and the elderly are allowed to marry. This case "does not involve" the issue of homosexual marriage only if one entertains the belief that principles and logic have nothing to do with the decisions of this Court. (*Lawrence v. Texas* 2003)[23]

Justice Scalia was right to worry. In November 2003, the highest state court in Massachusetts decided that "barring an individual from the protections, benefits, and obligations of civil marriage solely because that person would marry a person of the same sex violates the Massachusetts constitution" (*Goodridge v. Department of Public Health* 2003). The Massachusetts court thereby bestowed the sanctity of law on an arrangement that many Americans regarded as morally indefensible. A few months later, Gavin Newsom, the mayor of San Francisco, began to join same-sex couples in holy matrimony, in direct violation of existing statutes. Both the sober proceedings in Boston and the more flamboyant happenings in San Francisco were highly publicized.

Shortly thereafter, pressured by the Christian Right, President George W. Bush announced his support for a constitutional ban on gay marriage, declaring his irritation with a handful of judges who presumed "to change the most fundamental institution of civilization." Bush promised to bring moral clarity to this debate, but in fact his support was reluctant and tepid—perhaps because Senator John Kerry, Bush's Democratic opponent in the 2004 presidential election, said that he too opposed same-sex marriage, that the Massachusetts Supreme Judicial Court had gone too far, and that the Massachusetts Constitution should be amended to make gay marriage illegal.

Gay marriage disappeared from the presidential campaign, but it was very much alive in state politics. Proposals to make same-sex marriage illegal appeared on the November 2004 ballot of eleven states.[24] With the Christian Right supplying money and organizational, the defenders of traditional marriage prevailed in every case.

The question for us is whether the effect of ethnocentrism on opposition to same-sex marriage increased as a consequence of these campaigns. Such campaigns, it seems reasonable to assume, would have raised the salience of same-sex marriage and provided a bounty of ethnocentric frames (Wald and Glover 2007). These conditions, in turn, should have activated ethnocentrism.

Six of the eleven states that passed antigay marriage ballot proposals in 2004 were part of the NES sample in that year. The six were scattered across the country, including the Pacific Coast (Oregon), the Mountain West (Utah), the industrial Midwest (Michigan and Ohio), and the South (Arkansas and Georgia). All in all, about one in six respondents in the 2004 NES sample came from states that featured a proposal to outlaw same-sex marriage. To test for activation, we added two new terms to the standard model: [Same-Sex Ballot Initiative] and [Ethnocentrism × Same-Sex Ballot Initiative], where Same-Sex Ballot Initiative = 1 if a proposal to prohibit same-sex marriage is on the 2004 November ballot; 0 otherwise. The results are summarized in table 7.5.

As the table shows, ethnocentrism is indeed more important to opinion on same-sex marriage in states with antigay marriage campaigns than in states without them. In fact, the estimated impact of ethnocentrism more than doubles.[25]

TABLE 7.5. The effect of ethnocentrism on American opposition to gay rights in 2004 in states with/without same-sex ballot initiatives

	Marriage	Adoption	Military	Employment
Ethnocentrism (**E**)	0.77*	1.04***	1.03***	0.51
	0.40	0.40	0.35	0.34
E × same-sex ballot initiative	0.96	0.35	0.65	0.27
	0.97	0.99	0.80	0.77
Same-sex ballot initiative	−0.11	0.14	0.17	0.19
	0.14	0.15	0.13	0.12
N	889	849	860	859
Effect of **E**, *No Same-Sex Ballot*				
Initiative	0.45→0.66	0.31→0.59	0.06→0.20	0.15→0.24
Effect of **E**, *Same-Sex Ballot*				
Initiative	0.37→0.81	0.35→0.72	0.07→0.39	0.19→0.37

Source: 2004 NES.

Note: Table entry is the ordered probit regression coefficient with standard errors below. Models also control for importance of religion, religious doctrine, partisanship, education, authoritarianism, egalitarianism, religious denomination, race, ethnicity, and sex. Full results appear in the Web appendix. The bottom rows of the table give the effect associated with a shift in Ethnocentrism from Low (−0.1) to High (0.6) in the predicted probability of opposing gay rights.

***$p < 0.01$; **$p < 0.05$; *$p < 0.10$, two-tailed.

The effect is large, but it is also quite specific. We estimated the identical model for three other gay rights issues: whether gay couples should be allowed to adopt children, the desirability of laws to protect gays and lesbians from discrimination at work, and whether homosexuals should be allowed to serve in the U.S. armed forces. These results are also presented in table 7.5. As indicated there, activation is limited to opinion on gay marriage. It is strong there, but it does not spill over to other policies within the same domain.

If this really is a campaign effect—activation due to well-financed and highly visible efforts in some states to make same-sex marriage illegal—then we should see the effect increase as exposure to the campaign increases. The 2004 NES followed the customary design; this means that respondents were interviewed both before and after the election. As it happens, the question on same-sex marriage appeared in the preelection interview. On average, Americans were interviewed about one month before the election. But some were interviewed the day before, and some were interviewed nearly two months before. Those in the former group, questioned right before the election, would have had the opportunity to be exposed to a much larger "dose" of the campaign than would have those in the latter group.

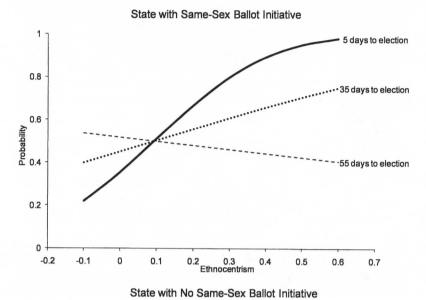

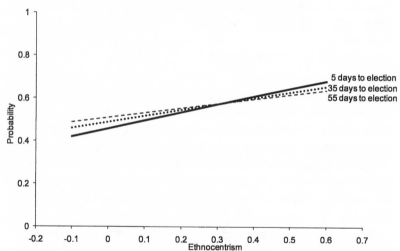

FIGURE 7.3. Activating ethnocentrism: the effect of ethnocentrism on American opposition to same-sex marriage by exposure to an antigay marriage campaign. Predicted probabilities. Estimation results appear in the Web appendix. Source: 2004 NES.

Our delicate prediction here, then, is that the effect of ethnocentrism on opposition to same-marriage in states with a proposal on the ballot to make same-sex marriage illegal should increase as date of interview approaches Election Day. And it does. This result is presented in graphical form in figure 7.3.

The top panel of the figure displays three curves. All three are predictions for those Americans who happened to live in states featuring an anti-gay marriage campaign. One curve represents the effect of ethnocentrism on opposition to same-sex marriage among persons interviewed fifty-five days before the election, another represents persons interviewed thirty-five days before the election, and a third represents persons interviewed five days before the election. The first curve is essentially flat, indicating no relationship between ethnocentrism and opposition to same-sex marriage, among those questioned before the campaign really gets rolling. The second tilts upward from left to right, indicating a moderate effect. The third curve ascends steeply, indicating a very strong effect of ethnocentrism among those questioned right before Election Day, at the close of the campaign.

In the meantime, among Americans living in states *without* a ballot proposition on same-sex marriage, date of interview proves to be utterly irrelevant. Ethnocentrism influenced opposition to same-sex marriage for these Americans, but this was so regardless of when they were interviewed. This is shown in the bottom panel of figure 7.3. Taken together, these results are consistent with the claim that the importance of ethnocentrism for public opinion depends on circumstances—in particular, that it depends on the degree to which issues that lend themselves to ethnocentric thinking capture public attention.[26]

The 2004 campaigns to make same-sex marriage illegal offer us one more test. The activation of ethnocentrism in matters of opinion is one thing; the activation of ethnocentrism in matters of action is another. Could it be that ethnocentrism motivated people to take part in politics who might not otherwise when they were offered the chance to vote in defense of marriage?

Under normal conditions ethnocentrism and engagement in politics are negatively associated. Those who are ethnocentrically disposed are generally a bit less likely to take part in political life. In keeping with this general pattern, in the fall of 2004, in states without a same-sex marriage proposal on the ballot, ethnocentrism predicts a reduction in voter turnout. It does so in the context of a standard model of turnout, one that includes measures of education, age, strength of partisanship, sex, race, and more. In the six states with gay marriage on the ballot that fell within the NES sample, however, the relationship reverses. Now ethnocentrism predicts an *increase* in voter turnout. These results appear in figure 7.4.[27]

Based on these results, we calculate that voter turnout in ballot states increased over what it would have been in the absence of same-sex ballot initiatives by about two percentage points. Other researchers, working from entirely independent sources of evidence, come to virtually the identical conclusion (Ansolabehere and Stewart 2005; Althaus 2005; McDonald

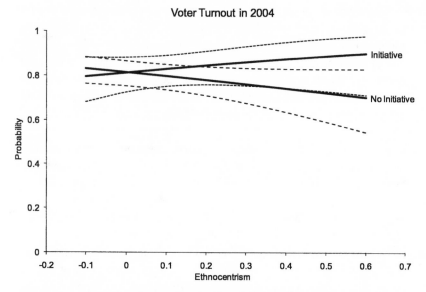

FIGURE 7.4. Activating ethnocentrism: the effect of ethnocentrism on voter turnout in 2004 in states with/without same-sex ballot initiatives. Predicted probabilities with 95 percent confidence intervals. Estimation results appear in the Web appendix. Source: 2004 NES.

2004). Our results indicate, moreover, that this increase comes very disproportionately from the mobilization of the ethnocentric into politics.[28]

In sum, the campaign to defend heterosexual marriage, carried on vigorously in some states but not in others, appears to have increased the importance of ethnocentrism for opinion and for action alike.

CONCLUSIONS AND IMPLICATIONS

Efforts to curb human appetites and enforce moral standards have been a notable feature of American politics, from abolition and temperance on up to contemporary conflicts over gambling, prostitution, pornography, drugs, and more. A preoccupation with impropriety is perhaps especially prominent in the United States. What Daniel Bell has called America's talent for "extremism in morality" (1955, p. 17) may stem from our religious fundamentalism, on the one hand, and our affluence, on the other. Prosperity, as Richard Hofstadter (1955, p. 99) once put it, "liberates the public for the expression of its more luxurious hostilities."

Whether the United States sees more than its fair share of conflicts of this kind, there is certainly plenty of it to see here. Our purpose in this chapter has been to investigate what part, if any, ethnocentrism plays in the politics of morality, taking the struggle over gay rights as a case in point.[29]

Disputes over moral questions are often fought out as appeals to government, as struggles over policy. Far from being a bystander in moral conflict, government is often an active participant in adjudicating recognition and respect among the contending groups. So it seems to be here. Ethnocentric Americans tend to disapprove of gays serving in the military and of laws designed to protect gays against discrimination on the job. They stand against allowing gay couples to adopt children. They say they want no part of same-sex marriage—and they say this especially when mobilized by campaigns that seek recognition and legal protection for marriage as traditionally conceived.

CHAPTER 8

Women's Place

Starting in the late 1960s, the issue of women's rights rose rapidly to national prominence. Suddenly there were press conferences, meetings, protests, marches, and demonstrations. More and more women declared themselves sympathetic to feminism, enlisted in feminist organizations, and ran for public office. Hearings on women's rights became commonplace in Congress. Women's rights became a salient subject in national party platforms and conventions. Bills representing various aspects of women's rights agenda were routinely introduced and very often passed. The most notable accomplishment of the time, or so it seemed, was the equal rights amendment (ERA). Promising that "equality of rights under the law shall not be denied or abridged by the United States or by any State on account of sex," the ERA sailed through both houses of Congress by overwhelming majorities. This (apparent) triumph was followed in short order by *Roe v. Wade* (1973), the Supreme Court's ruling that efforts to regulate abortion by the states were unconstitutional.[1]

Together, congressional action on the ERA and the Court's decision in *Roe v. Wade* triggered a powerful backlash. For many socially conservative Americans, "the ERA and abortion symbolized everything about feminism worth opposing" (Wolbrecht 2000, p. 40). Conservatives organized, entered the political fray, and often won. They blocked state ratification of the ERA, and through persuasion, pressure, litigation, and in some cases intimidation, they limited access to abortion.

This see-saw battle continues, and it takes many forms. In the end, however, the fight is primarily about one thing: whether the traditional place of women in society is a natural expression of their biological nature. Once the belief in biological destiny gives way, the whole arrangement between the sexes—a vast, entrenched, and integrated network of institutional rules and social practices—ceases to make much sense:

Women do and men don't gestate, breast-feed infants, and menstruate as a part of their biological character. So, too, women on the whole are smaller and lighter boned and muscled than are men. For these physical facts of life to have no appreciable social consequence would take a little organizing, but, at least by modern standards, not much. . . . It is not, then, the social consequences of innate sex differences that must be explained, but the way in which these differences were (and are) put forward as a warrant for our social arrangements, and, most important of all, the way in which the institutional workings of society ensured that this accounting would seem sound. (Goffman 1977, pp. 301–2)

From this point of view, the most important consequence of the modern women's movement is to weaken the doctrine that men and women are deeply and fundamentally different. For if it is conceded that the biological differences distinguishing men from women are slight, then the pervasive role that sex currently plays in the organization of society—from everyday interaction to the division of labor and reward—is open to challenge.

How does ethnocentrism enter this picture? Ethnocentrism, as we have said, is a readiness to divide society into in-groups and out-groups. As such, we expect to find an affinity between ethnocentrism, on the one hand, and the doctrine of biological differences between the sexes, on the other. Americans given to an ethnocentric outlook should be especially inclined to see the differences between men and women as natural. Insofar as that is true, then we should find ethnocentrism to be a source of opposition to the contemporary women's movement and to policies that challenge the sexual status quo.

ABORTION RIGHTS

We will start our empirical investigation with abortion, a focal point of contention and struggle. Before the Supreme Court decision in 1973, abortion was for the most part a private dilemma, not a political problem. After *Roe v. Wade*, abortion moved from the shadows to center stage. On the one side was the emergent women's movement, which claimed abortion as a right. This was a new argument: that the right to abortion was essential to the realization of women's full equality. From this side of the debate, abortion came to be seen as a "linchpin that held together a complicated set of assumptions about who women were, what their roles in life should be, what kinds of jobs they should take in the paid labor force, and how those jobs should be rewarded" (Luker 1984, p. 118). On the other side, mobilized in an important way by the *Roe v. Wade* decision (a "bolt out of the blue"), was the pro-life movement: Americans who were stunned and horrified by the

Court's decision. Pro-life activists regarded abortion as "unspeakable," the deliberate taking of innocent life.

Abortion is incendiary not just because of this one difference, sharp as it is, but also because activists on opposite sides of the issue hold radically different views about a whole range of consequential matters. As Luker (1984) adroitly shows, differences over abortion coexist with differences over the nature of men and women (whether they are naturally, intrinsically different), the meaning of motherhood, the place of sex in marriage, the importance of religion, and more. In short, the debate over abortion is not an academic exercise; it goes to the core of how people define their place in society, the value and worth they attach to how they live their lives.

This debate, of course, is far from over. It has become a recurrent matter of partisan politics (Adams 1997), and it continues to draw serious attention from the courts. In the spring of 2007, in a five-to-four decision, the Supreme Court outlawed a particularly gruesome procedure: intact dilation and extraction to the medical profession; partial-birth abortion to its opponents; late-term abortion to its (relatively few) supporters.

From the National Election Study, we have available a good range of questions on abortion: five distinct questions in all, scattered across several studies from 1992 to 2004.[2] By these various measures, public opinion on abortion seems to be moderate and qualified. Americans generally support a woman's right to make this decision for herself: 36.1 percent say that a woman should always be able to obtain a legal abortion as a matter of personal choice, while only 14.3 percent say that abortion should *never* be permitted. A clear majority—55.8 percent—strongly support a ban on partial-birth/late-term abortion. More than one-third of the American public (35.7 percent) strongly favors a statute that would require a married woman who intends to have an abortion to notify her husband beforehand. A near majority (47.8 percent) strongly oppose using government funds to help pay for abortions for women who cannot afford them. And an overwhelming majority of Americans—69.2 percent—strongly favors a law in their state that would require women under the age of eighteen to obtain parental consent before undergoing an abortion.

To what degree are differences in opinion on these matters due to ethnocentrism? To find out we estimated a standard model in the standard way.[3] The results, presented in table 8.1, reveal that ethnocentrism and opinion on abortion are completely unconnected to one another. Religion makes a huge difference, as we expected. Education, partisanship, and egalitarianism matter as well. But ethnocentrism does not. The estimated effect of ethnocentrism is positive in three cases, negative in the other two, and in only one case exceeds statistical significance.

TABLE 8.1. Ethnocentrism and opposition to abortion

	Abortion right	Late-term/ partial-birth	Government subsidy	Spousal notification	Parental consent
Ethnocentrism	0.22	−0.47	−0.57*	0.18	0.34
	0.29	0.32	0.31	0.21	0.27
Importance of	1.32***	0.85***	0.99***	0.73***	0.69***
Religion	0.15	0.17	0.16	0.13	0.15
Religious	0.63***	0.27*	0.56***	0.50***	0.29**
Doctrine	0.15	0.16	0.15	0.12	0.14
Partisanship	−0.50***	−0.77***	−0.84***	−0.18*	−0.41***
	0.13	0.14	0.14	0.10	0.12
Education	−0.38**	0.07	−0.37**	−0.60***	−0.41**
	0.17	0.19	0.18	0.14	0.17
Authoritarianism	0.43***	0.09	0.13	0.46***	0.38**
	0.16	0.17	0.16	0.12	0.15
Egalitarianism	−0.29	−0.46*	−0.63***	−0.17	−.55***
	0.23	0.25	0.24	0.18	0.21
Female	−0.34***	−0.01	0.02	−0.51***	0.02
	0.08	0.09	0.09	0.07	0.08
N	875	838	847	1511	1258
Effect of E	0.30→0.36	0.62→0.49	0.64→0.48	0.58→0.62	0.78→0.85

Source: 2004 NES (columns 1–3); 1992 NES (column 4); and 2000 NES (column 5).

Note: Table entry is the ordered probit regression coefficient with standard errors below. The model also controls for religious denomination, race, ethnicity, and political awareness. Full results appear in the Web appendix. The bottom row of the table gives the effect associated with a shift in Ethnocentrism from Low (−0.1) to High (0.6) in the predicted probability of opposing abortion.

***$p < 0.01$; **$p < 0.05$; *$p < 0.10$, two-tailed.

What we see in table 8.1, moreover, holds for men and women alike. In a second round of analysis, we reestimated the standard model testing the idea that the effects of ethnocentrism on opinion in this domain might differ between men and women—in particular, that the effect of ethnocentrism might be positive for men and negative for women. This test requires adding a single interaction term to the standard model:

$$y^* = \beta_0 + \beta_1 \text{Ethnocentrism} + \beta_2[\text{Ethnocentrism} \times \text{Female}]$$
$$+ \beta_3 \text{Importance of Religion} + \ldots + \varepsilon$$

where β_1 gives the effect of ethnocentrism for men and $\beta_1 + \beta_2$ gives the effect of ethnocentrism for women.[4] In all five cases of opinion on abortion, we found the estimated effect of ethnocentrism to be essentially the same for men as for women. This means that for men and women alike, ethnocentrism has nothing to do with opinion on abortion.[5]

The same disconnect appears when we turn to the General Social Survey. The 1990 and 2000 editions of GSS that include our standard measure of ethnocentrism also carry a set of questions on abortion that complements those from the NES that we have just analyzed. The GSS questions take up a series of circumstances under which abortion might be legally permitted (for example, rape, birth defect, an unplanned and unwanted pregnancy).[6] Most Americans appear to be moral relativists on abortion. Very few say that abortion should be legal under *no* circumstances. Very few say that abortion should be legal under *all* circumstances. Most Americans say that abortion should be legal under some circumstances and illegal under others.

Does ethnocentrism predict a relatively hard line on abortion, measured in this way? No, it does not. Not in 1990 and not in 2000. And once again, not for men and not for women.[7]

WOMEN'S ISSUES

By "women's issues" we mean to point to those policies that have greater and more immediate impact on women than on men—issues, one could say, that concern women as women.[8] Ransacking recent editions of the NES and GSS, we found five policy questions that fit the bill. Together, the set offers reasonably comprehensive coverage, taking up equal opportunity in employment, affirmative action, sexual harassment, child care, and family leave.[9]

A number of these policies have their origins in the 1960s. Equal employment opportunity, for example, goes back to the contentious debate in Congress over civil rights legislation. In 1964, in a desperate effort to sabotage the Civil Rights bill, then before the floor of the House, one Howard W. Smith, Democrat from Virginia, moved that a ban on sex discrimination in employment be added to Title VII. Smith's aim "was to complicate the debate and confuse the liberals" (Burstein 1985, p. 23), to sink Title VII through ridicule. His maneuver failed; the measure passed; and when Lyndon Johnson signed the Civil Rights Act into law later on that summer, discrimination on grounds of race, color, religion, national origin, or *sex* became illegal.

Forty years later, the American public is not yet entirely sold on this idea. In the fall of 2004, something short of a majority of Americans (45.6 percent) said that if women were not getting equal treatment in jobs, the government in Washington ought to see to it that they do.

A year after passage of Title VII and the Civil Rights Act, in his famous commencement address at Howard University, President Johnson argued that the country was entering a new stage in the struggle for racial justice, and that this would entail "not just equality as a right and a theory but equality as a fact and as a result." Later on that fall, Johnson issued Executive

Order 11246, which required federal contractors to develop "affirmative action programs" to comply with Title VII. Guidelines for compliance were
drawn up in a crisis atmosphere—"when," as Christopher Jencks (1992, p. 58)
put it, "cities were burning and racial warfare seemed a real possibility." Under these circumstances, affirmative action came to mean the imposition of
numerical goals and strict timetables necessary for the "prompt achievement of full and equal employment opportunity." In October 1967, under
pressure from the National Organization of Women, Johnson added sex as
a category covered by his executive order. In principle at least, women became beneficiaries of federal affirmative action programs.

In the fall of 2000, by a large majority (64.8 percent), Americans endorsed a relatively mild form of affirmative action for women, agreeing that
due to past discrimination, employers should make special efforts to hire
and promote qualified women.[10]

By 1980, the Equal Employment Opportunity Commission (EEOC) was
interpreting harassment as a form of unlawful employment discrimination
under Title VII. Few claims were brought, however, and the issue was seldom discussed. Then, in the fall of 1991 came the confirmation hearings of
Clarence Thomas, President George H. W. Bush's selection to replace Thur-
good Marshall on the Supreme Court. Anita Hill's detailed accusations that
Thomas had harassed her when she was working as an attorney under his
supervision, first in the civil rights division of the Department of Education
and then at the EEOC itself, caused a sensation. Complaints poured into
EEOC, and public concern rose.

In the wake of the Thomas-Hill hearings, most Americans (57.2 percent)
thought that too little was being done to protect women from being sexually harassed in the workplace.[11]

Child care, the subject of our fourth question, came relatively late to the
women's rights agenda. Bills began to appear in Congress in the early 1980s.
The political parties tended to agree on the importance of child care but
split over how it should be provided. Democrats favored a strong federal
role to guarantee universal access to certified child-care programs; Republicans preferred giving tax credits for child care and encouraging private enterprises to expand child-care facilities.

In the fall of 1992, a majority of Americans (50.5 percent) wanted the
government to spend more on child care; only 9.9 percent wanted to spend
less.

Finally, proposals on family leave emerged a bit later still. Patricia Schroeder introduced the first bill in Congress in 1985. It was formulated to require all businesses to provide job-protected leaves for employees with urgent family responsibilities. A Democratic Congress passed a mild version
of family leave, but it was vetoed by President Bush. The next Congress

TABLE 8.2. Ethnocentrism and opposition to "women's issues"

	Employment discrimination	Affirmative action	Sexual harassment	Spending on child care	Family leave
Ethnocentrism	−0.28	−0.54	−0.10	0.26	0.02
	0.30	0.52	0.21	0.20	0.23
Partisanship	−0.44***	−0.72***	−0.54***	−0.50***	−0.73***
	0.12	0.22	0.10	0.10	0.11
Egalitarianism	−2.51***	−1.14***	−1.15***	−1.47***	−0.94***
	0.24	0.40	0.18	0.17	0.20
Female	0.19**	−0.52***	−0.22***	−0.21***	−0.08
	0.08	0.14	0.07	0.07	0.08
N	876	278	1456	1536	1532

Source: 2004 NES (column 1); 2000 GSS (column 2); and 1992 NES (columns 3, 4, and 5).

Note: Table entry is the ordered probit regression coefficient with standard errors below. The model also controls for importance of religion, race, ethnicity, education, authoritarianism, and political awareness. Full results appear in the Web appendix. The bottom row of the table gives the effect associated with a shift in Ethnocentrism from Low (−0.1) to High (0.6) in the predicted probability of opposing "women's issues."

$***p < 0.01$; $**p < 0.05$; $*p < 0.10$, two-tailed.

passed the bill again, and as he had promised on the campaign trail, early in his first term, President Bill Clinton signed the Family and Medical Leave Act into law.

In the fall of 1992, only about one-third of the public (32.0 percent) favored a version of family leave that would require companies to allow up to six months of unpaid leave to employees who wished to spend time with their newborn child.[12]

What role does ethnocentrism play in motivating opposition to these various initiatives of special concern to women? The results, estimated in the usual way[13] and shown in table 8.2, suggest no role at all. In two cases the coefficient on ethnocentrism is positively signed (the predicted direction); in three cases the coefficient is negative; in none of the five does the coefficient on ethnocentrism attain statistical significance.[14] Opinions on women's issues reflect first and foremost the importance and priority Americans assign to egalitarianism. Partisanship and gender matter as well. But once again we see that ethnocentrism matters not at all. And once again, this conclusion holds for men and women in equal measure.[15]

"PUSHY WOMEN"

So far this chapter has told a story of failure. To our surprise, ethnocentrism has little to do with opposition to policies that challenge the traditional arrangement between the sexes. Terrorists, foreigners, illegal immigrants, homosexuals, and the like trigger ethnocentrism, but women do not. Perhaps because abortion rights or family leave do not conjure up, for most Americans, a clear and demonizable adversary, ethnocentrism falls out of the picture.

If this is right, at least to a first approximation, then ethnocentrism might still be activated by women of a particular kind: namely, radical feminists. In current folklore, radical feminists are angry, see harassment and discrimination everywhere, and are constantly pushing for change. They are "feminazis," to use the talk radio term.

One question present in the 2004 NES gets close to what we have in mind. There respondents were asked whether women who complain about sexual harassment cause more problems than they solve. The issue here would appear to be not women in general, and not even sexual harassment as a problem, but rather the trouble made by the kind of woman who complains about sexual harassment.

And on this proposition we find a very powerful effect of ethnocentrism. As shown in figure 8.1, ethnocentric Americans are much more likely to say that women who complain about harassment cause more problems than they solve. (The effect is as strong for women as it is for men.) Nothing else

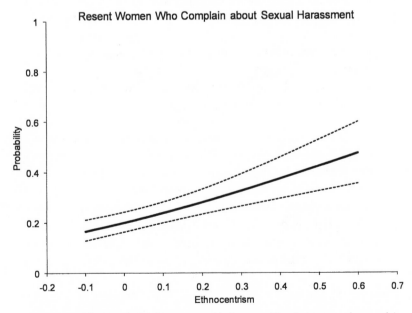

FIGURE 8.1. Ethnocentrism and agreement with the proposition that women who complain about sexual harassment cause more problems than they solve. Predicted probabilities with 95 percent confidence intervals. Source: 2004 NES.

in our analysis of issues raised by the women's movement is remotely like this. Not women in general, but women of a particular kind, trigger ethno-centrism.[16]

CONCLUSIONS AND IMPLICATIONS

The gay rights movement, examined in the previous chapter, poses a chal-lenge to conventional values and institutions that many Americans claim as fundamental. The same can be said for the contemporary women's move-ment, the subject of our analysis in this chapter. The similarities do not end there. In both cases, the challenge to the conventional moral order was ini-tially expressed through contentious political action, operating largely out-side of regular partisan party politics. The two challenges arose at roughly the same time. Both took inspiration and tactics from the civil rights move-ment. Both were greeted with widespread moral indignation. And both pro-voked a fierce and organized reaction from the Christian Right. And yet, de-spite these similarities, from the perspective of ethnocentrism, the gay rights movement and the women's movement could hardly be more different.

We found, on the one hand, that ethnocentrism plays a powerful role on gay rights. Ethnocentric Americans want no part of same-sex marriage or adoption of children by gay couples. They tend to disapprove of gays serv-ing in the military and of laws designed to protect gays against discrimina-tion on the job. They are apprehensive about catching AIDS. They find gay sex immoral. Predisposed as they are to divide the social world into qualita-tively distinct types, they believe that homosexuality is inborn and impos-sible to alter.

On the other hand, when it comes to the various issues raised by the women's movement, ethnocentrism simply vanishes. We found no effect of ethnocentrism on public opinion on policy dealing with women's place—not on abortion, not on equal opportunity in employment, affirmative ac-tion, sexual harassment, child care, or family leave.

Why might this be? We have already tipped our hand, suggesting that compared to homosexuals or immigrants, women as a broad social group-ing are less susceptible to demonization. This is a reflection, in part, of the unusual way that gender is spatially organized. Rather than being seques-tered away into enclaves of their own kind, women spend much of their adult lives in intimate relationship with men. This means that women are

separated from one another by the stake they acquire in the very organiza-tion which divides them. For instead of an employer or master, a woman is likely to have (through the course of her life) a father, a husband, and sons. And these males transmit to her enough of what they themselves possess or acquire to give her a vested interest in the corporation [of the family]. Defined as deeply different from men, each is yet linked to particular men through fundamental social bonds, placing her in a coalition with her menfolk against the whole of the rest of the world. (Goffman 1977, p. 308)

Out of this special arrangement emerge complicated emotions. Women are defined as less than men, but at the same time they are in certain respects idealized. Through gesture and various courtesies, men signal to women that they regard them as fragile and valuable, to be protected from the harsher sides of life. They are shown reverence for their role as mothers and placed on pedestals for their innocence, sensitivity, and kindness. If this is a lesser pantheon of virtues than the one reserved for men, it is a pantheon nonetheless (Goffman 1977). Insofar as men depend on women for sexual pleasure, progeny, and intimacy, hostility is not a winning play. "Men do not want solely the obedience of women," as John Stuart Mill famously put it, "they want their sentiments."[17]

In the next chapter we take up another contentious domain of domestic politics—welfare—which, as we will see, contains surprises of its own.

CHAPTER 9

Us versus Them in the American Welfare State

Writing in 1834, Charles Burroughs drew a distinction between the poor who deserved a helping hand and the "able-bodied poor" who did not. On one side, according to Burroughs, was the poverty that resulted from chance and the vagaries of fate; these unfortunate people should "claim our tenderest commiseration, our most liberal relief." And on the other side was the poverty "of wilful error, of shameful indolence, of vicious habits"; these poor deserve only our contempt.[1]

Burroughs's language may strike us as antique, but his sentiments are modern. Today, as in Burroughs's time, Americans are skeptical about government providing assistance to those in poverty. Today, as in Burroughs's time, support for welfare seems to depend on seeing the poor as victims of misfortune, people who are like us in some fundamental way.

This point is made more sharply by Ralph Waldo Emerson in his famous essay on self-reliance (1841). There Emerson argues for isolation and detachment, and for the necessity of renouncing society's fads and false obligations. He rejects sympathy and commiseration:

> Do not tell me, as a good man did to-day, of my obligation to put all poor men in good situations. Are they *my* poor? I tell thee, though foolish philanthropist, that I grudge the dollar, the dime, the cent I give to such men as do not belong to me and to whom I do not belong.[2]

As a general matter, we expect ethnocentrism to play an important role in public opinion on welfare. Why? Because the ethnocentrically inclined will be least likely to consider Americans in poverty as "their" poor.

More precisely, we expect ethnocentrism to play an important role in public opinion for certain kinds of welfare. The modern American welfare state is complicated, and we need to take this complexity into account. In particular, we must distinguish among three kinds of programs.[3]

The first is means-tested income transfers, programs like Aid to Families with Dependent Children (AFDC), food stamps, and Medicaid, which redistribute resources directly to poor and near-poor households. Many of these programs were either established or substantially enhanced as part of Lyndon Johnson's vision of the Great Society (Finegold 1988; Levitan and Taggart 1976; Patterson 1981). Since LBJ, government spending on these various forms of means-tested assistance has dramatically increased, interrupted on only two occasions: in the early 1980s as part of Ronald Reagan's goal to reduce the size and scope of the federal government; and in Bill Clinton's first term, as the president and Congress attempted to "end welfare as we know it." In 2005, total government outlays on means-tested transfer programs amounted to some $356 billion.[4]

The second broad category of programs is social insurance, financed largely by payroll taxes paid by the currently employed and their employers, with benefits going primarily to the retired, disabled, and unemployed. Social Security and unemployment insurance were established in the New Deal. After 1935, additional programs were placed under the broad umbrella of social insurance: benefits for surviving dependents in 1939; benefits for disabled workers in 1956; and in 1965, as part of President Johnson's War on Poverty, medical care for retirees, or Medicare. Over the same period, coverage and benefits provided by Social Security expanded, as more and more people were incorporated into the programs and as Congress repeatedly raised benefit levels (Derthick 1979). Since the 1960s, spending on social insurance has shot up enormously. In 2005, the federal government paid out more than $850 billion of benefits on Social Security and Medicare alone.[5]

The third aspect of the American welfare state consists of policies designed to enhance human capital. Head Start is perhaps the best-known example; other such programs include targeted aid to elementary schools, basic educational opportunity grants, the Job Corps, and the Job Training Partnership Act. Compared to means-tested welfare and social insurance, spending on human capital programs is modest. The federal government spent about $81 billion in fiscal year 2005 on all such education and training programs put together.[6]

If food stamps, Social Security, and Head Start are all part of the American welfare state, they differ from one another in significant ways: in their goals; in how they are funded and administered; in their scope and magnitude; and, most importantly for our purposes, in *whom they serve*. With this last difference in mind, let's revisit what we should expect of ethnocentrism in public opinion on welfare.

Our clearest expectation has to do with means-tested transfer programs. This part of the welfare state has few defenders. Public assistance is offensive to Americans who believe there is virtue in hard work and immorality in idleness. Derelict fathers, unwed mothers, so-called welfare queens: these are the undeserving poor, working the system, exploiting the misguided generosity of government. Ethnocentric Americans should be particularly prone to seeing the poor as categorically different, as deficient and undeserving. On this basis, we expect that the ethnocentric will be inclined to favor reducing welfare benefits, tightening eligibility, and otherwise turning welfare into work.

What to expect of relationships between ethnocentrism and opinion toward the other two types of social welfare programs is less clear. Unlike the undeserving poor, the beneficiaries of these programs escape denigration in popular discourse. On the contrary. In the case of social insurance programs, the beneficiaries are typically celebrated: they are hard-working, ordinary Americans who have paid their taxes and earned their due. In the case of human capital programs, investments are targeted primarily on young people who happen to have been born poor and who are taking steps to better themselves in that most endearingly American way, through education. Heading into the analysis, we saw no good reason why ethnocentrism would be an important force in opinion for these two aspects of welfare policy. On social insurance and human capital, we expected little of ethnocentrism. As we will see shortly, we were wrong.

PUBLIC OPINION ON WELFARE

The first thing to say about contemporary American opinion on welfare is that means-tested transfer policies are very unpopular. If it is not quite the case, as David Ellwood (1988, p. 4) once put it, that "everyone hates welfare," certainly many Americans do. They wish to cut back spending on food stamps, they would like to do the same to welfare programs (AFDC), and they strongly favor reforms that would restrict welfare benefits and tighten eligibility. In this way, programs like AFDC and food stamps are striking exceptions to the otherwise amply documented claim of Americans' operational liberalism. The American people say yes to roads and schools and to protecting the environment. But they say no, emphatically, to welfare.[7]

At the same time, most Americans treasure their social insurance programs. They want federal spending on Social Security to be increased or at least held constant. They reject the idea that Social Security benefits be taxed. They favor expanding the Medicare program to pay for nursing home care and long hospital stays. And in the late 1990s, most Americans wanted to spend the federal budget surplus to shore up Social Security and Medicare.[8]

Americans are also favorably inclined toward government programs designed to build human capital. They want to spend more on public schools and more on early education for poor children. They want government to provide college scholarships for good students from economically disadvantaged backgrounds. And they want to increase federal spending on Head Start. On these questions, the legendary American faith in education comes shining through.[9]

In sum, the American welfare state is complex, and at least some of that complexity in registered in public attitudes. The American people distinguish sharply among means-tested transfer programs like AFDC, social insurance programs like Social Security, and human capital programs like Head Start.[10] Of course, not everyone says no to welfare. And not everyone says yes to preschool education for poor children. Can variation in Americans' views on these topics be accounted for, at least in part, by ethnocentrism?

ETHNOCENTRISM AND THE WELFARE STATE AMONG WHITE AMERICANS

The answer is yes—more accurately, the answer is yes when it comes to the opinions of white Americans. Among black and Hispanic Americans, on issues of welfare, ethnocentrism matters not at all. Why this is so we will try to explain in the conclusion of the chapter. In the meantime, we will focus our attention on ethnocentrism and welfare among white Americans.

We estimate the effect of ethnocentrism on opinion in this domain in the usual manner.[11] In the domain of welfare, the standard model for opinion begins with partisanship. The American welfare state was created and expanded primarily by Democrats, and criticized and reformed in recent decades primarily by Republicans. It would be surprising if we did not see corresponding partisan differences in the general public. Also important within the standard model are political principles. Limited government and egalitarianism have played prominent roles in public debates over welfare. Americans have been encouraged to think about welfare and welfare reform in these terms, and our analysis of opinion will take this into account.[12] To the standard model we also add measures of benefits and costs, on the idea that those who rely on social welfare programs, or who may be likely to rely on them in the future, will be more likely to support them, whereas those who bear the costs of the programs with little expectation they will benefit from them, other things equal, will be least favorably disposed (Cook and Barrett 1992). We represent the benefits side of the ledger in several ways: recent bouts of unemployment, worries about losing one's job in the future, recent deterioration in family economic conditions, and age. Costs we measure in three ways: household income, home ownership (a proxy for wealth), and occupational status.[13]

TABLE 9.1. Ethnocentrism and white opinion on means-tested welfare

	Increase spending on welfare	Increase spending on food stamps	Provide more benefits with additional kids	Oppose time limit on welfare
Ethnocentrism	−0.73***	−0.48*	−1.19***	−1.44***
	0.27	0.25	0.26	0.27
Partisanship	0.56***	0.33**	0.13	0.25*
	0.14	0.13	0.13	0.13
Egalitarianism	1.53***	1.34***	1.19***	0.96***
	0.25	0.24	0.23	0.23
Limited government	−0.58***	−0.61***	−0.40***	−0.40***
	0.12	0.11	0.11	0.11
N	1034	1030	1005	1027
Effect of **E**	0.64→0.81	0.58→0.71	0.73→0.92	0.74→0.95

Source: 1996 NES.

Note: Table entry is the ordered probit regression coefficient with standard errors below. Dependent variables are coded such that higher values indicate more economically liberal views. Models also control for employment status, concerns about job security, household economic evaluations, household income, homeownership, occupational status, age, sex, education, and political awareness. Full results appear in the Web appendix. The bottom row of the table gives the effect associated with a shift in Ethnocentrism from Low (−0.1) to High (0.6) in the predicted probability of opposing means-tested welfare.

***$p < 0.01$; **$p < 0.05$; *$p < 0.10$, two-tailed.

Ethnocentrism and Means-Tested Welfare

Table 9.1 presents the findings on ethnocentrism and white Americans' views on means-tested social welfare programs, as assessed in the 1996 NES. As expected, ethnocentric whites are more likely to push for cuts in food stamps, to favor reductions in spending on welfare, to oppose increasing benefits to women on welfare if they have additional children, and to favor strict time limits on public assistance. Partisanship, egalitarianism, and limited government also contribute to opinion on welfare, and in the expected way. But with controls on partisanship and principles (and on costs, benefits, and all the rest), the effects of ethnocentrism are statistically significant and sizable in every case.[14]

Ethnocentrism and Social Insurance

Ethnocentrism also influences white Americans' opinions on social insurance programs, but here the effects run in the opposite direction. These results appear in table 9.2. On social insurance, ethnocentric whites support more benefits, not less. They favor increases in spending on Social Security, they oppose taxing Social Security benefits, they believe that Medicare coverage should be expanded, and they recommend that federal budget surpluses be used to insure the fiscal integrity of Social Security and Medicare. These results surprised us. We expected to find no systematic relationship between ethnocentrism and support for social insurance programs; what we found, instead, is a positive relationship. Granted, the positive effects of ethnocentrism on support for Social Security and Medicare are less impressive than are the negative effects of ethnocentrism on AFDC and food stamps. Granted, too, the positive effects do not always surpass conventional levels of statistical significance. So we could treat these unexpected results as anomalous, not worth puzzling over, and move on.

TABLE 9.2. Ethnocentrism and white support for social insurance

	Spend more on Social Security	Oppose Social Security tax	Expand Medicare	Spend surplus on Social Security/ Medicare
Ethnocentrism	0.56**	0.49**	0.43*	0.82***
	0.23	0.25	0.23	0.29
Partisanship	0.20*	−0.14	0.37***	0.23*
	0.11	0.12	0.11	0.14
Egalitarianism	0.39**	−0.00	0.61***	0.49**
	0.19	0.20	0.19	0.23
Limited government	−0.36***	0.02	−0.36***	−0.61***
	0.10	0.11	0.10	0.12
Age	0.10	0.47***	0.05	0.59***
	0.13	0.14	0.13	0.16
Education	−0.35**	−0.81***	−0.46***	−0.61***
	0.16	0.17	0.16	0.19
Political awareness	−0.78***	−0.38**	−0.57***	−0.68***
	0.16	0.17	0.16	0.16
N	1309	1285	1276	1012
Effect of **E**	0.41→0.56	0.86→0.92	0.83→0.89	0.89→0.96

Source: 1992 NES (first three columns) and 2000 NES (last column).

Note: Table entry is the ordered probit regression coefficient with standard errors below. Models also control for employment status, concerns about job security, household economic evaluations, household income, homeownership, occupational status, and sex. Full results appear in the Web appendix. The bottom row of the table gives the effect associated with a shift in Ethnocentrism from Low (−0.1) to High (0.6) in the predicted probability of supporting social insurance.

***$p < 0.01$; **$p < 0.05$; *$p < 0.10$, two-tailed.

That would be a mistake. We are convinced that the positive effects of ethnocentrism on support for social insurance are real. We uncovered the same result—that ethnocentrism helps to build support for social insurance programs among white Americans—wherever we looked, and we looked in quite a few places. For example, in the 1990 General Social Survey, Americans were asked (among many other things) whether government was spending too little on Social Security, whether government bore responsibility for the well-being of the elderly, and whether government should increase retirement benefits. In each of these cases, ethnocentric whites were more likely to say yes: spend more, help more, give more. Similarly, we find ethnocentric whites recommending that the federal government invest more on Social Security not only in the 1992 NES (as shown in table 9.2), but in the 1996, 2000, and 2004 installments of the NES as well. When it comes to providing pensions and health care to the retired and elderly, ethnocentrism appears to be a force for liberalism, for a more generous welfare state.[15]

Why might this be? The answer, we suspect, has to do with the way that Social Security is framed by elites and understood by the public (Winter 2006). From the very beginning, Social Security has been presented as social insurance in return for work and investment. In this way, Social Security is understood to be an *earned* right, earned by virtue of a lifetime of effort. In his message to Congress in 1935, President Franklin D. Roosevelt argued that social insurance programs "derive their social legitimacy from the achievements of beneficiaries." More than forty years later, President Gerald Ford made the same point, calling Social Security "a vital obligation each generation has to those who have worked hard and contributed to it all their lives." A second important aspect of the framing of Social Security for our purposes is the repeated invocation of in-group terminology. In defending and praising Social Security (a popular activity in and out of Washington), political leaders say that Social Security is for *us*: for the people, for our parents, for our children, for ourselves, for Americans, for us all.

Both these features—the connection between Social Security and work and the connection between Social Security and in-group vocabulary—imply, in a subtle way, that Social Security is for white people. In the American context, work, effort, determination, and the avoidance of idleness are all linked to whiteness. As Winter puts it, "Work—and the independent ownership of the fruits of that labor—has historically been at the center of what it has meant to be white in America" (2006, p. 402; on this point, see Roediger 1999). Likewise, the presentation of Social Security as benefiting "everyone," expressed over and over by white politicians, may build a symbolic association between Social Security and whiteness (Gaertner and Dovidio 2000; Winter 2006).

TABLE 9.3. In-group pride, out-group hostility, and white support for social insurance

	Spend more on Social Security	Oppose Social Security tax	Expand Medicare	Spend surplus on Social Security/ Medicare
In-group pride	0.79***	0.78***	0.66**	0.98***
	0.26	0.28	0.26	0.31
Out-group hostility	0.13	−0.06	−0.01	0.46
	0.31	0.34	0.32	0.36
N	1309	1285	1276	1012

Source: 1992 NES (first three columns) and 2000 NES (last column).

Note: Table entry is the ordered probit regression coefficient with standard errors below. In-group pride is coded from 0 (negative) to 1 (positive assessments). Out-group hostility is coded from 0 (positive) to 1 (negative assessments). Models also control for partisanship, egalitarianism, limited government, employment status, concerns about job security, household economic evaluations, household income, homeownership, age, occupational status, sex, education, and political awareness. Full results appear in the Web appendix.

***$p < 0.01$; **$p < 0.05$; *$p < 0.10$, two-tailed.

If this argument is on track, then the positive effect of ethnocentrism on white Americans' support for Social Security and for social insurance programs more broadly should be a manifestation, principally, of in-group favoritism. And if this turned out to be true, it would represent an exception to the general rule. We claim that the effects of ethnocentrism on public opinion reflect *both* attachment to the in-group *and* disdain for out-groups. For the most part, this is what we have found. The war on terrorism, Desert Storm, foreign aid and humanitarian assistance, immigration, gay rights: in all these cases, the important role played by ethnocentrism entails both in-group loyalty and out-group hostility.

But here we expect something different. When it comes to Social Security and Medicare among white Americans, we expect the positive effects of ethnocentrism to be channeled primarily through in-group pride—on the idea that these programs are understood to be for hard-working, tax-paying, white people—and rather little through out-group hostility.

To see if this is so, we repeated the analysis reported in table 9.2, after first breaking the ethnocentrism scale into two separate components, one pertaining to in-group pride, the other to out-group hostility. The findings, shown in table 9.3, could hardly be clearer. White support for Social Security and Medicare arises importantly from in-group favoritism and little or not at all from denigration of out-groups. When white Americans, under the influence of ethnocentrism, say do more, spend more on social insurance programs, they seem to be saying, in effect, do more, spend more, on *us*.

TABLE 9.4. Ethnocentrism and white opinion on human capital programs

	Increase spending on public schools	Increase spending on preschool enrichment	Increase spending on early education in poor neighborhoods	Increase spending on college Scholarships	Increase spending on Head Start
Ethnocentrism	-0.03	-0.07	-0.53	-0.33	-0.72**
	0.54	0.50	0.47	0.48	0.34
Partisanship	-0.18	0.28	0.40*	0.08	0.24
	0.25	0.25	0.22	0.22	0.16
Egalitarianism	1.14***	1.38***	0.52*	0.45	0.68***
	0.41	0.45	0.29	0.29	0.20
Limited government	-0.86***	-0.72***	-0.23	-0.40	-0.38**
	0.22	0.24	0.26	0.26	0.19
N	348	338	263	264	465
Effect of **E**	0.78→0.78	0.68→0.66	0.93→0.86	0.94→0.91	0.79→0.61

Source: 2000–2002 NES Panel (first two columns) and 1990 GSS (last three columns).

Note: Table entry is the ordered probit regression coefficient with standard errors below. Models also control for employment status, household economic evaluations, household income, age, occupational status, sex, education. NES models also control for concerns about job security, homeownership, and political awareness. Full results appear in the Web appendix. The bottom row of the table gives the effect associated with a shift in Ethnocentrism from Low (−0.1) to High (0.6) in the predicted probability of supporting increased spending on human capital programs.

***$p < 0.01$; **$p < 0.05$; *$p < 0.10$, two-tailed.

Ethnocentrism and Human Capital

Turning now to the third type of welfare policy, table 9.4 reveals that ethnocentrism is largely irrelevant for white Americans' views on programs that invest in human capital. Funding for public schools, support for preschool programs and educational enrichment for poor children, college scholarships for high-achieving students from poor families: none of these seems to engage ethnocentrism. The effect of ethnocentrism in this domain of welfare policy is notable in only a single case: Head Start, where increasing ethnocentrism is associated with decreasing support. In general, however, and in line with our original expectations, ethnocentrism has little or nothing to do with white opinion on government programs designed to build human capital.

Why, alone among the various welfare policies concerned with human capital, does Head Start activate ethnocentrism? Why does Head Start activate ethnocentrism but federal spending on preschool and early education for poor children does not—since Head Start *is* federal spending on preschool and early education for poor children?

Operation Head Start began as part of Lyndon Johnson's War on Poverty. It was based on the premise that positive preschool experiences could teach poor children the skills they needed to compete on an equal footing in elementary school. Hundreds of Head Start programs were run out of community agencies. Although the programs were intended to reach poor children without regard to race, they primarily served poor black children. Head Start became embroiled in the sharp debates that arose over the management and effectiveness of the Johnson administration's antipoverty policies generally. As the policies became controversial, and as riots spread through American cities, news coverage and political rhetoric racialized the War on Poverty: the poor were black, and the policies were failing (Burtless 1994; Gilens 1999; Quadagno 1994). Perhaps Head Start activates ethnocentrism because, alone among the policies presented in table 9.4, Head Start is presumed to be for black children.[16]

RÉSUMÉ OF RESULTS

We have seen that on matters of welfare, ethnocentrism propels white Americans in opposite directions: toward a smaller, more frugal welfare state when it comes to redistributing resources to the poor, but toward a more complete and magnanimous welfare state when it comes to providing pensions and health care to the elderly. Figure 9.1 provides a convenient summary. The graphs present the relationship between ethnocentrism and opinion on three different aspects of the welfare state: government spending on (means-tested) welfare, on Social Security, and on Head Start.

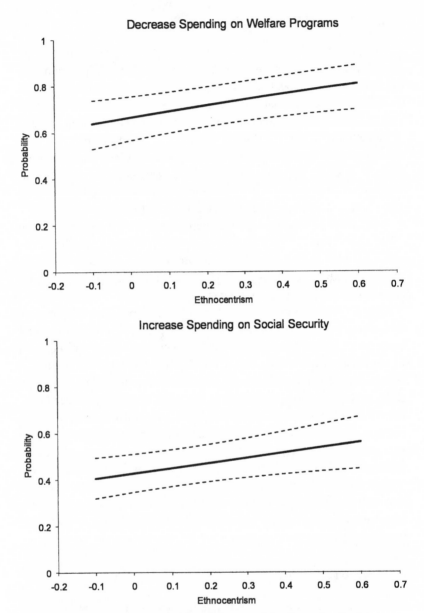

FIGURE 9.1. Ethnocentrism and white opinion on social welfare policy. Predicted probabilities with 95 percent confidence intervals. Estimates from tables 9.1, 9.2, and 9.4. Source: 1992 and 1996 NES; 1990 GSS.

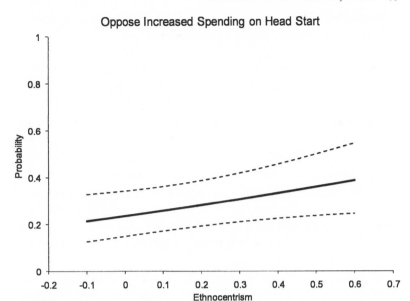

FIGURE 9.1. (*continued*)

ACTIVATION (THE COLOR OF WELFARE)

We have suggested that ethnocentrism becomes relevant for white Americans' views on welfare policy when policy is racialized: that is, when the benefits of the various programs are understood to go not to poor or elderly or children, but to poor who are black, elderly who are white, and to children who are black. Under the influence of ethnocentrism, when white Americans consider welfare policy, they seem to be asking themselves: welfare for whom? And in answering this question, they seem to have racial distinctions very much in mind. Put in our theoretical vocabulary, the activation of ethnocentrism in the realm of welfare requires resonance, and resonance is well provided when the beneficiaries of policy are understood in racial terms—when the beneficiaries of policy are like us or different from us in racial terms.

Is this really so? We can test this conjecture in a sharp and pointed way by analyzing a set of four experiments—real experiments, ones that feature random assignment to precisely designed treatments. Two of these were embedded in the 1990 GSS and the other two were designed as part of the 2000–2002 NES Panel. All deal with polices designed to build human capital of the sort that we have been examining here. In each case, the experiment entails varying the description of the beneficiaries of the policy, with respondents randomly assigned to one version of the question or the other. For example, in one of the experiments present in the 2002 NES interview, those interviewed were asked either:

Should federal spending on pre-school and early education for *poor chil-dren* be increased, decreased, or kept about the same?

or

Should federal spending on pre-school and early education for *black chil-dren* be increased, decreased, or kept about the same?

The other three experiments draw similar contrasts: between college scholarships *for children from economically disadvantaged backgrounds* who maintain good grades as against college scholarships *for black children* who maintain good grades; between spending more money on the schools in *poor* neighborhoods, especially for preschool and early education programs as against spending more money on the schools in *black* neighborhoods, especially for preschool and early education programs; and, in a subtle at-tempt at racialization, between federal spending on *public schools* and fed-eral spending on *big city schools.*

What happens when programs designed to build human capital are tar-geted on black children? The first thing that happens is white support de-clines sharply: 70.1 percent of white Americans want to increase federal spending on preschool and early education for poor children; just 44.4 per-cent want to do the same for black children. While 35.2 percent strongly fa-vor providing special college scholarships for students from economically disadvantaged backgrounds, just 15.9 percent want to do the same for high-achieving black students. Next, 27.5 percent strongly favor spending more on schools in poor neighborhoods; only 17.1 percent strongly favor spend-ing more on schools in black neighborhoods. And finally, while 71.4 per-cent of white Americans favor increasing government spending on public schools, just 48.5 percent favor increasing government spending on big city schools.[17]

The other thing that happens when human capital programs are targeted on black children is that ethnocentrism suddenly becomes a powerful force behind white opinion. These results, presented in coefficient form in table 9.5 and in graphical form in figure 9.2, reveal a striking transformation in the power of ethnocentrism. Ethnocentrism, by and large, is irrelevant to support for human capital programs when the benefits go to poor children, but highly relevant when the benefits are intended for black children.[18]

These results support our specific conjecture concerning the importance of ethnocentrism for Head Start—that Head Start activates ethnocentrism because it is understood to be a program serving black children. More im-portant, they support our general claim that the activation of ethnocentrism in the realm of welfare requires that the beneficiaries of welfare policy are understood in racial terms.

TABLE 9.5. Ethnocentrism and white opinion on human capital programs—Targeted either on poor Americans or on black Americans

	Increase federal spending on early education for		Provide college scholarships to		Increase spending on early education programs in		Increase federal spending on	
	Poor children	Black children	Poor students	Black students	Poor neighborhoods	Black neighborhoods	Public schools	Big city schools
Ethnocentrism	−0.07	−1.13**	−0.33	−0.69†	−0.53	−1.42***	−0.03	−0.79*
	0.50	0.52	0.48	0.46	0.47	0.46	0.54	0.48
N	338	345	264	257	263	257	348	334
Effect of E	0.68→0.66	0.46→0.18	0.94→0.91	0.87→0.74	0.93→0.86	0.91→0.64	0.78→0.78	0.58→0.37

Source: 2000–2002 NES Panel (first two columns and last two columns) and 1990 GSS (third through sixth columns).

Note: Table entry is the ordered probit regression coefficient with standard errors below. Models also control for employment status, household economic evaluations, household income, age, occupational status, sex, education. NES models also control for concerns about job security, homeownership, and political awareness. Full results appear in the Web appendix. The bottom row of the table gives the effect associated with a shift in Ethnocentrism from Low (−0.1) to High (0.6) in the predicted probability of supporting increased spending on human capital programs.

***$p < 0.01$; **$p < 0.05$; *$p < 0.10$, two-tailed.

†$p < 0.13$, two-tailed.

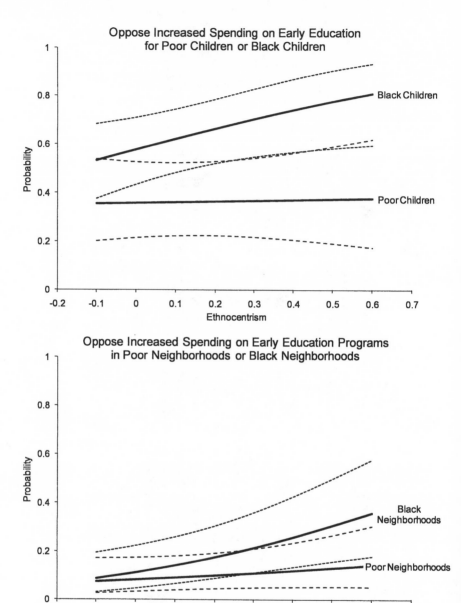

FIGURE 9.2. Ethnocentrism and white opposition to human capital programs—targeted either on poor Americans or on black Americans. Predicted probabilities with 95 percent confidence intervals. Estimates from table 9.5. Source: 2000–2002 NES Panel; 1990 GSS.

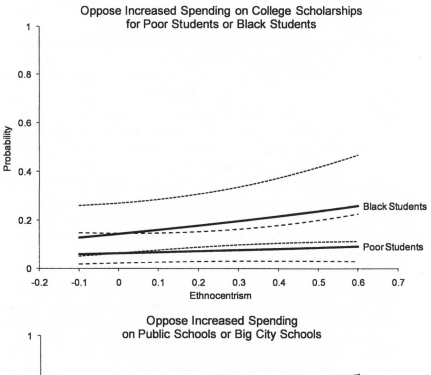

Oppose Increased Spending on College Scholarships for Poor Students or Black Students

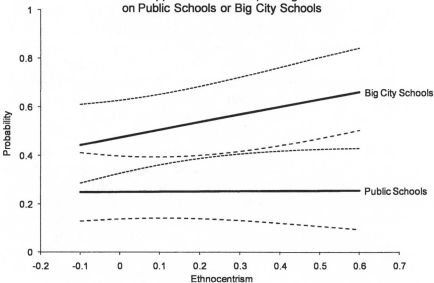

Oppose Increased Spending on Public Schools or Big City Schools

FIGURE 9.2. (*continued*)

CONCLUSIONS AND IMPLICATIONS

The notion that government might be responsible for the welfare of its citizens came late to the United States. Apart from a generous pension plan for elderly Civil War veterans and their dependents, the U.S. government played little direct role in the social and economic well-being of its citizens until FDR and the New Deal. Even then, forceful government action required a remarkable convergence of circumstance: a deepening economic crisis, the failure of unregulated capitalism, a titanic realignment of political forces, and strong public pressure (Orloff 1988; Skocpol 1992).

Under these extraordinary conditions, the Roosevelt administration moved cautiously. The president worried that federal initiatives might be found unconstitutional by the Supreme Court. He anticipated the states' rights arguments that the southern wing of his party would launch against his proposals. And he was mindful that state programs of social relief were well entrenched. In the end, his recommendations were measured. Roosevelt proposed a federal old-age insurance program, paid for by worker and employer contributions (what we think of today as Social Security); unemployment insurance, with considerable state discretion; and public assistance, administered by the states and subsidized by the federal government, directed to the needy, aged, dependent children, and the blind.

During the ensuing congressional deliberations, southern Democrats succeeded in overruling the president's recommendation that all employed persons be included in the unemployment and old-age insurance programs; agricultural and domestic workers were set to one side. Southern Democrats defeated plans to impose national standards in the old-age assistance program. And they prevailed as well by investing states with wide discretion in setting benefit levels and eligibility requirements for public assistance. All this had the consequence of drastically limiting the benefits black Americans would be able to claim from their government. That from the very beginning the welfare state was, in effect, for white people has a strong contemporary resonance with public attitudes, as we have seen here (Orloff 1988; Quadagno 1988, 1994; Finegold 1988; Lieberman 1998; Davies and Derthick 1997).

Indeed, race has been a persistent and notable theme throughout our analysis. It is the reason why (among white Americans) ethnocentrism goes one way on public assistance and the opposite way on social insurance. Ethnocentrism pushes Americans—white Americans—toward a smaller, more tight-fisted welfare state when it comes to redistributing resources to poor black people, but simultaneously toward a more complete and magnanimous welfare state when it comes to providing pensions and health care to elderly white people. And race supplies the reason why ethnocentrism is switched on or off when it comes to programs designed to build human capital.

Race also identifies where ethnocentrism has important effects (among whites) and where it does not (among blacks and Hispanics). Among blacks and Hispanics, we turn up no effect of ethnocentrism at all. It is not that black and Hispanic opinion on welfare policy is unpredictable. On the contrary, opinion is quite predictable, but the prediction comes entirely from considerations other than ethnocentrism. It comes from partisanship: Democrats are consistently more inclined to spend more on welfare and spend more on Social Security than are Republicans; from belief in limited government: those pressing for smaller government want to reduce spending on means-tested welfare and on social insurance programs; and from self-interest: income predicts opinion on public assistance while age predicts opinion on Social Security. For black and Hispanic Americans, the standard model works fine.[19] Yet for these Americans, on matters of welfare, ethnocentrism matters not at all. Why?

Here's our best guess. We have argued that ethnocentrism works the way it does among white Americans in the domain of welfare because this domain is racialized: means-tested programs like AFDC and food stamps are understood by whites to largely benefit shiftless black people; social insurance programs like Social Security and Medicare are understood by whites to largely benefit hard-working white people. Such racialization takes place through repeated pairings of race and welfare, first in elite discourse and then in everyday conversation and thinking. It is subtle, in that race is usually only implied. In the aftermath of the civil rights movement, political appeals based in white supremacy or fears of racial amalgamation are no longer acceptable. Public speech on race has become calibrated, cautious. Officials are careful what they say. They speak in a kind of code (Kinder and Sanders 1996; Mendelberg 2001).

Such language conveys the idea that means-tested welfare goes to the undeserving—individuals of color—and that Social Security goes to the deserving—individuals who are white. Racial code is concocted by white speakers and intended for white audiences. For the most part, neither black nor Hispanic American leaders speak this language; nor are black and Hispanic people tuned into this language. They may make the understandable mistake of believing that poverty, pension, and health care programs are for all Americans—not just for their racial group, and not just for other racial groups, but for the public as a whole. And so partisanship matters, and principles matter, and interest matters, but ethnocentrism does not.

CHAPTER 10

Ethnocentrism in Black and White

Beginning with constitutional arguments over the definition of citizenship, issues of race have often taken center stage in American politics. The debate over slavery and secession, the Civil War and Reconstruction, the civil rights movement, on up to contemporary arguments over affirmative action and fair representation: race has been and remains today a central theme of American political life.

Put another way, race in America is a nearly perfect instance of what Charles Tilly (1998) calls a "durable inequality." Inequality refers to differential access to valued resources: wealth, social standing, and power. Durable means that such inequalities are reproduced across generations and time. According to Tilly, durable inequalities are generated and perpetuated by two basic social mechanisms: discrimination and exclusion. Working together, discrimination and exclusion make possible the entrenchment of severe, categorical inequality.

Perhaps the most extreme example of American categorical inequality is provided by chattel slavery. Slavery is long gone, of course, and racial discrimination and segregation are declining. Nevertheless, important inequalities across racial lines remain, and they often find expression in politics. That racial categories are social constructs, not biological ones, does nothing to diminish this point. Today, as in the past, social, legal, economic, and political opportunities are structured, in part, by race.[1]

Taking up the role of ethnocentrism in American public opinion on race has the virtue of forcing us to confront a fundamental issue. Two fundamental issues, actually. In the public opinion literature, the standard explanation for black Americans' views on such matters as school integration or affirmative action emphasizes the primacy of in-group attachment (e.g., Dawson 1994; Gurin, Hatchett, and Jackson 1989; Tate 1993). Black Americans identify more or less closely with their racial group, and this, according to the standard account, explains variation in their policy opinions on race. At the same time, the standard explanation for white Americans' views on matters of race emphasizes the primacy of prejudice (e.g., Kinder and Sanders 1996; Sears, Sidanius, and Bobo 2000). White Americans feel more or less animosity toward blacks, and this, according to the standard account, explains variation in their policy opinions on race. This means that examining ethnocentrism in the realm of race requires us to clarify the relationship between ethnocentrism and group identification (among African Americans), and between ethnocentrism and prejudice (among white Americans).

Ethnocentrism, group identification, and prejudice bear a family resemblance to one other—they are conceptual cousins—but they are not the same. The domain of race policy provides an excellent venue for sorting out the differences.[2]

OPINION IN THE REALM OF RACE

In recent years, the National Election Study has carried an extensive set of policy questions relevant to race. Before we are through, we will analyze seven in all: school integration, fair employment, federal spending on programs for blacks, affirmative action in hiring, racial quotas in college admissions, affirmative action for companies that discriminate, and the government's obligation to make special efforts to assist blacks. These questions touch new and evolving issues (like affirmative action) as well as mature and stable ones (school integration). Some invoke the federal government, others do not. Some refer to employment or income, others to education. And some emphasize equality of opportunity, others equality of result. All this variety is an asset; it means that we can ascertain whatever role ethnocentrism plays in the domain of race free from the worry that our results are limited to a particular kind of policy. Put more positively, in the realm of race, we can test the power of ethnocentrism broadly.[3]

A striking feature of opinion within this realm is how decisively blacks and whites disagree with each other. We see this vividly on each of the seven policies under examination here. Consider this typical example: whereas 89.2 percent of African Americans in the fall of 2000 supported the idea that the government in Washington should see to it that black people get fair treatment in jobs, just 38.1 percent of whites did so. As a general matter, racial differences in opinion dwarf differences associated with other social cleavages—class, generation, religion, or sex. The difference between blacks and whites over matters of race policy add up to more than a gap or a simple disagreement; they constitute, as Kinder and Sanders (1996) once put it, a racial divide.[4]

We expect ethnocentrism to contribute to the racial divide in opinion in two ways: first, by moving African Americans to the left on matters of race; and second, by moving white Americans to the right. Let's see.

ETHNOCENTRISM IN THE REALM OF RACE AMONG BLACK AMERICANS

We'll begin with African Americans, estimating the effect of ethnocentrism in the standard way. Here the standard model includes measures of education, equality, limited government, moral traditionalism, political awareness, and sex, as well as ethnocentrism. Estimating effects among African Americans alone runs us into a problem—too few cases—and we solve it by combining NES surveys to build an adequate sample. Pooling the 1992, 1996, 2000, and 2004 editions of the NES generates nearly six hundred cases of African Americans. With the pooled data, we can analyze black Americans' opinions on three of the NES race policy questions: fair employment (which appeared on all four surveys), affirmative action in hiring (appearing in every survey but the 2000 NES), and the government's obligation to make special efforts to assist blacks (appearing in all four).[5]

The results, presented in table 10.1, indicate that ethnocentrism has a consistent and sizable effect on opinion. The more ethnocentric African

TABLE 10.1. Ethnocentrism and support for liberal racial policy among African Americans

	Fair employment	Hiring preferences	Government assistance
Ethnocentrism	0.66*	1.11**	1.01***
	0.39	0.43	0.36
Egalitarianism	1.57***	0.69*	0.84***
	0.33	0.36	0.31
Limited government	−0.65***	−0.32	−0.24
	0.21	0.24	0.20
Moral traditionalism	−0.63**	−1.15***	−0.50*
	0.31	0.33	0.27
N	588	417	578
Effect of **E**	0.60→0.77	0.51→0.79	0.42→0.70

Source: 1992, 1996, 2000, and 2004 NES.

Note: Table entry is the ordered probit regression coefficient with standard error below. Dependent variables are coded such that higher values indicate racially liberal responses. Models also control for political awareness, education, sex, and year. Full results appear in the Web appendix. The bottom row of the table gives the effect associated with a shift in Ethnocentrism from Low (−0.1) to High (0.6) in the predicted probability of supporting liberal racial policies.

***$p < 0.01$; **$p < 0.05$; *$p < 0.10$, two-tailed.

TABLE 10.2. Ethnocentrism and black opinion on policies targeted on Blacks, Hispanics, or Asians

	Job training	Affirmative action	Job training	Affirmative action	Job training	Affirmative action
	For Blacks		For Hispanics		For Asians	
Ethnocentrism	1.12***	1.27***	−0.75***	−0.37*	−1.21***	−0.68***
	0.25	0.23	0.22	0.21	0.21	0.21
Partisanship	0.30**	0.20	0.22*	0.15	0.19	0.10
	0.14	0.13	0.13	0.12	0.12	0.12
Liberal	0.09	0.02	−0.11	−0.10	−0.08	−0.08
	0.09	0.08	0.08	0.08	0.08	0.08
Conservative	0.11	0.06	−0.08	−0.05	0.02	0.12
	0.10	0.09	0.09	0.09	0.09	0.08
N	1030	1029	1030	1029	1030	1029
Effect of E	0.88→0.97	0.65→0.90	0.82→0.66	0.62→0.52	0.64→0.31	0.45→0.27

Source: Los Angeles component of the 1992–94 MCSUI.

Note: Table entry is the ordered probit regression coefficient with standard error below. Dependent variables are coded such that higher values indicate racially liberal responses. Models also control for education, income, employment status, and sex. Full results appear in the Web appendix. The bottom row of the table gives the effect associated with a shift in Ethnocentrism from Low (−0.1) to High (0.6) in the predicted probability of supporting liberal racial policies.

***$p < 0.01$; **$p < 0.05$; *$p < 0.10$, two-tailed.

Americans are, they more they favor policies that benefit their own: fair employment, affirmative action in hiring and promotion, government assistance. Egalitarianism, limited government, and moral traditionalism play significant parts as well, but controlling for these effects, ethnocentrism makes an important and independent contribution to support for racial liberalism.[6]

We can expand this test by capitalizing once more on the Multi-City Study of Urban Inequality (MCSUI). The Los Angeles component of the MCSUI included interviews with large numbers of African Americans ($N >$ 1000). As expected, we find in the MCSUI data that ethnocentrism among blacks is consistently and significantly associated with support for programs intended to help their own group. These results appear in table 10.2. Among African Americans in Los Angeles, as in the country as a whole, on issues of race, ethnocentrism is a force for in-group favoritism. In this instance, ethnocentrism promotes liberalism.

A second virtue of the MCSUI for our purposes is that the survey included questions about policies designed to help Hispanics and Asians as well as black Americans. Table 10.2 shows that when it comes to policies designed to assist *other* minority groups, ethnocentrism becomes a force for conservatism. Among African Americans, ethnocentrism is consistently and significantly associated with animosity toward policies targeting Hispanics and Asians. Ethnocentric blacks tend to oppose job training and educational assistance for Hispanics or for Asians; and they tend to object to affirmative action in employment policy for them as well. In this way, ethnocentrism seems to be operating among blacks as a general predisposition, one oriented to protecting the in-group and penalizing out-groups.

Ethnocentrism and Group Identification among Black Americans

As we noted in the beginning of the chapter, standard accounts of black public opinion often start with the notion of group identification. The fundamental claim here is that the political consequences of group membership are accentuated among those who belong to their group psychologically, who identify with their group for reasons of shared interests or common values (e.g., Conover 1988; Tajfel 1982). Group identification is thought to be especially powerful among African Americans, a reflection of the black experience in America. Insofar as African Americans identify strongly with their racial group, so the argument goes, they will be inclined to adopt liberal positions on policies that are seen to affect their group directly. For African Americans, politics is viewed primarily through the prism of the interests and aspirations of their racial group (Dawson 1994; Gurin, Hatchett, and Jackson 1989; Tate 1993).

This means that we must make sure that we are not confusing ethnocentrism with group identification. Can we be confident that the results for African Americans we have just presented really reflect ethnocentrism, as we say, rather than group identification?

Yes, we can, on two grounds. First, when we break ethnocentrism into its two components—in-group favoritism and out-group animosity—we find that both components play a role in black opinion on race policy. This is true in both the NES and the MCSUI analyses. If anything, the out-group component of ethnocentrism is often more important. But the key result is that both matter. This evidence works against the hypothesis that the effects we have attributed to ethnocentrism really belong to group identification.[7]

The second reason, and perhaps the more convincing, has to do with the results that emerge when we estimate the effect of ethnocentrism while controlling on racial group identification. The best test here, the one that provides the stiffest challenge to the claim of ethnocentrism, makes use of the 1996 National Black Election Study (NBES).[8] The 1996 NBES carries a version of the NES thermometer scale, including ratings of blacks, whites, Asian Americans, and Hispanics, and so we can build our standard backup

TABLE 10.3. Ethnocentrism and black support for race policy with [2] or without [1] controlling on sense of common fate

	Affirmative action	School busing	Government assistance	Proportional representation
[1] Ethnocentrism	0.90***	0.41*	0.39*	0.44*
	0.22	0.22	0.21	0.26
[2] Ethnocentrism	0.86***	0.45**	0.21	0.30
	0.23	0.22	0.21	0.26
Common fate	0.21	−0.07	1.15***	0.83***
	0.19	0.19	0.18	0.22
N	659	658	670	655

Source: 1996 NBES.

Note: Table entry is the ordered probit regression coefficient with standard error below. Dependent variables are coded such that higher values indicate racially liberal responses. Models also include measures of political awareness, education, and sex. Full results appear in the Web appendix.

***$p < 0.01$; **$p < 0.05$; *$p < 0.10$, two-tailed.

measure of ethnocentrism. It also includes a set of policy questions in the realm of race, some modeled after the NES questions we have been analyzing (affirmative action, government providing special assistance to black Americans), and some not (busing for the purposes of school integration, a proposal for proportional representation). The 1996 NBES also includes a good set of measures relevant to racial group identification, centered on the idea of common fate. Some blacks see their personal prospects linked with the fortunes of their racial group while others do not, and this difference turns out to be important in understanding their support for redistributive policies and nationalist initiatives (Dawson 1994; Tate 1993). For the purpose of analysis, we created a simple composite scale of common fate, based on equally weighted replies to four standard questions.[9]

Using as close to our standard model as the 1996 NBES allows, we find ethnocentrism to have a consistent and positive effect.[10] Ethnocentric black Americans tend to favor affirmative action, endorse busing as a means for integrating public schools, support the idea that the federal government has a special obligation to provide assistance to blacks, and subscribe to a proportional representation scheme likely to give black Americans a stronger say in government. The NBES results thereby replicate what we see in both the NES and the MCSUI.

Fine—but the important result here is that adding common fate to the model has virtually no consequence for the potency of ethnocentrism. This is shown in table 10.3. The estimated effect of ethnocentrism remains essentially unchanged for school busing and affirmative action. It declines only gently on government assistance and proportional representation when group identification is added to the model.[11] The story we have told in this chapter, as in chapters past, is a story of ethnocentrism.

ETHNOCENTRISM IN THE REALM OF RACE AMONG WHITE AMERICANS

What about white Americans? Here we estimate the effect of ethnocentrism in the usual manner, except that we make special allowance in the cases of school integration and fair employment, where significant numbers of whites said that they did not know what their opinion was. In these two instances, we corrected for selection bias by using the bivariate probit selection model.[12]

In table 10.4, sizable effects of ethnocentrism show up across the board. Ethnocentric whites are generally inclined against government stepping in to ensure that public schools are integrated or to make certain that blacks do not suffer discrimination at work; they think reserving openings for black students in college admissions is wrong; they oppose giving blacks any advantage in employment decisions; they are inclined against imposing affirmative action policies on companies that have been shown to discriminate; they would prefer to cut back on spending for programs that assist blacks; and they believe that the federal government has no special responsibility to black citizens. In short, consistent and noteworthy effects are the rule on race, just as has been true in other domains of policy.[13]

Ethnocentrism and Prejudice among White Americans

Are these effects due really to ethnocentrism? Might not they be due, instead, to prejudice?

In our view, ethnocentrism and prejudice are related, but they are not the same. Ethnocentrism is broader. Ethnocentrism is a reaction to outsiders in general. In extreme cases, the condescension or disdain that the ethnocentric feels for others is virtually indiscriminant. Prejudice, in contrast, is condescension or resentment focused on a single group. Moreover, while ethnocentrism is a universal human appetite, prejudice is both an expression of, and a justification for, a set of specific practices of racial exclusion and oppression. The one has its origins, in part, in the distant evolutionary past; the other is much more a creature of immediate historic and social contingency.[14]

The argument we are making here runs parallel to the one advanced by John Higham in *Strangers in the Land* ([1955] 1988), his classic history of

TABLE 10.4. Ethnocentrism and white opposition to race policy

	School integration (1992)	Fair employment (2000)	Hiring preferences (1992)	Quotas in college admissions (1992)	Affirmative action for offending companies (2000)	Spending on programs for blacks (2000)	Government assistance for blacks (2004)
Ethnocentrism	−0.59*	−0.96***	−0.64***	−1.28***	−0.98***	−0.90***	−1.33***
	0.30	0.30	0.22	0.21	0.26	0.25	0.31
Partisanship	0.18	0.07	0.09	0.14	−0.08	0.18	0.63***
	0.15	0.13	0.11	0.10	0.13	0.12	0.13
Egalitarianism	1.78***	1.38***	1.08***	1.46***	1.77***	1.57***	1.43***
	0.30	0.23	0.19	0.18	0.22	0.22	0.24
Limited government	−0.60***	−0.43***	−0.18*	−0.19**	−0.38***	−0.28**	−0.39***
	0.15	0.12	0.10	0.10	0.11	0.11	0.11
N	1383	1095	1390	1359	965	1033	679
Effect of E	0.31→0.41	0.38→0.57	0.84→0.93	0.65→0.90	0.47→0.73	0.23→0.46	0.38→0.74

Source: 1992, 2000, and 2004 NES.

Note: First two columns: Table entry is the bivariate probit regression coefficient, modeling nonresponse, with standard error below. Remaining columns: Table entry is the ordered probit regression coefficient with standard error below. Dependent variables are coded such that higher values indicate racially liberal responses. Models also control for partisanship, education, political awareness, sex, limited government, and egalitarianism. Full results appear in the Web appendix. The bottom row of the table gives the effect associated with a shift in Ethnocentrism from Low (−0.1) to High (0.6) in the predicted probability of *opposing* liberal racial policies. For models with selection equations, the cell provides the probability of opposing policies given that the respondent has an opinion.

***p < 0.01; **p < 0.05; *p < 0.10, two-tailed.

American nativism from the Civil War to the second decade of the twentieth century. Higham distinguishes between ethnocentrism and nativism, much as we distinguish between ethnocentrism and prejudice. Higham regards ethnocentrism as pervasive, indeed a universal human reaction to strangers, one characterized primarily by distrust and suspicion. But nativism, according to Higham, combines the general ethnocentric suspicion of outsiders with the political fear that outsiders pose a threat to the nation: that they are subversive, or disloyal, or fundamentally alien, unwilling or unable to be assimilated to the American way of life. In Higham's framework, nativism draws on ethnocentrism, but it is also separate and distinct. Likewise for ethnocentrism and prejudice.

One implication of this difference, as we make it out, is that the substantial effects due apparently to ethnocentrism in the domain of race should be traceable in roughly equal portion to in-group favoritism and out-group denigration. White opposition to school integration or affirmative action should arise from out-group animosity and in-group pride. This turns out to be true. If we break ethnocentrism into its two components—in-group favoritism and out-group denigration—and repeat the analysis summarized in table 10.4, we find that both components have effects, and that the effects are roughly equal.[15]

Another implication of the difference we see between ethnocentrism and prejudice is that ethnocentrism should predict white opposition to racial change in general, beyond just black and white. In the MCSUI, ethnocentric whites tend to oppose job training and affirmative action programs targeted specially on blacks. These results, presented in table 10.5, mimic those we found in the NES data. What is new in table 10.5 is that ethnocentrism appears to work the same way for opinions about policies designed with other racial groups in mind. Ethnocentric whites tend to oppose job training programs for Hispanics and Asians—just as they oppose comparable programs for blacks. And ethnocentric whites are inclined to stand against affirmative action in hiring and promotion for Hispanics and Asians—just as they are inclined to stand against affirmative action programs for blacks. In short, when we expand the test of ethnocentrism in the realm of race beyond black and white, we continue to find strong effects. By these results, ethnocentrism appears to be, once again, a general predisposition.[16]

Ethnocentrism and prejudice are not the same, but they are related. In particular, we think they are *causally* related. Ethnocentrism is a general readiness to partition the world into allies and adversaries, a way of looking at the social world that paves the way to prejudice. Putting the same point in a different way, the appeal of any particular prejudice will be greater if a person is already ethnocentrically predisposed. Prejudice is all the more

T A B L E 1 0 . 5 . Ethnocentrism and white opinion on policies targeted on Blacks, Hispanics, and Asians

	Job training	Affirmative action	Job training	Affirmative action	Job training	Affirmative action
	For blacks		For Hispanics		For Asians	
Ethnocentrism	−0.50*	−1.69***	−0.60**	−1.58***	−0.39	−1.58***
	0.29	0.29	0.29	0.29	0.29	0.29
Partisanship	0.43***	0.50***	0.37***	0.46***	0.27***	0.37***
	0.11	0.11	0.10	0.11	0.10	0.10
Liberal	0.08	0.12	0.04	0.11	−0.03	0.07
	0.10	0.10	0.10	0.10	0.10	0.10
Conservative	−0.18*	−0.10	−0.21**	−0.16	−0.26***	−0.17*
	0.10	0.10	0.10	0.10	0.10	0.10
N	757	756	757	756	757	756
Effect of E	0.09→0.16	0.33→0.77	0.10→0.19	0.37→0.78	0.12→0.18	0.36→0.77

Source: Los Angeles component of the 1992–94 MCSUI.

Note: Table entry is the ordered probit regression coefficient with standard error below. Dependent variables are coded such that higher values indicate racially liberal responses. Models also control for education, income, employment status, and sex. Full results appear in the Web appendix. The bottom row of the table gives the effect associated with a shift in Ethnocentrism from Low (−0.1) to High (0.6) in the predicted probability of *opposing* liberal racial policies.

***$p < 0.01$; **$p < 0.05$; *$p < 0.10$, two-tailed.

comfortable, all the more satisfying, and all the more sensible for someone given to ethnocentrism. Such a person is

> prepared to reject groups with which he has never had contact; his approach to a new and strange person or culture is not one of curiosity, interest, and receptivity but rather one of doubt and rejection. The feeling of difference is transformed into a sense of threat and an attitude of hostility. The new group easily becomes an out-group. (Adorno et al. 1950, p. 149)

If this is right—if prejudice arises out of ethnocentrism—then certain empirical consequences follow.

First of all, we should find that ethnocentrism and prejudice are correlated. To find out if this is so, we made use of a measure of prejudice included in recent installments of NES. As a general matter, prejudice presumes the existence of differences between whites and blacks in achievement and status and offers an account of those differences that is denigrating to blacks. The NES measure in particular proposes that racial differences arise because of deficiencies in black culture—because of imprudent choices, unhealthy values, and bad habits. It is especially concerned with black Americans' supposed individualistic shortcomings. From this point of view, blacks fail to display the virtues of hard work and self-sacrifice that white Americans claim as central to the moral ordering of their own lives and to the life of their society.[17]

In the 2000 NES, the correlation between our standard measure of ethnocentrism, on the one hand, and this measure of prejudice, on the other, is 0.33. The correlation runs a bit stronger in 1992 (0.38) and a bit weaker in 2004 (0.29). When we substitute the thermometer-based measure of ethnocentrism for the one based on stereotypes, we find essentially the same thing. And when we correct these estimates for unreliability in measurement, the "true" correlation between ethnocentrism and prejudice comes in at about 0.45. In short, consistent with expectations, ethnocentrism and prejudice are correlated but distinct.[18]

A second observable implication of our claim that ethnocentrism is a cause of prejudice is this: if we add prejudice to the standard model, the estimated effect due to ethnocentrism on opinion should diminish. These results are summarized in table 10.6. The first row of the table simply reprints the estimates of the effect of ethnocentrism from the standard model—those that do not take into account whatever effects might be due to prejudice (presented earlier in table 10.4). The second row of the table then displays the effect of ethnocentrism with prejudice held constant.

As predicted, the effect of ethnocentrism diminishes when prejudice is taken into account. It diminishes *dramatically*. This happens on all seven policies; in four instances, the direct effect of ethnocentrism, after controlling on prejudice, cannot be confidently distinguished from zero. Meanwhile, the direct effect of prejudice on opinion is large, and it is large in each and every case.

These results are consistent with our claim that ethnocentrism should be conceived of as a cause of prejudice. Ethnocentrism gives rise to prejudice. Prejudice, in turn, drives opposition to policies intended as remedies for segregation, discrimination, and inequality. The substantial effect of ethnocentrism on white opinion is almost entirely indirect, mediated by prejudice.[19]

This is the way things work in the realm of race—but they should *not* work this way in other policy domains. This is the final observable implication of our understanding of the relationship between ethnocentrism and prejudice. The prediction is that across the various domains of policy we have investigated here, adding a measure of prejudice to the standard model will have little or no consequence for the effects we have been attributing all along to ethnocentrism. On policies having to do with confronting enemies abroad, providing assistance to foreign countries, controlling immigration,

TABLE 10.6. The impact of ethnocentrism on white opposition to race policy with [2] or without [1] controlling on race prejudice

	School integration (1992)	Fair employment (2000)	Hiring preferences (1992)	Quotas in college admissions (1992)	Affirmative action for offending companies (2000)	Spending on programs for blacks (2000)	Government assistance for blacks (2004)
[1] Ethnocentrism	-0.59*	-0.96***	-0.64***	-1.28***	-0.98***	-0.90***	-1.33***
	0.30	0.30	0.22	0.21	0.26	0.25	0.31
[2] Ethnocentrism	-0.20	-0.34	0.03	-0.62***	-0.49*	-0.29	-0.71**
	0.31	0.32	0.23	0.22	0.27	0.27	0.32
Prejudice	-1.03***	-1.67***	-2.32***	-2.72***	-1.38***	-1.98***	-2.45***
	0.26	0.25	0.19	0.18	0.20	0.21	0.23

Source: 1992, 2000, and 2004 NES.

Note: First two columns: Table entry is the bivariate probit regression coefficient, controlling for nonresponse, with standard error below. Remaining columns: Table entry is the ordered probit regression coefficient with standard error below. Dependent variables are coded such that higher values indicate racially liberal responses. Models also control for partisanship, education, political awareness, sex, limited government, and egalitarianism. Full results appear in the Web appendix.

***$p < 0.01$; **$p < 0.05$; *$p < 0.10$, two-tailed.

Oppose Government Involvement in Fair Hiring

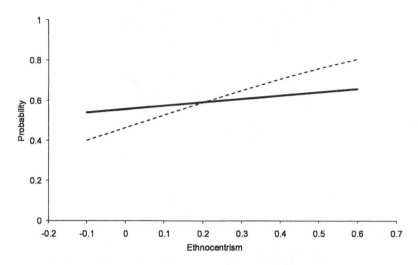

Spend More on War on Terror/Homeland Security

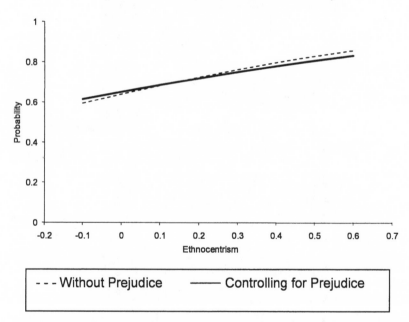

- - - Without Prejudice   ——— Controlling for Prejudice

FIGURE 10.1. Ethnocentrism and white opinion on policy—with and without controlling for prejudice. Predicted probabilities. Source: 1992, 2000, 2000–2002, and 2004 NES.

Cut Spending on Foreign Aid

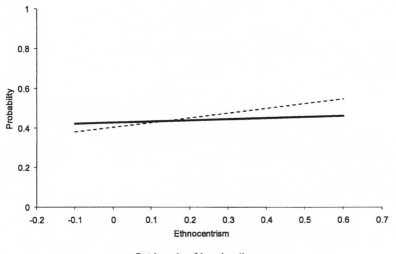

Cut Levels of Immigration

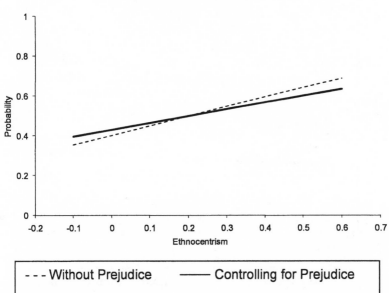

- - - Without Prejudice   —— Controlling for Prejudice

FIGURE 10.1. (*continued*)

Oppose Same-Sex Marriage

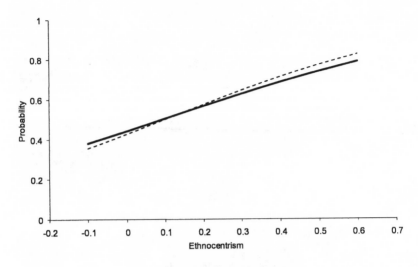

Cut Spending on Welfare

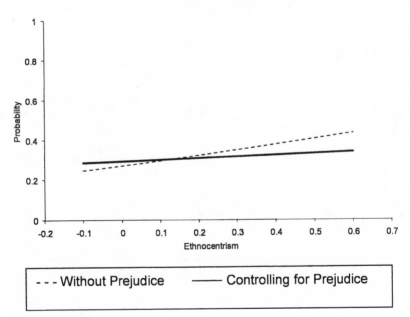

- - - Without Prejudice   —— Controlling for Prejudice

FIGURE 10.1. (*continued*)

and all the rest, we expected it would matter little whether the standard model took prejudice into account.

Figure 10.1 tells the tale. Each graph in figure 10.1 represents a distinct policy domain. Each displays two curves: one representing the effect of ethnocentrism on white opinion without controlling for prejudice; the other representing ethnocentrism's effect after controlling on prejudice.

The first graph features the effect of ethnocentrism in the realm of race: on government involvement in fair hiring. Here, the effect of ethnocentrism is mediated by prejudice. In this instance, the two curves are easy to distinguish. Without prejudice taken into account, the curve ascends steeply, indicating that as ethnocentrism increases, so does opposition to racial change. With prejudice added in, however, the curve flatlines. Taking prejudice into account, ethnocentrism has nothing to do (directly) with opinion on matters of race.

Elsewhere, prejudice plays no such role. By and large, across the various policy domains we have investigated, the two curves are hard to distinguish. The effect of ethnocentrism on white Americans' support for the war on terrorism, for cutting foreign aid, for putting a stop to immigration, for prohibiting same-sex marriage, and more, is essentially the same, whether prejudice is taken into account or not. The domain of welfare supplies a partial exception to this conclusion. In all other domains, it is ethnocentrism in general—prejudice, broadly conceived—that is the driver of opinion.[20]

CONCLUSIONS AND IMPLICATIONS

On such contentious matters as school integration and affirmative action, ethnocentrism motivates opposition among white Americans and support among African Americans. This pattern is neatly summarized in figure 10.2. For white Americans, the curves displayed in figure 10.2 climb from left to right: opposition grows as ethnocentrism increases. For black Americans, the curves fall from left to right: opposition declines as ethnocentrism increases. Differences on race policy between blacks and whites are modest among those who reject (or overcome) ethnocentrism, but very large among those who embrace ethnocentrism. Put differently, if ethnocentrism could be erased from American society, the racial divide on fair employment and school integration and affirmative action would narrow appreciably. Racial differences would not disappear entirely, but they would no longer be extraordinary. In the absence of ethnocentrism, differences between blacks and whites would resemble the differences we have grown accustomed to seeing between rich and poor, or between young and old, or between men and women: that is to say, differences, not divides.

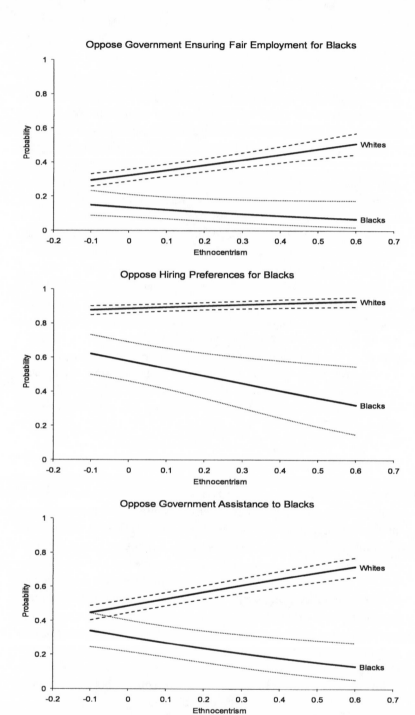

FIGURE 10.2. Ethnocentrism and opinion on policies designed to help blacks, separately by race. Predicted probabilities with 95 percent confidence intervals. Source: 1992, 1996, 2000, and 2004 NES (pooled).

Is the apparent effect of ethnocentrism among African Americans really just group identification at work? No. Ethnocentrism and group attachment represent conceptually separate and empirically distinct explanations. Among African Americans, ethnocentrism plays an important and independent role in motivating liberal views on race policy. Regardless of their partisanship, principles, interests, and intensity of racial group identification, ethnocentric African Americans want more from government for their group.

Is the apparent effect of ethnocentrism among white Americans really just prejudice at work? No. Ethnocentrism and prejudice are correlated but distinct. Race prejudice, like other specific animosities, arises, in part, from ethnocentrism. Ethnocentrism is a general readiness to partition the world into allies and adversaries, and as such, makes adoption of particular prejudices more likely. On matters of policy that deal explicitly and unambiguously with race, prejudice largely mediates the effect of ethnocentrism. When policy shifts away from race as a central consideration, ethnocentrism's influence remains, while prejudice's mediating role vanishes.

Race represents one of America's most tenacious and intractable problems. A few years before William Graham Sumner ([1906] 2002) introduced the idea of ethnocentrism, W. E. B. Du Bois was completing *The Souls of Black Folk*. Du Bois began his famous book with a bold prophecy: that the problem of the twentieth century would be the "problem of the color-line— the relation of the darker to the lighter races of men in Asia and Africa, in America and the islands of the sea" ([1903] 1907, p. 13). Du Bois wrote authoritatively about the black experience in America, with a fine sense of history, and he was right, accurately foretelling the struggle for freedom and equality that came to mark much of the last hundred years.

Much has changed in race relations since Du Bois, of course, much of it very good: the rising of the civil rights movement; landmark federal legislation outlawing discrimination; the emergence of a black middle class; the dismantling of the legal foundations of segregation; striking gains in political participation and representation among black Americans, illustrated vividly by Barack Obama's astonishing rise to prominence, power, and the presidency.

But the struggle for freedom and equality continues. Race is, as Tilly would say, a durable inequality. Black Americans have made significant inroads into the middle class, sharing in the economic prosperity and educational opportunities that came to most of American society following World War II. Nevertheless, sharp racial disparities in employment, income, and especially wealth remain. Discrimination, sometimes subtle and sometimes not, continues. Segregation by race is still a central organizing principle of American social life. And policies designed to level the playing field—desegregating public schools, eliminating discrimination in the workplace, imposing affirmative action on companies that discriminate— remain controversial. Some policies to promote racial equality are actually less popular now than they were a decade or two ago. For others, there is modest movement in the liberal direction. All generate a huge and persistent divide between whites and blacks—a divide rooted, in part, as we have seen here, in ethnocentrism.[21]

Ethnocentrism and Political Life

In this final chapter, we step back from the details of particular cases to offer an assessment of our project as a whole. To set the stage for this stock taking, we begin with a summary—mercifully brief—of our findings. The heart of the chapter then explores the implications of the findings. We take up, in turn, the issue of demarcating where ethnocentrism matters and where it does not; the moderating effect of political knowledge; the distinction between ethnocentrism and authoritarianism; cosmopolitanism as a counterweight to ethnocentrism; the likelihood of ethnocentrism at work in other places; and finally, the consequences of ethnocentrism's pervasive effect on public opinion for the character and quality of democratic politics. But first, a quick review of the journey we have taken.

SUMMARY OF FINDINGS

We define ethnocentrism to be a way of thinking that partitions the world into in-groups and out-groups—into us and them. Ethnocentrism is an attitude—perhaps, as Lévi-Strauss would have it, "the most ancient of attitudes" (1961, p. 19)—constituting a readiness to act in favor of in-groups and in opposition to out-groups.

Back in the introduction, we claimed that ethnocentrism, defined this way, is for all practical purposes invisible in studies of American public opinion. We said that this was a mistake and that we aimed to correct it. Whether we have succeeded in this purpose is, as always, up to the reader to decide. On behalf of our project, we will say this:

- Across a diverse and wide-ranging set of policy domains, ethnocentrism emerges time and again as an important force in American public opinion. Protecting the homeland; dealing harshly with enemies abroad; withholding help to foreign lands; stemming the tide of immigration; pushing back against gay rights; cutting welfare while expanding social insurance; putting an end to affirmative action: in all these cases, ethnocentrism plays a significant and sizable role.

· Ethnocentrism is a durable attitude. People differ reliably from one another in the degree to which they approach the social world with an ethnocentric point of view, and this difference is rooted in fundamental processes: genetic inheritance, personality formation, and the values and skills imparted by higher education. Like other core aspects of personality and political identity, ethnocentrism displays substantial and increasing stability in adulthood.

· Ethnocentrism is pervasive in society but its importance for politics depends on circumstances. Ethnocentrism carries more or less weight in public opinion depending on the ability of the issue in question to command the public's limited and fickle attention and on the closeness of fit between ethnocentrism, on the one hand, and how the particular issue is framed, on the other.

We conclude that ethnocentrism is a foundational element of public opinion. Americans' views on the issues that give life to the politics of our time—peace and security, immigration and citizenship, poverty and inequality—are an expression, in important part, of ethnocentrism.

Not of ethnocentrism alone, of course. Ethnocentrism is not the only engine driving public opinion. To grasp the magnitude of ethnocentrism's effect on opinion more precisely, we went back through all our empirical tests, comparing in each instance the effect due to ethnocentrism with the effect due to party identification. For this purpose party identification is a good and obvious choice. When it comes to political predispositions, partisanship stands first among equals.

Most Americans think of themselves as Democrats or Republicans. For many, this is a lifelong commitment—and (within the domain of politics) a highly consequential one. "To the average person," as Donald Stokes once put it, "the affairs of government are remote and complex, and yet the average citizen is asked periodically to formulate opinions about these affairs. . . . In this dilemma, having the party symbol stamped on certain candidates, certain issue positions, certain interpretations of reality is of great psychological convenience" (Stokes 1966, pp. 126–27; also see Bartels 2000; A. Campbell et al. [1960] 1980; Converse 1966; Green, Palmquist, and Schickler 2002). To the extent that the issues taken up here—from the war on terrorism to affirmative action in college admissions—generate strong disagreements between Democratic and Republican elites, rank and file Democrats and Republicans should disagree as well. And as we have seen, generally they do. The question we raise here is how the effects on opinion attributable to partisanship compare in magnitude to the effects attributable to ethnocentrism.[1]

Across all tests, the most common outcome is for opinion to be influenced both by ethnocentrism and by party identification, and for this influence to be roughly equal. Occasionally the effect of ethnocentrism is smaller, especially on flagrantly partisan matters (for example, ratings of George W. Bush's performance as president). More often, the effect on opinion due to ethnocentrism exceeds the effect due to party identification. This includes a fair number of cases where ethnocentrism is quite important while party identification is utterly unimportant.[2]

In short, ethnocentrism stands up well to a strong comparison. If party identification has come to provide a standard and illuminating approach to the analysis and understanding of public opinion, perhaps ethnocentrism should too.

THE WOMEN'S MOVEMENT AND OTHER FAILURES

Does the ethnocentrism effect *always* hold? No. A powerful (and perhaps surprising) example of the failure of ethnocentrism is provided by the cluster of issues associated with the modern women's movement—the so-called second wave of feminism that came ashore in the 1960s. As we discovered in chapter 8, on abortion, equal opportunity in employment, affirmative action, sexual harassment, child care, and family leave, ethnocentrism had no effect on public opinion. We suggested that ethnocentrism's failure might be attributable to the absence of a dehumanizable adversary. Who in the struggle over abortion rights is the enemy? Most Americans take moderate, qualified positions on abortion. Many Americans are acquainted with women who have struggled with the decision of whether to proceed with a pregnancy. Without a clear and demonizable adversary, ethnocentrism never becomes engaged.

Environmentalism supplies another example of ethnocentrism's failure. Issues in this domain are not neatly reducible to a struggle between us and them, between virtue and depravity. Indeed, on protecting the environment and preventing climate change, the enemy, for the most part, is us. And as things turn out, ethnocentrism is generally unrelated to opinion on environmental issues. Ethnocentrism has no bearing on the choice between environmental protection and economic development, is likewise irrelevant to opinion on the need for tougher government regulation to protect the environment, and is of no consequence on whether federal spending on the environment should be increased or cut back.[3]

Ethnocentrism is a general predisposition with wide-ranging effects on public opinion. But we should not expect ethnocentrism to influence public opinion in every case. Its activation in particular instances requires resonance: a good fit between ethnocentrism, on the one hand, and how the particular issue is framed and understood, on the other. Much of politics *can* be framed this way, but not all. It seems to us that the issues raised and challenges posed by environmentalism and the women's movement generally fail to fulfill the necessary condition of resonance, and therefore generally fail to activate ethnocentrism.

ETHNOCENTRISM AND KNOWLEDGE

As we have seen over the preceding chapters, ethnocentrism predisposes Americans to think in certain ways about policy. The ethnocentrism effect holds not for every issue, as we have just been reminded, but it holds for many: the war on terrorism, same-sex marriage, affirmative action, and much else besides. According to these results, ethnocentrism is a central ingredient in public opinion.

Ethnocentrism, we should have said, is a central ingredient in public opinion *on average*. That is, the empirical relationships that we have reported so far between ethnocentrism, on the one side, and views on the war on terrorism, same-sex marriage, affirmative action, and all the rest, on the other, are estimates of the average relationship between predisposition and opinion, ignoring whatever differences there might be across individuals. Put another way, the ethnocentrism effect takes the average American for granted.

But, of course, there really is no such thing as the average American. Americans differ from one another in all sorts of ways, and such differences may have implications for the importance of ethnocentrism. Ethnocentrism is a pervasive human habit, but its application to the domain of politics may not be for everyone. In particular, we say that the political activation of ethnocentrism requires a minimal investment—time, attention, thought—in public affairs, an investment not all citizens care to make. For ethnocentrism to shape opinion on policy, citizens must be sufficiently engaged in matters of politics. Absent sufficient motivation and knowledge, we expect the power of ethnocentrism to diminish sharply if it does not disappear altogether. As motivation and knowledge increase, we expect the power of ethnocentrism to increase correspondingly.

To test this claim we need a measure of political engagement, and on this point we took instruction from John Zaller's (1992) influential work on opinion formation and change. Zaller defines political engagement to entail both attention and comprehension: engagement means the degree to which people pay attention to politics *and* understand what they have encountered.[4] Engagement, defined this way, is best measured by tests of factual information. Such tests assess "political learning that has actually occurred—political ideas that the individual has encountered, understood, and stored" (Zaller 1992, p. 335).[5]

Persuaded by Zaller's argument and evidence, the Board of Overseers of the National Election Study decided to include tests of political information in the election study series. In the 2004 NES, for example, respondents were asked to identify, in turn, Dennis Hastert, Dick Cheney, Tony Blair, and William Rehnquist. Answers to these questions are positively correlated. So, if a person happened to know that Dennis Hastert was the Republican Speaker of the House, she was also quite likely to know that William Rehnquist was the Chief Justice of the Supreme Court. Command of political knowledge appears to be a general trait.[6] This means that we can create reliable and comparable scales of political knowledge in all NES presidential-year studies since 1992.[7]

To see whether engagement moderates the effect of ethnocentrism, all we need do is add two new terms to what we have been calling the standard model: political knowledge and the interaction between political knowledge and ethnocentrism. In mathematical form:

$$y^* = \mathbf{x'\beta} + \varepsilon$$
$$= \beta_1 \text{Ethnocentrism} + \beta_2 \text{Political Knowledge}$$
$$+ \beta_3 [\text{Political Knowledge} \times \text{Ethnocentrism}] + \ldots + \varepsilon$$

As throughout, y^* refers to opinion on a particular policy, represented as an unobserved latent variable.

With Political Knowledge scored 0 to 1, where 0 is the least informed, our predictions can be written:

$\beta_3 > 0$ (that is, the effect of ethnocentrism increases with increases in knowledge)

$\beta_1 = 0$ (that is, among those with the least involvement and information—where Political Knowledge equals zero—the effect of ethnocentrism is zero)

We estimated this model wherever measures allowed. We started with military intervention (from chapter 4), ended with affirmative action (chapter 10), and took up everything[8] in between, carrying out 85 tests in all. The results are summarized in figure 11.1.[9]

The figure shows that, as predicted, the effect of ethnocentrism generally increases with increases in knowledge. The swarm of points displayed in figure 11.1 is centered above zero. In more than one-third of the cases (31 out of 85, or 36.5 percent), the interaction term (β_3) surpasses statistical significance.[10] And in virtually all of these cases (29 out of 31, or 93.5 percent), the interaction term is positive (that is, $\beta_3 > 0$). In general, the political power of ethnocentrism increases with increases in knowledge.

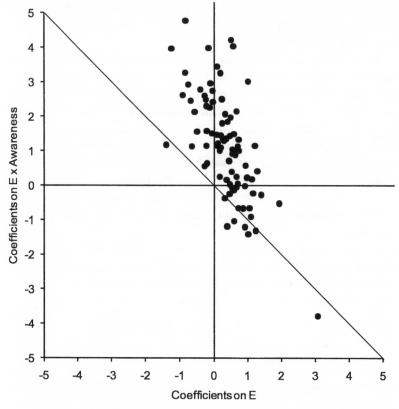

FIGURE 11.1. Political knowledge and the effect of ethnocentrism on opinion. Estimated coefficients on **E** and **E** × **Awareness**, across 85 tests.

Figure 11.1 also shows that, in line with our second prediction, the effect of ethnocentrism generally heads toward zero at low levels of knowledge. In figure 11.1, the points cluster in a band around the vertical axis. In more than 67 percent of the cases (57 out of 85), we find the effect of ethnocentrism among the least knowledgeable to be statistically indistinguishable from zero. Ethnocentrism may be a universal predisposition, but its application to the political realm seems to require some minimal command of political knowledge.[11]

That we find political knowledge to be consequential is perhaps not all that surprising. In some respects, our results just add to a mountain of evidence already in, for we know that the well-informed differ from the poorly informed in all kinds of significant ways. They are more likely to express opinions. They are more likely to possess stable opinions—real opinions, opinions held with conviction. They are more likely to use ideological concepts correctly, to cite evidence in political discussions, and to process information sensitively. They are better at retaining new information. And they are more likely to vote consistently with their presumptive interests. In some ways, our results are old news.[12]

But there is new news here as well. Political knowledge is widely regarded as a universal good. Every election season, commentators deplore the sad state of American democracy, how little voters know about the choices they face, how few of them can (say) find Iraq on a map. Possessing more facts about the world of politics, it is assumed, is always better than possessing fewer. As Delli Carpini and Keeter (1996) put it, facts in hand "prevent debates from becoming disconnected from the material conditions they attempt to address. They allow individuals and groups with widely varied experiences and philosophies to have some common basis of comparison— some common language with which to clarify differences, identify points of agreement, and establish criteria for evaluation. They tether public discourse to objective conditions" (p. 11). But here, command of facts means something quite different: that people are sufficiently invested in public affairs that ethnocentrism becomes a routine part of their thinking.

DISTINGUISHING ETHNOCENTRISM FROM AUTHORITARIANISM

As recently reimagined by Karen Stenner and Stanley Feldman (Stenner 2005; Feldman and Stenner 1997; Feldman 2003), authoritarianism arises out of a basic and recurring dilemma. Living alongside others is an inescapable feature of human society and leads inevitably to tension between personal autonomy and social cohesion. The persistent challenge is to strike a proper balance between group authority and uniformity, on the one side, and individual autonomy and diversity, on the other. Authoritarians choose the former over the latter: they glorify uniformity while disparaging difference.

Authoritarianism, defined this way, and ethnocentrism, as we see it, are congenial predispositions. They share a temperamental aversion to difference. Back in chapter 2, we suggested, with Stenner's and Feldman's work in mind, that ethnocentrism might come, in part, from authoritarianism, conceived of as a personality-based taste for conformity over autonomy. Put another way, authoritarians should find ethnocentrism naturally appealing. Back in chapter 3, we found that authoritarianism and ethnocentrism *were* empirically related, but quite modestly (Pearson $r = 0.20$). We concluded that ethnocentrism may arise in part—in rather small part—from authoritarianism.

Authoritarianism could be a source of ethnocentrism, as we have just seen; but it could also be a rival. Stenner finds authoritarianism to be a consistent and often powerful predictor of political intolerance. This empirical regularity encouraged us to include a measure of authoritarianism in many of our analyses, to guard against the possibility that the effects we would otherwise attribute to ethnocentrism really "belong" to authoritarianism. When we did so, we found, first of all, that the effect due to ethnocentrism remained essentially the same. We have not been confusing one for the other. Our results are about ethnocentrism, not authoritarianism.

Second, authoritarianism often has an effect of its own. When both ethnocentrism and authoritarianism influence opinion, they usually do so in the same way. For example, ethnocentrism enhances Americans' support for stricter control of U.S. borders; authoritarianism does the same. Sometimes, however, the predispositions work against one another. For example, ethnocentrism pushes Americans in the direction of thinking that homosexuality is a biological condition and cannot be changed; authoritarianism pushes in the opposite direction, to the idea that homosexuality is a choice and can be reversed. Or again, while authoritarians take conservative positions on sexual matters generally—they oppose adultery, sex education in the schools, teenage sex, sex before marriage, and more—ethnocentrism comes into play in this domain really only where gay men and women are concerned. From an ethnocentric point of view, gay sex is immoral and must be prohibited, just as other aspects of the "gay agenda" must be resisted. These results reinforce the distinction between ethnocentrism and authoritarianism. And they suggest again that if ethnocentrism arises in part from authoritarianism, that part must be small.

An additional distinction is that ethnocentrism and authoritarianism appear to be activated by different conditions. Stenner and Feldman (Stenner 2005; Feldman and Stenner 1997; Feldman 2003) present threat as the key trigger for authoritarianism. They argue that authoritarianism becomes relevant when social cohesion is threatened: when the culture appears to be fragmenting, or when leaders prove themselves unworthy of public trust. This is the authoritarian dynamic, and Stenner and Feldman have assembled an impressive amount of empirical support for it. Our account of activation heads off in a different direction. Our analysis is rooted in limitations in human attention and framing effects in human judgment.[13]

One last point here: to measure authoritarianism, Stenner's method is simply to ask people to choose values that children should be encouraged to learn at home. Those who select "good manners" and "obedience" as primary virtues for children are authoritarian; those who choose "imagination" and "independence" are not. It turns out that measured this way, authoritarianism in the United States has been declining over much of the twentieth century (Alwin 1984, 1988). That is, Americans have been increasingly likely to select imagination and independence over good manners and obedience as primary virtues for children. We do not have comparable evidence for ethnocentrism (we wish we did), but it would be surprising and theoretically disconcerting to discover that ethnocentrism was on the same path—that it too was in sharp decline.[14]

In sum, authoritarianism and ethnocentrism share in common a temperamental aversion to difference, but they are otherwise distinct. Authoritarianism and ethnocentrism are conceptually independent. They are only weakly correlated with one another. They exert independent effects on public opinion. They occasionally work in opposition to one another. And they are set in motion by different precipitating conditions.

COSMOPOLITANISM AGAINST ETHNOCENTRISM

Cosmopolitanism derives from the ancient Greek term *kosmopolites* meaning "citizen of the world." A genuine cosmopolitan's primary allegiance is to the worldwide community of human beings. Such a person gives serious attention, in ethical and political matters, "to the good of all humanity—and not just individuals, families, or specific communities" (R. Smith 2008, p. 40).

There is some reason to think that the social, economic, and political factors that might encourage a cosmopolitan outlook are gathering strength. Such factors would include, in the view of Rogers Smith,

> the spread of world-spanning communications, information, and transportation systems; the transnational networks and organizations these systems enable; the deregulation of capital markets, the proliferation of international free trade agreements, and the accompanying rise of multinational corporations and heightened flows of capital, labor, and goods; the development of regional and international security alliances; the growing awareness of environmental trends that endanger populations around the globe; and the rise in international human rights agreements and institutions. (2008, p. 42)

Such forces should be pushing more and more people to see themselves as joined to others around the globe in larger and larger "overlapping communities of fate" (Held 2000, p. 396). Maybe so.

And *should* be so, according to a number of prominent public intellectuals, including most notably Martha Nussbaum (1996, 2008; Cheah and Robbins 1998; R. Smith 2008). Each of us, Nussbaum argues, "dwells, in effect, in two communities—the local community of our birth, and the community of human argument and aspiration" (1996, p. 7). Differences of nationality or class or ethnicity or gender can be powerful, but should be overcome. "We should recognize humanity wherever it occurs and give its fundamental ingredients, reason and moral capacity, our first allegiance and respect" (1996, p. 7).[15]

Nussbaum sees education as the principal instrument for generating cosmopolitan citizens. Civic education must focus not on national or democratic citizenship, she argues, but on world citizenship. In Nussbaum's view, this would have many benefits. Through cosmopolitan education, Americans would learn not just about the world but about themselves, would make forward progress on the serious problems that require international cooperation, would recognize moral obligations to the rest of the world otherwise invisible, and would erase irrelevant considerations—nation, ethnicity, and so on—from ethical deliberation and judgment.

It is easy enough to agree with Nussbaum that American children should "learn a good deal more than they frequently do about the rest of the world in which they live, about India and Bolivia and Nigeria and Norway and their histories, problems, and comparative successes" (p. 6). But it is hard to see, especially as we mull over the results on ethnocentrism, how civic education alone could generate a nation whose citizens pay first allegiance to humanity. Nussbaum acknowledges some of the difficulty. She concedes that becoming "a citizen of the world is often lonely business" (p. 15)—and not just because there are so few making the journey. Cosmopolitanism, Nussbaum says, is "a kind of exile—from the comfort of local truths, from the warm, nestling feeling of patriotism, from the absorbing drama of pride in oneself and one's own" (p. 15). Patriotism and other particularistic commitments—other attachments to in-group, as we would put it—are full of color and intensity and passion. Cosmopolitanism, by contrast, is cool, neutral, abstract.

Nussbaum is a most perceptive and agile ethical philosopher—but she fails, we think, to make a plausible case on how to create a cosmopolitan citizen. She is more persuasive on the obstacles that stand in the way than she is on the efficacy and realism of the remedies she offers. And we think this even though she did not even consider the most fundamental obstacle to her wish: the persistence and durability of ethnocentrism. Ethnocentrism is a deep and powerful habit, a part of human nature, and therefore not easily reengineered or evaded. To in-group members, it delivers first-order benefits: trust, comfort, coordination, and cooperation. And ethnocentrism is, as Nussbaum might say, full of color and intensity and passion. It seems to us that the road to cosmopolitanism is steep and long—and that perhaps the only hope for arriving at this lofty destination would be the sudden appearance of an alien enemy, one that threatens us all. Under this unhappy circumstance, ethnocentrism might serve as the instrument for creating the cosmopolitan citizen that Nussbaum yearns for.

ETHNOCENTRISM ELSEWHERE?

Insofar as ethnocentrism is concerned, our analysis has taken up a hard case. Of all the nations in the world, the United States has endured as a democracy the longest. Its record of political tolerance, though far from perfect, is relatively enlightened. The people of the United States are, compared to the rest of the world's population, astonishingly rich and extraordinarily well educated. By establishing the importance of ethnocentrism for contemporary American politics, our results suggest that ethnocentrism is likely to thrive in other places as well.

We wish we could point to a developed literature on the political uses of ethnocentrism outside the United States to support our speculation. But there is none to point to. For the most part, analysts of politics elsewhere, like their American counterparts, have been focused on other questions and preoccupied with other concepts. We did come across three suggestive examples, however. The first concerns French voters' support for Jean LePen and the National Front. Founded in 1972, the National Front has campaigned on a platform of open anti-Semitism and ferocious opposition to immigration. It has been LePen's wish, one might say, to return France to the French. And among the factors that drive voters to the National Front, the most important appears to be ethnocentrism (N. Mayer 1993).

A second example focuses on hostility to immigration among Italians in the 1990s. Such hostility was widespread and strikingly indiscriminant. Recent arrivals from Somalia, Albania, or Tunisia elicited essentially the same reaction. More generally, the "signature feature" of anti-immigrant prejudice in contemporary Europe, according to Paul Sniderman and his colleagues, is its "enveloping character" (2000, p. 53).

A third and less certain example concerns the recent surge of anti-Americanism around the world. Especially visible in the Islamic Middle East, North Africa, and Pakistan, anti-Americanism has been on the rise just about everywhere (Katzenstein and Keohane 2007; Chiozza 2007). The phenomenon is surely due in part to outrage over U.S. foreign policy, but it also rests, according to Markovits, "on a substantial sediment of hatred toward, disdain for, and resentment of America" (2007, p. 4)—a reaction not merely to what America does, but what it is. Markovits finds common threads running through Western European anti-Americanism: "anti-Americanism in Germany does not differ at all in its texture, its topics, its features, and also its social carriers from that in Britain, France, Italy, Spain, or any other West European country" (p. 28). In these societies, disdain and condescension fall on all things American: film, language, theater, sports, food, media, and more. It is the sameness and especially the wide reach of anti-Americanism that suggests the possibility that hostility toward America may be drawing strength from an underlying general predisposition—from a prejudice, generally conceived, or, as we would say, from ethnocentrism.

By citing these examples we do not mean to suggest that ethnocentrism is at work in all societies and in just the same way. Cultural differences surely matter. For example, as far as American ethnocentrism is concerned, we have argued for the primacy of race. Given historical experience and current conditions, delineations based on race are likely to catch the inclination to ethnocentrism more effectively than any other social cleavage.[16] In other societies (and perhaps in the United States at some point in its future), other differences—defined by religion, language, caste, or region—are likely to loom larger.

Differences in institutional arrangements are important too. By political institutions we mean the formal rules, regulations, and policies that structure social and political interactions. An institutionalist analysis proceeds from the assumption that what happens in politics is shaped by the institutional structure within which politics takes place. Among other things, political institutions create "islands of imperfect and temporary organization," parcel out responsibility, provide regular procedures for the division and specialization of labor, define rules of political competition, and coordinate and aggregate individual choice.[17] With Elster (1989) we say that institutions enable certain actions and inhibit others.

Here, of course, we are interested in institutional arrangements that enable or inhibit the expression of ethnocentrism in politics. This interest draws us to institutions that shape the nature of party systems. Writing about Italy after the collapse of communism, Paul Sniderman and his colleagues put the general point well: "The articulation of private grievances into political demands thus depends not simply on the intensity of individual resentments, but conjointly on the availability of a political vehicle that permits their public expression" (2000, p. 92). In terms relevant to our project, ethnocentrism is more likely to be expressed in politics insofar as parties and candidates have incentive to fashion appeals to grievances rooted in ethnocentrism.

It turns out there is no simple relationship between the cultural heterogeneity of a society and the number of political parties that compete for control of government in the society. The relationship is conditional on electoral rules. In particular, district magnitude—the average number of seats to be filled in an electoral district—intervenes between heterogeneity and parties. When district magnitude equals one, as it does in U.S. House elections, the party system is relatively unresponsive to ethnic or linguistic or other forms of cultural difference. Under these circumstances, even large cultural differences are unlikely to be converted into multiple parties (Orde-shook and Shvetsova 1994). This is an important result from our point of view, on the idea that multiple party systems allow space for the emergence of parties and candidates that traffic in ethnocentric appeals. The National Front in France is, perhaps, a good case in point. In the limit, when multiple parties reflect cultural divisions perfectly, elections are little more than as-sertions of cultural identity (Horowitz 1985).[18]

In a rough way, this analysis suggests that the United States may turn out to be relatively lackluster in its place among nations in the prominence and power of ethnocentrism in politics. In a *very* rough way. We hope our results and analysis will encourage others to investigate ethnocentrism in other settings. Comparative work poses special challenges, but it can de-liver special rewards too: in the present case, a systematic understanding of how differences in culture and institution produce differences in the role of ethnocentrism in politics.

POLITICAL IMPLICATIONS

In *Public Opinion and American Democracy*, V. O. Key (1961) set out his bril-liant reconnaissance of research on public opinion. Key was both impressed and worried by the state of the literature:

> During the past two decades the study of public opinion, once a major concern of political scientists, has become the preoccupation of sociolo-gists and social psychologists. By the application of the techniques of their trade these specialists have made substantial contributions to the under-standing of public opinion. Yet as they have done so, they have also in large measure abstracted public opinion from its governmental setting. We have, consequently, a large body of research findings characterized often by methodological virtuosity and on occasion even by theoretical felicity, whose relevance for the workings of the governmental system is not always apparent. (p. vii)

Key's goal was to place the findings on public opinion in their proper context. To Key's way of thinking, this was a necessary and urgent endeavor. The scientific study of public opinion was pointless, Key wrote, "unless the findings about the preferences, aspirations, and prejudices of the public can be connected with the workings of the governmental system" (1961, p. 535).

Key goes too far here, but he has a point, and his admonition has been in the backs of our minds throughout. Now, in this final section, we put po-litical relevance front and center. We take up three aspects of the possible connection between ethnocentrism and politics in particular:

- Ethnocentrism as a remedy for ideological innocence
- The relationship between ethnocentrism and the "good citizen"
- The prospect that ethnocentrism, by shaping public opinion, gives focus and direction to government policy

Ethnocentrism as an Imperfect Solution for Ideological Innocence

For the most part, Americans come to the political world without an ideological axe to grind. Most have little acquaintance with sweeping ideas on government and society. They possess no broad outlook on public policy. They hold real opinions on just some of the pressing issues of the day. And they know precious little about political life.

This is the argument advanced by Philip Converse, in his extraordinary essay on belief systems written more than forty years ago. After a masterly analysis of American national election surveys carried out in the 1950s, Converse concluded that qualitative, perhaps unbridgeable, differences separated the political thinking of elites from the political thinking of ordinary people. Most Americans, in Converse's judgment, were incapable of following—much less actually participating in—what might be called democratic discussion.

Not everyone agreed. In short order, Converse's powerful analysis and unsettling conclusions set off a huge scholarly commotion.[19] As we read the evidence and sort through the arguments, Converse's claim of ideological naiveté stands up well, both to transformations in politics and to scores of challenging analysis. Most Americans *are* ideologically innocent. So it was in the Eisenhower years, and so it is, by and large, today.[20]

This was a *problem*, as Converse saw it, since his analysis was motivated by the attractions of ideological reasoning. In Converse's view, if Americans thought about politics this way, then new political events would have more meaning, retention of political information from the past would be far more adequate, and political judgments and actions would more closely approximate rational models.[21] But as things turned out, the great debate over ideology, the consuming preoccupation of public opinion studies for more than a generation, has taught us more about how Americans do not think about politics than about how they do.

Now in some respects, ethnocentrism resembles the kind of ideological framework that Converse looked for and could not find. Americans are more or less ethnocentric—as they might have been more or less liberal or more or less conservative. And more pertinent here, differences in ethnocentrism appear to motivate the opinions Americans take on a wide range of policies. From a certain perspective, ethnocentrism supplies what public opinion needs: structure, coherence, stability. Remove structure, coherence, and stability from public opinion and democratic theory loses its starting point (cf. Achen 1975).

But democratic aspirations require public opinion to be more than structured, coherent, and stable. The issue here is not just whether citizens possess genuine preferences, but *why* they do. In our case, the systematizing principle that stands behind public opinion is itself antidemocratic. Ethnocentrism divides the social world into two classes. This invites violation of the first principle of democratic government: political equality. In the results we have presented here, public opinion is structured in a way that denies equal standing—democratic standing—to others. And it is structured in a way that tempts leaders to mobilize antidemocratic sentiments.

In short, our analysis and findings suggest a systematic but distasteful base for public opinion, a decidedly mixed message for democratic aspirations.

Ethnocentrism and the Good Citizen

Some observers of democratic politics have taken comfort in the indifference and apathy that generally characterize modern mass publics. Too much participation from the wrong sorts can be dangerous, producing more conflict, contention, and demand than democratic governments can handle (e.g., Almond and Verba 1963; Berelson 1952; Berelson, Lazarsfeld, and McPhee 1954; Huntington 1976; Lipset 1959). The specific question here for our purposes is whether ethnocentric Americans are inclined to sit on the sidelines. Perhaps those predisposed to ethnocentrism find politics off-putting or boring and so their voices are seldom heard.

To see if this is so, we examined as much of the complete repertoire of civic and political action available to citizens in the United States today as the evidence allowed.[22] We investigated turning out to vote, working on campaigns, making financial contributions to political parties and interest groups, and organizing communities to take action on local problems. These distinct forms of political action vary in all sorts of ways: in the resources—time, money, skill—they require; in the clarity of the information they convey and the pressure they apply; and in whether they are carried out alone or with others (Verba, Schlozman, and Brady 1995).[23]

Figure 11.2 summarizes the relationship between ethnocentrism and general political participation. The latter is a simple count of activities that people said they had engaged in over the previous year. The figure provides some consolation for those who might hope that ethnocentrism, though common in society, would be rare in politics. We find that participation declines with increases in ethnocentrism. We see this for white and black and Hispanic Americans alike. We see it for participation overall and for each

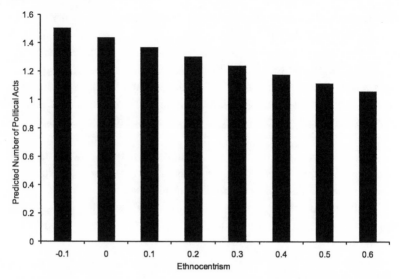

FIGURE 11.2. Ethnocentrism and political participation. Columns display the predicted mean number of political activities. Estimation results appear in the Web appendix. Source: 1992, 1996, 2000, and 2004 NES (pooled).

individual aspect of participation—turning out to vote, attending rallies, and so on—taken separately.[24]

This is good, as far as it goes. But it doesn't go too far. The differences in participation are statistically significant but small—which is to say, ethnocentric Americans are nearly as likely to take an active part in politics as are their less ethnocentric counterparts.[25] And remember also in this respect that we have uncovered at least one instance—state-based campaigns to make same-sex marriage illegal—where ethnocentrism can become a source of political activism. Taken all around, our results offer some consolation, but not too much.

Ethnocentrism and Policy

In nations the size and complexity of the United States, pure forms of democracy are impractical. Instead of the citizen's assembly of the ancient city-state, we find the various institutions and practices of representative government. Notably among these are that control over the policies of government is constitutionally vested in official representatives, and that such representatives are chosen through fair and frequent elections (Dahl 1989).

Thought about this way, a crucial test of representative democracy is the responsiveness of elected officials to the views of their constituents. Representatives must decide how to spend their time, focus their activities, and ultimately vote on matters of policy. As they go about their business, what weight do they give to the views of their constituents?[26]

Quite a bit, it turns out. Correspondence between public opinion and government action is impressive. Stimson, MacKuen, and Erikson summarize their work on the quick response of government to swings in the national mood with this arresting metaphor: "Politicians are keen to pick up the faintest signals in their political environment. Like antelope in an open field, they cock their ears and focus their full attention on the slightest sign of danger" (1995, p. 559). When public opinion shifts, elected officials adjust their positions and modify their votes accordingly. The movement of public opinion over time is, according to James Stimson, the "drive wheel" (2004, p. xvi) of politics, the single most important factor in American political life.[27]

In short, if we have succeeded in establishing an important role for ethnocentrism in public opinion, then we are likely on to something of real social consequence, for public opinion influences the shape and direction of government policy. How might ethnocentrism influence the shape and direction of government policy?

We might surmise, first of all, that the ready availability of ethnocentrism makes military intervention and vigorous defense of the homeland more compelling than they would otherwise be.

We might point out that ethnocentrism undermines foreign aid and humanitarian assistance. We began chapter 5 by invoking the memory of the Rwandan genocide and pointing out that the United States did nothing to stop the slaughter that took place there in the spring and summer of 1994. The same can now be said about Darfur and Sudan.

We might better appreciate the obstacles in the way of more open and generous policies on immigration.

We might wonder what happened to American concern over AIDS. As of August 2006, 65 million people around the world were infected with HIV/AIDS; 22 million had already perished. According to a recent UN sponsored report, AIDS has "reversed the course of human development" and "eroded improvements in life expectancy." The problem is still with us—but its epicenter has moved to sub-Saharan Africa. The further away culturally and geographically AIDS appears to be, the more difficult it will be for AIDS to capture the American public's attention and interest.[28]

Finally, we might notice that the United States spends relatively little of its gross domestic product on the provision of social welfare; it offers no national health insurance or family assistance; its public aid and unemployment insurance programs are, comparatively speaking, stingy (Weir, Orloff, and Skocpol 1988). There are two striking—and expensive—exceptions to the general pattern: old-age pensions (Social Security) and health care for the elderly (Medicare), where U.S. policy is relatively generous. The overall shape of the American welfare state, of course, corresponds closely to the way ethnocentrism operates in this domain. On the one hand, Americans (white Americans, for the most part) seem to regard most welfare programs as government handouts to (nonwhite) people who are trying to get something for nothing. Help for *them*, in short. On the other hand, they see Social Security and Medicare as governmental obligations to deserving (white) workers earned through a lifetime of hard work. Rewards for *us*. Thus it could be said that when it comes to welfare policy, the (white) public, motivated partly by ethnocentrism, seems to be getting just what it wants.[29]

Ethnocentrism is not the sole determinant of public opinion. It is often important, but public opinion is shaped by a multiplicity of forces. Equally important to keep in mind, public opinion is not simply and automatically translated into public policy. Other forces are operating, some working against opinion. Conceding this, it remains likely that insofar as ethnocentrism's influence is registered on opinion, it registers on policy as well. If ethnocentrism could be erased (a most unlikely prospect) or its importance for politics diminished (more likely), Americans would be living in a different country than they do now—and in a different world as well.

Appendix

Information about the National Election Studies can be found at its home page: http://electionstudies.org. Datasets are available for public download directly from the NES Web site and by researchers at ICPSR member institutions at http://icpsr .umich.edu.

Information about the General Social Surveys can be found at http://gss.norc .org. The General Social Surveys cumulative datafile is available for download by researchers at ICPSR member institutions at http://icpsr.umich.edu (Study #4697).

Information about the Political Socialization Study can be found in Jennings and Niemi (1981, appendix A) and Jennings and Stoker (1999). The youth and parent datasets are available for download by researchers at ICPSR member institutions at http://icpsr.umich.edu (Study #7286 [youth-parent 1965]; #7779 [youth-parent 1965–1973]; #9553 [youth-parent 1965–1982]; #4037 [youth 1965–1997]).

The 1992–94 Multi-City Study for Urban Inequality is available for download by researchers at ICPSR member institutions at http://icpsr.umich.edu (Study #2535).

The 1996 National Black Election Study is available for download by researchers at ICPSR member institutions at http://icpsr.umich.edu (Study #2029).

Ethnocentrism: Surveys, Variables, and Coding

2004 NES

Stereotypes of Whites, Blacks, Hispanics, and Asians on three traits: lazy to hard-working, unintelligent to intelligent, and not trustworthy to trustworthy: v045222 to v045233.

Feeling thermometers of Whites, Blacks, Hispanics, and Asians: v045086, v045077, v045056, v045075.

Race/ethnicity of respondent: v043303x, v043305, v03306, v043299.

2000 NES

Stereotypes of Whites, Blacks, Hispanics, and Asians on three traits: lazy to hard-working, unintelligent to intelligent, and not trustworthy to trustworthy: v001574 to v001585.

Feeling thermometers of Whites, Blacks, Hispanics, and Asians: v001309, v001308, v001316, v001327.

Race/ethnicity of respondent: v001011, v001012, v001013, v001006a, v000066, v001030.

1996 NES

Stereotypes of Whites, Blacks, and Hispanics on three traits: lazy to hard-working, unintelligent to intelligent, and not trustworthy to trustworthy: v961311 to v961319.

Feeling thermometers of Whites, Blacks, and Hispanics: v961029, v961030, v961037.

Race/ethnicity of respondent: v960703, v960705, v960706, v960708, v960709, v960067.

1992 NES

Stereotypes of Whites, Blacks, Hispanics, and Asians on three traits: hard-working to lazy, unintelligent to intelligent, and violent to peaceful: v926221 to v926232.

Feeling thermometers of Whites, Blacks, Hispanics, and Asians: v925333, v925323, v925327, v925339.

Race/ethnicity of respondent: v924116, v924118, v924119, v924122, v924123, v924202.

1988 NES

Feeling thermometers of Whites, Blacks, and Hispanics: v880625, v880617, v880613.

Race/ethnicity of respondent: v880537, v880541, v880539, v880412.

2000 GSS

Stereotypes of Whites, Blacks, Hispanics, and Asians on three traits: hard-working to lazy, unintelligent to intelligent, violent to peaceful: work[whts/blks/hsps/asns]; intl[whts/blks/hsps/asns]; viol[whts/blks/hsps/asns]. *Violence* item was administered to only half the sample; ethnocentrism measure combines all available items for each respondent.

Race/ethnicity of respondent: race, hispanic.

1990 GSS

Stereotypes of Whites, Blacks, Hispanics, and Asians on five traits: hard-working to lazy, unintelligent to intelligent, violent to peaceful, patriotic to not patriotic, self-supporting to not self-supporting: work[whts/blks/hsps/asns]; intl[whts/blks/hsps/asns]; viol[whts/blks/hsps/asns]; patr[whts/blks/hsps/asns]; fare[whts/blks/hsps/asns]

Race/ethnicity of respondent: race, hispanic.

1992–94 Multi-City Study of Urban Inequality

Stereotypes of Whites, Blacks, Hispanics, and Asians on four traits: intelligent to unintelligent, easy to get along with to hard to get along with, treat others equally to discriminate against others, and involved in drugs and gangs to not

involved in drugs and gangs: dintl[wht/blkhis/asn]; deasy[wht/blk/his/asn]; dtret[wht/blk/his/asn]; ddrug[wht/blk/his/asn]. The MCSUI also included three additional traits (rich to poor, prefer to be self-supporting to prefer to live off welfare, speak English well to speak English poorly). These items were not used, as they were either "factual" rather than trait assessments or they were too close in content to the dependent variables we analyzed.
Race/ethnicity of respondent: crace, chispan.

1996 NBES
Feeling thermometers of Whites, Blacks, Hispanics, and Asians: b1p, b1n, b1w, b1u

1965 Political Socialization Study (Youth-Parent Dyad)—Study #7286
Feeling thermometers (Youth Respondents) of Whites and Blacks; Catholics, Jews, and Protestants: v197, v199, v194, v196, v198
Race/ethnicity of Youth: v297
Religious denomination of Youth: v265
Feeling thermometers (Parent Respondents) of Whites and Blacks; Catholics, Jews, and Protestants: v441, v443, v438, v440, v442
Race/ethnicity of Parent: v584
Religious denomination of Parent: v557

1965–1973 Political Socialization Study (Youth)—Study #7779-001
Feeling thermometers of Whites and Blacks; Catholics, Jews, and Protestants: v259, v261, v256, v260, v258 (in 1965); v773, v775, v770, v772, v774 (in 1973)
Race/ethnicity of respondent: v232
Religious denomination of respondent: v200; v748

1965–1973 Political Socialization Study (Parents)—Study #7779-002
Feeling thermometers of Whites and Blacks; Catholics, Jews, and Protestants: v287, v289, v284, v286, v288 (in 1965); v465, v467, v456, v464, v466 (in 1973)
Race/ethnicity of respondent: v268
Religious denomination of respondent: v241; v693

1965–1973–1997 Political Socialization Study (Youth)—Study #4037
Feeling thermometers of Whites and Blacks; Catholics, Jews, and Protestants: v259, v261, v256, v260, v258 (in 1965); v773, v775, v770, v772, v774 (in 1973); v5608, v5611, v5612, v5614, v5615 (in 1997)
Race/ethnicity of respondent: v232
Religious denomination of respondent: v200; v748; v6500

Independent Variables: Surveys, Variables, and Coding

These independent variables are used in multiple chapters. Less commonly used independent variables are described in the Notes. Where exceptions to these codings occur, they are described in the Notes.

Age: A set of dummy variables with ages 40–49 serving as the suppressed reference group or a single variable with six categories, ranging from 0 (17–29) to 1 (70 or over).

Authoritarianism: An additive index ranging from 0 (not) to 1 (authoritarian).

Education: A seven-category variable ranging from 0 (< 9 years) to 1 (advanced degree).

Egalitarianism: An additive index ranging from 0 (not) to 1 (egalitarian).

Female: A dummy taking on a value of 1 (female); 0 (male).

Household Economic Evaluations: A scale (if available) or single item ranging from 0 (much worse than one year ago) to 1 (much better).

Household Income: A series of dummies (including a dummy for refusals) with $40K–$50K serving as the suppressed reference group in 2004 and $35K–$50K serving as the suppressed reference group for other years. Or, in pooled analysis, a series of dummies referring to percentile within the sample, with the 0–25th percentile serving as the suppressed reference group.

Ideological Identification: A series of dummies (including a dummy for DK/ refused to choose), typically with moderates serving as the suppressed reference group; or a seven-category variable ranging from 0 (extremely conservative) to 1 (extremely liberal).

Limited Government: An additive index ranging from 0 (want more active government) to 1 (want less active government).

Moral Traditionalism: An additive index ranging from 0 (not) to 1 (traditional).

National Economic Evaluations: A scale (if available) or single item ranging from 0 (much worse than one year ago) to 1 (much better).

Occupation: A series of dummies indicating the degree of occupational threat (low/medium/high and out of the labor market) with the suppressed reference group indicating those with medium threat jobs. Or, in select analyses, dummies indicating the nature of occupation.

Partisanship: A seven-category variable ranging from 0 (strong Republican) to 1 (strong Democrat).

Political Awareness: An additive index ranging from 0 (low) to 1 (high).

Race/Ethnicity: Black: A dummy taking on a value of 1 (black); 0 (Hispanic or white).

Race/Ethnicity: Hispanic: A dummy taking on a value of 1 (Hispanic); 0 (black or white).

Racial Resentment: An additive index ranging from 0 (not) to 1 (resentful).

Religiosity: An additive index ranging from 0 (not) to 1 (religious).

Religious Denomination: A series of dummies, with mainline Protestants serving as the suppressed reference group.

Religious Doctrine: A measure of how literally the respondent reads the Bible, from 0 (not) to 1 (Bible is the word of God).

Social Trust: An additive index ranging from 0 (not) to 1 (highly trusting).

Variable codes appear in the tables that follow.

TABLE A.1. Variable codes: National election studies

	2004 NES	2000 NES	1996 NES	1992 NES	1990 NES	1988 NES
Age	v043250	v000908	V960605	v923903	v900548	v880414
Authoritarianism	v045208- v045211	v001586- v001589	—	v926019- v926022	—	—
Education	v043254	v000913	V960610	v923908	v900554	v880422
Egalitarianism	v045212- v045217	v001521- v001526	v961229- v961234	v926024- v926029	v900426- v900431	v880924- v880928
Female	v043411	v001029	V960066	v924201	v900547	v880413
Household economic evaluations	v043062	v001412a	V960338	v923426 v923430	v900417	v880207
Household income	v043293x	v000994	V960701	v924104	v900663	v880520
Ideological identification	v045117 v045118	v001368 v001370	V960365	v923509 v923513	v900320	v880274
Limited government	v045150- v045152	v001420- v001422	v961144- v961146	v925729- v925731	v900331, v900333, v900335	—
Moral traditionalism	v045189- v045192	v001530- v001533	v961247- v961250	v926115- v926119	v900500- v900502	v880951- v880954
National economic evaluations	v043098	v00491	v960386 v961478	v923528 v923530 v923532	v900423	v880244
Occupation	v043262b v043260a	v000980 v000919	v960665 v960616	v923922 v923914	—	—
Partisanship	v043116	v000523	V960420	v923634	v900320	v880274
Political awareness	v045162- v045165	v001446a/b, v001449a/b v001452a/b, v001455a/b	v961189- v961192 v961072 v961073	v925915- v925921 v925951 v925952	v900395- v900401	v880871- v880879
Racial resentment	v045193- v045196	v001508- v001511	v960487 v961207 v961210	v926126- v926129	v900520- v900523	v880961- v880964
Religiosity	v043219 v043220 v043223- v043225	v000872, v000873, v000877, v000879, v000880	v960571 v960572 v960576 v960578	v923820- v923822 v923826 v923828 v923829	—	v880932 v880933 v880530- v880531
Religious denomination	v043247 v043247a	v000904	v960602 v960600	v923850 v923846	—	—
Religious doctrine	v043222	v000876	V960575	v923824	—	—
Social trust	v045186- v045188	v001475- v001477	v960567 v960569	v926139 v926140	—	—

—: Not available or not used.

	1990 GSS	2000 GSS	1992–94 MCSUI	1996 NBES
Age	age	age	—	—
Authoritarianism	ownthing	obey	—	—
	talkback	thnkself		
	twoclass	helpoth		
	openmind	spanking		
	obey			
	spanking			
Education	degree	degree	eedudeg	qy3
Egalitarianism	socdif4	inequal3	—	—
		inequal5		
		inequal7		
Female	sex	sex	crespex	qz2
Political awareness	—	—	—	ql4
				ql4aa
				ql4ba
				ql5
Household economic evaluations	satfin finalter finrela	satfin finalter finrela	—	—
Household income	income86	income98	efaminc	—
Ideology	polviews	polviews	clibcons	—
Limited government	helpnot	helpnot	—	—
Moral traditionalism	premarsx	premarsx	—	—
	teensex	teensex		
	xmarsex	xmarsex		
	homosex	homosex		
National economic evaluations	—	—	—	—
Occupation	occ80	occ80	fwkstat	—
	wrkstat	wrkstat		
Partisanship	partyid	partyid	cpolprty	—
Racial Resentment	racdif1	racdif1	—	—
	racdif4	racedif4		
		racpush		
		wrkwayup		
Religiosity	pray	pray	—	—
	attend	attend		
Religious denomination	relig	relig	—	—
Religious doctrine	bible	bible	—	—
Social trust	—	trust	—	—
		fair		
		helpful		

—: Not available or not used.

Notes

Introduction

1. The comprehensive sociology imagined by Sumner was completed by his associates following his death and published in four volumes by Yale University Press (Sumner, Keller, and Davie 1927).

Sumner was energetic in his political pursuits as well. Awakened in his middle years to the dangers of socialism, Sumner spoke forcefully and wrote prolifically against the interference of government in the splendid human struggle for survival so vividly underway in the new industrial age. Much like his inspiration Herbert Spencer across the Atlantic, Sumner believed that in the absence of government meddling, market forces and ferocious competition would handsomely reward those who displayed courage, enterprise, and good training, while depositing those who lacked the requisite virtues at the bottom of society, precisely where they belonged. A fine account of Sumner's career as an advocate of social Darwinism can be found in Hofstadter ([1944] 1959).

2. For more recent evidence on this point, see M. Brewer and Brown (1998); M. Brewer and Campbell (1976); D. Campbell and LeVine (1961); and Tajfel et al. (1971). This literature is persuasive, as far as it goes, but what is missing, perhaps surprisingly, is systematic evidence on ethnocentrism in postindustrial societies like the United States.

3. So says LeVine (2001). To assure ourselves that this was so—that ethnocentrism is essentially invisible in empirical studies of American public opinion—we examined the *American Political Science Review*, the *American Journal of Political Science*, the *Journal of Politics*, and *Public Opinion Quarterly*, from 1975 to 2000. We sought first to identify any article that included the terms *ethnocentrism* and *public opinion*. This search turned up a grand total of 25 articles—roughly one paper per year, or, in another metric, .5 percent of the 4,735 articles published in these journals over this time period. We looked closely at this set of 25 and found that not a single one addressed ethnocentrism in a direct or sustained way. Outside the purview of this search, we found two examples from outside the United States: one on ethnocentrism and support for LePen and the National Front in France (Mayer 1993), and the other on ethnocentrism and hostility to immigration among Italians (Sniderman et al. 2000).

Chapter One

1. Geertz (1973, p. 196). Geertz offered this parable as a comment on the glaring inadequacies, as he saw it, in the conceptualizations of ideology then dominating the social sciences. His warning is entirely general, however.

2. Our conception of ethnocentrism is broadly consistent with standard views across the social sciences. For example, in *The Dictionary of Anthropology*, Michael Rhum writes that ethnocentrism is "the belief that one's own culture is superior to others, which is often accompanied by a tendency to make invidious comparisons" (1997, p. 155). According to Robert LeVine in the *International Encyclopedia of the Social and Behavioral Sciences*, ethnocentrism refers "to culturally biased judgment, i.e., applying the frame of reference provided by one's culture to an object, action, person, or group of a different culture" (2001, p. 4852). In a chapter prepared for the *Harvard Encyclopedia of American Ethnic Groups*, Thomas Pettigrew, a social psychologist by training, defines ethnocentrism to be "the unquestioned belief in the superiority of one's own ethnic group and the consequent inferiority of other groups" (1982, p. 3). The historian John Higham conceives of ethnocentrism as a universal inclination to greet outsiders with disdain and suspicion; to regard the "manners, mere habits of life, and social practices" of foreigners as inferior to one's own ([1955] 1988, p. 24). And finally, to Lévi-Strauss, ethnocentrism "consists in the pure and simple repudiation of cultural forms (moral, religious, social, and aesthetic) which are the most remote from those with which we identify" (1983, p. 328).

3. On the difference between typological and population thinking in biology, see Mayr (2001).

4. It may be useful here to distinguish ethnocentrism from other related terms as well. Ethnocentrism is related to, but not the same as, *intolerance*, which Thomas Pettigrew defines as "a rejection of out-groups because of their differences from the in-group" (1982, p. 3), and from *xenophobia*, defined by Donald Campbell (1947) as a generalized fear and hatred toward strangers. While ethnocentrism includes both out-group hostility and in-group loyalty, intolerance and xenophobia refer to hostility toward out-groups alone.

Nor, by the same logic, should ethnocentrism be confused with *racism*, a point made forcefully by William J. Wilson in *Power, Racism, and Privilege* (1973). In Wilson's view, ethnocentrism is disdain for out-groups on account of their biological or cultural deficiencies. But racism is this and more: it is also a philosophy of exploitation and exclusion. Racism puts ethnocentrism to political purpose, providing justification for inequality and motivation for policies of exclusion.

Nor is ethnocentrism the same as *nativism*. In *Strangers in the Land* ([1955] 1988), the classic historical work on patterns of American nativism from the Civil War to the second decade of the twentieth century, John Higham regards ethnocentrism as pervasive, indeed a universal human reaction to strangers, one characterized primarily by distrust and suspicion. But nativism is something else again; it is meaner and more dangerous. Nativism, according to Higham, combines the general ethnocentric suspicion of strangers with the political fear that certain strangers pose a threat to the nation: that they are subversive, or disloyal, or fundamentally alien, unwilling or unable to be assimilated to American ways. In Higham's framework, nativism draws on ethnocentrism; ethnocentrism is "the cultural subsoil" from which nativism grows" (p. 24), but nativism is also something more, a political ideology. Higham wants to reserve suspicions of political habits and loyalties for nativism. There is nothing in "mere" ethnocentrism, according to Higham, about threats to country, national cohesion, or American identity.

Finally, ethnocentrism is not the same as *group identification* since group identification is concerned entirely with the in-group and has nothing to say, one way or the other, about out-groups (e.g., Centers 1949; Converse 1958; Gurin, Hatchett, and Jackson 1989).

5. After Sumner completed *Folkways*, Georg Simmel (1923/translated 1955) published a more systematic statement on social conflict, one that subsumed most of what Sumner claimed. In

later works, Sumner is not always cited, but his insight into the origins of ethnocentrism remains present: in Blalock (1967), Bonacich (1972, 1973), Coser (1956), Blumer (1958), Sherif and Sherif ([1953] 1966), Bobo (1988), Olzak (1992), Olzak and Nagel (1986), among others. Our purpose here is to accentuate the similarities among these various positions, to identify central tendencies and consolidate the strong family resemblances. Donald Campbell (1965) gave this family of related ideas the single name realistic group conflict theory, a practice we follow here.

6. This basic finding—competition inducing out-group animosity—has been replicated in a number of other well-designed field experiments. The classic Robbers Cave study is described in detail in Sherif et al. (1961). Essentially the same results were found in an earlier field experiment carried out in the summer of 1949 in northern Connecticut (Sherif and Sherif [1953] 1966). Additional replications are reported in Blake and Mouton (1962, 1979). We should mention that Robbers Cave included a third stage in which cooperation toward a shared goal replaced competition, which largely succeeded in reducing tensions and hostilities between the groups.

7. Key's observations in *Southern Politics* have been corroborated by scores of subsequent investigations. This work demonstrates the lingering significance of the black belt in southern politics and establishes the more general point of the political importance of numbers. As the great migration carried blacks out of the rural South into the cities, South and North, black belts were created everywhere. And time and again, as the black share of the population increased, whites' political reaction became more hostile. For a sampling of this literature, see Kousser (1974); Matthews and Prothro (1963); Black and Black (1987); Heard (1952); G. Wright (1976, 1977); Sundquist ([1973] 1983); Giles and Evans (1986); Pettigrew (1959); Smith (1981); Glaser (1994); Blalock (1967); and Giles and Hertz (1994).

More generally, disputes over school integration, affirmative action, immigration, fishing rights for Native Americans, and more, have all been profitably analyzed in group conflict terms (e.g., Bobo 1999; Bobo and Hutchings 1996; Bobo and Tuan 2006; Kinder and Sanders 1996; Quillian 1995).

8. Realistic group conflict theory has other problems. One is a preoccupation with conflict over exclusively material resources (Horowitz 1985); another is the assumption that conflict is realistic, that participants are always clear-eyed (Kinder and Sanders 1996); and a third is that when conflict is removed, or even replaced by incentives to cooperate, in-group favoritism is "remarkably hard to eradicate" (Brewer and Brown 1998, p. 566).

9. Principal sources, in addition to the study itself, include Christie (1954), Altemeyer (1981), and, most important, Roger Brown's essay (1965), written as a chapter for the first edition of his splendid textbook, *Social Psychology*, which remains to this day the most insightful discussion of *The Authoritarian Personality*, the methodological hue and cry that it incited, and what remained after the dust settled.

10. Daniel Levinson was also primarily responsibly for the portions of the study on the meaning and measurement of ethnocentrism. See, for example, Levinson's paper on ethnocentrism that appeared in the *Journal of Psychology* in 1949.

11. Levinson combed through "the writing of virulent anti-Semites; technical, literary, and reportorial writings on anti-Semitism and fascism; and, most important, everyday anti-Semitism as revealed in parlor discussion, in the discriminatory practices of many businesses and institutions, and in the literature of various organizations which are trying, with small success, to counter numerous anti-Semitic accusations by means of rational argument" (Adorno et al., 1950, p. 58).

12. In more technical language, the scale is highly reliable—split-half reliability coefficients for the ten-item version of the anti-Semitism scale run 0.90 or higher—and responses to the various propositions appear to reflect a single factor.

13. Here are some examples:

Negroes have their rights, but it is best to keep them in their own districts and schools and to prevent too much contact with whites.

The main threat to American institutions during this century has come from the infiltration of foreign ideas, doctrines, and agitators.

Filipinos are all right in their place, but they carry it too far when they dress lavishly, buy good cars, and go around with white girls.

European refugees may be in need, but it would be a big mistake to lower our immigration quotas and allow them to flood the country.

14. A fourteen-item version of the ethnocentrism scale has a reliability of about 0.80. Adorno et al. report a Pearson correlation between the anti-Semitism scale and the ethnocentrism scale of 0.80 (1950, p. 122). When corrected for attenuation due to random error in measurement (Carmines and Zeller 1979), the correlation rises to 0.87.

15. Here are a few sample items:

Obedience and respect for authority are the most important virtues children can learn.

An insult to our honor should always be punished.

Nowadays when so many different kinds of people move around so much and mix together so freely, a person has to be careful to protect himself against infection and disease.

The thirty-eight-item version of the F scale has a reliability of about 0.75.

16. This quotation appears in *The Authoritarian Personality*'s opening paragraph (p. 1). Anti-Semitism, ethnocentrism, and authoritarianism are also associated with conservative economic and political beliefs (as assessed by the Politico-Economic-Conservatism scale). The relationships are less striking here than in the social realm: Adorno et al. say that the relationships are "qualitatively imperfect . . . and qualitatively complex" (p. 207).

As for the origins of authoritarianism, Adorno, Frenkel-Brunswik, Levinson, and Sanford looked to the family. They argued that predispositions to authoritarianism were created out of a harsh and punitive home life. Children raised by parents who were strict, emotionally distant, and preoccupied with status and who organized family life around clearly defined and rigidly enforced roles of domination and submission were thereby excellent candidates for authoritarianism.

17. Especially devastating were the essays collected in Christie and Jahoda (1954), particularly Hyman and Sheatsley's masterly critique.

18. Classic papers on response set include Cronbach (1946) and Couch and Kenniston (1960). For how acquiescence cripples the empirical work presented in *The Authoritarian Personality*, see Christie, Havel, and Seidenberg (1958); D. Campbell, Siegman, and Rees (1967); and Altemeyer (1981).

19. Over the years, investigation into authoritarianism continued, though with a few important exceptions, this work drifted away from the theoretical framework and grand ambition of the original (Altemeyer 1981; Meloen 1993). A notable exception is the research program

of Altemeyer, which kept the hypothesis of the authoritarian personality alive almost single-handedly for more than a decade: *Right-Wing Authoritarianism* (1981), *Enemies of Freedom* (1988), and *The Authoritarian Specter* (1996).

20. The most important studies are D. Campbell and McCandless (1951); Selznick and Steinberg (1969); Prothro (1950); McFarland, Ageyev, and Abalikina (1993); and McFarland, Ageyev, and Abalikina-Paap (1990). Some of Altemeyer's results can be read as support for an ethnocentric syndrome as well (Altemeyer 1981, 1988, 1996), as can some of the results reported by Stenner (2005).

None of these results unfortunately has anything to say about in-group loyalty, about whether hostility toward out-groups is accompanied by reverence toward in-groups, as William Graham Sumner insisted and as argued in *The Authoritarian Personality*.

21. One might have thought that this connection had already been established by Altemeyer. In a series of careful studies, he developed a reliable and balanced scale of authoritarianism. He then proceeded to demonstrate that authoritarianism, so measured, is systematically associated with a variety of social and political beliefs, including both specific prejudices and general ethnocentrism.

These various results are reported in *Right-Wing Authoritarianism* (1981), *Enemies of Freedom* (1988), and *The Authoritarian Specter* (1996). Altemeyer's studies almost always entail comparisons between his measure of authoritarianism and related measures: the original F scale, a balanced F scale, a dogmatism scale, and a conservatism scale, among others. (Altemeyer refers to such studies as "pitting experiments.") Almost always, Altemeyer's measure outperforms the rest.

In some respects this evidence is quite impressive, but it falls short of proving that ethnocentrism has its roots in personality. Altemeyer was careful in developing a superior measure of authoritarianism. It is balanced to avoid the problem that sank the original scale. And it is demonstrably reliable. But Altemeyer's measure has problems of its own. Most important, it is full of propositions that make explicit social and political claims, such as these:

A "woman's place" should be wherever she wants it to be. The days when women are submissive to their husbands and social conventions belong strictly in our past.

The only way our country can get through the crisis ahead is to get back to our traditional values, put some tough leaders in power, and silence the troublemakers spreading bad ideas.

Gays and lesbians are just as healthy and moral as anybody else.

The problem here is partly that such propositions seem far from their claimed destination: the configuration of unconscious drives, wish fulfillments, and emotional impulses that make up personality. And it is partly that Altemeyer's measure of authoritarianism bears an uncomfortably close resemblance to the social and political beliefs that authoritarianism is supposed to explain.

22. The measure is reasonably reliable (typical Cronbach's $alpha = 0.60$). It avoids the response set problem that plagued the original measure (while remaining true to the core concept of authoritarianism introduced by Adorno and his colleagues). And it avoids tautology. It is a long way to go from the view that children should be taught obedience and respect for authority to, say, support for the proposal that people with AIDS should be quarantined. It is not at all obvious that the two should be related. If it turns out that the one predicts the other, we have learned something surprising, something that calls out for explanation.

Feldman (2003) develops a more complex inventory. It includes virtues that children should be taught ("It may well be that children who talk back to their parents respect them more in the long run" versus "Obedience and respect for authority are the most important virtues children can learn"), but also encompasses an abstract preference for conformity over autonomy ("It's best for everyone if people try to fit in instead of acting in unusual ways" versus "People should be encouraged to express themselves in unique and possibly unusual ways"), fear of disorder over expanding freedom ("Society is always on the verge of disorder and lawlessness and only strict laws can prevent it" versus "It is more important to give people control over their lives than to create additional laws and regulations"), general respect for norms and traditional values ("Rules are there for people to follow, not to change" versus "Society's basic rules were created by people and so can always be changed by people"), and giving priority to social cohesion ("In the long run, our cultural and ideological differences will make us a healthier, more creative, and stronger society" versus "It is unlikely that this country will survive in the long run unless we can overcome our differences and disagreements"). All of this—five components, seventeen pairs of items ($alpha$ = 0.80)—is then combined with a measure abstracted from Schwartz's value inventory (twenty items or so) to form one general and highly reliable measure of authoritarianism.

23. Here we are passing over—but only temporarily—Stenner's main point, on the activation of authoritarianism. We will pick up her argument in the next chapter.

24. To be fair, Levinson and his associates initiated their investigation hoping to illuminate the nature and origins of anti-Semitism and its implications for democratic society. They deliberately restricted their attention to why some were more ready than others to accept anti-Semitic ideology. Their object was to develop a psychology of prejudice, to understand why some people accept prejudice while others reject it. They never intended their study, massive as it was, to provide a comprehensive account of prejudice.

25. To reconstruct social identity theory, we draw principally on Tajfel and Turner (1979; John Turner was at the time a Bristol colleague); Hogg and Abrams (1988), a textbook devoted to social identity theory; and *Human Groups and Social Categories* (1981), a collection of Tajfel's own essays that represent the evolution of his thinking (and, not coincidentally, a picture of the parallel development of the European perspective on social psychology).

For reviews of this literature, see Brewer and Brown (1998); Huddy (2003); and Turner and Reynolds (2003). For applications of social identity theory to political analysis, see Huddy and Khatib (2007); Conover (1984); Fowler and Kam (2007); Gibson and Gouws (2000); Kam and Ramos (2008); and Sniderman, Pierangelo, De Figueiredo, and Piazza (2000).

26. Assignment to treatment in these experiments is, of course, always random.

27. The original minimal group experiment is reported in Tajfel, Billig, Bundy, and Flament (1971). Versions of the ultimate minimal group experiment were carried out by Billig and Tajfel (1973) and by Locksley, Ortiz, and Hepburn (1980). For reviews of the now extensive work on the minimal group experiment (more than one hundred studies have been published), see Brewer (1979); Brewer and Kramer (1985); Brown (1986); Messick and Mackie (1989); Hewstone, Rubin, and Willis (2002); Mullen, Brown, and Smith (1992); and Brewer and Brown (1998).

28. The early minimal group experiments confounded favoritism that took the form of absolute profit for the in-group with favoritism that sought relative profit. Brewer and Silver (1978) designed an experiment that disentangled the two and found a clear preference for relative profit. A technical literature has grown up dedicated to the specific task of drawing inferences about which strategies of reward are being employed by participants in the minimal group experiments (cited and reviewed by Messick and Mackie 1989).

29. This seems a promising starting point, from a variety of perspectives. In John Rawls's theory of justice, for example, self-esteem is regarded as "perhaps the most important primary good" (1971, p. 440). In *Power and Society* (1950), Harold Lasswell and Abraham Kaplan treat self-respect as a superordinate value, an end in itself. And Roger Brown insists that a general psychological theory of ethnocentrism must "start with motives deeply rooted in individual psychology, motives that are primitive and universal" (1986, p. 542), and then points out that this is precisely where social identity theory begins.

On the other hand, the pursuit of positive self-esteem turns out to be much more important in some cultures than in others (Heine et al. 1999).

30. Tajfel (1981, p. 255).

31. Tajfel also emphasizes social comparison processes: social comparison refers to the process whereby individuals evaluate their own virtues and shortcomings. How beautiful or intelligent or successful people judge themselves to be depends on the standards they employ. On this point, social identity theory owes a clear debt to Festinger (1954). But Tajfel modifies Festinger's theory in several ways, the most important of which is to introduce and underscore the group basis of comparison. Festinger was primarily concerned with the comparisons individuals make among themselves and others. But, as Tajfel points out, this "neglects an important contributing aspect of an individual's self-definition: the fact that he is a member of numerous social groups and that this membership contributes, positively or negatively, to the image he has of himself" (1981, p. 254).

32. See evidence summarized by Brewer (1999, 2007).

33. The most important works here are M. Brewer and Campbell (1976); M. Brewer (1999, 2007).

34. On the automatic activation of in-group bias, see Farnham, Greenwald, and Banaji (1999); Otten and Moskowitz (2000); Otten and Wentura (1999); Perdue et al. (1990). In a review of studies of the development of group attitudes in children, Cameron et al. (2001) find that children routinely display in-group favoritism but not hostility toward out-groups.

35. Favoring Brewer's position is the evidence that in-group bias is expressed most commonly in claims about mutual trust. The best evidence on this point is supplied by the Cross-Cultural Study of Ethnocentrism, organized by Robert LeVine and Donald Campbell, and reported on in detail in Brewer and Campbell's *Ethnocentrism and Intergroup Attitudes* (1976). For experimental evidence consistent with this point, see Leach et al. (2007).

36. Brewer acknowledges that in-group loyalty can serve as a platform for out-group hate. This is likely to happen (1) when in-group moral superiority becomes entrenched and institutionalized, (2) under conditions of threat (when the out-group threatens the interests, values, and the very survival of the in-group), (3) with "proper" political engineering, and (4) when societies are divided by a single social cleavage.

37. Indeed, had we been tuned to see it, we might have noticed minimal group ethnocentrism even in Sherif's famous field experiment, which was dedicated to the creation of real conflicts over scarce resources. At the close of stage one, after the Eagles and Rattlers had undergone a series of activities intended to build in-group solidarity, the two groups were made aware for the first time of each other's existence. This knowledge, prior to any actual competition and prior even to any expectation of competition, was apparently enough to set off a round of derogatory name calling—ethnocentrism in the absence of real conflicts of interest (see Brewer 1979, p. 308).

38. Quote by Theodosius Dobzhansky (1964, p. 115). For an edifying presentation of the theory and evidence on evolution through natural selection, see Futuyma (1998).

39. Absent evolution, the social sciences resemble "astronomy without physics, biology without chemistry, and mathematics without algebra" (E. O. Wilson 1978, pp. 1–2).

40. *Sociobiology* spawned a new scientific discipline and was hailed by the International Animal Behavior Society as the most influential book of the twentieth century. Still, not everyone has cared to cross the bridge Wilson built between natural selection and human society. When *Sociobiology* was initially released, it was greeted with alarm and criticism. Some critics saw it as laying the groundwork for eugenics; others saw it as promoting biological determinism and stripping human beings of free will. Has it grown less controversial with time? Perhaps, but controversies remain (see, e.g., Freese, Li, and Wade 2003).

41. Technically speaking, the question here is whether ethnocentrism should be regarded as an *adaptation*: "a property of an organism, whether a structure, a physiological trait, a behavior, or any other attribute, the possession of which favors the individual in the struggle for existence" (Mayr 2001, p. 149).

42. E. O. Wilson (1978) also suggests how ethnocentrism might be adaptive in his analysis of the evolutionary origins of aggression. Wilson argues that aggression is an innate predisposition; that under certain specifiable conditions, humans are ready to fight; and that such aggression is facilitated by an irrationally exaggerated allegiance of individuals to their kin and tribe—that is, by ethnocentrism.

43. See especially the critique offered by George C. Williams, *Adaptation and Natural Selection* (1966).

44. See Sober and Wilson (1998) for a nontechnical presentation and defense of group selection; Mayr (2001) for an account of "hard" group selection; and Wilson and Wilson (2007) for an argument on behalf of multilevel natural selection.

Group members need not be related genetically for altruism to evolve. Group selection requires variation between groups—the more variation the better—but this variation need not be due to genealogical relatedness. *Cultural processes* can also cause offspring to resemble their parents, and this kind of heritable variation can also serve as the raw material for natural selection (Boyd and Richerson 1985). Cultural differences between human groups are often stable over long periods of time and are regularly and faithfully transmitted to descendent groups. They are heritable in the sense that offspring resemble parents—which is all that matters as far as the process of natural selection is concerned.

45. There are two other explanations for altruism worth mentioning.

In a series of influential papers, William Hamilton (1964, 1970, 1971a, 1971b, 1972) launched the modern genetic theory of altruism. The pivotal concept in Hamilton's analysis is *inclusive fitness*. Inclusive fitness is the sum of an individual's own fitness plus all its influence on fitness in the individual's relatives other than direct descendents—hence, the total effect of kin selection with reference to an individual. Relatives are related in a particular and important way: by common descent they share some fraction of genes in common. Like other animals, humans can duplicate their genes directly through survival and reproduction or indirectly, through the survival and reproduction of biological relatives, with whom genes are shared. Hamilton's key result is that, under the right conditions, genetically based altruism can evolve.

Pierre van den Berghe's (1978, 1981, 1995) theory of ethnocentrism argues that ethnic sentiments are extensions of kinship sentiments and that ethnocentrism is an extended form of nepotism—the universal propensity to favor kin over nonkin. Race and ethnicity, van den Berghe argues, are "extensions of the idiom of kinship" and therefore "ethnic and race sentiments are to be understood as an extended and attenuated form of kin selection" (1978, p. 403). For nearly all of human history—all but the last few thousand years, so virtually all of evolutionary time—human society consisted of tribes, or superfamilies: inbred populations of a few hundred people, sharing common descent, and maintaining clear territorial and social boundaries with outsiders. Within these small human societies, peace and cooperation prevailed; relations between groups, on the other hand, were characterized by mistrust and either avoidance or open conflict over scarce resources. Ethnocentrism evolved as an extension of kin selection. Eventually, kinship selection, a primordial model of social organization, was extended to much larger societies, partly through what van den Berghe calls "cultural inventions": unilineal descent, the idea of tracing descent either through the maternal or paternal line only; and lineage exogamy, the idea that marriage outside of a group is traced to a common progenitor.

It is no accident, van den Berghe would say, that cooperative ties among ethnic group members resemble the intense and emotional bonds of family or that public rhetoric about ethnicity commonly appeals to kinship, blood, and common descent. *All* human societies, van den Berghe says, practice kin selection and *all* are ethnocentric.

46. The founding of the field is usually traced to publication of Fuller and Thompson's monograph in 1960, though some regard Sir Francis Galton as the true founder of behavioral genetics: for his pioneering work on correlation, for his fascination with the inheritance of genius, and for the design and execution of the first twin study, carried out in an effort to separate the effects due to nurture from those due to nature, reported in 1883 (McClearn and DeFries 1973).

47. Paraphrasing Dobzhansky (1964, p. 55).

48. An example is the Minnesota Study of Twins Reared Apart (MISTRA), established in 1979. MISTRA's sample is drawn predominantly from the United States and the United Kingdom, but also from Australia, Canada, China, New Zealand, Sweden, and Germany, and is roughly representative of the broad middle class. Participants in MISTRA complete fifty hours of medical and psychological assessment, carried out at the University of Minnesota Department of Psychology and University Hospital. This assessment includes a zygosity analysis (based on assessments of blood groups, serum proteins, blood cell enzymes, fingerprint ridge counts, and standard anthropometric indicators) to determine whether the twin pair is identical or fraternal; intensive clinical interviews (which, among other things, pick up information about the pair's birth, separation, adoption, reunion, degree of contact, as well as information about the quality of the family environment); and extensive inventories on occupational interests, cognitive ability, personality traits, and social attitudes.

Human behavioral genetics is no longer exotic. It has taken its place in standard reviews (for example, in chapters prepared for the *Annual Review of Psychology* or for the *Handbook of Social Psychology*). Reports of behavioral genetic findings appear in the top field journals (*American Political Science Review, Journal of Personality and Social Psychology*, not to mention *Science*).

49. One exception to the presumption that attitudes are wholly learned is provided by William McGuire (1985) in his essay in the third edition of the *Handbook of Social Psychology*. After acknowledging that "attitude theorists typically abhor hypothesizing genetic influence," McGuire suggests that this is an excellent reason to open the question. He goes on to cite Donald Campbell and E. O. Wilson, and to suggest, further, that one place where the theory of evolution through natural selection might have a role to play is in ethnic hatred. Nowadays, "evolutionary psychology" has taken a seat at the table (not always entirely welcome, but definitely present): e.g., Buss and Kenrick (1998); and Sidanius and Kurzban (2003). There is now even some writing and research from this point of view on attitudes specifically: e.g., Tesser (1993); Crelia and Tesser (1996).

50. This study is presented in book-length detail in *Genes, Culture, and Personality* (Eaves, Eysenck, and Martin 1989). It was a seminal piece, but not the first. That honor goes to a brief

report by Eaves and Eysenck that appeared in *Nature* in 1974. In their comparison of MZ and DZ twins, they concluded that political ideology (stretching from radicalism on the left to conservatism on the right, based on a lengthy and reliable inventory) was largely inherited. That is, h^2 (or V^G/V^P, the fraction of the observed variance in conservatism that is caused by differences in heredity) = 0.65.

51. To be exact, $h^2 = 0.62$. Conservatism means what here? Most studies rely on the same measure: the so-called Wilson-Patterson Conservatism Scale. According to G. Wilson (1973), the scale is intended to tap conservatism in a very broad sense. This is conservatism as a kind of temperament, encompassing resistance to change, a preference for tradition, and an attachment to conventional forms of institutional arrangements and social practices. The fifty items that comprise the complete scale reflect these various aspects of conservatism (test-retest correlation of the complete scale is about 0.90). Responses to the items fall into correlated but distinct clusters, and one of these resembles ethnocentrism (or more precisely, out-group hostility), indicated by support for such things as white superiority, apartheid, and empire building, and rejection of such things as "colored" immigration, mixed marriages, and working mothers. Martin and colleagues (1986) present heritabilities for each individual item. These results suggest that these aspects of out-group hostility are, comparatively speaking, of middling heritability—neither extraordinarily genetic nor extraordinarily environmental in origin. And middling, remember, means that roughly half of the observed variation can be ascribed to genetic factors.

52. Research in behavioral genetics has also taken up the heritability of personality. It turns out that central personality traits appear to be substantially inherited, just as conservatism and ethnocentrism seem to be. Across a large number of studies, heritability estimates are centered at about 0.5. Differences in extraversion, conscientiousness, and so forth are due in important part to genetic endowments. Major studies in this tradition include Loehlin (1992) and Bouchard et al. (1990). Excellent reviews are provided by Bouchard and Loehlin (2001) and by Caspi, Roberts, and Shiner (2005).

Chapter Two

1. Sumner missed this point completely. His analysis treated membership as necessary and sufficient to the establishment of in-groups and out-groups. For Sumner, any and all membership groups are in-groups, any and all membership groups inspire solidarity and loyalty, and any and all membership groups necessarily and inevitably generate hostility toward those outside. For an effective critique of Sumner from the point of view of reference group theory, see Merton (1957) and Merton and Rossi (1957).

2. In *Party Systems and Voter Alignments* (1967), Lipset and Rokkan trace the origins of such cleavages back to the "two revolutions"—the national and the industrial—that mark the onset of modernity. The rise of the nation-state, Lipset and Rokkan argue, generated a pair of conflicts of high and continuing relevance to the practice of politics: one that opposed the nation-building center against the ethnically, linguistically, and religiously diverse subject populations in the provinces; the other that set the State against the Church. According to Lipset and Rokkan, the conflicts arising from the national revolution primarily concerned moral values and cultural identities. In contrast, the Industrial Revolution gave rise to conflict between economic interests. The expansion of markets and the rapid spread of new technologies opened up new and enduring cleavages: first between landed interests and the rising class of industrial entrepreneurs, and later between owners and employers, on the one side, and tenants and workers, on the other.

3. For variations on this argument, see Gelman (2003); Gelman and Hirschfeld (1999); Gil-White (2001); and Hirschfeld (1996). According to Lumsden and Wilson (1981), the inherited machinery of the brain includes the strong inclination to divide the world into binary categories (for example, in-group and out-group).

Natural kinds—such as tiger or tree—are distinguished from human artifacts—such as car or sweater (H. Putnam 1970; Quine 1977). Rothbart (Rothbart and Taylor 1992; Rothbart and Park 2004) suggests that categories for social groups—such as race—are typically understood (misunderstood) to be natural kinds. This is important because to categorize a particular instance into a natural kind category is to presume to know a great deal about it. Natural kind categories are rich in inductive potential; they are "laden in theory." As a consequence, "the imposition of natural kind structure onto our thinking about social categories gives disproportionate strength to category differences correlated with physical appearance" (Rothbart and Taylor 1992, p. 26).

4. Children either inherit a blueprint directly for ethnocentrism, or they inherit a blueprint for authoritarianism that makes ethnocentrism more appealing (McCourt et al. 1999; Scarr and Weinberg 1981; Stenner 2005), or both.

5. For an account of political socialization in terms of social learning theory, see Jennings and Niemi (1974) and Sears (1975).

6. Feldman (2003) thinks of this as a choice between competing values. He points out that systematic studies of social values across many countries repeatedly turn up a dimension that runs from social conformity, on the one side, to self-direction, on the other (Kohn 1977; Schwartz 1992). Stenner (2005) thinks of it in terms of personality. Hers is the stronger claim: that authoritarianism is a universal predisposition—deep-seated, perhaps innate, and difficult to alter. That is, Stenner looks at authoritarianism much as we look at ethnocentrism.

7. The most important studies in this tradition include, in addition to Stouffer (1955): Sullivan, Piereson, and Marcus (1982); McClosky and Brill (1983); Nunn, Crockett, and Williams (1978). For a review of the literature, see Kinder (1998).

8. *Almost* always, we should say. Sullivan, Piereson, and Marcus (1982) find that political tolerance has little to do with education. This is an important result: demoralizing, in fact, for liberal theorists who argue that education produces a more competent and responsible public. But the failure of Sullivan, Piereson, and Marcus to find a positive association between education and tolerance may be due to their procedure, which requires citizens to contemplate not just disagreeable groups but *exceedingly* disagreeable groups. The well educated may be more prepared than the less well educated to grant protection to run-of-the-mill objectionable speech and assembly, but not to extremists who practice intolerance themselves (Bobo and Licari 1989).

9. See, for example, Fraley and Roberts (2005); Kagan and Snidman (2004); Roberts and DelVecchio (2000). Test-retest correlations, uncorrected for measurement error, rise from roughly 0.40 in childhood to roughly 0.70 by late middle age. In their review, Caspi, Roberts, and Shiner (2005) regard this level of stability as "remarkably high" (p. 466), noting that only measures of cognitive ability are more stable. In this literature, stabilization is attributed variously to (i) genetic set points, to which people increasingly return; (ii) settling into congenial, reinforcing niches; and (iii) consolidation of identity.

10. See Jennings and Markus (1984); Jennings and Stoker (1999).

11. What we are trying to do here for ethnocentrism is what Stenner attempted to do for authoritarianism. Stenner (2005), and Feldman too (Feldman and Stenner 1997; Feldman 2003), argue that authoritarianism becomes especially relevant when social cohesion is threatened: when the culture appears to be fragmenting or when leaders prove themselves unworthy of

public trust. Then a whole ensemble of psychological tendencies—glorification of the in-group, denigration of the out-group, obedience to higher authority, conformity to traditional norms, intolerance toward those who fail to abide by society's rules—comes into play. This is the authoritarian dynamic (Stenner 2005), and Feldman and Stenner have accumulated an impressive amount of empirical support for it. Our interest in the activation of ethnocentrism is identical in spirit to Stenner's enterprise, but our argument takes a very different form.

12. We know a lot about this, thanks in large part to the fundamental contributions made in recent decades by Daniel Kahneman and Amos Tversky. Kahneman and Tversky follow in Simon's tradition in the sense that they take bounded rationality and satisficing for granted. Their work can be read as providing detail and specificity to Simon's claim. When confronted with "complexity and uncertainty, lacking the wits to optimize" (H. Simon 1979, p. 3), what is it, Kahneman and Tversky ask, that people actually do? In a series of influential experiments, Kahneman and Tversky show the following:

People routinely rely on simple heuristics to reduce the complexity of judgment tasks they confront. They do this even when they should know better, even when they do know better, and even when relying on heuristics is likely to lead them astray. (Tversky and Kahneman 1974)

Faced with simple choices, people are risk averse over the prospect of gains, risk-seeking in the domain of losses, and are generally more responsive to the possibility of loss than of gain. (Kahneman and Tversky 1979)

The judgments people reach and the decisions they make are subject to systematic and pervasive framing effects. Just how the problems people face and options available to them happen to be described play a large role—even when these alternative descriptions ("frames") are logically equivalent. (Tversky and Kahneman 1981)

These experiments caused a sensation. They gave rise to an industry of research; spawned an entire new field (called, somewhat oddly, "behavioral economics"); and, in time, delivered to Kahneman the Nobel Prize in Economic Science (Kahneman was awarded the Nobel Prize in 2002 for the work he did with Tversky, who died in 1996).

For summaries and reviews of this work, see Gilovich, Griffin, and Kahneman (2002); Kahneman (2003a); Kahneman and Frederick (2002); Kahneman, Slovic, and Tversky (1982); and Kahneman and Tversky (2000).

13. On the architecture for cognition in general, see Anderson (1983); Atkinson and Shiffrin (1968); and Broadbent (1958, 1971, 1982). On the characteristics of working memory in particular, see Miller (1957); Payne (1982); and H. Simon (1978).

Simon believed that emotion played an important role in agenda setting. He argued that intense and unexpected environmental events produce emotion, and emotion interrupts ongoing thinking and redirects attention to new problems (1967). In a less technical presentation, Simon (1983) offers Rachel Carson's *Silent Spring* as an example of emotion's role in fixing human attention. Why, Simon asks, was the book so influential? The problems she described were already known to biologists of the time. The book was influential, Simon suggested, because Carson described ecological problems "in a way that aroused emotion, that riveted our attention. . . . That emotion, once aroused, wouldn't let us go off and worry about other problems until something had been done about this one. At the very least, emotion kept the problem in the back of our minds as a nagging issue that wouldn't go away" (H. Simon 1983, p. 30). More generally, Simon argues that people "are able to attend to issues longer, to think harder about them, to receive deeper impressions that last longer, if information is presented in a context of emotion—a sort of hot dressing—than if it is presented wholly without affect" (1983, p. 32), a point not lost on politicians and journalists.

14. For evidence on the typically low salience of politics in everyday life, see A. Campbell, Converse, and Rodgers (1976); A. Campbell (1981). Levels of information about public affairs "are astonishingly low" (Converse 1975, p. 79; on this point, also see Delli Carpini and Keeter 1996; Price and Zaller 1993). On the notion of "nonattitudes," see Converse (1964, 1970). Evidence and arguments relevant to nonattitudes are reviewed in Kinder (1998, 2006).

15. For this point we are drawing primarily on the theoretical work of Robert Abelson (e.g., 1959, 1963, 1968, 1975, 1981; Schank and Abelson 1976). Abelson took as his original point of departure the exciting work on computer simulation of cognitive processes led by Herbert Simon and Allen Newell. Abelson found much to admire in this research, but also one glaring limitation. To Abelson's way of thinking, computational modeling was occupied entirely with the simulation of logical problem solving: with simulating how people prove theorems or play chess. There was as yet no provision for the study of cognition dealing with affect-laden objects—what Abelson (1963) called "hot cognition."

Abelson's aim was to specify a psychologically realistic model of opinion formation and change in sufficient detail so that it could be computationally simulated. He drew for theoretical inspiration from the seminal contributions of Heider (1944, 1946, 1958). Heider argued that mental representations can be characterized as balanced or imbalanced, as harmonious or discordant, and that people prefer the former to the latter. If an admired person commits a virtuous act, the two elements are perceived together without strain (they are balanced). But if a virtuous person commits a heinous crime, the two elements are imbalanced; "the factors in the situation 'do not add up'; they seem to pull in different directions. They leave us with a feeling of disturbance." (Heider 1958, p. 180). Such feelings instigate mental activity in the service of restoring balance: perhaps, we say to ourselves, the person is not so virtuous, perhaps the crime is not so horrible, perhaps the person did not commit the crime after all.

Working with Milton Rosenberg (1958; Rosenberg and Abelson 1960), Abelson developed and formalized Heider's intuition in a general model of "subjective rationality." Subjective rationality takes for granted that people tolerate a fair amount of imbalance; they simply don't notice it. Moreover, when people do notice imbalance, they often resolve it in a variety of ways that protect and preserve their original opinion. When a strongly held opinion is challenged by new information—when an imbalance is created—people have readily at their disposal a repertoire of defensive mental mechanisms. Under such circumstances, people may engage in denial, bolstering, rationalization, differentiation, and more—in order to restore balance and protect the original opinion (Abelson 1959, 1963, 1968).

Abelson and others went on to develop more realistic models of opinion formation and change, drawing on the development of connectionist theories of constraint satisfaction (Abelson 1975, 1976; Carbonell 1981; Read and Miller 1994; Schank and Abelson 1976; D. Simon and Holyoak 2002). The important point for our purposes is to note the widespread agreement within psychology that reasoning is motivated in ways that are broadly consistent with Abelson's original claims (Kahneman 2003a; Kunda 1990; Molden and Higgins 2005); that prominent models of public opinion take for granted that political reasoning is motivated (Sears and Whitney 1973; Taber and Lodge 2006; Zaller 1992); and that careful empirical studies have demonstrated that people are inclined to engage in active counterarguing with communications that challenge their opinions, dismissing such communications as weakly argued, unconvincing, and laced with error, much as Abelson would predict (e.g., Cacioppo and Petty 1979;

Edwards and Smith 1996; Tetlock 1998; Taber and Lodge 2006; Lord, Ross, and Lepper 1979; Pomerantz, Chaiken, and Tordesillas 1995).

We are not saying that the information appraisal process is *entirely* defensive; that people are utterly lost inside their own heads. The dynamic force behind consistency is modest, closer to a preference than a drive. As Robert Zajonc put it, in his fine review of the early work in consistency theory, "there is no anxiety when structures are imbalanced; imbalanced states are not noxious; a compelling need for balance is not assumed. Forces toward balance have the same character as Gestalt forces toward 'good figures' in the perception of forms" (1968, p. 341).

16. Agenda-setting effects are robust. They show up in studies that control on the possibility that news organizations are responding to the public's priorities (and not just the other way round); that take into account the independent effects due to real world conditions (e.g., changes in prices or interest rates); and that (in effect) translate the variation in news coverage that occurs naturally over time to contemporaneous variation across experimental conditions. Under stringent conditions and for a wide variety of problems, the American people's political priorities reflect what is showing up in their newspapers and on their television sets (e.g., Fan 1988; Funkhouser 1973; Iyengar and Kinder 1987; MacKuen 1981; McCombs and Shaw 1972; Neuman 1990; Protess et al. 1991; Semetko 2007).

17. Baumgartner and Jones (1993) acknowledge that media attention sometimes leads and sometimes follows changes in government agendas. Causality can likely go both ways. Their analysis is part of an effort to develop a model of policy change—what they call a "punctuated equilibrium model of policy change." The model is intended to account both for long periods of stability in policy (policy domination by entrenched elites) and for rapid change in policy (periods of short bursts of even violent change, where ostensibly entrenched elites find themselves on the losing side). Periods of change entail the destruction of "policy monopolies" (stable institutional arrangements supported by a powerful idea). This process is typically (almost always) set in motion by changes in the intensity of interest: "People, political leaders, government agencies, and private institutions which once had shown no interest in a particular question become involved for some reason. That reason is typically a new understanding of the nature of the policies involved" (1993, p. 8). Baumgartner and Jones conclude that shifts in media attention are often an important element in monopoly destruction.

18. Framing effects expose a particularly unrealistic assumption of rationality: namely, that rational agents make their choices after a *comprehensive* review—a review that takes into account *all* the relevant details of the present situation along with expectations about *all* future opportunities and risks. Instead, choices are made in light of a particular way of looking at the problem. People generally fail to construct a canonical representation for all extensionally equivalent descriptions of a state of affairs.

19. This is also what Simon finds in research on human problem solving (Newell and Simon 1972). It turns out that problem descriptions are consequential for problem solving, just as frames are consequential for decision making. Even "rather minor and seemingly 'innocent' changes" (H. Simon 1979, p. 372) in the cover story for a problem—for example, a change from active to passive voice—can dramatically alter the problem's difficulty, and people generally merely accept the given representation of the problem (Hayes and Simon 1977; H. Simon and Hayes 1976; Greeno 1977; Novick and Bassok 2005).

20. For reviews of the literature, see Chong and Druckman (2007) and Kinder (2003, 2007). For key empirical tests of framing effects in political communication, see Cappella and Jamieson (1997); Jacoby (2000); Kinder and Sanders (1990); Nelson, Clawson, and Oxley

(1997); Price (1989); Sniderman and Theriault (2004); and Zaller (1990). Framing effects can be erased when the alternative frames are attributed to ludicrous sources (Jerry Springer on government programs for the poor or the *National Enquirer* on constitutional protection of hate speech) (Druckman 2001); when frame recipients are induced to talk to others recently armed with opposing frames (Druckman and Nelson 2003); and when frames are presented simultaneously with their transparently logically equivalent opposites (Druckman 2004).

Chapter Three

1. More details about the surveys we analyze appear in the appendix.

2. We undertook four comparisons to support this assertion: the 1992 NES and 1990 GSS were compared to the 1990 Census; the 2000 NES and 2000 GSS were compared to the 2000 Census. The comparisons employed weighted analysis. Compared to the Census baseline, GSS and NES samples somewhat overrepresent married people, the middle aged, the college educated, women, and whites; and somewhat underrepresent the young, the poor, and the rich. The differences here are generally small. For example, according to the 2000 Census, 50.9 percent of the American adult population was female; according to the 2000 GSS, 54.8 percent of the American adult population was female.

Note too that the GSS and the NES differ in the populations to which inferences are intended to be made. For the GSS, the population consists of the adult, English-speaking household population of the continental United States. For the NES, the population is confined to adult *citizens* in the continental United States (and in some years, interviews were conducted in Spanish).

3. The notion of stereotype was introduced into the social sciences by Walter Lippmann in *Public Opinion* (1922), his influential and skeptical rumination on the capacity of common citizens to develop informed views on the issues of the day. On the one side, politics was "altogether too big, too complex, and too fleeting for direct acquaintance" ([1922] 1997, p. 11). And on the other, citizens of the day, in Lippmann's estimation, were preoccupied with private affairs, assaulted by the clamor and disorder of modern life, parochial in interest, and modest in intellect. Under these conditions, citizens tended to rely on stereotypes to reach their opinions (if they managed to reach opinions at all). In Lippmann's analysis, a stereotype was a kind of mental map, one that gave direction to ordinary people as they attempted to navigate, none too successfully, through the confusions of politics. As Lippmann put it:

> the attempt to see all things freshly and in detail, rather than as types and generalities, is exhausting, and among busy affairs practically out of the question.... There is neither time nor opportunity for intimate acquaintance. Instead we notice a trait which marks a well known type, and fill in the rest of the picture by means of the stereotypes we carry around in our heads. ([1922] 1997, p. 59)

4. On the definition of stereotype, see Allport (1954); McCauley, Stitt, and Segal (1980); and Stangor and Lange (1994).

5. For evidence on the power of stereotypes to shape judgment and behavior, see M. Brewer (1988); Devine (1989); Fazio and Dunton (1997); and Fiske (1998).

6. The GSS questions were developed by a team headed by Lawrence Bobo as part of a larger effort to assess contemporary racial attitudes. This research and development project is described in Bobo et al. (1988).

7. The stereotype question retains the same formatting across studies, but varies a bit in the details. For example, the 1992 NES asks about how hard-working, intelligent, and prone to violence groups are. In subsequent NES studies, the last item is replaced by trustworthiness (an improvement, we think). Details appear in the appendix.

8. It is instructive to compare the stereotype questions we use here to those developed by Levinson and his colleagues in *The Authoritarian Personality* (Adorno et al. 1950) in their effort to measure ethnocentrism. From our point of view, remember, Levinson's team went too far: their questions mixed together ethnocentric sentiments with opinions about exclusion and suppression. Levinson's questions conflate attitude toward the group and opinion on policy, and it is the relationship between the two that we want to assess empirically.

9. Again, race is not the only way to partition the social world, and so not the only way to define ethnocentrism. Indeed, one of ethnocentrism's distinctive features is its versatility (e.g., Levinson 1949). Depending on circumstances, in-group and out-group might be defined by religion, language, sex, occupation, nationality, and more. In general, how the lines are drawn between in-group and out-group and how prominent and important such lines turn out to be in politics are no doubt situationally specific and historically contingent. Given the history of conflict organized around race in the United States, and the marked racial inequalities that continue to characterize U.S. society, ethnocentrism based in race seemed to us the most propitious place to begin. In the final chapter, we will say more about ethnocentrism based on criteria aside from race.

10. At the most rudimentary level, these questions work. That is, for the most part, people answer them. In the 2000 NES, nonresponse ("Don't know" or "Refused to say") ranges from 3.0 to 6.7 percent across the twelve stereotype items (mean = 4.7 percent). This represents a bit more "missingness" than on some standard NES questions (federal spending on various programs); a bit less than on some standard NES questions (influence wielded by various groups); and about the same as on some other standard NES questions (attitudes toward various government policies). "Don't know" and "Refused to say" responses were most common in response to questions about Asian Americans and least common in response to questions about whites (6.2 percent on average in the first case and just 3.4 percent on average in the second), with questions about Hispanic Americans and black Americans in between.

Nonresponse was a bit more common in the 1992 NES (range = 3.9 to 11.0 percent, mean = 7.5 percent), and a bit less common in the 2004 NES (range = 1.5 to 4.3 percent, mean = 2.7 percent).

Nonresponse appears to be invariant to mode of interview. In the 2000 NES, roughly half the respondents were interviewed face to face; the other half was interviewed over the telephone. For those interviewed face to face, average nonresponse across the twelve items was 4.6 percent; for those questioned over the telephone, average nonresponse was 4.7 percent. Another way to make the point is through a *t*-test on the average level of nonresponse across the twelve stereotype questions. The difference in means is not statistically distinguishable from zero across mode of interview, at $p \sim 0.83$.

Whether people answered the stereotype questions is not predictable from standard political predispositions. Failure to answer is unrelated to partisanship, ideological identification, racial prejudice, social trust, authoritarianism and more.

Finally, our results are unaffected by how we treat the modest amount of missing data that the stereotype questions generate. Excluding respondents who are missing on any of the ethnocentrism components; including all those who answer only a few items from the full battery;

imputing scores on ethnocentrism using information from other parts of the interview (King et al. 2001): all these yield essentially the same results.

11. For an argument on the separateness of cognitive and emotional processes, see Zajonc (1980, 1981). For political applications, see Abelson et al. (1982); and Conover and Feldman (1986).

12. The thermometer scale has its own limitations, of course. Most notably, its unusual format almost certainly picks up systematic response error (Winter and Berinsky 1999). Our measure of ethnocentrism avoids this problem because it is based on difference scores, so response set should wash out.

Perhaps surprisingly, "Don't know" responses are no more common on the stereotype measures than on the thermometer score. (This is surprising on the idea that feelings are easier, more accessible, than beliefs.) For the feeling thermometer, nonresponse is counted as any of "Don't recognize," "Don't know where to rate," and "Refusal" or "NA." The table below presents nonresponse rates for the feeling thermometer (FT) and for the stereotype (ST) questions, averaged across the trait assessments for each group.

	FT 1992 (%)	ST 1992 (%)	FT 1996 (%)	ST 1996 (%)	FT 2000 (%)	ST 2000 (%)	FT 2004 (%)	ST 2004 (%)
Evaluations of whites	2.6	4.7	3.9	3.9	6.2	3.4	2.3	1.8
Evaluations of blacks	2.9	5.2	2.8	4.4	6.6	3.8	2.3	2.2
Evaluations of Hispanics	5.7	9.1	4.7	6.9	7.5	5.4	2.7	3.3
Evaluations of Asians	5.3	10.8	NA	NA	8.9	6.2	3.8	3.5

13. In addition, all 30 groups attributed more favorable characteristics to their own group than out-groups, on average, attributed to them. And, taking this test further, 29 of 30 attributed more favorable characteristics to their own group than *any* group attributed to them.

14. For experimental evidence consistent with this point, see Leach, Ellemers, and Barreto (2007).

15. Other surveys include 1996 NES, 2000 NES, 2004 NES, 1990 GSS, and 2000 GSS.

16. The stereotype battery included in the Multi-City Study of Urban Inequality represented the target group to be evaluated in one of three (randomly assigned) forms: either the racial group as a whole, female members of the racial group, or male members of the racial group. For example, MCSUI respondents were asked about "blacks," or about "black women," or about "black men." This variation turned out to make little or no difference for our purposes, and so we pooled responses across the three forms.

17. In-group favoritism holds for Asians generally and in particular for Asians of Chinese, Korean, and Japanese descent.

18. Much the same result emerges under an alternative way to test for in-group favoritism. We counted the number (proportion) of out-groups that are deemed inferior, on balance, to the in-group. The new measure of ethnocentrism (E_o) represents the proportion of occasions that the respondent (R) favors the in-group over a particular out-group. The 1992 NES, for example, offers three occasions (that is, three traits) for each of three different out-groups. We counted the number of times the in-group is favored over each out-group and converted this to a proportion ranging from 0 (R never prefers the in-group to a particular out-group) to 1 (in all comparisons, R prefers the in-group to the out-group).

To cover the other side of the spectrum, we calculated the proportion of occasions where R favors an out-group over the in-group ($\sim E_o$).

Then, for each out-group, if $E_0 > \sim E_0$, then $E^*_0 = 1$; otherwise $E^*_0 = 0$.

Finally, we counted E^*_0 over out-groups and converted this to a proportion (0–1).

Using the 1992 NES stereotype measure, 37.9 percent of whites are "genuinely ethnocentric" (that is, regard their own group as superior to all three out-groups); another 29.1 percent are partially ethnocentric (that is, regard their own group as superior to two of three out-groups). The corresponding percentages for blacks are 12.3 percent and 22.7 percent; for Hispanics, the percentages are 5.3 percent and 24.5 percent.

Another approach is to explore the prevalence of ethnocentrism when in-groups and out-groups are defined in terms other than race. This takes advantage of the feeling thermometer instrumentation and the NES time series.

In general, what we find with race (white, black, Hispanic, Asian), we find with most other cleavages: that is, in-group favoritism. We see this for religion (Protestant, Catholic, Jewish), partisanship (Republican, Democrat), and ideological identification (liberals and especially conservatives). The ethnocentric pattern shows up only partially for gender: women feel more warmth for women compared to men, but men also feel more warmth for women compared to men.

19. Tajfel (1982) treats this discovery as a problem for realistic group conflict theory—and it is—but it is also a problem for his own social identity theory. According to empirical investigations outside the minimal group experimental paradigm, social identity is not always positive; the universal striving for a favorable identity is not always successful. How can this be explained?

Tajfel's remedy is to invoke the notion of ideology. By this term, Tajfel refers to systems of beliefs that are socially shared and that justify and confer legitimacy on existing social inequalities. Such belief systems often include invidious distinctions that members of subordinate groups nonetheless internalize. As a consequence, they do not display the anticipated patterns of ethnocentrism: they do not regard out-groups with hostility or their in-group with pride. Instead, they swallow the view of their own group's shortcomings. In the process, existing patterns of privilege and power are protected from challenge.

20. For evidence consistent with this from experimental psychology, see Jost (2001); Jost, Banaji, and Nosek (2004); Sachdev and Bourhis (1991); and Leach, Ellemers, and Barreto (2007).

21. As a practical matter, looking elsewhere means analyzing the 1996 NES, 2000 NES, and 2004 NES.

And what if we do here what we did with the stereotype measure and give more weight to the idea that ethnocentrism requires generalized malice? This means counting the number (proportion) of out-groups that are deemed inferior, on balance, to the in-group, but this time using the thermometer scale. We find roughly the same pattern for whites. Using the 1992 NES thermometer score ratings, 32.9 percent of whites are "genuinely ethnocentric" (that is, regard their own group as superior to all three out-groups), and another 12.0 percent are partially ethnocentric (that is, regard their own group as superior to two of three out-groups). This is roughly what we saw using the stereotype measures.

But the patterns for blacks and Hispanics shift dramatically. By the thermometer score ratings, blacks are substantially more ethnocentric than whites and Hispanics are slightly more so: 54.5 percent of blacks are "genuinely ethnocentric," and another 18.0 percent are partially ethnocentric; for Hispanics, the corresponding percentages are 33.7 percent and 17.2 percent. This shift is dramatic, but it is anticipated, of course, by the difference we saw earlier between the measure of ethnocentrism based on stereotypes and that based on thermometer score ratings.

22. To specify systematic error, the model allows (some) error terms to correlate. In particular, error term covariances are estimated when a trait is shared in common (e.g., whites' views about the intelligence of Asian Americans and their views about the intelligence of black Americans), consistent with the anchoring and adjustment heuristic. Error covariances are otherwise assumed to be zero. We rely on maximum likelihood estimation of the variance/ covariance matrix, with all indicators coded 0–1. To provide a scale for the latent variables, we set their variances to 1.0.

23. Chi-square with 30 degrees of freedom = 133.90 ($p < 0.01$), adjusted goodness of fit index = 0.961, root mean square residual = 0.051. The model estimated in table 3.3 fits much better than a model that makes no allowance for systematic response error (that is, assumes that error terms are uncorrelated): chi-square with 48 degrees of freedom = 2271.74 ($p < 0.01$), adjusted goodness of fit index = 0.626.

It is possible, of course, to tinker with the model, to improve the fit. Most immediately, we could relax assumptions regarding the factor loadings. Some of these that we set to zero are not quite. But while this would improve the fit a bit, it would not change the basic story: the nonzero coefficients in the factor loading matrix are uniformly small (none exceeds 0.25 and only one would exceed 0.20).

24. Moreover, in the chapters that follow, we find little or no evidence that any one trait is more important in accounting for ethnocentrism's effect on opinion than any other. This is more evidence in support of ethnocentrism as a general predisposition.

25. In the 1990 GSS, the corresponding CFA correlations between the out-group factors are 0.36, 0.40, and 0.69. In the 1996 NES, the estimated correlation between views of blacks and views of Hispanics (only two out-groups present in the 1996 NES) is 0.79. And in the 2000 GSS, the estimated correlations are 0.16, 0.36, and 0.83. We would have liked to have analyzed the 2000 NES and the 2004 NES in this fashion, but the questions were administered with questions all pointing in the same direction (higher values always indicating less charitable assessments). This consistency in the direction of the questions eliminates our ability to peel off systematic measurement error from underlying evaluations of the group.

The result of generalized prejudice also fits the patterning of correlations generated by the judgments offered by whites, blacks, Hispanics, and Asians in Los Angeles, taken from the Multi-City Study of Urban Inequality.

Finally, we see the same pattern when we analyze thermometer score ratings.

26. In the 1990 GSS, the correlations between in-group (whites) and out-groups are 0.22, 0.05, and −0.03. As before, the only nonzero correlation is between views of whites and views of Asian Americans, and as before, the correlation is positive, opposite to that predicted. In the 1996 NES, the estimated correlation between in-group (whites) and Hispanics is 0.34 and between in-group (whites) and blacks is 0.30. Both these are reliably different from zero and positive, and so once again run in the opposite direction to that predicted by Sumner. In the 2000 GSS, more of the same: the CFA correlations are 0.49, −0.05, and 0.23.

We also find little connection between in-group attachment and out-group prejudice when we estimate the relationship using different measures, which allows us to extend our test to blacks, Hispanics, and Asians: using closeness measures to tap in-group sentiments, using stereotype measures to tap out-group sentiments, and pooling over NES surveys to build up cases. For whites, the correlation between in-group attachment and out-group prejudice ranges from 0.07 to 0.09; for blacks, the corresponding correlation ranges from 0.01 to 0.12;

for Hispanics, the correlation ranges from –0.03 to 0.09; and for Asians, the correlation ranges from –0.01 to 0.04. All the correlations are small: most do not even pass the statistical significance test; those that do run in a direction opposite to that predicted by Sumner.

27. Sometimes strong in-group loyalty is accompanied by out-group animosity (Gibson and Gouws 2000; Perreault and Bourhis 1999); sometimes not (de Figueiredo and Elkins 2003; Feshbach 1994). Sumner's claim about a close and inextricable connection between in-group loyalty and out-group animosity was formulated with groups, not individuals, in mind. But the results are no brighter at the group level (M. Brewer and Campbell 1976).

28. E is more reliable for whites (0.79) than for blacks (0.55), Hispanics (0.59), or Asians (0.60), pooling the 1992, 1996, 2000, and 2004 NES.

We explored several alternative measures of ethnocentrism, mostly in order to give greater priority to the idea that ethnocentrism requires generalized prejudice.

One way to do this is to weight out-group sentiment in our standard measure by its variance. The ethnocentric pattern is consistent hostility. People should get "credit" for consistency in their hostility across groups; they should "suffer" if their hostility is inconsistent (e.g., hating one out-group but liking two others, or disliking two out-groups but admiring a third). We created such a measure, but it turned out to be virtually indistinguishable from the original measure of E (Pearson $r > 0.95$).

Another possibility is to create a measure that counts the number (proportion) of out-groups that are deemed inferior, on balance, to the in-group (the procedural details are spelled out in note 18). This version of the ethnocentrism scale also correlates quite highly E (Pearson $r = 0.73$). And if in later analysis we substitute this scale (coded 0, 0.33, 0.67, 1.0) for E, we find much the same results.

In short, alternative ways of assembling an overall scale of ethnocentrism appear to lead to the same place. This is reassuring: our results seem not to depend on a particular and perhaps peculiar method of measurement.

29. By this manner of accounting, ethnocentrism is more common among whites (62.6 percent) and especially Asians (81.2 percent) than among blacks (42.7 percent) or Hispanics (43.4 percent).

30. E* is slightly more reliable for whites (0.89) than for blacks (0.83), Hispanics (0.81), or Asians (0.80), pooling the 1992, 1996, 2000, and 2004 NES.

31. Using this measure, 55.7 percent of respondents locate themselves on the ethnocentric side of the scale. Ethnocentrism seems quite prevalent among blacks (75.6 percent locating to the right of zero) and Hispanics (58.0 percent). About half of whites (52.4 percent) and Asians (53.1 percent) locate to the right of zero.

32. Partisanship is measured with v923634, v960420, v000523, v043116. It ranges from 0 (strong Republican) to 1 (strong Democrat).

33. On this theme, see Tocqueville ([1848] 1994), Myrdal (1944), Lipset (1959), Hofstadter (1948), and especially Louis Hartz's *The Liberal Tradition in America* (1955). Limited government is measured by a three-item scale that has become a regular part of NES, thanks to research and development work by Gregory Markus (2001).

In 1992 NES, the limited government scale consists of an additive index of v925729–v925731. In 1996 NES, it consists of v961144–v961146. In 2000 NES, it is comprised of v001420–v001422. In 2004 NES, it consists of v045150–v045152. The scale is fairly reliable (*alpha* averages 0.73 across the years). The index ranges from 0 (want more active government) to 1 (want less active government).

34. On the meaning and measurement of equality, see Feldman (1988); Kinder and Sanders (1996); Feldman and Zaller (1992); McClosky and Zaller (1984); Schlozman and Verba (1979); and Sears, Henry, and Kosterman (2000).

In 1992 NES, the egalitarianism scale consists of an additive index of v926024–v926029. In 1996 NES, it consists of v961229–v961234. In 2000 NES, it is comprised of v001521–v001526. In 2004 NES, it consists of v045212–v045217. The scale is reasonably reliable (*alpha* averages 0.70 across the years). The index ranges from 0 (not) to 1 (egalitarian).

35. Ideological identification is measured with v923509, v960365, v001368, and v045117. It ranges from 0 (extremely conservative) to 1 (extremely liberal).

36. Here are the three standard social trust questions:

Generally speaking, would you say that most people can be trusted, or that you can't be too careful in dealing with people?

Do you think most people would try to take advantage of you if they got the chance or would they try to be fair?

Would you say that most of the time people try to be helpful, or that they are just looking out for themselves?

The three-item additive scale appears in 2000 and 2004. It ranges from 0 (least trusting) to 1 (most trusting), with a mean of 0.63 and 0.57, and standard deviation of 0.39 and 0.39 in 2000 and 2004, respectively. Cronbach's reliability is 0.73 in 2000 and 0.72 in 2004. Only two of the items appeared in 1992 and 1996 (the first and third items in 1992; the first and second items in 1996).

37. Notice that the expected relationship between ethnocentrism and social trust is stronger among white Americans and much stronger among whites than among blacks or Hispanics (table 3.4). Perhaps when white Americans are asked to render "sweeping judgments of human nature" in matters of trust, they have mainly white Americans in mind. That is, for whites, the social trust questions are really about their own group. As a consequence, we see a relatively strong (and of course negative) association between social trust and ethnocentrism. Black and Hispanic Americans may be less likely to regard the social trust questions to be directed at their own group. As a consequence, among blacks and Hispanics, we see virtually no relationship between social trust and ethnocentrism. For experimental evidence that whites implicitly define American as white while African Americans do not, see Devos and Banaji (2005).

38. See, for example, Eaves, Eysenck, and Martin (1989); McCourt et al. (1999); and Maccoby (2000).

39. Jennings's study starts with a national probability sample of 97 secondary schools (public, private, parochial); the schools were selected with probability proportionate to their size. Within each selected school, 15–21 randomly designated seniors were interviewed in person. Independently, face-to-face interviews were also carried out with the fathers of one-third of the seniors, the mothers of one-third, and both parents of the remaining third. Where the designated parent was permanently absent, the other parent or a parent-surrogate was interviewed instead. Interviews with at least one parent were obtained for 94 percent of the students. For more details on design and quality of the samples, see Jennings and Niemi (1981, app. A) and Jennings and Stoker (1999).

40. See the appendix for the measures of ethnocentrism in this dataset.

41. Here are the complete distributions:

	Ethnocentric on both race and religion (%)	Partially ethnocentric (%)	Not ethnocentric (%)
Offspring ($N = 1547$)	48.0	32.3	19.7
Parents ($N = 1811$)	50.6	27.8	21.7

Source: 1965 Political Socialization Study Cross-Section Youth and Parent File.

The main file (ICPSR dataset #7286) is organized with the youth-parent dyad as the unit of analysis. The 430 youth whose parents were both interviewed appear twice in the original datafile. The N for offspring represents the 1150 youth for whom only one parent was interviewed and 430 youth for whom both parents were interviewed (these 430 appear only once in our analysis). The N for parents reflects all parental respondents.

42. The abbreviated measure is also correlated with **E**: in the 2000 NES, Pearson $r = 0.35$.

43. To ascertain the relationship between youth and parent **E**, we used ordered probit to regress youth **E** on parent **E**, yielding $b = 0.43$; se = 0.07.

44. By design, interviewers in the Jennings's socialization study were instructed to interview the fathers of one-third of the seniors, the mothers of one-third, and both parents of the remaining third. (As a practical matter, something short of a full third of the high school seniors had both parents interviewed: 430/1669.) For the estimate of parental influence we just presented, the last-mentioned seniors appear twice, once with their fathers and once with their mothers. An alternative estimation strategy is to (1) randomly sample from these twice-appearing seniors (that is, take either the mother or the father); (2) reestimate correspondence between parents and offspring; and (3) repeat (200 replications was our standard practice). Following this procedure, we found virtually identical results to those presented in the text: in particular, the median b indexing the impact of parental ethnocentrism on offspring ethnocentrism = 0.47. The median standard error is 0.08.

This estimate of the impact of parental ethnocentrism on offspring ethnocentrism is attenuated insofar as our measure of parental ethnocentrism contains error. And we can be certain that it contains error—probably quite a bit of error. At best, the measure distinguishes only among three broad classes of ethnocentrism (complete, partial, and none).

We explored how attenuated our estimate might be due to measurement error by reestimating the impact of parental ethnocentrism on offspring ethnocentrism, using errors in variables regression across a range of plausible reliabilities. Without correcting for unreliability, the least-squares regression estimate of parental ethnocentrism is 0.15 (se = 0.02). This is the estimate of parental impact under the (highly suspect) assumption that parental ethnocentrism is measured without error (reliability = 1.0). Under the more plausible assumption that parental ethnocentrism is measured very imperfectly (reliability = 0.40), the regression estimate of the impact of parental ethnocentrism more than doubles, to 0.36 (se = .06). If parental ethnocentrism is measured a bit better than that (reliability = 0.50), then the estimate of parental ethnocentrism is 0.29 (se = 0.05). And if the measurement is actually a bit worse (reliability = 0.30), then the estimate of parental ethnocentrism increases accordingly, to 0.49 (se = 0.07). We conclude from these experiments that parents exercise a considerable influence over their high school senior-aged children's ethnocentrism.

45. For an account of political socialization in terms of social learning theory, see Jennings and Niemi (1974) and Sears (1975).

46. Political activity by parents consists of an additive scale of participatory acts (voting, persuading others, attending a rally, participating in other electoral activities, wearing a button, donating to a campaign, joining a political organization: v387–v393), rescaled to range from 0 (none) to 1 (all 7). Family discussion of politics is based on the youth report of frequency of political conversation in family (v141), ranging from 0 (low) to 1 (high). Youth interest in politics is measured with v206, rescaled to range from 0 (low) to 1 (high). Youth political information is an additive scale consisting of knowledge of political figures and political institutions (v221–226), ranging from 0 (low) to 1 (high). Closeness to parents is an average of closeness to father (v176) and closeness to mother (v180), ranging from 0 (not close to either) to 1 (very close to both). Full results appear in the Web appendix.

47. Alas, the socialization study does not include information on whether offspring are biological or adopted.

48. Is there any reason to think the sample of offspring with both parents interviewed is different from the sample of offspring with just one parent interviewed? No: the two samples are indistinguishable on ethnocentrism, closeness to parents, following politics, intended participation in politics, and political information (Hotelling's test of the vectors of means, by whether one or two parents were interviewed, suggests $p \sim 0.83$: the null hypothesis of equal means cannot be rejected). Likewise, parents in the two samples resemble one another closely: they are indistinguishable on ethnocentrism, they participate in politics at similar rates, and they talk with their spouses about politics to similar degrees (Hotelling's test yields $p \sim 0.55$; the means are indistinguishable).

Parents tend to agree when it comes to ethnocentrism. For 49 percent of offspring for whom both parents were interviewed, the parents shared the same score. For 37 percent of offspring for whom both parents were interviewed, the parents were one category apart (that is, one parent was not ethnocentric and the other was mildly ethnocentric, or one parent was mildly ethnocentric and the other completely ethnocentric). Complete disagreement is relatively rare: only 14 percent of offspring had parents who were polar opposites (one completely ethnocentric and the other not at all).

49. In ordered-probit regression, $b = 0.28$ for father's contribution and $b = 0.31$ for mother's. The interaction term testing whether these two coefficients are different = 0.03, se = 0.21, $p \sim 0.88$.

We could take this analysis one step further, under the expectation of independent and equal parental effects *regardless of sex of offspring*. High school senior boys and high school senior girls should be influenced equally by their mothers and by their fathers, from the point of view of genetic transmission. We find, to the contrary, that boys are influenced somewhat more by their mothers than their fathers, while girls are influenced somewhat more by their fathers than by their mothers. However, the interaction testing this difference is not significant (a consequence, perhaps, of insufficient cases).

50. Here's the exact question:

Although there are a number of qualities that people feel that children should have, every person thinks that some are more important than others. I am going to read you pairs of desirable qualities. Please tell me which one you think is more important for a child to have:

Independence *or* Respect for elders
Curiosity *or* Good manners
Obedience *or* Self-reliance
Being considerate *or* Well-behaved?

The virtue of this question is that it captures the conceptual core of authoritarianism while avoiding the problems—acquiescence response set, explicit references to social and political arrangements—that crippled the original measure (Altemeyer 1981; Hyman and Sheatsley 1954; Stenner 2005). The scale is reasonably reliable. Cronbach's *alpha* = 0.67 in 1992, 0.60 in 2000, and 0.61 in 2004. Pooling across NES surveys, Cronbach's *alpha* = 0.64.

51. More precisely, authoritarianism and ethnocentrism are positively correlated, except among African Americans:

	Full sample	Whites	Blacks	Hispanics
NES 1992	0.18	0.29	0.04	0.21
	(N = 1690)	(N = 1339)	(N = 208)	(N = 143)
NES 2000	0.22	0.30	0.04	0.23
	(N = 1329)	(N = 1108)	(N = 138)	(N = 83)
NES 2004	0.24	0.35	0.01	0.15
	(N = 940)	(N = 709)	(N = 148)	(N = 83)
NES Pooled	0.20	0.30	0.03	0.18
	(N = 3959)	(N = 3156)	(N = 494)	(N = 309)

52. Social isolation is a dummy that represents lack of membership in social organizations (v961454). Increased social distance from neighbors is coded 1 for those who report having talked with neighbors in 1992 but no longer doing so in 1996 (v926141 and v961260). Divorced since 1992 is coded 1 for those who were married in 1992 but report being divorced in 1994 or 1996 (v923904, v941204, v960606). Disabled since 1992 is coded 1 for those who were not disabled in 1992 but report being disabled in 1994 or 1996 (v923914, v941216, v960616).

53. With authoritarianism scored 0–1, an ordinary least-squares regression of **E** on authoritarianism yields b = 0.10, se = 0.02. We find essentially the same result with **E***, where b = 0.06, se = 0.02. Full results appear in the Web appendix.

54. See the appendix for the coding of these variables and Kam and Franzese (2007) for a discussion of slope-shift models.

55. It could have been otherwise. Individuals who pursue higher education differ systematically from those who do not (Kam and Palmer 2008). This means that the various characteristics that propel individuals to pursue higher education (e.g., superior cognitive skills, engagement in school and community life, self-confidence, politically engaged and active parents, privileged backgrounds) might actually be responsible for the observed correlation between education and ethnocentrism.

The Jennings socialization study provides an excellent venue for attacking this causal conundrum. The design allows us to observe individual and family characteristics in 1965, before the offspring cohort leaves the family nest. And the 1973 follow-up allows us to identify those who did and did not go to college, and to ascertain whether their ethnocentric sentiments have changed.

As for analysis, we rely on propensity score matching to estimate the causal effect of education. Typical regression analyses assume that independent variables are "fixed in repeated sampling." Another way to think about this assumption is that the levels on independent variables are randomly assigned; observations hold particular levels of X's, and variation in other covariates or other unobserved processes would not alter these levels of these X's. Educational attainment, however, is not randomly assigned. Regression analyses that ignore nonrandom assignment, where the process underlying assignment is correlated with the outcome of interest, face the threat of biased and inconsistent statistical estimates (Achen 1986). The traditional manner of dealing with nonrandom assignment is through instrumental variable estimation; the weakness of such a technique is that credible instruments, that is, exogenous variables that are used to identify the system of equations and that predict assignment but not the outcome of interest, are difficult to find (Achen 1986; Bartels 1991b).

We rely instead on propensity score matching. Propensity matching pairs up offspring who attended college to those who did not by their propensity score—that is, the predicted likelihood of attending college based on characteristics of the individual, the individual's parents, and the individual's high school. Matching mimics random assignment; it generates two groups (those who attended college, those who did not) who are comparable in important respects. Through propensity score matching, treated respondents (for the purposes of this study, attending college or not) are paired with "essentially equivalent" control respondents, and the average treatment effect consists of the mean difference in ethnocentrism between the matched groups. Propensity score matching allows us to analyze observational data as if we had carried out an experimental design (to a first approximation). For a more detailed discussion of matching, see Rubin (1974); Rosenbaum and Rubin (1985); Sekhon (2004); Diamond and Sekhon (2005); Ho et al. (2007); and for an application to an important political puzzle, see Kam and Palmer (2008).

The first step in this analysis is creating the propensity score. We estimate a logistic regression that predicts college attendance using a (long) series of relevant covariates. We then generate a predicted probability that an individual will attend college for each respondent. We predict college attendance, as ascertained in the 1973 re-interview, using a series of covariates theorized to be substantively related to the decision to attend college. The underlying process for selecting covariates for the propensity score regression is the same as for any other model specification: all covariates that would be included in the logistic regression predicting the treatment, even if only weakly predictive, should be included in the propensity score equation (Ho et al. 2007).

Step two is examining *balance*: in order for comparisons between matched groups to be sound, the groups must be "essentially equivalent" on a range of relevant characteristics. A successful match requires us to determine whether the matched pairs of treatment and control observations are distributionally similar on a series of substantively relevant covariates. To produce the final propensity score model we report here, we identified the model that produced maximal balance on covariates relevant for our research question.

Balance tests typically examine the univariate distributions of single variables across the matched treatment and control groups as well as multivariate distributions across a collection of variables, comparing the matched treatment and control groups. Univariate tests are t-tests of difference of means between the matched treatment and control groups and difference of variance tests. Where applicable, we have also used Kolgomorov-Smirnov tests of distributional similarity (these cannot be used on dichotomous indicators).

The propensity score generation, matching and balancing were implemented using R-code developed by Sekhon (2007). After propensity score matching, our matched control and treatment groups are indistinguishable on grade point average, political information, parental education, parental homeownership, parental political information, and, most important, parental ethnocentrism.

Step three, assuming balance has been achieved, is a simple comparison in means between the treated and matched control group. For our purposes, the key statistic is a comparison of means on ethnocentrism between those who went to college and those who did not:

Effect of college on ethnocentrism before and after propensity score matching

	Before matching	After matching
Estimated effect	−0.080***	−0.081
(se)	(0.030)	(0.076)
N	684	1255

Source: 1965–1973 Political Socialization Panel Study.

Note: Table entry is the estimated average effect of college on ethnocentrism, before and after matching.

***$p < 0.01$; **$p < 0.05$; *$p < 0.10$, two-tailed.

In the first column of the table is the comparison of means *before* propensity score matching. As shown and as expected, this comparison of means indicates that those high school seniors who went to college expressed significantly less ethnocentrism than their fellow cohort members who did not (mean difference before matching = −0.080). In the second column of the table is the comparison of means *after* propensity score matching: that is, after pairing the college-educated group with an "essentially equivalent" control group. This comparison shows that high school seniors who went to college expressed less ethnocentrism than their comparable cohorts who did not, and by exactly the same margin (mean difference after matching = −0.081).

Read one way, the propensity score matching results support the conclusion that education inhibits ethnocentrism—the point estimate for the "effect" of education is essentially the same. But read another way, the propensity score matching results could be interpreted as providing little positive evidence that education actually inhibits ethnocentrism—the "effect" of education after matching takes place cannot be distinguished from zero.

56. The Wiley-Wiley model requires observations at three points in time. The model assumes errors of measurement are well behaved: in particular, that they are homoscedastic, that their mean is zero, and that they are uncorrelated with each other. Further, the model assumes that all unreliability can be attributed to the instrument; most psychometricians would say that unreliability belongs both to instrumentation and to respondents. See Palmquist and Green (1992); D. Wiley and J. Wiley (1970); J. Wiley and M. G. Wiley (1974); Heise (1969); Converse and Markus (1979); and Achen (1983).

57. These estimates are generated from samples of whites only. The full-sample models were similar for the 2000–2002–2004 and 1965–1973–1997 datasets. The full-sample model generated inadmissible values for the 1992–1994–1996 NES.

Here are the reliability estimates for the models that we discuss:

	1965–1973–1997 Socialization study	1992–1994–1996 NES	2000–2002–2004 NES
Time 1	0.29	0.61	0.82
Time 2	0.39	0.65	0.55
Time 3	0.37	0.41	0.62

58. Here are the results (table entry is the Wiley-Wiley stability coefficient):

Stability of ethnocentrism by age, 2000–2002

Youngest cohort	Middle cohort	Oldest cohort
0.41	0.64	0.83

Source: 2000–2002 NES Panel.

Here are the reliability estimates for the 2000–2002–2004 NES, by age:

	Youngest cohort	Middle cohort	Oldest cohort
2000	0.93	0.92	0.67
2002	0.74	0.70	0.41
2004	0.72	0.81	0.40

The youngest cohort consists of those aged 17–38 in 2000. The oldest cohort consists of those 55 and older in 2000.

What other kinds of experiences might be able to alter ethnocentrism? One general answer is suggested by Tajfel's social identity theory. According to Tajfel, remember, ethnocentrism arises out of need for positive identity, a need that can be satisfied at least partially by thinking of one's own group as superior to others. This implies that ethnocentrism should increase, other things equal, when setbacks are encountered in personal life. Ethnocentrism should be more common among the unsuccessful, for whom ethnocentrism provides compensating satisfactions.

Perhaps, but we could turn up very little evidence in support of this claim. For the most part, personal troubles and ethnocentrism are unconnected. Divorce, disability, illness, loneliness, crime: none of these powerful personal experiences produced an increase in ethnocentrism. We pursued many possibilities and turned up only a single positive case. In both the 1992–1996 NES Panel and in the Jennings socialization study, Americans whose economic condition had recently deteriorated registered a small but statistically significant increase in ethnocentrism. Apart from this one result, we found no empirical support for the expectation drawn from social identity theory of a connection between ethnocentrism and the trials and tribulations of private life.

Chapter Four

1. See Clodfelter (1992); Philips and Axelrod (2005); Patterson (1996); Correlates of War Project, http://correlatesofwar.org/.

2. Text of President Bush's Speech (Cincinnati Museum Center–Cincinnati Union Terminal, Cincinnati, Ohio, October 7, 2002), Associated Press Online, http://www.lexis-nexis.com.

3. The 2000–2002 American National Election Panel Study was conducted by the Center for Political Studies at the Institute for Social Research at the University of Michigan. Data collection was carried out by the Indiana University Center for Survey Research. In 2002, all interviews were conducted in English and over the telephone, using Computer-Assisted Telephone Interviewing (CATI) technology. The panel component of the 2000–2002 study consists of 1187

respondents, all of whom had previously participated in the 2000 NES. Of these, 1070 were also interviewed in the 2002 postelection wave.

The 2002 leg of the NES Panel would not have been possible without the financial support of a consortium of organizations: the Carnegie Corporation, the Center for Information and Research on Civic Learning and Engagement (CIRCLE), the Russell Sage Foundation, the University of Michigan Institute for Social Research, the University of Michigan Office of the Provost, and the University of Michigan Office of the Vice President for Research.

4. The federal spending battery begins with the following introduction:

Next I am going to read you a list of federal programs. For each one, I would like you to tell me whether you would like to see spending increased or decreased.

(What about) homeland security? (Should federal spending on homeland security be increased, decreased, or kept about the same?)

(What about) the war on terrorism? (Should federal spending on the war on terrorism be increased, decreased, or kept about the same?)

(What about) tightening border security to prevent illegal immigration? (Should federal spending on tightening border security to prevent illegal immigration be increased, decreased, or kept about the same?)

(What about) defense? (Should federal spending on defense be increased, decreased, or kept about the same?)

By random assignment, respondents were asked either about federal spending on homeland security or about federal spending on the war on terrorism. The distributions for all the terrorism policy questions appear in the Web appendix.

Now it turns out that Americans generally say government should spend and do more. They complain about government in the abstract, but they tend to support most programs in particular (Free and Cantril 1967). A completely standard result from the NES spending battery is that Americans favor increases in federal spending over cuts. This has been so for as long as the questions have been asked, and it is so in 2002. However, of the sixteen domestic programs included in the 2002 spending battery, just two generated more support than did the policies intended to make the country safe from terrorism: public schools and early education programs for poor children (74.6 percent of the sample said that federal spending on public schools should be increased; the identical percentage said the same about federal spending on early education programs for poor children). Setting these two programs aside, Americans were concerned most of all about terrorism in 2002. They wanted increases in spending for the war on terrorism, and more Americans wanted this than wanted to increase spending on environmental protection or on unemployment insurance or on building highways and bridges or a host of other domestic programs. From this perspective, American support for the war on terrorism seems substantial.

5. These questions read:

After the September 11 terrorist attacks, President Bush declared a war on terrorism. A first step was to launch air strikes against the Taliban government of Afghanistan that was providing aid and protection to Osama bin Laden and the Al-Qaeda terrorists responsible for the September 11 attacks. Taking everything into account, do you think the U.S. war against the Taliban government in Afghanistan was worth the cost or not?

As you may know, President Bush and his top advisers are discussing the possibility of taking military action against Iraq to remove Saddam Hussein from power. Do you favor or oppose military action against Iraq—or is this something you haven't thought about? Do you [favor/oppose] this policy strongly or not strongly?

6. These questions read:

All things considered, do you approve or disapprove of the way George W. Bush has responded to the terrorist attack of September 11?

All things considered, do you approve or disapprove of the way George W. Bush is handling the war on terrorism?

Do you approve or disapprove of the way George W. Bush is handling his job as president?

Each question included a follow-up:

Do you [approve/disapprove] strongly or not strongly?

Respondents to the 2002 NES were randomly assigned to evaluate either President Bush's response to the terrorist attacks of September 11 or his handling of the war on terrorism.

7. Also see, on the persistent power of partisanship, Bartels (2000); Green, Palmquist, and Schickler (2002). Partisanship is measured in 2000 (v000523) with a seven-category variable, where 0 corresponds with strong Republican and 1 with strong Democrat.

8. Education is a seven-category measure of schooling (v000913), rescaled from 0 (less than nine years of schooling) to 1 (advanced degree).

9. Perception of threat is measured with v023118; 23.7 percent of respondents saw another attack as somewhat unlikely and 9.4 percent saw it as very unlikely. It is coded from 0 (very unlikely) to 1 (very likely).

10. All independent variables in the model are coded to range from 0 to 1.

The model we use to estimate the effect of ethnocentrism is actually a bit more complicated than shown in the text. It includes a short list of control variables in addition to partisanship, threat, and education: (1) political awareness, under the hypothesis that those Americans who pay the greatest attention to elite debate might be most prepared to follow the president's lead in wartime (J. Mueller 1973, p. 122); (2) sex, on the idea that women are more wary than men about the deployment of violence for political purposes (e.g., Conover and Sapiro 1993; Shapiro and Mahajan 1986); (3) race, based on the empirical regularity that white Americans have generally been more enthusiastic in their support for U.S. military interventions than black Americans (Holsti 1996; J. Mueller 1973, 1994); and (4) in equations predicting support for President Bush, we add in standard survey measures of economic well-being, following the well-established result that a president's popularity depends in an important way on economic conditions (e.g., Kinder 1981; Rosenstone 1983; Alesina, Londregan, and Rosenthal 1993).

Political awareness is an additive scale of four information items, following Zaller (1992), scaled from 0 (low) to 1 (high). Cronbach's *alpha* is 0.64; the items are v001446a/b, v001449a/b, v001452a/b, v001455a/b.

Sex is a dummy coded 1 for females and 0 for males.

Race and ethnicity are represented with a dummy for black (1 if black, 0 otherwise) and Hispanic (1 if Hispanic, 0 otherwise), with whites serving as the suppressed reference group.

Economic well-being is measured by assessments of change in the family's economic condition as well as change in the country's economic condition (Kinder and Kiewiet 1981).

Retrospective national economic evaluations are measured with v023028, scaled from 0 (negative evaluation of the performance of the national economy over the past year) to 1 (positive evaluation). Retrospective household economic evaluations are measured with v023026, scaled from 0 (negative evaluation of household economic conditions over the past year) to 1 (positive evaluation). Both variables appear in the 2002 survey.

These variables are included in the analysis, but their estimated effects are typically not presented in the tables that accompany the text. Nor are they discussed. Full results for all the analyses appear in the Web appendix.

11. In models of presidential approval, economic evaluations are also from the 2002 interview.

12. Bartels (2006) has recently made this point as part of a broader argument on behalf of panel designs. According to Bartels, covariates measured in the prior time period "may more plausibly be considered 'exogenous' rather than 'endogenous,' making interpretations of their apparent effects a good deal more straightforward and compelling" (p. 148).

13. In the 2000 NES, Cronbach's coefficient *alpha* for **E** = 0.88 among whites, 0.81 among blacks, and 0.77 among Hispanic Americans.

14. Because our dependent measures are categorical, we analyze the data using ordered probit, not ordinary least-squares (OLS) regression. Although OLS regression has excellent statistical properties and is robust to departures from several of its assumptions, the ordinal nature of the observed measures argues against utilizing OLS. The primary objection to using OLS is that OLS assumes that the dependent measure is interval: that is, the categories in the scale are equally spaced from each other. We (and most public opinion scholars) believe this assumption is untenable. For example, if a question contains four categories (strongly agree, agree, disagree, and strongly disagree), OLS assumes that the distance from "strongly agree" to "agree" is exactly the same as the distance from "agree" to "disagree." Ordered probit provides a different conceptualization of the response. Respondents' opinions are seen as falling onto an underlying, latent continuous scale, and the survey question maps this underlying latent scale onto a set of categories. The response categories need not be equally spaced from each other; in fact, ordered probit (and its counterpart, ordered logit) estimates a series of cutpoints that estimate how far apart the response categories are. Ordered probit uses the cumulative normal distribution to map the underlying continuous scale onto observable response categories (the more familiar probit and logit estimators can be thought of as special cases of these models, where there are only two response categories).

Interpretation of results typically proceeds by examining predicted probabilities: the probability that a given respondent with some set of characteristics would fall into a particular response category. OLS, in contrast, proceeds by examining predicted values, which can easily take on out-of-sample and substantively implausible values. By using a cumulative normal functional form, ordered probit assumes that a change in a particular X will induce relatively greater changes in the probabilities ranging at the midpoint ($p = 0.5$) and smaller changes at the tails ($p = 0$, $p = 1$), and this assumption substantively makes sense to us. Relatedly, the effect of a particular X will depend on the values of each of the other variables included in the model. Typical OLS models (when variables are entered linearly) assume uniform effects across all values of the dependent variable, regardless of the values of the other independent variables. OLS also assumes homoscedastic (constant variance) and normally distributed disturbances, and both assumptions are likely to be violated given that the dependent variable is categorical. One disadvantage of these models that we are quick to concede is that these results are not as immediately interpretable as OLS coefficients. As a consequence, we will discuss predicted probabilities in the text and present results graphically at the end of the chapter, providing predicted probabilities that a respondent with a given set of characteristics would espouse a particular view. For more on ordered probit, we refer the reader to its original introduction to the social sciences by McKelvey and Zavoina (1975) and to a lucid exposition in Long (1997).

In table 4.1 as well as most of the others in the book, we have featured coefficients from some of the key variables in the model. The notes at the bottom of the table indicate the other variables that are controlled for in the model but that are not shown. Full results are available in the Web appendix.

15. We also analyzed feelings toward President Bush, as ascertained using the feeling thermometer. Ethnocentrism significantly predicted warmth toward Bush as well.

16. Here we are following the logic and practice of simulation spelled out by Gary King and his colleagues (King, Tomz, and Wittenberg 2000). The simulations here and throughout set the values of the other variables as follows: white, female, Independent-leaning Democrat, and otherwise average in education, political awareness, sense of threat, and economic evaluations (where relevant).

17. In the aftermath of 9/11, George Bush made fighting terrorism the mission of his presidency. So we expected and so we see that support for the president came disproportionately from ethnocentric Americans. What about support for prominent members of the Bush administration other than the president?

As it turns out, ethnocentrism also predicts positive evaluations of Dick Cheney and Richard Ashcroft, though only among the relatively well informed—only among those, that is, most likely to be in command of the vital fact that Cheney and Ashcroft were principal architects of the war on terrorism.

In the standard model, the coefficient on ethnocentrism is 0.16 (se = 0.26) for evaluations of Cheney and 0.29 (se = 0.29) for evaluations of Ashcroft. When we include an interaction between ethnocentrism and political awareness, the coefficient on ethnocentrism is −0.20 (se = 0.36) and −0.31 (se = 0.41). This means that the effect of ethnocentrism at the lowest level of political awareness is indistinguishable from zero. The estimated coefficient on the interaction term on political awareness and ethnocentrism is 1.55 (se = 1.06, $p < 0.15$, two-tailed) and 2.29 (se = 1.13, $p < 0.05$, two-tailed). Ethnocentrism has nothing to do with evaluations of prominent political figures outside the Bush team: not Bill Clinton ($b = 0.37$, se = 0.26); not Ralph Nader ($b = 0.31$, se = 0.27); not Jesse Jackson ($b = −0.06$, se = 0.26); not Al Gore ($b = 0.22$, se = 0.26); and not Hillary Clinton ($b = 0.10$, se = 0.26)—and this is so regardless of how much or little about politics a person knows. See Gilens (2001) for similar results from experimental studies.

18. The effects of partisanship shown in tables 4.1 to 4.3 are accentuated as political awareness increases. The interaction between partisanship and political awareness is negative in every model, sizable in most, and statistically significant in over half. In all cases, the implication is that the gap between Democrats and Republicans grows with greater levels of political awareness. This means that among the most aware, the effect of partisanship is comparable to the effect due to ethnocentrism. See Kam and Kinder (2007).

19. The results on threat are generally consistent with those reported by Huddy et al. (2005). And in the full set of results (see the Web appendix), women wanted to spend more on defense and more on the war on terrorism than men did (presumably in order to keep the country safe), but they were less keen than men on using military force to eradicate the sources of terrorism. Finally, compared to whites, African Americans supported military intervention less and criticized President Bush more.

20. This conclusion holds however we carry out the analysis.

First, we reestimated our models relying on OLS rather than ordered probit, and found essentially the same results.

Second, we corrected for errors-in-variables. Measurement error is inevitable when using survey data. Comparing ethnocentrism and perception of threat, ethnocentrism is likely measured more reliably, given that it is comprised of a set of items and perception of threat is measured only with a single item. As a consequence, we may be underestimating the effect due to threat and overestimating the effect due to E. To address this possibility, we conducted errors-in-variables regression. The amount of error in a survey item can be estimated with Cronbach's *alpha* (which we have estimated for our E measure), when multiple items tapping the construct are available. When only one item is available, reliability can be measured with a test-retest correlation (having the same individuals answer the question on two "identical" occasions and estimating the correlation between time 1 and time 2). Unfortunately, there are neither multiple items to tap threat nor multiple measures of the same threat item under identical conditions. So we have estimated errors-in-variables regression across a range of plausible reliability values for perceptions of threat (from 0.2 to 0.5) and for ethnocentrism (based on Cronbach's *alpha*, we use a value of 0.8). These analyses suggest that (1) under reasonable assumptions about error, the estimates in tables 4.1 to 4.3 underestimate the real effect due to threat (the precise amount depends, of course, on how much error we assume is present in the threat variable); (2) but the effect attributed to ethnocentrism is for the most part unchanged. For more on reliability and errors-in-variables, see Bollen (1989).

And third, the results are robust across missing data algorithms. Our measure of ethnocentrism relies on respondents' ratings of their own group and out-groups. The stereotype measure, for example, is constructed from responses to twelve separate questions (three stereotype questions, across four groups). Occasionally, respondents decline to answer these questions. So long as respondents answer the majority of questions about each group, we have averaged across their valid responses. Respondents who do not answer the majority of questions about each group are eliminated from the analysis. In this way, we have included respondents who have answered most, if not all, of the questions in the battery. We tested the robustness of this strategy in two ways. First, we used more stringent criteria for inclusion in the analyses. We ran the analyses with only respondents who provided valid answers to every single question in the battery. The results were no different in substantive or statistical significance. Second, we used more relaxed criteria for inclusion in the analyses. We used AMELIA (King, Honaker, Joseph, and Scheve 2001) to implement multiple imputation of missing data on all covariates. The results, again, were no different in substantive or statistical significance.

21. As described in more detail in chapter 3, we built the thermometer scale version of ethnocentrism exactly as we did the stereotype-based measure. So it too ranges in principle from –1 to 1. Measured by the thermometer score ratings, ethnocentrism is centered at 0.08 with sd = 0.18 and Cronbach's coefficient *alpha* = 0.89 for whites, 0.82 for blacks, and 0.82 for Hispanic Americans. The correlation between the two versions of ethnocentrism, one based on stereotypes, the other based on feeling thermometer ratings, is 0.43.

22. These results appear in the Web appendix.

23. Full results appear in the Web appendix.

24. Moral traditionalism is a four-item scale, comprised of v001530–33, with a mean of 0.60, sd of 0.22, and Cronbach's *alpha* = 0.64. Limited government is an additive scale consisting of responses to v001420–22, with a mean of 0.41, sd = 0.40, and Cronbach's *alpha* = 0.74. Egalitarianism is comprised of v001521–26, with a mean of 0.60, sd = 0.20, and Cronbach's *alpha*

= 0.68. Ideological identification is derived from v001370. The results of adding them into the standard model appear in the Web appendix.

We also considered adding measures of religious faith to the standard model, on the idea that some Americans see the conflict with terrorism in religious terms. To some, the Islamic world is engaged in a "holy war." To others, the response of the United States to terrorism carried out by religious fanatics should be thought of as a "crusade." As such, strength of religious faith may supply an additional motivation behind support for the war on terrorism. To test this claim, we developed a measure of strength of religious faith. Strength of religious faith consists of a three-item scale, all three items appearing in the 2000 NES: how much guidance religion provides to the respondent (v000872, v000873), how often the respondent prays (v000874), and how regularly the respondent attends religious services (v000877, v000879, v000880). For the three-item scale, Cronbach's *alpha* = 0.87. It turns out that religious conviction did have occasional effects on support for the war on terrorism—on support for the president and for increased spending on defense—but whether this measure was included in the analysis made no difference to the estimated effect of ethnocentrism. These results also appear in the Web appendix.

25. On this point, see Altemeyer (1981); Hyman and Sheatsley (1954); and Stenner (2005). For the authoritarianism scale, Cronbach's *alpha* = 0.60, using v001586–v001589.

26. Complete results appear in the Web appendix. The persistence of the effect of ethnocentrism is not attributable to the more reliable measurement of ethnocentrism compared with authoritarianism. We estimated errors-in-variables regression, setting the reliability value for authoritarianism and ethnocentrism both to 0.8 (to put them on equal footing). Rerunning the analyses suggests that when we assume that ethnocentrism and authoritarianism are equally reliable, the estimates in tables 4.1 to 4.3 underestimate the real effect due to both variables, but the relative magnitudes of the effects are for the most part unchanged, as are the statistical significances of the variables.

27. Here are the exact wordings:

The United States should do everything it can to prevent the spread of communism to any other part of the world.

Some people feel it is important for us to cooperate more with Russia, while others believe we should be much tougher in our dealings with Russia. Where would you place yourself on this [seven-point] scale, or haven't you thought much about this? [Try to cooperate more with Russia (1); Get much tougher with Russia (7).]

The United States and the Soviet Union have recently reached agreements to reduce the number of nuclear arms. Do you approve or disapprove of these agreements? Do you approve/disapprove strongly or not strongly?

28. In the 1988 NES, respondents were asked to report their feelings toward whites, blacks, and Hispanic Americans but not, unfortunately, Asian Americans. This means our measure of ethnocentrism is a bit thinner than we would like—and thinner than what we use in most of our other analyses. Ethnocentrism is centered at 0.17 and has a standard deviation of 0.22. Cronbach's *alpha* is 0.86 for whites, 0.66 for blacks, and 0.66 for Hispanic Americans.

29. The effect of ethnocentrism is unchanged if we add to our standard model measures of religious conviction, to capture the likelihood that some Americans see the conflict with

the Soviet Union and communism in religious terms. It also withstands inclusion of standard measures of conservatism available in the 1988 study (moral conservatism, egalitarianism, and ideological identification).

30. In most respects, the model we use to estimate the effects presented in table 4.6 is identical to the model we used in estimating the impact of ethnocentrism on support for the war on terrorism. The one notable departure is that because the stereotype battery was present in the 1992 NES but not in the 1990 NES, here we are predicting "backward," against time's arrow: ethnocentrism as assessed in 1992 predicting opinions on Desert Storm expressed in the summer of 1991.

31. These three policy questions read:

Now, turning to the troubles in the Middle East. . . . Before the war in the Persian Gulf started, Congress debated whether to continue economic sanctions or to give President Bush the authority to use military forces to get Iraq out of Kuwait. At that time, were you for continuing to rely on sanctions, or were you in favor of authorizing the President to use military force, or didn't you have an opinion on this?

Do you think we did the right thing in sending U.S. military forces to the Persian Gulf or should we have stayed out?

Some people think that the U.S. and its allies should have continued to fight Iraq until Saddam Hussein was driven from power. Others think that the U.S. was right to stop fighting after Kuwait was liberated. What do you think? Should the war have continued or should it have stopped?

32. This boost in public support showed up vividly in all the polls, and it shows up as well in the NES Panel. In November 1990, less than 30 percent of the Americans who participated in the NES survey gave Bush their strong approval on his performance as president; in the summer of 1991, with memories of Desert Storm presumably still lingering, nearly 50 percent did so. The president's ratings on the war itself were even more glowing. Fully two-thirds of Americans strongly approved of President Bush's management of the Persian Gulf crisis in the summer of 1991, double the percentage from the preceding fall. Such increases are quite predictable, given what we know about the impact of sharply focused international crises on presidential popularity (e.g., J. Mueller 1973; Kernell 1978; MacKuen 1983). And in the Gulf crisis in particular, once the fighting began, virtually no American of national importance dissented (Brody 1991, 1994). Furthermore, judged as a military operation, the war seemed at the time to be little short of miraculous. American military hardware appeared to work magnificently, while American losses were astonishingly light: fewer than 150 American troops died on the battlefield (J. Mueller 1994, p. 69).

33. These predictions set the values of the other variables as follows: white, female, Independent-leaning Democrat, and otherwise average in education, political awareness, sense of threat, and economic evaluations (where relevant). The dotted lines represent 95 percent confidence intervals.

34. To preserve cases, we combined respondents who received slightly different versions of the defense spending question in the 2000 NES (one version was formatted as a seven-point Likert question; the other as a five-point branch-stem question). Their responses were recoded into three categories, to correspond with 2002.

35. The increase in Bush's ratings on the thermometer scale from 57 to 66 is substantial: for example, a nine-point difference in thermometer score ratings of major party presiden-

tial candidates would signal a landslide of historic proportions (Kinder and McConnaughy 2006). In both years, we average the pre- and post-election evaluations of Bush. We use the pre-election evaluation if the respondent did not complete the post-election interview. In table 4.7, we recode the continuous measure into nine categories, to analyze it using ordered probit. OLS produced similar results.

36. Can we be sure that this is so? Are the effects of ethnocentrism in 2002 significantly greater than the effects of ethnocentrism in 2000? Pretty sure. Here's how we conducted the test.

First of all, we converted the panel data into two stacked, independent cross-sections, by arbitrarily splitting the sample in half. In one, the independent variables and dependent variable were all measured in the 2000 NES. In the other, the independent variables came from the 2000 NES and the dependent variables from the 2002 NES. We then estimated a fully interactive model, where each predictor was multiplied by a dummy variable, coded 0 if the respondent belonged to the first "sample" and coded 1 if the respondent belonged to the second (the "2002 sample"). To provide a sampling distribution for the coefficient interacting ethnocentrism with the 2002 sample, we split our original sample in half in multiple iterations. For each of the three opinions—border security, national defense, and evaluations of President Bush—we reran the model 50,000 times, dividing the sample a different way each time. The results of this test suggest that we can be quite certain that the increase in the effect of ethnocentrism is real in the case of ratings of President Bush ($p < 0.10$); a bit less certain for spending on defense ($p < 0.16$); and less certain still for tightening border security ($p < 0.40$), where the effect of ethnocentrism was already significant in 2000. See the Web appendix for more details.

37. We are interested in the activation of ethnocentrism as a consequence of 9/11; we focus on determining whether the effect of ethnocentrism rises between 2000 and 2002. A separate question concerns whether ethnocentrism plays a role in opinion change between 2000 and 2002. One expectation is that in the post–9/11 world, ethnocentrism will drive foreign policy opinions in the conservative direction. Indeed, it does. To test this expectation, we reran our model predicting foreign policy opinions in 2002, with a lagged dependent variable measured in 2000. As predicted, ethnocentrism plays a significant role ($p < 0.01$ in all three cases) in shifting American support in favor of increased spending on defense, in favor of increased spending on patrolling the borders, and in support of the sitting president, above and beyond where individuals stood in the pre–9/11 era. In each of our three test cases, after controlling for opinion in 2000, ethnocentrism increases support for policies made relevant by the post–9/11 environment.

38. The predictions set the values of the other variables as follows: white, female, an Independent-leaning Democrat, and otherwise average in political awareness, authoritarianism, strength of religious faith, and economic evaluations.

39. To provide a statistical test of our claims, we repeated the process detailed in note 36. Each fully interactive model was reestimated 50,000 times. Throughout, we found that the effect of ethnocentrism was larger, on average, in 1991 than in 1990. We can be certain that this difference is nonzero when it comes to respondents' preference for a military solution ($p < 0.07$); a bit less certain when it comes to the view that sending the troops was right thing to do and approval of George Bush's performance as president ($p < 0.21$ in both cases); and less certain still when it comes to respondents' support for strengthening defense ($p < 0.34$).

All questions are asked identically in 1990, 1991, and 1992, with one exception. In 1990, when it comes to preference for a military solution, respondents were asked, "Which of the following do you think we should do now in the Persian Gulf: pull out U.S. forces entirely; try harder to find a diplomatic solution; tighten the economic embargo; or take tougher military action?"

Respondents were permitted to provide more than one answer. We have coded the answers such that a 1 corresponds with a sole mention of "take tougher military action" and a 0 corresponds with all other possibilities.

In 1991, the question was asked a bit differently: "Now, turning to the troubles in the Middle East. . . . Before the war in the Persian Gulf started, Congress debated whether to continue economic sanctions or to give President Bush the authority to use military forces to get Iraq out of Kuwait. At that time, were you for continuing to rely on sanctions, or were you in favor of authorizing the President to use military force, or didn't you have an opinion on this?" Respondents who were in favor of authorizing the President to use military force were coded a 1; those who responded with continuing sanctions were coded a 0; all others were set to missing (this was a very small number of respondents—less than 1.5 percent).

40. To determine whether the differences in effects from 1991 to 1992 are statistically significant, we engaged in the same type of analysis as outlined in note 36. Throughout, we found that the effect of ethnocentrism in 1992 was, on average, less than it was in 1991. After 50,000 simulations, we can conclude that the effect of ethnocentrism declined in 1992 with the following levels of certainty: for whether sending the troops was the right thing to do ($p < 0.31$); for whether we should have carried the fight to Baghdad ($p < 0.14$); strengthen defense ($p < 0.34$); and approval of George Bush's performance as president ($p < 0.37$).

41. The rise in the effect of national economic evaluations from 1991 to 1992 is statistically significant at $p < 0.001$, based on 50,000 iterations of stacked panel data. In 50,000 iterations, not a single iteration suggested that national economic conditions became less important in 1992.

42. As noted earlier, because the stereotype battery was present in the 1992 NES but not in the 1990 NES, here we are sometimes predicting "backward": ethnocentrism as assessed in 1992 predicting opinions offered either in 1990, or in 1991, or in 1992. The 1991 versus 1992 comparison is impressive since the E measure appears on the 1992 interview—by that fact alone, we would expect to see bigger effects in 1992 than in 1991. But we do not.

Chapter Five

1. On the Rwandan genocide and the American "response" to Rwanda, see Gourevitch (1998); Melvern (2000); and Power (2002). Power argues that Rwanda is part of a general pattern, that throughout the twentieth century, the United States has chosen to remain on the sidelines in the face of unambiguous evidence of genocide.

2. Quoted in an article written by James Bennet: "Clinton Declares U.S., with World, Failed Rwandans," New York Times, March 26, 1998, pp. A6, A12. At another time and on a less public occasion, Clinton also said that American voters cared more about the color of his tie than they did about what went on in a tiny African county (according to Samantha Power's Tanner Lecture, delivered at the University of Michigan, March 9, 2007).

3. Figure 5.1 presents Lowess plots of the percentage of respondents saying the United States is spending "too little." Lowess is the acronym for "locally weighted scatterplot smoother." It is a technique for smoothing data, especially useful in time-series graphical presentations (Fox 1997).

4. Model specification is identical to what we used in chapter 4. The dependent variable is coded such that higher values indicate support for *decreased* spending on foreign aid. The shift in predicted probability refers to the probability that a respondent will support *decreased* spending on foreign aid.

5. The results for limited government and equality appear in the Web appendix. Additional tests reinforce the robustness of the basic result.

The effect of ethnocentrism on opposition to foreign aid is completely unaffected if we add a measure of authoritarianism into the analysis (the estimated coefficient for ethnocentrism, holding constant authoritarianism, is 0.69 with standard error 0.30). These results also appear in the Web appendix.

The effect due to ethnocentrism is unaffected if we add perceptions of threat.

It is likewise unaffected if we add measures of moral conservatism and ideological identification into the analysis.

The effect due to ethnocentrism is also maintained when the stereotype measure of ethnocentrism is replaced by one based on thermometer scores (the estimated coefficient is 0.65, se = 0.25, significant at $p < 0.01$).

If we partition the sample by race and carry out the analysis among white, black, and Hispanic respondents separately, the effect appears to be uniform across groups (though the limited number of cases in the black and the Hispanic subsamples reduces the sensitivity of the test).

Finally, the effect of ethnocentrism on opposition to foreign aid holds generally. It shows up in various National Election Studies (the 1990–1992 NES Panel, 1996 NES, and 2004 NES), and it comes through clearly in the 2000 General Social Survey as well, regardless of whether the program is described as "foreign aid" or as "assistance to other countries."

6. These predictions are generated for a white, female Independent-leaning Democrat, with average political awareness and education.

7. Here is the exact wording of the two foreign aid questions:

Do you think the United States should give economic assistance to those countries in Eastern Europe which have turned toward democracy, or not? (v912401).

Should federal spending be increased, decreased, or kept about the same on aid to countries of the former Soviet Union? (v923731)

8. Figure 5.2 is based on ordered probit results from a standard model (full results appear in the Web appendix). These predictions are generated for a white, female Independent-leaning Democrat, with average political awareness and education. Dashed lines represent the 95 percent confidence intervals.

Does it matter whether authoritarianism is added to the analysis? No. The effect of authoritarianism is either small or statistically insignificant, and in neither case is the estimated effect due to ethnocentrism altered. Likewise, neither limited government nor egalitarianism predicts opposition to foreign aid in these two instances.

Finally, the question on whether the United States should give economic assistance to those countries in Eastern Europe that have turned toward democracy appeared in both the 1990 and 1991 interviews. In figure 5.2 and the Web appendix, we present results for the latter only. The results for the 1990 version are virtually identical. Specifically, the estimated coefficient for ethnocentrism on opposition to economic assistance to Eastern Europe expressed in 1990 is 0.72, with standard error of 0.36, $p < 0.05$.

9. We are drawing here on George M. Fredrickson's *Racism* (2002) and especially on Leonard Thompson's *A History of South Africa* (2001).

10. Here is the exact wording of the two questions:

Have you read or heard enough about what's going on there to have an opinion about what US policy toward South Africa should be?

Some people think that the US should apply economic sanctions to get the South African government to change its racial laws. Others think that the US should not do this. What do you think—should the US apply economic pressure or not? Do you hold this opinion strongly or not strongly?

The 1990 question was preceded by a weaker preamble to filter out no opinions and was asked in one of two formats (seven-point scale versus branching). Either as:

Some people feel that the economic sanctions against South Africa should be decreased a lot in light of changes in the treatment of blacks that have taken place there recently. (Suppose those people are at one end of the scale, at point number 1.) Other people feel that sanctions should be increased a lot in order to pressure the government to make further changes. (Suppose these people are at the other end at point 7. And, of course, other people have opinions in between at points 2, 3, 4, 5, or 6.) Where would you place yourself on this scale, or haven't you thought much about this?

Or:

Some people feel that the economic sanctions against South Africa should be decreased a lot in light of changes in the treatment of blacks that have taken place there recently. Other people feel that sanctions should be increased in order to pressure the government to make further changes. And still others feel that the US should continue to impose about the same sanctions it imposes now. What about you? Do you feel that sanctions against South Africa should be decreased, should be increased, should be kept about the same, or haven't you thought much about this?

(If increased or decreased:) Should sanctions be decreased/increased a lot or a little?

(If kept about the same:) Would you lean toward decreasing sanctions, increasing sanctions, or do you oppose any change in sanctions?

In the 1990 NES, the branching format seems to spreads out opinion a bit more than the seven-point scale does, and it elicits somewhat more "no opinions." For our purposes, such differences are uninteresting, so we created a new composite variable, one that combines opinion across the two formats.

11. On each question, blacks were less likely to say they had no opinion than whites were, reversing the usual race difference (e.g., Delli Carpini and Keeter 1996). The percentage of blacks saying that they had no opinion on sanctions for South Africa was 56.2 percent in 1988 and 27.9 percent in 1990; the corresponding figures for whites were 58.0 percent in 1988 and 35.3 percent in 1990. The racial difference in 1990 is statistically significant.

12. For the analysis of black Americans, we estimate the impact of ethnocentrism in the usual way (using ordered probit to estimate the standard model, which includes partisanship, education, awareness, and sex). Here is the estimated effect of ethnocentrism on opposition to sanctions among blacks: in 1988 ($N = 75$), $b_1 = -3.39$, se = 1.53; in 1990 ($N = 89$), $b_1 = -0.31$, se = 0.65. The small N makes the more complicated selection model less credible.

13. The results portrayed in figure 5.3 are based on a bivariate probit selection model, which corrects for the glaring fact that a substantial fraction of NES respondents claimed to have no opinion on apartheid and so were not asked what their opinion might be. In the equa-

tion predicting who has an opinion and who does not, the estimated coefficient on ethno-centrism is –0.72 with a standard error of 0.19 in 1988; in 1990, the values are –0.57 and 0.28, respectively.

Alternatively, we could have simply used listwise deletion, removing respondents who failed to give an opinion from the analysis entirely. Listwise deletion may be the most convenient so-lution to missing data, but it assumes that the respondents who are missing on the particular covariate are missing at random. When missingness affects a small proportion of cases, listwise deletion may not be very dangerous to statistical estimates. However, in this case, a substantial proportion of respondents failed to provide an opinion on the issue. Further, we worried that simply dropping these individuals would lead to *selection bias* in who we analyze. One alterna-tive solution would have been to retain these individuals and assign them a value in between those who support sanctions against the South African regime and those who oppose sanc-tions. This missing data solution makes a strong assumption about what it means to be miss-ing on (or to have refused to answer) the question: that these individuals should be located somewhere between the two valid responses. A better solution is to model the missingness: to estimate why some people express an opinion and others do not, and to take what we learn from that examination into account when we examine why some people support sanctions and others oppose sanctions. This is what selection models accomplish (for selection models gen-erally, see Heckman 1979; for the bivariate probit selection model, Dubin and Rivers 1989; for an excellent application to public opinion, see Berinsky 2004).

We could have modeled this in a couple of different ways, and we did. First, we used a Heck-man selection model, where the assignment equation (predicting whether respondents ex-press an opinion) is dichotomous and the outcome equation is "continuous." The Heckman model uses a probit in the first stage and ordinary least-squares (OLS) in the second stage. For all of the reasons discussed in the previous chapter, we disliked the OLS treatment of the de-pendent variable (views on sanctions) in the second stage. Hence, we elected to use a bivari-ate probit selection model, which differs from the Heckman in that it treats the second stage as a dichotomous variable. Because of the inconsistency across the years in question wordings, this seemed like a reasonable choice. We collapsed the views on sanctions into two categories: favor or oppose economic sanctions in 1988, and decrease/keep same or increase sanctions in 1990. For the 1990 data, we experimented with grouping individuals who provided the mid-point option with the liberal option and with the conservative option; those who elected the midpoint option seemed to cluster better with those providing more conservative responses, but the results are substantively and statistically similar when we omit those who were at the midpoint.

The Heckman model and the bivariate probit model provided substantively and statisti-cally similar results.

For the bivariate probit model, we included in the "assignment equation" (predicting whether people express an opinion) variables that represent the conventional wisdom about who is interested in politics and who is not (Krosnick and Milburn 1990; Delli Carpini and Keeter 1996), plus a measure of ethnocentrism (E^*, based on thermometer score ratings in 1988; E, based on stereotypes drawn from the 1992 interview, in 1990). In equation form:

Expressing an Opinion on South Africa = $\beta_0 + \beta_1$Ethnocentrism + β_2Sex +
β_3Ethnicity + β_4Education + β_5Awareness + β_6Discuss Politics + β_7Strength
of Partisanship + β_8Refused to Report Income + β_9Ideological Innocence +
β_{10}Race of Interviewer + ε_1

Where Opinion on South Africa = 1 if yes and 0 if no; ethnocentrism is measured in the standard way and coded –1 to 1; sex = 1 if female and 0 if male; education is coded onto the 0–1 interval, where 0 = 8 grades or fewer and 1 = postgraduate degree; awareness is a standard information scale, following Zaller (1990, 1992), coded 0–1 (with the proviso that the 1990 NES knowledge item asking people to identify Nelson Mandela was excluded from the scale in that year); discuss politics ranges from 0 (never) to 1 (every day); strength of partisanship is coded into four categories, ranging from 0 (pure independent) to 1 (strong partisan); refused to report income = 1 if refused and 0 if reported; ideological innocence = 1 if "apolitical" or refused to say when asked to identify as a liberal or a conservative, and 0 otherwise; and race of interviewer = 1 if black and 0 if white. Black respondents are excluded from this analysis.

The "outcome equation" (predicting whether people oppose sanctions) is the familiar standard model, except that parameters are estimated by bivariate probit selection (and black Americans, for reasons spelled out in the text, are excluded).

Full results, for both assignment and outcome, and for both surveys, are presented in the Web appendix.

The predictions in figure 5.3 are calculated for a white, female Independent-leaning Democrat, of average education and political awareness. For the assignment equation, we also set political discussion to its mean, and income refusal, ideological innocence, and race of interviewer to zero.

14. In 1988, b_1 = 0.84, se = 0.39; in 1990, b_1 = 1.05, se = 0.41.

15. If our story is right here, we should find that the inhibiting effect of ethnocentrism on opinion expression should *not* be general; in particular, it should not apply to prominent aspects of domestic U.S. policy. To see if this was so, we looked for cases in the 1990 NES of domestic policy where a significant fraction of the public admitted that they had no opinion. We found three: spending more on national defense; government's responsibility to provide a job and a decent standard of living for all Americans; and the tradeoff between cutting federal spending, on the one hand, and maintaining essential services, on the other. Does ethnocentrism predict no opinion on these matters? Not really. We turn up a positive coefficient on ethnocentrism in all three instances, but the coefficient never reaches statistical significance: for defense, b_1 = 0.15, se = 0.44; for employment, b_1 = 0.49, se = 0.34; and for cuts in spending versus services, b_1 = 0.52, se = 0.34. These results offer additional support for our account: that the relatively ethnocentric are more likely to say they have no opinion on applying sanctions on South Africa because ethnocentrism breeds an indifference to the suffering of faraway others.

16. Presidential address to the nation on U.S. policy in Central America, May 9, 1984.

17. What is surprising, perhaps, is that aid to the contras was no more unpopular than foreign aid in general. Here is the exact question:

Should federal spending on aid to the contras in Nicaragua be increased, decreased, or kept about the same?

18. These results come from the standard model, estimated in the standard way, except that because the 1988 NES does not carry the stereotype battery, we make do with E^* (based on thermometer score ratings of whites, blacks, and Hispanic Americans). The dependent variable is coded such that higher values indicate support for spending. As usual, complete results appear in the Web appendix.

19. A cautionary note: heteroscedastic probit results are not straightforward to interpret and may be sensitive to misspecification (Keele and Park 2004). On the other hand, the results presented here are quite robust across alternative specifications. Because the heteroscedastic

probit model seems less sensitive to misspecification than the heteroscedastic ordered probit, we use the former, recoding the dependent variable such that 0 corresponds with decreased spending and 1 corresponds with keeping spending the same or increasing it.

20. The results are based on the standard model, predicting opinions expressed in the summer of 1991 from ethnocentrism (E) measured in the 1992 NES. Full results appear in the Web appendix.

21. Gender differences in the expression of emotion is a general result. See Brody and Hall (2000).

22. Based on foreign aid opinion assessed in the 2000 NES, b_1 =0.11, se = 0.30; with opinion assessed in 2002, b_1 = 0.72, se = 0.30. To determine whether the effect of ethnocentrism in 2002 is *significantly* greater than the effect of ethnocentrism in 2000, we carried out the same test described in chapter 4. The result of the test suggests that we can be quite certain that the increase in the effect of ethnocentrism is real ($p < 0.12$). See the Web appendix for the details.

23. Emphasis added. Our account of the Marshall Plan and its politics relies on Patterson (1996). The Gallup poll results are cited in Holsti (1996).

Chapter Six

1. We take the title of this chapter from John Higham's masterly history of American nativism from the Civil War to the early decades of the twentieth century: *Strangers in the Land: Patterns of American Nativism, 1860–1925* ([1955] 1988).

2. Noted by Nicolaus Mills (1994, p.15). A year after the act's passage, the Commissioner of Immigration at Ellis Island was able to announce that "virtually all immigrants now looked exactly like Americans" (Higham [1955] 1988, p. 325).

3. Data for figure 6.1 come from Gibson and Lennon (1999, table 1), amended with Census data from 2000 and 2005. For state-level immigration data from 2000 to 2005, see U.S. Census Bureau (2005). On the causes of the new immigration, see Espenshade (1995); Massey and Espinosa (1997); and Massey et al. (1993, 1994).

4. Ronald Takaki titled his history of Asian Americans *Strangers from a Different Shore* (1989). As recently as 1960, three-quarters of American immigrants were European born and only 5 percent were born in Asia. By the 1990s, however, Asian immigrants outnumbered those of European descent, and Latin American immigrants nearly outnumbered both (Gibson and Lennon 1999). Between 1990 and 2000, the foreign-born population in the United States increased by over 50 percent, from 19.8 million to 31.1 million. Of the 31.1 million foreign born, over one-half hailed from Latin American countries, about one-fourth from Asian countries, and 16 percent from Europe (Malone et al. 2003).

5. More than a decade ago, as we embarked on this project, we chose immigration as our first case. We figured that if we could not find effects of ethnocentrism in the domain of immigration, then we should fold up our tent and go home. As it happened, we did find effects, and we presented them in a paper delivered at the annual meeting of the Midwest Political Science Association in April 1997: "Closing the Golden Door? Exploring the Foundations of American Opposition to Immigration" (Kinder and Deane 1997).

6. *Asian* and *Hispanic* are generic categories, convenient for some administrative purposes perhaps, but ones that conceal enormous diversity. Portes and Truelove (1987, p. 360) put this point well, writing about Hispanic Americans:

Under the same label [Hispanic], we find individuals whose ancestors lived in the country at least since the time of independence and others who arrived last year; we find substantial numbers of professionals and entrepreneurs, along with humble farm laborers and unskilled factory workers; there are whites, blacks, mulattos, and mestizos; there are full-fledged citizens and unauthorized aliens; and finally, among the immigrants, there are those who came in search of employment and a better economic future and those who arrived escaping death squads and political persecution at home.

7. Roughly half of those interviewed in the 1992 NES were also questioned first in the 1990 NES and again in the 1991 NES Persian Gulf War study; the remainder constitutes a fresh cross-section. A short form of the questionnaire was designed to be used over the telephone with respondents first interviewed in 1990 who had since moved "out of range" of the NES interviewing staff. As a result, 6.2 percent were interviewed in the preelection period with a short-form questionnaire; 8.4 percent were taken through a short form in the postelection interview. A final wrinkle in the 1992 NES study design is that while the great majority of participants were interviewed in person, some were questioned over the phone: roughly 11 percent in the preelection interview and 21 percent in the post. Fortunately, differences in the quality of data supplied by those interviewed over the telephone as against those interviewed in person are virtually impossible to find (Rosenstone, Petrella, and Kinder 1993), and so the various analyses we report here ignore mode of interviewing.

8. On the 1992 presidential campaign, see Arterton (1993), Frankovic (1993), and Pomper (1993). In our own analysis of presidential approval (in chapter 4), we found strong evidence for the activation of concerns about national economy in 1992 relative to 1991.

9. Here are the exact wordings for the four key policy questions:

Do you think the number of immigrants from foreign countries who are permitted to come to the United States to live should be increased a little, increased a lot, decreased a little, decreased a lot, or left the same as it is now?

Do you think that immigrants who come to the US should be eligible as soon as they come here for government services such as Medicaid, Food Stamps, welfare, or should they have to be here for a year or more?

There are several different ideas about how to teach children who don't speak English when they enter our public schools. Which one of the following statements best describes how you feel? One, all classes should be conducted only in English so that children have to learn English right from the start. Two, children who don't know English should have classes in their native language just for a year or two until they learn English. Three, there should be one set of classes in English and another set in Spanish or other languages all the way through high school so that children can keep up their native languages and culture if they choose.

Do you favor a law making English the official language of the United States, meaning government business would be conducted in English only, or do you oppose such a law?

Frequency distributions appear in the Web appendix, for the sample as a whole, and for whites and blacks and Hispanics taken separately.

Most Hispanic Americans are Mexican by descent: according to a March 1989 Current Population Survey, 62.6 percent of Hispanics claim Mexican American heritage. (By comparison, 11.6 percent are Puerto Rican, 5.3 percent are Cuban, and 12.7 percent trace their origins to a variety of Central and South American countries.) Roughly one-half of the Hispanics interviewed in the 1992 NES are Mexican American, and their opinions on immigration resemble closely the views expressed by Hispanics in general, with a consistent but modest shift in the more generous direction.

10. On the Massachusetts colony, see Kraut (1994). For a review of the evidence from public opinion surveys, see Harwood (1986); R. J. Simon and Alexander (1993); and Lapinski et al. (1997).

11. Based on Rosenstone, Hansen, and Kinder (1986). For family economic conditions, the items are v923426 and v923430. We began with an eight-item scale that used v923426, v923430, v923433, v923434, v923435, v923437, v923438, and v923439, but the battery of questions from v923433 to v923439 was not asked on the short form of the questionnaire, resulting in missing data for about 170 cases. To keep these cases in the analysis, we used an abbreviated, two-item scale. The correlation between the abbreviated scale and the eight-item scale was 0.63. Analyses using the eight-item scale and the abbreviated scale did not vary appreciably from each other. The measure is scaled from 0, indicating many economic difficulties, to 1, indicating few economic difficulties.

12. For evidence consistent with this proposition, see Citrin et al. (1990); Espenshade and Calhoun (1993); Nie, Junn, and Stehlik-Barry (1996); R. J. Simon and Alexander (1993); and Quillian (1995). Political knowledge is based on a series of nine information items (for example, who is William Rehnquist?), with responses averaged into a composite scale. The scale is approximately normally distributed and reasonably reliable (Cronbach's *alpha* = 0.81; scale items are v925915 to v925921, v925951, and v925952).

13. See, on this point, Abowd and Freeman (1991); and Borjas and Freeman (1992). For this purpose, we transformed the NES detailed coding of occupation (v923922) into three dummy variables: top of the occupation structure, bottom, and out of the labor market altogether, with those occupying middling positions serving as the omitted reference group. We also included a measure of weekly occupational wages, under the idea that workers who earn less will find themselves more vulnerable to being threatened by immigrant laborers (Scheve and Slaughter 2001). When this variable was included without education, it had a significant effect such that low-wage workers were significantly more opposed to immigration policy. Once education was included, however, the effect of wages was indistinguishable from zero.

14. We relied here on 1990 Census data, taking the log value of the proportion of each state that is Hispanic and Asian. There is huge variation in these proportions. For example, Hispanics and Asians constituted just 0.09 percent of the population of West Virginia in 1990, but 34.9 percent of the population of California.

15. We represent such economic optimism through Americans' assessments of recent changes in the national economy—so-called sociotropic assessments (Kinder and Kiewiet 1981)—based on three questions, averaged into a single scale (*alpha* = 0.72; v923528, v923530, and v923532).

16. See Adorno et al. (1950); and Stenner (2005). To test this idea, we took advantage of a five-item moral traditionalism scale (Cronbach's *alpha* = 0.66; v926115 to v926119), originally developed by Conover and Feldman (1986b).

17. For arguments and evidence on the importance of principles (or values) to public opinion, see Feldman (1988); Feldman and Zaller (1992); Kinder (1998); Kinder and Sanders (1996); and Markus (2001). Equal opportunity is a six-item scale (v926024 to v926029; *alpha* = 0.71) developed and refined by Feldman (1988). Limited government, the conviction that market solutions trump governmental interventions, is a three-item scale (v925729 to v925731, *alpha* = 0.71), based on Markus (1993, 2001).

18. Based on the pooled NES 1992–2004, we find that 87.7 percent of white Americans and their parents were born in the United States; 94.2 percent of black Americans; 46.6 percent of Hispanic Americans; and just 25.0 percent of Asian Americans.

19. Just thirty Asian Americans were questioned in the 1992 NES.

We also investigated whether ethnocentrism might operate differently among black Americans. Over several surveys and many policy questions, we mostly found no differences. When we did occasionally uncover a significant racial difference, the effect of ethnocentrism was sometimes greater among blacks; sometimes the effect was greater among whites. We concluded that on matters of immigration, there was no good reason to treat whites and blacks separately. And so we do not.

20. Here's the full equation:

$$y^* = \mathbf{x'\beta + \varepsilon}$$

$$= \beta_0 + \beta_1\mathbf{Ethnocentrism} + \beta_2[\mathbf{Ethnocentrism} \times \text{Hispanic}] + \beta_3\text{Family Economic}$$
Conditions $+ \beta_4$Unemployed $+ \beta_5$Divorced $+ \beta_6$Education $+ \beta_7$Political
Awareness $+ \beta_8$Occupation $+ \beta_9$Proportion Hispanic and Asian $+ \beta_{10}$Beneficiary of
Government Program $+ \beta_{11}$Economic Optimism $+ \beta_{12}$Moral Traditionalism $+$
β_{13}Egalitarianism $+ \beta_{14}$Limited Government $+ \beta_{15}$Partisanship $+ \beta_{16}$Black $+$
β_{17}Hispanic $+ \beta_{18}$Female $+ \varepsilon$

$$\Pr(y = m) = \Pr(\tau_{m-1} < y^* < \tau_m) = \Phi(\tau_m - \mathbf{x'\beta}) - \Phi(\tau_{m-1} - \mathbf{x'\beta})$$

In the expressions above, y refers to opinion on immigration (in our analysis, each issue is taken up separately). The term y^* represents the unobserved latent variable in each case. That is, we assume that the opinion expressed on any particular question arises from a latent, continuous opinion, and that our survey questions segment this continuum at a series of ordered thresholds (y^* falls into one of m categories).

The "effect" of ethnocentrism among *Hispanics* is given by $\beta_1 + \beta_2$. *Effect* is used loosely here since the marginal effect of ethnocentrism in an ordered probit model would also entail differentiating the normal cumulative density function.

21. All other right-hand side variables are coded on the 0–1 interval as well, with one exception: the measure of the logged proportion of each state's population accounted for by Hispanics and Asians, which ranges from −4.74 (West Virginia) to −1.05 (California).

22. The effect of a shift in ethnocentrism from −0.1 to +0.6 appears in the last row of table 6.1 to illustrate the substantive effects of ethnocentrism. We generated these predicted probabilities for a white, female, Independent-leaning Democrat, who has average (or modal, in the case of dummy variables) scores on all other variables.

23. Our analysis uncovered no effects of partisanship, no effects of personal troubles, and, perhaps surprisingly, no effects of threat.

Contrary to realistic group conflict theory, Americans working low-wage, low-skill jobs were not any more likely to take a hard stand on immigration policy. In their study of southern Californians' attitudes toward illegal immigration, Espenshade and Calhoun (1993) found little support for this hypothesis either. Nor did Citrin and colleagues (1997). For one study that does report a link between occupation and opinion on immigration, see Scheve and Slaughter (2001).

Americans receiving government assistance were *more* likely, not less, to support the idea that immigrants should have immediate access to government aid, they were more supportive of bilingual education in the schools, and they were less enthusiastic about establishing English as an official language.

Finally, Americans living in states with comparatively high proportions of Hispanics and Asians were significantly more likely to push for establishing English as an official language, but were actually *less* negative in their views on other aspects of immigration. This surprised us. Group conflict theory has proven valuable in application to American race relations in a line of empirical work that extends back to V. O. Key's *Southern Politics in State and Nation* (1949). The basic result, relying for the most part on measures like the one we use here, is that as the nearby population becomes increasingly black, whites become more reactionary in their views on race (e.g., Giles and Evans 1986; Glaser 1994). Furthermore, Quillian (1995) found that aggregate differences among Western European publics in anti-immigrant prejudice could be traced to national variation in the sheer presence of immigrants: the larger the immigrant population, the stronger the prejudice. In light of these positive results, we pushed harder in our analysis to see if we could turn up some support for group conflict theory. We experimented with various formulations of this population variable, hoping to turn up more positive evidence, but with no success. We added a set of terms to the analysis [Occupation × Proportion Hispanic and Asian] on the idea that *real* threat means working at the bottom of the occupational structure in states with large immigration populations. We found no support for this claim either. Finally, neither Occupation, nor Proportion Hispanic and Asian, nor their interaction, predicts ethnocentrism, so we were also unable to uncover an indirect route by which threat might influence immigration opinion.

24. Again, the effect, loosely speaking, of ethnocentrism among Hispanic Americans is given by $\beta_1 + \beta_2$; more precisely, the substantive effects (given by differences in predicted probabilities) for non-Hispanic Americans and for Hispanic Americans appear in table 6.1.

25. Here are the questions:

Many different groups of people have come to the United States at different times in our history. In recent years, the population of the United States has been changing to include many more people of Hispanic and Asian background. I'm going to read a list of things that people say may happen because of the growing number of Hispanic people in the United States. For each of these things, please say how likely it is to happen.

How likely is it that the growing number of *Hispanics* will improve our culture with new ideas and customs?

(How likely is it) to cause higher taxes due to more demands for public services?

(How likely is it) to take away jobs from people already here?

How likely is it that the growing number of *Asians* will improve our culture with new ideas and customs?

(How likely is it) to cause higher taxes due to more demands for public services?

(How likely is it) to take away jobs from people already here?

Frequencies appear in the Web appendix. Hispanic Americans were much less alarmist about the harm done to American culture by Hispanic immigrants' ideas and customs, but in other respects they were not much different from the rest of the American public.

26. These computations assume individuals who, apart from their scores on the ethnocentrism scale, are typical of the population as a whole: moderate threat occupation, Independent-leaning Democrat, female, and average (or modal) on all other predictor variables. We could have plotted the effects of ethnocentrism among whites or blacks; our statistical model combines them. Here, we have plotted the lines for whites. The lines for blacks are similar, just with slightly different intercepts. The dashed lines represent 95 percent confidence intervals.

27. This conclusion holds however we carry out the analysis. The effect of ethnocentrism is substantial whether estimated with cross-sectional or panel data (where ethnocentrism is measured four years before opinion). And it remains substantial when we replace the stereotype-based measure of ethnocentrism with the parallel measure created out of thermometer score ratings. This last result is reassuring in at least two respects. First, convergence between the two measures removes the worry that our findings turn on one particular and perhaps peculiar way of measuring ethnocentrism. Second, convergence erases a technical problem (or potential problem). It turns out that in the 1992 NES interview, the stereotype questions immediately precede the measures of opinion on immigration. Such placement might artificially enhance the relationship we report between opinion on matters of immigration and ethnocentrism, measured through group stereotypes. Relying instead on the thermometer ratings allows us to estimate the effect of ethnocentrism, free of this particular worry. Using the thermometer-based measure, we find consistent and large effects of ethnocentrism on white opinion, across every aspect of immigration policy. In raw terms, the ordered probit coefficients are somewhat smaller than those displayed in tables 6.1 and 6.2, but still sizable.

28. The 1992 NES included four questions designed to measure authoritarianism. Following Stenner and Feldman, the questions ask about the values most important for parents to emphasize in the raising of their children, with each posing a choice between the authority of parents and the autonomy of children. The virtue of these questions is that they capture the conceptual core of authoritarianism while avoiding the problems that crippled the original measure. On this point, see Altemeyer (1981); Hyman and Sheatsley (1954); and Stenner (2005). For the authoritarianism scale as a whole, Cronbach's *alpha* = 0.67, using v926019 to v926022.

29. When asked the general question, 44.3 percent of Americans favored a decrease in immigration, as against just 9.6 percent who favored an increase. In the case of immigration from Latin America, 44.2 percent of Americans favored a decrease in immigration, as against just 8.9 percent who favored an increase. In the case of immigration from Asia, 43.0 percent favored a decrease in immigration, while just 8.9 percent favored an increase. And as for Europe: 35.5 percent of Americans favored a decrease in immigration versus 9.9 percent who favored an increase.

30. Here are the relevant results (complete results appear in the Web appendix):

Ethnocentrism and opposition to immigration . . .

	In general	From Latin America	From Asia	From Europe
Ethnocentrism	1.91***	2.06***	2.13***	1.17***
	0.27	0.28	0.28	0.27

Source: 2000 GSS.

Note: Table entry is the ordered probit coefficient with standard error below. Model includes measures of partisanship, education, employment status, household economic conditions, sex, and race.

***$p < 0.01$; **$p < 0.05$; *$p < 0.10$, two-tailed.

31. This result replicates if we measure ethnocentrism through thermometer scores and when we analyze different surveys (including the 1996, 2000, and 2004 NES; the 1992–1996 and 2000–2004 NES Panels; and the 2000 GSS).

32. These results also replicate in the 1996, 2000, and 2004 NES and the 2000–2004 NES Panel.

33. For this section, we recoded the dependent variables such that higher values indicate *support* for immigration. On increasing immigration, the ordered probit coefficient on ethnocentrism is estimated to be 1.38 (se = 0.43); on spending (less) on the borders, the estimate is = 1.11 (se = 0.59). Full results appear in the Web appendix. These effects are robust. They are unaffected by controlling on measures of immigrant status (whether the survey respondent or the survey respondent's parents were born outside the United States), nation of origin, class, family economic conditions, and more.

34. Is this ethnocentrism at work, or is it group identification? The theory of group identification contends that the political consequences of group membership are accentuated among those who belong to the group psychologically, not just objectively, who identify with their group for reasons of shared interests or common values (Conover 1988; Dawson 1994; Price 1989; Tajfel 1982). In the particular case before us here, among Hispanic Americans, conventional measures of group identification are correlated with the in-group component of ethnocentrism, as one would expect, but the correlations are surprisingly weak. Moreover, when we add these conventional measures to our standard model, we find that group identification is generally irrelevant to Hispanic Americans' opinions on immigration, and that the presence of group identification does nothing to the sizable effects we have previously assigned to ethnocentrism.

35. To provide a statistical test to determine whether the effects of ethnocentrism in 1996 were significantly greater than the effects in 1992, we first converted the panel data into two stacked, independent cross-sections, by arbitrarily splitting the sample in half. In one cross-section, the dependent variable was measured in the 1992 NES. In the other, the dependent variable was measured in the 1996 NES. We then estimated a fully interactive model, where each predictor was multiplied by a dummy variable, coded 0 if the respondent belonged to the first "sample" and coded 1 if the respondent belonged to the second (the "1996 sample"). To provide a sampling distribution for the coefficient interacting ethnocentrism with the 1996 sample, we split our original sample in half in multiple iterations. For the two dependent variables—decreasing the level of immigration and requiring immigrants to wait before being eligible for assistance—we reran the model 50,000 times, dividing the sample a different way each time.

For opinion on decreasing the level of immigration, the mean interaction term between $E \times 1996$, produced by these 50,000 iterations, was 0.06 (sd = 0.76); nearly half of the analyses produced a negative interaction term and nearly half of them produced a positive one. We cannot say with any certainty that the effect of ethnocentrism rises in 1996 for this dependent variable.

For opinion on requiring immigrants to wait, the results are a bit more promising, but they still did not meet conventional significance levels. We can reject the null hypothesis of no effect at $p < 0.23$ (one-tailed).

For more details, see the Web appendix.

36. According to a member of the state central Republican Party Committee, McCain's weak position eliminated him as a serious contender: "When I go county to county visiting 29 counties in my area, I believe almost without exception that immigration is that issue that puts fire in their eyes. They just really are livid that we have allowed this to happen to the point it has" (Nagourney 2007).

That McCain was attacked on immigration in Iowa may actually not be that surprising. Patterns of immigration settlement have shifted across the country in the past few decades, with immigrants settling in "New Destinations"—nontraditionally receiving states in the South and Midwest. Between 1990 and 2000, the Hispanic population grew at a rate of 300 percent or above in North Carolina, Arkansas, and Georgia (Kochhar, Suro, and Tafoya 2005). From 2000 to 2005, 41,000 Iowans took up residence in other states; this population loss was not entirely offset by international in-migration of 30,000 residents (U.S. Census Bureau 2005). The state government in Iowa has tried (not without controversy) to encourage immigration in order to curtail its falling population.

37. The (one-sided) *p*-values are as follows: 0.15 (decreasing the level of immigration), 0.43 (wait for benefits), 0.05 (English-only instruction), and 0.12 (English as official language).

38. We do *not* see this triggering effect of increasing immigration on opposition to immigration in 2000—perhaps because by 2000, every state but Maine had experienced gains in foreign-born population.

39. We also analyzed Asian Americans, whose views on immigration seem harder to predict. On the one hand, like Hispanic Americans, many Asian Americans may find themselves "in between two nations." On the other hand, for Asian Americans, "home" is further away geographically and may be so psychologically as well, and so the myth of return may be less compelling. We expect in-group pride to be a force for positive views on immigration among Asian Americans, though perhaps not quite so one-sidedly as it appears to be for Hispanic Americans.

The practical problem for investigating this question is cases—more precisely, insufficient cases. The Asian American population in the United States is growing rapidly, but even large representative national samples of the sort carried out by NES or GSS scoop up so few Asians to make serious analysis impossible. We needed to find another source.

The best we managed to turn up is the Multi-City Study of Urban Inequality (MCSUI), which we put to use back in chapter 3. MCSUI, remember, was carried out between 1992 and 1994 in four American cities: Atlanta, Boston, Detroit, and Los Angeles. In Los Angeles, the Asian population was deliberately oversampled. More than eight hundred Asians, mostly of Korean, Japanese, or Chinese descent, were interviewed. And each was asked, following our familiar format, to offer judgments about the character of four racial groups—whites, blacks, Hispanic Americans, and Asian Americans—with respect to each of five characteristics—intelligent, friendly, fair, law-abiding, and independent. As we learned in chapter 3, Asian Americans living in Los Angeles displayed considerable ethnocentrism: they regarded their group to be superior, on average, to *all* other groups on *each* of these characteristics.

Fortunately for our immediate purposes, the MCSUI also asked two questions on immigration. Neither one concerns policy per se, but each seems to capture sentiments that are close to, and perhaps even interchangeable with, support for immigration in general. Both begin from the same premise: that immigration to the United States continues at the same (high) rate into the foreseeable future. Respondents are then asked to guess what would happen under this condition to their own group's political power. In the second and exactly parallel question, they were asked what would happen to their group's economic opportunity.

Here are the exact questions:

If immigration to this country continues at the present rate, how much political influence do you believe people like you, that is Asian American people, will have?

Much more than now
Some but not a lot more

No more or less than now
Less than now
A lot less than now?

What about economic opportunity? If immigration to this country continues at the present rate, do you believe people like you, that is Asian American people, will probably have

Much more economic opportunity than before
Some but not a lot more
No more or less than now
Less than now
A lot less economic opportunity than now?

Keep in mind that the sample we are analyzing here is not intended to be representative of Asian Americans nationwide; nor is it necessarily a fully representative sample of Asian Americans living in Los Angeles (see the MCSUI codebook for details on sampling).

Asian Americans were generally positive in their assessment of immigration's consequences. On average, they thought that immigration would mean greater political power and expanded economic opportunity. More precisely, 17.4 percent of Asian Americans said that their political influence would increase sharply with continuing high rates of immigration; another 56.6 percent claimed that they would gain some influence; 14.2 percent said that economic opportunity for Asian Americans would expand dramatically if immigration continues; 45.8 percent said that their economic opportunity would expand somewhat. Hispanic Americans saw immigration in much the same way. In contrast, whites and blacks looked at immigration and saw trouble for their group: political influence diminished, economic opportunity narrowed.

The key question here is whether, as we expect, ethnocentrism among Asian Americans is associated with more favorable assessments of immigration. The answer is yes, as the top row of the following table demonstrates:

Ethnocentrism and immigration among Asian Americans

	Political power	Economic opportunity	Political power	Economic opportunity
Ethnocentrism	0.71***	1.01***		
	0.27	0.27		
In-group			0.52	0.82***
pride			0.32	0.31
Out-group			1.17***	1.29***
hostility			0.42	0.41
N	733	735	733	735

Source: Los Angeles component of the 1992–1994 MCSUI.

Note: Table entry is the ordered probit regression coefficient with standard errors below. In-group pride is coded from 0 (negative) to 1 (positive assessments). Out-group hostility is coded from 0 (positive) to 1 (negative assessments). Dependent variables are coded such that higher values correspond with *favorable* views of immigration's consequences. Models also control for ideological identification, partisanship, education, sex, family income, and employment status. Full results appear in the Web appendix.

***$p < 0.01$; **$p < 0.05$; *$p < 0.10$, two-tailed.

Among Asian Americans, ethnocentrism generates positive views on immigration. The more Asian Americans regard their own group to be superior, the more likely they are to say that immigration is good—that it enhances their group's political influence and expands their group's economic opportunity.

On matters of immigration and ethnocentrism, then, Asians resemble Hispanics. The resemblance is strong but imperfect. Among Hispanic Americans, most of the power of ethnocentrism to influence opinion on immigration arises from in-group pride. Among Asian Americans, both aspects of ethnocentrism are working. Both in-group pride and out-group hostility motivate Asian Americans toward a positive view of immigration.

Chapter Seven

1. In response to exit polls following the election, many journalists and political pundits declared that the election turned decisively on moral issues (Seelye 2004). Some attributed President George W. Bush's success in the presidential election to state-level ballot initiatives on same-sex marriage (Dao 2004). Senator John Kerry's advisers blamed voters' preoccupation with moral values for Kerry's loss (Nagourney 2004). This seems largely mistaken. Although same-sex referenda seem to have increased turnout by two to three percentage points (Althaus 2005; McDonald 2004), it is unclear whether this surge in voters actually benefited Bush. And while some political scientists have found that moral issues contributed to Bush's victory (D. E. Campbell and Monson 2005; Lewis 2005), most seem skeptical (see, e.g., Abramowitz and Stone 2006; Ansolabehere and Stewart 2005; Burden 2004; Fiorina 2004; Hillygus and Shields 2005).

2. Here is the text of the questions (distributions appear in the Web appendix):

Should same-sex couples be allowed to marry, or do you think they should not be allowed to marry?

Do you think gay or lesbian couples, in other words, homosexual couples, should be legally permitted to adopt children?

Do you think homosexuals should be allowed to serve in the United States Armed Forces or don't you think so? (Strongly or not strongly?)

Do you favor or oppose laws to protect homosexuals against job discrimination? (Strongly or not strongly?)

3. Public opinion on this issue has become much more progressive in recent years. In 1992, as Clinton's recommendation was being first discussed, Americans on balance favored the idea of gays being allowed to serve in the military, but by a narrow margin: 32.1 percent strongly favored military service for gays; 32.4 percent strongly opposed it. Twelve years later, opinion favored the idea of gays serving in the military overwhelmingly. On the evolution of policy in this domain, see D'Amico (2000); and Herek, Jobe, and Carney (1996).

4. On policy and opinion on employment discrimination against gays, see Button, Rienzo, and Wald (2000); Donovan, Wenzel, and Bowler (2000); Gamble (1997); Haider-Markel and Meier (1996); Lewis and Edelson (2000); and Wald, Button, and Rienzo (1996).

5. Here again we see a sharp and rapid shift in opinion. As recently as 1992, when the identical question was asked, the American public was much more divided. Then 32.4 percent of Americans said that they strongly supported laws that would protect gays and lesbians from

job discrimination, with 24.6 percent in strong opposition. This shift in opinion is part of a more general pattern. In the last twenty years, American public opinion on homosexuality and on policies addressing the rights of homosexuals has shifted dramatically to the left (e.g., Wilcox and Norrander 2002; P. Brewer 2003a; Loftus 2001).

6. Here is the coding of the variables in the standard model:

Partisanship. The political parties have taken distinct stands on homosexual rights, with the Christian conservatives steering the Republicans to the right and, for the most part, gay and lesbian rights activists finding themselves under the big tent of the Democratic Party (Ellis 2005). *Partisanship* is coded from 0 (strong Republican) to 1 (strong Democrat), based on vo43116.

Education is coded from 0 (<9 years) to 1 (advanced degree), using vo43254.

Female is coded 1 for female and 0 for male, based on vo43411.

Religion. Importance of Religion is an additive scale comprised of *Guidance* (vo43220) and *Attendance* (vo43223 to 043225). The scale ranges from 0 (low) to 1 (high), has a mean of 0.48, a standard deviation of 0.33, and Cronbach's reliability of 0.74. *Religious Doctrine* consists of responses to vo43222, ranging from 0 ("Word of man") to 1 ("Word of God"). *Religious Denomination* consists of responses in vo43247 and vo43247a, coded into five dummy variables: Baptist/Fundamentalist; Catholic; Jewish; Other Religion; Agnostic/No Religion), with mainline Protestants set as the baseline reference group.

Authoritarianism. Following Stenner (2005), we measure *Authoritarianism* with respondents' choices of the values that children should be encouraged to learn at home (an additive scale based on vo45208 to vo45211). Those who select "good manners" and "obedience" as primary virtues for children are authoritarian; those who choose "imagination" and "independence" are not. The measure ranges from 0 (not authoritarian) to 1 (authoritarian), has a mean of 0.58, standard deviation of 0.29, and Cronbach's reliability of 0.61.

Egalitarianism. While proponents of gay rights have often framed their cause as one of securing equal rights, opponents use equality to argue against "special rights" (P. Brewer 2003b; Wilcox and Wolpert 2000). Hence, what to expect of the empirical relationship between egalitarianism and opinion on gay rights is unclear. *Egalitarianism* consists of an additive scale of items vo45212 to vo45217. The scale, bounded from 0 (less egalitarian) to 1 (highly egalitarian), has a mean of 0.63, a standard deviation of 0.20, and a Cronbach's reliability of 0.72.

All dependent variables are coded such that higher values represent more conservative views.

7. These effects hold up in several national surveys in addition to the 2004 NES. For example, here are the ordered probit coefficients (and standard errors) for ethnocentrism estimated by the standard model. Identical dependent variables are available in the 1992 and 2000 NES:

	Adoption	Military	Employment
NES 1992	1.20***	0.86***	0.66***
	0.24	0.20	0.19
NES 2000	0.93***	0.24	0.59***
	0.29	0.23	0.23

***$p < 0.01$; **$p < 0.05$; *$p < 0.10$, two-tailed.

The effect of ethnocentrism is unaffected by various alternative specifications. Suppose, for example, we add a measure of moral traditionalism to the standard model. We have made good use of moral traditionalism before, in our analysis of opposition to immigration in chapter 6. According to Pamela Conover and Stanley Feldman (1986b, p. 1), moral traditionalism reflects "a general dimension of traditional (conservative) to modern (liberal) moral values." Conceived of in this way, moral traditionalism would seem to belong to the standard model for predicting public opinion on gay rights. But we have reservations about its operationalization (see Stoker 1987). In the NES measure of moral traditionalism, respondents are asked whether they agree or disagree with the following series of propositions:

The newer lifestyles are contributing to the breakdown of our society.

The world is always changing, and we should adjust our view of moral behavior to those changes.

This country would have many fewer problems if there were more emphasis on traditional family ties.

We should be more tolerant of people who choose to live according to their own standards, even if they are very different from our own.

Conover and Feldman offer these items as a general predisposition, a way to distinguish between the generally traditional and the generally modern. But in content the measure is not all that general. Two of the items in particular (the first and third) implicate, by our reading, a specific moral issue: namely, the challenge to traditional marriage and family posed by the gay rights movement. The "newer lifestyles" referenced in the first question and "traditional family ties" referenced in the third seem to us to be code. From this point of view, adding moral traditionalism to our analysis will certainly add predictive power to the standard model, but without adding appreciably to our understanding of the foundations of public opinion on gay rights.

For our analyses, *Moral Traditionalism* consists of an additive scale of items v045189 to v045192. The scale, bounded from 0 (less traditional) to 1 (highly traditional), has a mean of 0.56, a standard deviation of 0.22, and a Cronbach's reliability of 0.67.

When we add moral traditionalism to the standard model, we find, as expected, that it has substantial independent effects on opinion, especially in matters of marriage and adoption. Bringing moral traditionalism in, however, has no consequence for our assessment of the part played by ethnocentrism. When moral traditionalism is added to the standard model, the effects due to ethnocentrism decline ever so slightly or they increase ever so slightly. Differences between the two sets of estimates are negligible (as shown in the Web appendix).

What about class? Here we draw on Lipset's (1959) argument that the precarious predicament of the working class "predisposes them to view politics as black and white, good and evil . . . a tendency to view politics and personal relationships in black-and-white terms, a desire for immediate action, an impatience with talk and discussion, a lack of interest in organizations which have a long-range perspective, and a readiness to follow leaders who offer a demonological interpretation of the evil forces (either religious or political) which are conspiring against [them]" (pp. 90, 115). By this reasoning, we might expect the working class to enlist most avidly in initiatives that would reassert moral order. But when we add to our standard model a high-performing measure of social class (Hout, Brooks, and Manza 1993, 1995, 1999), nothing in our results changes. Perhaps Lipset was wrong; perhaps we have applied his argument inappropriately; or perhaps insofar as Lipset was onto something, the tendencies he identified as associated with working-class experience are measured more directly by ethnocentrism.

We also investigated whether ethnocentrism might interact with other variables. Does ethnocentrism here work differently for blacks and Hispanic Americans? Not so far as we could tell, though our tests were limited by the relatively small number of black and Hispanic Americans in NES samples.

Does ethnocentrism interact with limited government, on the idea that ethnocentrism would matter more in the moral domain among those Americans who thought government had an important role to play in society? No.

Finally, what about gender? In the 2004 NES, we find large and statistically significant interactions between gender and ethnocentrism: big effects of ethnocentrism on gay rights among men; modest or negligible effects among women. There is independent evidence to suggest that straight men are especially agitated or threatened by gay men (Herek 2002), but before we head too far down this path we must report that the 2004 results do not replicate: not in the 1992 NES, not in the 2000 NES, not in the 1990 GSS, and not, finally, in the 2000 GSS. The general finding, then, is that ethnocentrism is as powerful a factor on issues of gay rights among women as among men.

8. Predicted probabilities are generated for a white female, Independent-leaning Democrat, who is a mainline Protestant, and is average on all other predictor variables. Dashed lines represent 95 percent confidence intervals.

9. From one perspective, the results presented in table 7.1 and displayed in figure 7.1 almost certainly underestimate the real effects of ethnocentrism. The coefficients shown there represent average effects; in particular, the standard model, as we have estimated it so far, assumes that ethnocentrism works the same way for gays and straights. This must be wrong. Among heterosexuals, ethnocentrism motivates opposition to policies meant to protect and extend civil rights for gay people; among homosexuals, we would expect ethnocentrism to work in the opposite direction. In-group favoritism—gay pride—should lead to support for same-sex marriage, the right of gays to serve in the military, and all the rest.

Unfortunately, the NES does not contain a measure of sexual orientation, so we cannot test this directly. We can, however, gain a sense of how much trouble this is likely to make for our estimates of ethnocentrism's impact in the domain of gay rights. Return for a moment to the last chapter and role of ethnocentrism in public opinion on immigration. There we faced an analogous situation to the one we encounter here. In chapter 6 we found that ethnocentrism motivates opposition toward a more generous immigration policy among white and black Americans, but support for a more generous immigration policy among Hispanic Americans. The advantage in that analysis is that NES provided instrumentation that allowed us to distinguish among whites, blacks, and Hispanics. Among other things, this means that can see what difference it would make to our estimate of the effect of ethnocentrism on immigration if we were to run the standard model on the entire sample—that is, assuming that the effect of ethnocentrism on immigration policy is the same regardless of race. We also know (or think we know) from the Census and the National Health and Social Life Survey the proportion of the American adult population that is gay. Putting these two pieces of information together, we believe that the coefficients shown in table 7.1 underestimate the real effects due to ethnocentrism among the heterosexual population by about 8 percent.

Technical details behind these calculations are spelled out in the Web appendix.

10. See C. Cohen (1999); Cook and Colby (1992); Shilts (1987); Rom (2000); and Centers for Disease Control and Prevention (2006a).

11. See Centers for Disease Control and Prevention (2006c).

12. For the most part, this is what the government was doing—spending more (Rom 2000). Included in the 7.9 percent who wanted a decrease in funding is a tiny group who volunteered the idea that spending on AIDS should be cut out entirely.

13. This speculation suggests that ethnocentric Americans might be ambivalent toward spending federal dollars on AIDS research. However, using the method spelled out by Alvarez and Brehm (2002), we turned up no evidence for this.

14. Here's the exact question from the 1993 NES Pilot Study:

Which comes closer to how you feel:

If I had a job working with a gay or lesbian, I would be worried about getting AIDS or some other disease.

I don't worry that working with a homosexual would pose any special danger of disease.

A follow-up question asks how worried the respondent is of contracting the disease or how confident the respondent is of not catching AIDS. Frequencies appear in the Web appendix. For evidence on the public's knowledge (ignorance) about AIDS, see Singer, Rodgers, and Corcoran (1987); and Sniderman, Brody, and Tetlock (1991).

15. The questions read:

There's been a lot of discussion about the way morals and attitudes about sex are changing in this country. If a man and woman have sex relations before marriage, do you think it is always wrong, almost always wrong, wrong only sometimes, or not wrong at all?

What if they are in their early teens, say 14 to 16 years old? In that case, do you think sex relations before marriage are always wrong, almost always wrong, wrong only sometimes, or not wrong at all?

What is your opinion about a married person having sexual relations with someone other than the marriage partner—is it always wrong, almost always wrong, wrong only sometimes, or not wrong at all?

What about sexual relations between two adults of the same sex—do you think it is always wrong, almost always wrong, wrong only sometimes, or not wrong at all?

Would you be for or against sex education in the public schools?

Do you strongly agree, agree, disagree, or strongly disagree that methods of birth control should be available to teenagers between the ages of 14 and 16 if their parents do not approve?

Frequencies appear in the Web appendix. In our analyses, the dependent variable is coded such that higher values represent more conservative responses.

16. When we carried out the identical analysis with the 1990 GSS, which included the same battery of questions, plus larger sample sizes, we found, once again, a significant and sizable effect of ethnocentrism on disapproval of gay sex but not, for the most part, elsewhere (results appear in the Web appendix).

17. On public opinion moving toward expert opinion, see Wilcox and Norrander (2002); Wilcox and Wolpert (1996).

18. Here are the exact questions:

Do you think being homosexual is something people choose to be, or do you think it is something they cannot change?

Which of these statements comes closer to your view: One, homosexuality is unnatural. Or, Two, for some people, homosexuality is their natural sexuality?

19. See Centers for Disease Control and Prevention (2006a). For an account of the politics of AIDS among black Americans, see C. Cohen (1999).

20. A national survey carried out by Kaiser Family Foundation/Harvard School of Public Health included a question asking whether the number of new AIDS infections among a series of groups (gay men under twenty-five, gay men twenty-five and older, women, intravenous drug users, people receiving blood transfusions, newborn babies, blacks, Hispanics, and teenagers) has "gone up," "gone down," or "stayed the same." Among black respondents, 73 percent said that the infection rate among blacks had "gone up" (compared with only 60 percent of whites). In contrast, blacks and whites were pretty similar in their views on the incidence rate among gay men under twenty-five (56 percent of blacks and 52 percent of whites say that it has gone up).

Blacks are also much more concerned about AIDS. When asked about how serious a problem it is "for people you know," 63 percent of blacks think AIDS is a serious problem compared with 40 percent of whites. With respect to being concerned about *personally* getting AIDS, 56 percent of blacks are "very concerned" whereas only 16 percent of whites are "very concerned." Among those with children under the age of twenty-one, 71 percent of black respondents are "very concerned" about their child becoming infected, whereas 50 percent of white respondents report the same.

21. In the 1992 NES, when we estimate the standard equation among black Americans alone, we find $b_1 = -1.16$, se = 0.78, $p < 0.15$ (two-tailed). In the 2000 NES, when we estimate the standard equation among black Americans alone, we find $b_1 = -1.70$, se = 0.88, $p < 0.06$ (two-tailed). Full results are in the Web appendix. We would have liked to have analyzed the 2004 NES as well, but the question on AIDS spending was not present on that study.

22. Consistent with these results, black Americans are also more inclined than the rest of the public to favor an increase in spending on AIDS. In the 1992 NES, 76.5 percent of black Americans said that federal spending on research on AIDS should be increased compared to 60.2 percent of the rest of the American public. By the fall of 2000, with the epidemic now centered in Africa, the racial divide in opinion had widened: 74.4 percent of black Americans said that federal spending on research on AIDS should be increased compared to just 49.6 percent among the rest.

As of an August 2008 CDC report, black Americans were seven times more likely than whites to contract AIDS.

23. According to John D'Emilio, the founding director of the Policy Institute of the National Gay and Lesbian Task Force, Scalia wrote his dissent not with the Court or constitutional scholars in mind. Rather, D'Emilio argues, Scalia intended "to sound an alarm, to mobilize the armies of the Christian right, to alert conservatives to a danger in [their] midst and to call them to action" (D'Emilio 2007, p. 44).

24. The eleven states are Arkansas, Georgia, Kentucky, Michigan, Mississippi, Montana, North Dakota, Ohio, Oklahoma, Oregon, and Utah. Two others—Louisiana and Missouri—passed amendments banning same-sex marriage prior to Election Day (Wilcox, Merolla, and Beer 2006).

25. Testing the statistical significance of the interaction term, $t = 0.99$, $p < 0.17$ (one-sided test).

26. We argue that the effect of ethnocentrism should be conditional upon *both* exposure to the campaign *and* the presence of a same-sex ballot initiative. To test these predictions, we estimated the standard model predicting opinion on same-sex marriage, plus four interaction terms: *E × Same-Sex Ballot Initiative × Exposure*; *E × Same-Sex Ballot Initiative*; *E × Exposure*; *Same-Sex Ballot Initiative × Exposure*. *Exposure* is coded from 0 (interviewed fifty-six days before Election Day) to 1 (interviewed the day before Election Day). If exposure to the campaign increases the effect of ethnocentrism within same-sex ballot initiative states, then the three-way interaction term should be positive and significant. The coefficient on *E × Same-Sex Ballot Initiative × Exposure* was 4.50, with standard error of 3.79, one-tailed $p < 0.12$. Full results appear in the Web appendix.

27. In the six states with gay marriage on the ballot that fell within the NES sample, the estimated effect of ethnocentrism is $b = 0.67$; in states without gay marriage on the ballot, $b = -0.67$. The interaction term testing for the difference between the two effects borders on statistical significance ($t = 1.45$, $p < 0.08$, one-sided test). Full results appear in the Web appendix.

28. We find a roughly 8 percentage point increase among those scoring in the highest quartile of E, and a slight decline—about 2.5 percentage points—among the least ethnocentric. To arrive at these estimates, we first apportioned our sample respondents into four quartiles: those who were more ethnocentric, mildly ethnocentric, indifferent between the in-group and out-groups, and those who favored out-groups over the in-group. We estimated each respondent's predicted probability of turning out, using each respondent's own sample values for each of the covariates in the model. Then we estimated an average predicted turnout level for each quartile. This provides us with a baseline set of values. To determine the "effect" of the same-sex marriage initiative for a given individual, we generated a new predicted probability for each respondent who lived in a same-sex marriage initiative state—by assigning them a value of 0 on *E × Same-Sex Marriage Initiative* and *Same-Sex Marriage Initiative*. The effect of the same-sex marriage initiative is thus the difference between the predicted probability, given that a same-sex marriage initiative was present, and the predicted probability, given that a same-sex marriage initiative was *not* present. For more details, see the Web appendix.

29. For general discussions of morality and politics in the United States from a variety of perspectives, see Hofstadter (1955); Gusfield (1963); Lakoff (1996); and Stoker (1992).

Chapter Eight

1. On these points, see Freeman (1975); Klein (1987); Mansbridge (1986); C. Mueller (1987); and Wolbrecht (2000).

2. The question text reads:

There has been some discussion about abortion during recent years. Which one of the opinions on this page best agrees with your view? You can just tell me the number of the opinion you choose.

1. By law, abortion should never be permitted.
2. The law should permit abortion only in case of rape, incest, or when the woman's life is in danger.
3. The law should permit abortion for reasons other than rape, incest, or danger to the woman's life, but only after the need for the abortion has been clearly established.

4. By law, a woman should always be able to obtain an abortion as a matter of personal choice.

There has been discussion recently about a law to ban certain types of late-term abortions, sometimes called partial birth abortions. Do you favor or oppose a law that makes these types of abortions illegal? (Strongly or not strongly?)

Would you favor or oppose a law in your state that would allow the use of government funds to help pay for the costs of abortion for women who cannot afford them? (Strongly or not strongly?)

Would you favor or oppose a law in your state that would require a married woman to notify her husband before she can have an abortion? (Strongly or not strongly?)

Would you favor or oppose a law in your state that would require a teenage girl under age 18 to receive her parent's permission before she could obtain an abortion? (Strongly or not strongly?)

Distributions appear in the Web appendix. In our regression analyses, the dependent variable is scaled such that higher values indicate more restrictive views on abortion.

3. For opinion on abortion, the standard model must take into account the possible impact of religion. We represent religion in three aspects. *Religious Denomination* is coded into five dummy variables (Catholic; Baptist/Fundamentalist; Jewish; Other Religion; Agnostic/No Religion), with mainline Protestants set as the baseline reference group. *Importance of Religion* is an additive scale comprised of the extent to which people say that their religion provides them guidance and the frequency with which they attend religious services. And *Religious Doctrine* distinguishes between those who believe that the Bible consists of the inerrant and infallible "Word of God" from those who do not.

4. *Effect* is used loosely here since the marginal effect of ethnocentrism in an ordered probit model would also entail differentiating the normal cumulative density function.

5. In all five cases, β_2, the coefficient testing for sex differences, was substantively small and statistically indistinguishable from zero.

Incidentally, differences between men and women in their opinion on these issues ranged from negligible to small. The largest difference shows up on the question of government subsidy, where women were a bit more likely to be strongly opposed to the government providing financial assistance to poor women who want to have abortions (51.5 percent of the women versus 43.4 percent of the men in strong opposition; the difference is significant at $p < 0.01$). But by and large, a gender gap on abortion policy is hard to find.

6. Here is the GSS question:

Please tell me whether or not you think it should be possible for a pregnant woman to obtain a legal abortion:

If there is a strong chance of serious defect in the baby?
If she is married and does not want any more children?
If the woman's own health is seriously endangered by the pregnancy?
If the family has a very low income and cannot afford any more children?
If she became pregnant as a result of rape?
If she is not married and does not want to marry the man?
If the woman wants it for any reason?

7. For this analysis, we constructed a dependent variable that counted the number of circumstances where abortion should not be legal. The variable ranges from 0 (in all seven circumstances it should be legal) to 1 (in no circumstance should it be legal). For the additive scales, $\alpha = 0.88$ in the 1990 GSS; $\alpha = 0.89$ in the 2000 GSS. The effect of ethnocentrism is estimated by least-squares regression, controlling on partisanship, education, sex, race, ethnicity, authoritarianism, egalitarianism, age, and religious attendance.

	GSS 1990	GSS 2000
Ethnocentrism	−0.05	0.18
	0.08	0.18
N	580	227

Note: Table entry is the estimated OLS regression coefficient with standard error below.

To determine whether ethnocentrism worked differently for women and men, we included an interaction between ethnocentrism and sex of the respondent. It did not. The estimated coefficients for the interaction terms were $b = 0.14$ (se = 0.15, $p \sim 0.32$) in 1990 and $b = -0.01$ (se = 0.34, $p \sim 0.98$) in 2000.

8. Here, we are drawing from Carroll (1985) and Wolbrecht (2000).

9. These questions read:

Some people feel that if women are not getting equal treatment in jobs, the government in Washington ought to see to it that they do. Others feel that this is not the federal government's business. Have you had enough interest in this question to favor one side over the other? How do you feel? Should the government in Washington see to it that women get equal treatment in jobs or is this not the federal government's business? Do you feel strongly or not strongly (that the government in Washington should see to it that women get equal treatment in jobs/that this is not the federal government's business)?

Because of past discrimination, employers should make special efforts to hire and promote qualified women. (Do you strongly agree, agree, neither agree nor disagree, disagree, or strongly disagree?)

Do you think enough is being done to protect women from being sexually harassed in the workplace, is too much being done, or too little being done?

Should federal spending be increased, decreased, or kept about the same on child care?

Do you think the government should require companies to allow up to six months unpaid leave for parents to spend time with their newborn or newly adopted children, or is this something that should be left to the individual employer?

10. Americans are generally more favorably disposed toward affirmative action programs designed to help women than they are toward comparable programs that are designed to help blacks. The differences run ten to twenty percentage points and show up for different kinds of programs and across differently formulated survey questions. The difference can be made to disappear by placing the question about affirmative action for women immediately before the question about affirmative action for blacks, which apparently activates a norm of reciprocity (Steeh and Krysan 1996; Schuman and Presser 1981).

11. For an excellent account of the Thomas nomination and confirmation, see Mayer and Abramson (1994).

12. On all of these "women's issues," women were more likely than men to favor the liberal position. The differences were consistent, statistically significant, and modest in size. The largest gap occurred on federal spending on child care: 56.7 percent of the women, compared to 43.7 percent of the men, favored increased federal spending on child care in 1992 ($p < 0.01$).

13. Some modifications were made for the GSS model. Authoritarianism was dropped to preserve cases. Religious attendance is used instead of religious importance.

14. Recall that the employment discrimination item included a filter question. In the results we present, we set those who said they were not interested in the issue to the midpoint. Explicitly addressing selection bias using a Heckman model produced substantively identical results: ethnocentrism is not a significant predictor of opinion on whether government should ensure equal treatment for women.

15. The interaction between ethnocentrism and sex of the respondent was insignificant in four of five cases. The one exception was on whether the government should see to it that women receive equal treatment in jobs. There the coefficient on ethnocentrism was 0.28 (se = 0.44, $p \sim 0.52$), while the interaction coefficient [$E \times Female$] was –0.99 (se = 0.57, $p \sim 0.08$, two-tailed). These results suggest that ethnocentrism works differently for men and women: that ethnocentrism motivates men to oppose and women to support government's stepping in to make sure that women are not discriminated on the job.

16. In the standard model, $b_1 = 1.29$, se = 0.28, $p < 0.01$.

17. From Mill's point in his famous essay on the subjection of women ([1869] 1998). Also see Glick and Fiske (1996, 1997); Jackman (1994); and Luker (1984).

Chapter Nine

1. Quoted in Katz (1986). On American attitudes toward poverty and work viewed historically, see Katz (1986) and Rodgers (1974).

2. Emerson (1841, p. 43).

3. Here we are following Burtless's (1994) helpful analysis of the American welfare state.

4. According to the Government Printing Office (2007, p. 227).

5. Social Security Administration (2007).

6. U.S. Bureau of the Census (2007, table 462, p. 309). http://www.census.gov/compendia/statab/tables/07s0462.xls.

7. To measure American opinion on welfare, we drew opportunistically from recent installments of the NES and GSS. As always, distributions appear in the Web appendix.

Means-tested welfare programs are *very* unpopular. In the 2000 NES, respondents were asked their opinion on federal spending across thirteen items. In 2000, the least popular spending item was foreign aid. Not far behind were welfare programs and food stamps. When asked about welfare programs, 37.9 percent of respondents wanted spending decreased or cut out entirely; 32.2 percent said so for food stamps. Less than half of respondents (45.0 percent) wanted spending maintained on welfare programs; slightly more (51.6 percent) favored maintaining spending for food stamps. In contrast, the item garnering the greatest support was spending on public schools: 76.5 percent of respondents wanted spending to be increased, 18.5 percent wanted it maintained, and only 5.0 percent wanted it decreased or cut out entirely. Social Security was almost as popular: 64.7 percent of respondents wanted increased spending; about a third (31.0 percent) wanted spending maintained, and only 4.2 percent wanted it decreased or cut out entirely. For more on the relative unpopularity of means-tested programs, see Cook and Barrett (1992) and Gilens (1999).

8. The questions read as follows:

Should federal spending on social security be increased, decreased, or kept about the same?

Do you favor or oppose expanding Medicare to pay for nursing home care and long hospital stays for the elderly? Strongly or not strongly?

Do you favor or oppose taxes on social security retirement benefits? Strongly or not strongly?

Some people have proposed that most of the expected federal budget surplus should go to protecting social security and Medicare. Do you approve or disapprove of this proposal? Strongly or not strongly?

9. The questions read as follows:

Should federal spending on public schools be increased, decreased, or kept about the same?

Should federal spending on pre-school and early education for poor children be increased, decreased, or kept about the same?

In the GSS, the series of questions is preceded with the following:

Here are several things that the government in Washington might do to deal with the problems of poverty and unemployment. I would like you to tell me if you favor or oppose them. Would you say that you strongly favor it, favor it, neither favor nor oppose it, oppose it, or strongly oppose it?

Spending more money on the schools in poor neighborhoods especially for pre-school and early education programs.

Provide special college scholarships for children from economically disadvantaged backgrounds who maintain good grades.

Here are some other areas of government spending. Please indicate whether you would like to see more or less government spending in each area. Remember that if you say "much more," it might require a tax increase to pay for it. . . . Preschool programs like Head Start for poor children.

10. Views within these categories of means-tested transfer programs, social insurance programs, and human capital programs are reasonably coherent. Using all available items in the 1992, 1996, 2000, and 2002 NES, and 1990 GSS, the average intra-category correlations between available means-tested opinion items is 0.39; the average intra-category correlation for social insurance items is 0.25, and it is 0.26 for human-capital opinion items. There is more coherence among items within categories than across categories: the average inter-category correlations between policy items are 0.12 (means-tested to social-insurance), 0.12 (means-tested to human-capital, and 0.14 (social-insurance to human-capital).

11. We use ordered probit regression, with all opinion measures coded such that higher values indicate more economically *liberal* views (typically, a preference for increased spending).

12. On principles and opinion on welfare, see Feldman and Zaller (1992); Feldman (1988); T. Smith (1987); Kinder and Sanders (1996); and Hasenfeld and Rafferty (1989). In our analysis, belief in limited government is a three-item scale (v961144–6, Cronbach's *alpha* = 0.75), based

on Markus (1993, 2001); egalitarianism is a six-item scale (v961229–34, Cronbach's *alpha* = 0.71), the measure developed and refined by Feldman (1988).

13. Assessments of family economic conditions are measured with v960338, with 0 indicating the household is "much worse off" than it was a year ago and 1 indicating that the household is "much better off" than it was a year ago. Occupational status is measured as it is in chapter 6: we transformed the NES detailed coding of occupation (v960665) into three dummy variables: top of the occupation structure, bottom, and out of the labor market altogether, with those occupying middling positions serving as the omitted reference group.

14. These results replicate in several other datasets. The 1990 GSS provides an excellent site for replication—for all the usual reasons and also because the 1990 GSS includes a related but distinct set of questions on welfare. The estimated ordered probit coefficients on ethnocentrism in models for welfare program spending, imposing work requirements, and reducing benefits to encourage work were, respectively: −0.72 (se = 0.51, significant at $p < 0.08$, one-tailed); $b_1 = -1.25$ (se = 0.35, $p < 0.01$); and $b_1 = -1.75$ (se = 0.34, $p < 0.01$). Significance is harder to achieve for the welfare spending item because it was administered to half as many respondents ($N = 252$ compared with $N = 520$). All models control for the covariates featured in table 9.1 (with the exception of concerns about job security and political awareness, which were not available in the GSS, and homeownership, which was half-sampled in the GSS).

In the 2004 NES, 33.7 percent of white Americans said that spending on welfare should be decreased or cut out altogether. In an augmented standard model (usual factors plus measures of class, moral conservatism, and the belief that government wastes a lot of taxes [the latter two have sizable effects]), the estimated coefficient on ethnocentrism is −0.75 (se = 0.36, $p < 0.05$; with the thermometer score measure, the estimate is −0.78, se = 0.29, $p < 0.01$).

The effect of ethnocentrism on opinion on means-tested assistance is robust to alternative specifications. The 1992 NES is interesting for our purposes because it included measures of whether the respondent's family was on the receiving end of government welfare programs: means-tested programs (food stamps, AFDC, and Medicaid) and social insurance programs (Social Security, Medicare, unemployment compensation, and worker's compensation). In our analysis, we found Americans in households currently receiving food stamps, AFDC, or Medicaid were much more likely to be supportive of increased government spending on food stamps and AFDC. These are big effects, though of course they are limited to the relatively small handful of people who are receiving assistance. Moreover, ethnocentrism was still a significant predictor of opinion even controlling for benefit receipt (these results appear in the Web appendix).

Means-tested benefits are not randomly assigned, and to the extent that the process of becoming a recipient of such benefits is correlated with opinion on social welfare programs, these estimates may be biased. As a check on this possibility, we ran supplementary analyses on the 1992 NES data, as suggested in Achen (1986), to take into account nonrandom assignment. These analyses yield similar results and in particular do not alter the estimates of the effects due to ethnocentrism. Finally, omitting these variables had virtually no effect on the estimated coefficients for ethnocentrism (for spending on welfare, $b_1 = -0.74$, se = 0.22; for spending on food stamps, $b_1 = -0.69$, se = 0.21, $p < 0.01$ in both cases).

15. The estimated ordered probit coefficients giving the effect of ethnocentrism for spending on Social Security, helping the elderly, and increasing retirement benefits in the 1990 GSS were, respectively: 0.71 (se = 0.36); $b_1 = 0.71$ (se = 0.38); and $b_1 = 0.58$ (se = 0.34), all significant at $p < 0.1$.

The estimated ordered probit coefficients on ethnocentrism in the models in the 1996, 2000, and 2004 NES were, respectively: 0.50 (se = 0.25, $p < 0.05$); 1.49 (se = 0.30, $p < 0.01$); and 0.71 (se = 0.41, $p < 0.1$).

Essentially the same result shows up in a panel test: ethnocentrism measured in the 2000 NES predicts support for spending more on Social Security two years later (as assessed in the 2002 NES reinterview). The estimated ordered probit coefficient when we predict opinion in 2002 using ethnocentrism measured in 2000 is 1.79 (se = 0.39, $p < 0.01$).

All these models control for the covariates featured in table 9.2 with these exceptions: in the 1990 GSS, homeownership was omitted because it was half-sampled; anxiety about job security was not measured; and political awareness was not available. In the 2000–2002 NES Panel analysis, economic variables (employment status, household economic evaluations, income, and homeownership) were measured in 2002.

16. Here's some evidence consistent with this conjecture. On the human capital programs listed in table 9.4, we find consistent and sizable differences by race. Whites are the most conservative, Hispanics the most liberal, with blacks in between. That's the general pattern, but there is one striking exception: on funding for Head Start, black Americans are far and away the most liberal: 43.0 percent of blacks say spend much more on Head Start, compared to 28.6 percent of Hispanics and just 14.4 percent of whites.

17. All four differences are significant by the χ^2 test ($p < 0.01$).

18. To determine whether the effect of ethnocentrism depends on how the question frames the beneficiaries of the policy, we estimated fully interactive models. This means that we added to our standard model a complete set of interaction terms: each covariate multiplied by a dummy variable indicating whether the respondent received a racialized version of the question or not. These models essentially uncover the same information as through separate-sample estimation, which we present for simplicity's sake in table 9.5, but they allow us to test precisely whether the effect of ethnocentrism is significantly greater in the racialized frame. The coefficient on the interaction between ethnocentrism and question frame for early education for poor children versus black children is –1.03 (se = 0.72, $p < 0.1$, one-tailed). For college scholarships for poor versus black children, the estimated coefficient for the interaction is –0.34 (se = 0.66, *ns*). For investing more in early education in schools in poor versus black neighborhoods, the relevant coefficient is –0.92 (se = 0.66, $p < 0.1$, one-tailed). And for spending on public schools versus big city schools, it is –0.78 (se = 0.72, $p < 0.15$, one-tailed).

19. Our analysis of welfare among black and Hispanic Americans is based on combining NES surveys from 1992, 1996, 2000, and 2004. Pooling the datasets is possible because each survey carries our standard measures of ethnocentrism, each includes the identical set of crucial control variables, and each includes two measures of social welfare policy: one from the domain of means-tested programs—opinion on federal spending on welfare—and one from the domain of social insurance—opinion on spending on Social Security. The results, estimating the effects of ethnocentrism for separate samples of blacks and Hispanics, are presented in the Web appendix.

The results from estimating an interactive model that estimates whether the effect of ethnocentrism is *significantly* different for whites as opposed to blacks and Hispanics also appear in the Web appendix; there, we see that the interactions between E and *Black* and between E and *Hispanic* are statistically significant, suggesting that not only is ethnocentrism statistically significant for whites, but also its effect is statistically different for whites versus blacks and whites versus Hispanics. This pattern—a strong effect of ethnocentrism for whites, no effect at all for blacks and Hispanics—shows up in no other policy domain that we have analyzed.

Chapter Ten

1. On this point, see Clotfelter (2004); Farley and Allen (1987); Jaynes and Williams (1989); and Massey and Denton (1993).

2. In this chapter we set aside the opinions of Hispanic Americans. We do this for two reasons. First, our expectations for how ethnocentrism might operate among Hispanic Americans on matters of race are far from clear. On the one hand, in-group favoritism among Hispanic Americans should encourage opposition to government help targeted specifically on blacks. On the other hand, insofar as such policies imply governmental intervention as a remedy for discrimination and inequality in general, ethnocentrism might encourage support for racial liberalism. In fact, among Hispanic Americans, ethnocentrism and opinion on matters of race turn out to be utterly unrelated. Second, setting Hispanic Americans to one side allows us to concentrate on the pressing analytic questions raised by blacks and whites—the relationship between ethnocentrism and group identification, which comes up as a point of urgency among blacks; and the relationship between ethnocentrism and prejudice, which arises as a point of urgency among whites.

3. Here are the exact question wordings (distributions are given in the Web appendix):

Some people feel that if black people are not getting fair treatment in jobs, the government in Washington should see to it that they do. Others feel that this is not the government's business. Have you been interested enough in this question to favor one side over the other? [IF YES] How do you feel? Should the government in Washington see to it that black people get fair treatment in jobs or is this not the government's business?

Some people say that the government in Washington should see to it that white and black children go to the same schools. Others claim that this is not the government's business. Have you been interested enough in this question to favor one side over the other? [IF YES] Do you think the government in Washington should see to it that white and black children go to the same schools or stay out of this area as it is not the government's business?

Some people say that because of past discrimination against blacks, preference in hiring and promotion should be given to blacks. Others say preferential hiring and promotion of blacks is wrong because it gives blacks advantages they haven't earned. What about your opinion—are you for or against preferential hiring and promotion of blacks?

Some people think that if a company has a history of discriminating against blacks when making hiring decisions, then they should be required to have an affirmative action program that gives blacks preference in hiring. What do you think? Should companies that have discriminated against blacks have to have an affirmative action program [or should companies not have to have an affirmative action program]?

Some people say that because of past discrimination, it is sometimes necessary for colleges and universities to reserve openings for black students. Others oppose quotas because they say quotas give blacks advantages they haven't earned. What about your opinion—are you for or against quotas to admit black students?

Should federal spending on aid to blacks be increased, decreased, or kept about the same?

Some people feel that the government in Washington should make every effort to improve the social and economic position of blacks. (Suppose these people are at one end of a scale, at point 1.) Others feel that the government should not make any special effort to help blacks because they should help themselves. (Suppose these people are at the other end, at point 7.) And, of course, some other people have opinions somewhere in between, at points 2, 3, 4, 5, or 6. Where would you place yourself on this scale, or haven't you thought much about this?

No single NES carries all seven questions. From the 1992 NES, we take school integration, affirmative action in hiring, and college quotas; from the 2000 NES, affirmative action for companies that discriminate, federal spending on blacks, and fair employment; and from the 2004 NES, whether the government in Washington is obliged to help blacks.

4. For additional evidence on racial differences on policy, see Jackman (1994); Kinder and Winter (2001); Kluegel and Smith (1986); and Sigelman and Welch (1991).

5. To accommodate differences in question format across and within surveys, the government assistance item is coded into three categories: respondents in favor of government help, those who are at the midpoint or offer no response, and respondents opposed to government help. Each dependent variable in this set of analyses is scored such that higher values indicate racially liberal responses. To preserve cases, we coded "don't know" responses into the middle (rather than estimate separate selection and outcome equations).

6. The emergence of a black middle class after World War II generated considerable interest in the possibility that class position would begin to compete with and eventually overcome racial identity as a force in politics (e.g., W. Wilson 1973, 1987). Class divisions in politics among the black rank and file have generally proven difficult to find, however (e.g., Dawson 1994; Kinder and Winter 2001), and the same turns out to be true here. Adding in measures of income, occupation, and homeownership to the standard model produces almost no significant effects, and even when significant effects do appear, they have absolutely no consequence for the estimated effect assigned to ethnocentrism.

7. These results appear in the Web appendix.

8. The Principal Investigator for the 1996 NBES was Katherine Tate. The study was supported by Ohio State University and the National Science Foundation, with field work carried out by Market Strategies. A probability sample of 1216 voting-eligible black Americans was interviewed over the telephone prior to the fall presidential election; 854 of these same respondents were successfully questioned again after the election, also by phone. Additional details on NBES can be obtained through the Inter-University Consortium for Political and Social Research (http://www.icpsr.umich.edu).

9. Cronbach's *alpha* = 0.56. Here are the relevant questions from the 1996 NBES:

What happens to black people in this country has a lot to do with what happens to me.

Being black determines a lot how you are treated in this country, more than how much money a person earns.

In this country, people treat you more on the content of your character than on your race.

Do you think what happens generally to black people in this country will have something to do with what happens in your life?

10. The model includes measures of political engagement, education, and sex, in addition to ethnocentrism.

11. Indeed, in the 1996 NBES, common fate and ethnocentrism were only weakly related (Pearson $r = 0.11$).

We find very much the same results in a parallel analysis of NES surveys, based on a different (and arguably weaker) measure of group attachment. Once again, adding in a measure of group attachment does nothing to our estimate of ethnocentrism's effects. Once again, ethnocentrism and group attachment are barely related (Pearson $r = 0.05$).

12. Mathematically, the standard model can be expressed as

$$y^* = \mathbf{x'}\boldsymbol{\beta} + \varepsilon$$
$$= \beta_0 + \beta_1 \text{Ethnocentrism} + \beta_2 \text{Partisanship} + \beta_3 \text{Education} + \beta_4 \text{Female} + \beta_5 \text{Political}$$
$$\text{Awareness} + \beta_6 \text{Limited Government} + \beta_7 \text{Egalitarianism} + \varepsilon$$
$$\Pr(y = m) = \Pr(\tau_{m-1} < y^* < \tau_m) = \Phi(\tau_m - \mathbf{x'}\boldsymbol{\beta}) - \Phi(\tau_{m-1} - \mathbf{x'}\boldsymbol{\beta})$$

where y refers to opinion on race policy (falling into one of m categories); y^* represents the unobserved latent variable.

We introduce one modification into the standard model in order to correct for selection bias for the two policies that elicited large numbers of "don't knows." When asked directly, a sizable number of people said that they had not really thought about school integration (30.3 percent); likewise for fair employment (36.7 percent). Having no opinion on these matters is no doubt partly a straightforward expression of ignorance and uncertainty. Citizens simply don't know enough to know what they think. But some of those who say, for example, they have no opinion on school segregation may in fact have an opinion but feel reluctant to share it. In particular, whites who oppose the government's stepping in to integrate public schools may decide to keep their opinions to themselves, for fear of being thought a racist. Berinsky (2004) has made a strong case that this in fact is so, and if he is right—that many people deny they have an opinion in response to the school integration questions for reasons that are systematically related to their views on race—then our estimation strategy must take this into account. One way to correct for selection bias is through the bivariate probit selection model (Berinsky 2004; Dubin and Rivers 1989). This is what we have done for the two dependent variables that feature sizable nonresponse. The Web appendix presents the complete results.

13. As before, dependent variables are coded such that higher values indicate a racially liberal response. These effects hold up under a variety of alternative specifications. They remain when we replace the measure of ethnocentrism based on stereotypes with one based on thermometer ratings. They also withstand the addition of measures of self-interest to our analysis. From the perspective of self-interest, white parents of teenage children who command middle-class resources should be most opposed to college quotas for blacks. But when we augment the standard model to take this and other such possibilities into account, we find, first of all, that self-interest rarely makes a detectable difference to opinion; and second, even when significant effects due to self-interest appear, they take nothing away from ethnocentrism. All these auxiliary results can be found in the Web appendix.

14. For discussions of the meaning of prejudice and racism (we will use the terms interchangeably), see Blumer (1958); W. Wilson (1973); Pettigrew (1982); Kinder and Sanders (1996); and Fredrickson (2002).

15. These auxiliary results can be found in the Web appendix.

16. The standard model is somewhat attenuated, in that no measures of limited government, equality, and political awareness were carried on the MCSUI survey. In partial compensation, we were able to include measures of ideological identification, family income, and employment status, in addition to the usual standbys of partisanship, education, and sex.

To see what difference this omission likely made, we went back to the NES surveys and re-estimated the results summarized in table 10.4, first deleting both limited government and equality. What happens? Sometimes nothing; more often, the effect of ethnocentrism increases somewhat—roughly 10 to 30 percent. The implication is that we are overestimating, but not egregiously, the effect due to ethnocentrism in the MCSUI data.

Finally, results shown in table 10.5 are virtually identical if we discard "law abiding" as a stereotyped feature of the standard measure of ethnocentrism (on the grounds that such beliefs might be too close in content to some of the opinions we wish to explain). The same holds when we analyze public opinion among black or Hispanic or Asian Americans—in all cases, whether law abiding is included in the measure of ethnocentrism is utterly innocuous.

17. The standard NES measure of prejudice—also known as "racial resentment" (Kinder and Sanders 1996), "symbolic racism" (Sears 1988), "modern racism" (McConahay 1982, 1986), and "laissez faire racism" (Bobo and Smith 1998)—consists of responses to four propositions:

Irish, Italian, Jewish and many other minorities overcame prejudice and worked their way up. Blacks should do the same without any special favors.

Generations of slavery and discrimination have created conditions that make it difficult for blacks to work their way out of the lower class.

It's really a matter of some people not trying hard enough; if blacks would only try harder they could be just as well off as whites.

Over the past few years, blacks have gotten less than they deserve.

White Americans respond to these various propositions consistently, as they should, if the propositions are in fact getting at the same thing. To create an overall scale of prejudice, we simply averaged each person's response to the four individual propositions, with each response weighted equally. Confirmatory factor analysis shows that a one-factor model fits the structure of responses to the four questions very well (Kinder 2009; Henry and Sears 2002). Averaging over the four responses, the reliability of the overall scale, given by Cronbach's coefficient *alpha*, is about 0.77 (a bit higher in some NES surveys and a bit lower in others).

18. Essentially the same estimate is given both by the simple correction due to attenuation ($r = 0.47$) and by confirmatory factor analysis ($r = 0.53$).

19. The same pattern of results shows up time and again, across different surveys carried out in different years, in cross-sectional and panel tests. It also shows up on racialized aspects of foreign policy. Recall that back in chapter 5, we analyzed opinion on whether the United States should apply economic pressure on the South African government to change its racial laws, as part of a broader analysis of the role ethnocentrism might play in suppressing support for humanitarian intervention abroad. We predicted that ethnocentrism would be a force against support for sanctions on South Africa, and that is what we found. Now, when we add prejudice into the analysis, the results look exactly like what we saw for school integration, fair employment, affirmative action in hiring, and all the rest: prejudice matters enormously, and the effect of ethnocentrism diminishes dramatically. These results appear in the Web appendix.

20. On welfare policy, adding prejudice to the standard model does occasionally make a noticeable dent in the effect due to ethnocentrism, especially on means-tested transfer programs. This makes sense: such programs are assumed to go disproportionately to blacks, recipients of such programs are commonly represented in racially stereotyped ways, and elite discussions of welfare policy and its reform traffic routinely in racial code (Gilens 1999; Kinder and Sanders 1996; Mendelberg 2001; and Peffley, Hurwitz, and Sniderman 1997).

21. On these points see, among others, Ayres (2001); Clotfelter (2004); Farley and Allen (1987); Jaynes and Williams (1989); Kellstedt (2003); Kinder and Sanders (1996); Massey and Denton (1993); Rhode (2004); Ross and Yinger (2002); Schuman et al. (1997); and Thernstrom and Thernstrom (1997).

Conclusion

1. Ethnocentrism and partisanship are virtually uncorrelated with each other (Pearson r = −0.06, shown in table 3.4) and so constitute independent explanations for public opinion.

2. A sample of these comparisons appears in the Web appendix.

3. These results appear in the Web appendix.

4. Zaller prefers the phrase "political awareness."

Zaller's model highlights three key elements: (1) a small set of stable political predispositions that citizens bring to politics (partisanship, ideology, core values); (2) elite discourse: the constantly changing flow of ideas, symbols, stereotypes, frames, and so forth that are made available to citizens through a variety of more or less public channels—television, newspapers, radio, magazines, the Internet, and more; and (3) the attention citizens pay to this ongoing stream of information and advice. Zaller's model recognizes that people differ from one another in their partisan and ideological predispositions. But at least as important to the model is the assumption that people differ from one another in the care and attention they invest in politics. This difference is crucial to the process of opinion change. People are more likely to receive a communication as a direct function of their level of general engagement in politics, where "receiving" entails both exposure to and comprehension of the given communication (the so-called Reception Axiom). And they resist communications that are inconsistent with their political predispositions—but only insofar as they command sufficient information to detect such inconsistency (the Resistance Axiom).

The model works: that is, it can account for a wide array of empirical cases. Shifts in opinion on school desegregation and on the Vietnam War, the dynamics of presidential primary election campaigns, the electoral advantages enjoyed by congressional incumbents, popular support for Ross Perot during his $73 million presidential adventure of 1992: all these (and more) can be accounted for within a common theoretical vocabulary (Zaller 1989, 1991, 1992; Zaller and Hunt 1994, 1995).

5. Zaller has compared the performance of political knowledge against a variety of standard measures of attention and interest—including education, media exposure, self-report, participation in politics, and professed interest in politics. Across a variety of empirical tests, political knowledge emerges as the decisive winner. See Zaller (1990, 1992 appendix); Luskin (1987); Price and Zaller (1993).

6. Based on an extensive series of independent tests, Zaller (1986, 1990, 1992 appendix) and Delli Carpini and Keeter (1996) reach the same conclusion: political knowledge should be thought of as a general trait.

7. Knowledge questions have been asked in all NES presidential-year studies since 1992. To create a scale, we simply counted the number of correct answers and divided by the number of questions. The scale is constrained to range in principle from 0 to 1. The actual range is 0 to 1 as well. The average score varies across studies as a function of the difficulty of the test items. The reliability of the overall scale varies as a function of the number of test items (k).

	Number of observations	Mean	Standard deviation	k	Cronbach's alpha
1992	2249	0.51	0.29	9	0.81
1996	988	0.60	0.27	6	0.69
2000	1555	0.27	0.28	4	0.64
2004	1066	0.48	0.29	4	0.66

As expected, engagement is negatively correlated with ethnocentrism—more knowledge goes with less ethnocentrism—but the relationship is slight: Pearson $r = -0.08$. (The correlation is based on combining the 1992, 1996, 2000, and 2004 NES.) The weak relationship is statistically convenient in that it enhances our power to detect interactions between the two if such interactions actually exist.

For more on the measurement of political knowledge, see Delli Carpini and Keeter (1996, appendix 2) and Zaller (1990, 1992). For an argument that knowledge scales of the sort we have created here substantially underestimate the actual variance in mass publics, see Converse (2000, pp. 333–35). For problems with the measure, see Mondak (1999, 2001); Sturgis, Allum, and Smith (2008); and Krosnick et al. (2008).

8. These analyses exclude chapter 8, where no "average" ethnocentrism effect was found.

9. We undertook a parallel analysis with an alternative measure of engagement, one emphasizing motivational commitment as opposed to intellectual mastery.

Motivational commitment to politics crops up regularly as an explanatory factor in the literature on political participation. Way back in *The Voter Decides* (1954), Campbell, Gurin, and Miller pointed to differences in motivation as the principal reason why some people turn out and others stay home. This theme was picked up and elaborated on in *The American Voter* ([1960] 1980). There, Campbell, Converse, Miller, and Stokes argued that variation in electoral participation from one person to the next was largely a matter of motivation. Those who were highly involved in politics—who expressed interest in the campaign and concern over its outcome—were much more likely to vote and otherwise participate. Essentially the same point is made by Verba, Schlozman, and Brady in *Voice and Equality* (1995). Verba, Schlozman, and Brady are usually cited for demonstrating the importance to participation of resources—time, money, and especially civic skills—as well as communication and organizational abilities developed at work or in religious or voluntary organizations. Fair enough, but Verba, Schlozman, and Brady also consider political involvement as a factor in participation. They conclude that involvement signals and supplies the desire that draws people to politics, while time, money, and civic skills provide the wherewithal to act, to turn interest into action (Verba, Schlozman, and Brady 1995, p. 354).

These studies establish the importance of political involvement and offer guidance on how it should be measured. Looking over recent National Election Studies, we identified eight questions as good candidates for a general measure of political involvement: the extent to which people follow public affairs; claim to be interested in the current campaign; care who wins the presidential election; are paying attention to the campaign on television, on television news, in newspapers, and on radio (in separate questions); and are discussing politics with family and friends. In a principal components analysis, each of the eight questions loads strongly on a single dominant factor. Equally weighting each response and averaging them all together generates a reliable scale of political involvement (Cronbach's $alpha = 0.79$).

The two components of engagement—involvement and knowledge—are positively correlated (as well they should be), but not so correlated that they can be taken as equivalent or interchangeable: $r = 0.43$.

And we tested our proposition about engagement in three rounds: first, with engagement measured as political involvement; second, with engagement measured as political knowledge; and third, with engagement measured as the combination of involvement and knowledge.

Not surprisingly, results across the three rounds of estimation were similar. What was surprising, at least to us, is that the results were strongest and most precise when engagement was measured as political knowledge: stronger and more precise than when engagement was measured as political involvement, and stronger and more precise even when engagement was measured as political involvement *and* political knowledge.

10. Here and immediately following, statistical significance set at $p < 0.10$, two-sided.

11. These findings are consistent with those reported by Goren (2003).

12. The best single source on this point is Delli Carpini and Keeter (1996). But also see Bartels (1988); Fiske and Kinder (1981); Fiske, Lau, and Smith (1990); Gilens (2001); Iyengar (1990); Lau and Redlawsk (2001); Mondak (2001); Price and Zaller (1993); and Zaller (1990, 1992).

13. Moreover, when we looked for evidence of threat triggering ethnocentrism, we were unable to find any. The effect of ethnocentrism on support for the war on terrorism was not any greater among those who said that another major attack on the United States was imminent. The effect of ethnocentrism on opposition to immigration was not any greater among those most likely to be personally harmed by increases in immigration, measured by such characteristics as occupation and state of residence.

14. Equally disconcerting, on theoretical grounds, would be evidence that ethnocentrism was sharply increasing.

15. *First* allegiance, but not one's only allegiance, according to Nussbaum: "We need not give up our special affections and identifications, whether ethnic or gender-based or religious. We need not think of them as superficial, and we may think of our identity as constituted partly by them. But we should also work to make all human beings part of our community of dialogue and concern, base our political deliberations on that interlocking communality, and give the circle that defines our humanity special attention and respect" (Nussbaum 1996, p. 9).

Kristen Monroe's (1998) conceptualization of altruism is relevant here as well. Monroe finds that individuals who are willing to engage in uncommon acts of altruism express a sense of universalism in viewing the human condition. Instead of viewing an individual (and the self, in particular) as tied to specific social groupings, altruists "share a view of the world in which all people are one" (p. 198).

16. Using the NES feeling thermometer instrumentation, we developed measures of ethnocentrism grounded in differences other than race: religion, age, gender, and political party. In general, what we found with race (white, black, Hispanic, Asian), we found with most other cleavages: that is, in-group favoritism. We see this most clearly for religion (Protestant, Catholic, Jewish) and partisanship (Republican, Democrat). And measures of ethnocentrism based on these alternative criteria are generally positively—but weakly—correlated with our primary measures of ethnocentrism based on race.

17. This conception follows Posner (2005). By excluding markets and norms, it is narrower than the definitions offered by Bates (1988) or by North (1990). Quoted passages come from March and Olsen (1989, p. 16).

18. For more work in this tradition, see Chhibber and Kollman (1998); Lijphart (1999); Posner (2004, 2005); Varshney (2002); and Weingast (1998).

19. For a time—quite a long time—it seemed that the commotion would never end. At the annual meeting of the American Political Science Association in Denver in 1982, one of us (the one not in elementary school at the time) presented a paper under the title "Enough Already

about Ideology" (Kinder 1982). It had no effect: the avalanche of papers and books dedicated to determining whether Converse had got the story right continued unabated.

20. For readings of the evidence supporting this conclusion, see Kinder (1983, 1998, 2006).

21. Lightly paraphrasing Converse (1964, p. 227).

22. Tilly (1978) develops the idea of a political action repertoire.

23. The participation scale (following Verba, Schlozman, and Brady 1995) consists of an additive index of the following acts: voting in the most recent election, wearing a campaign button, attending campaign meetings/rallies, volunteering in campaigns, donating to campaigns, and working on local issues in the community. Cronbach's *alpha* = 0.55.

24. And we see it for ethnocentrism measured by thermometer score ratings as well as the standard measure based on stereotyping. These results appear in the Web appendix.

25. Pooling across 1992, 1996, 2000, and 2004 NES surveys, we modeled participation as a function of ethnocentrism using ordered probit. In the bivariate regression, the estimated coefficient on ethnocentrism is -0.66 (se = 0.09), $p < 0.01$.

26. Elected officials are, in part, delegates, and they are required in that part to act in accordance with the views of the people who elected them. In extreme form, the delegate conception of representation demands that instruction from home always preempts other considerations. Here we are borrowing from Pitkin's (1967) well-known analysis of the idea of representation. The polar opposite to this position was given classic expression by Edmund Burke in his famous speech to the electors of Bristol. Burke argued for representative independence; that once elected, representatives should exercise their own considered judgment, taking into account the arguments advanced during the assembly deliberation. For Burke, the obligation of a representative was to discover and enact what was best for the nation, not serve as an errand boy for particular interests. Those drawn to the Burkean persuasion argue that representatives are selected to play the role of experts by voters who themselves possess neither the time nor the inclination to immerse themselves in the details and complications that naturally arise in deliberation over public policy.

27. For key studies in the realm of representation, see Achen (1978); Bartels (1991b, 2008); Burstein (1985); Converse and Pierce (1986); Erikson (1978); Fenno (1978); Fiorina (1974); Jackson (1974); Jackson and King (1989); Kingdon (1973); Miller and Stokes (1963); Page and Shapiro (1992); Rosenstone and Hansen (1993); Stimson, MacKuen, and Erikson (1995); Verba, Schlozman, and Brady (1995); and Weissberg (1978).

Evidence for representation comes disproportionately from high-profile cases, instances of legislative breakthroughs: the Civil Rights Act of 1964, major tax reform in 1978, the Reagan defense buildup of 1981. Such cases are important to understand, of course, but they may give a skewed picture of representation on average. Citizens no doubt have less voice, and probably less influence, on the many routine but consequential matters that come before government assemblies unaccompanied by public commotion.

28. See Centers for Disease Control and Prevention (2006b, 2006c). Here's a case where opinion and policy seem to diverge. President George W. Bush pledged substantial U.S. support for fighting AIDS in Africa; he did this quietly, in the absence of public pressure.

29. For recent efforts to estimate directly the link between social division and policy outcomes, see Alesina and Glaeser (2004); and Roemer, Lee, and Van Der Straeten (2007).

References

Abelson, Robert P. 1959. Modes of resolution of belief dilemmas. *Journal of Conflict Resolution* 3:343–52.

———. 1963. Computer simulation of "hot cognitions." In *Computer simulation of personality*, ed. Silvan S. Tomkins and Samuel Messick, 277–98. New York: Wiley.

———. 1968. Psychological implication. In *Theories of cognitive consistency: A sourcebook*, ed. Robert P. Abelson, E. Aronson, W. J. McGuire, T. M. Newcomb, M. J. Rosenberg, and R. H. Tannenbaum, 112–39. Chicago: Rand McNally.

———. 1975. Concepts for representing mundane reality in plans. In *Representation and understanding: Studies in cognitive science*, ed. Daniel G. Bobrow, and Allan Collins, 273–309. New York: Academic Press.

———. 1976. Script processing in attitude formation and decision-making. In *Cognition and social behavior*, ed. John S. Carroll, and John W. Payne, 33–46. Hillsdale, NJ: Erlbaum.

———. 1981. Psychological status of the script concept. *American Psychologist* 36:715–29.

———. 1995. The secret existence of expressive behavior. *Critical Review* 9 (Winter–Spring): 25–36.

Abelson, Robert P., Donald R. Kinder, Mark D. Peters, and Susan T. Fiske. 1982. Affective and semantic components in political person perception. *Journal of Personality and Social Psychology* 42:619–30.

Abelson, Robert P., and M. Rosenberg. 1958. Symbolic psycho-logic: A model of attitudinal cognition. *Behavioral Science* 3 (1): 1–8.

Abowd, John M., and Richard B. Freeman. 1991. Introduction and summary. In *Immigration, trade, and the labor market*, ed. John M. Abowd, and Richard B. Freeman, 1–25. Chicago: University of Chicago.

Abramowitz, Alan I., and Walter J. Stone. 2006. The Bush effect: Polarization, turnout, and activism in the 2004 presidential election. *Presidential Studies Quarterly* 36 (2): 141–54.

Achen, Christopher H. 1975. Mass political attitudes and the survey response. *American Political Science Review* 69:1218–31.

———. 1978. Measuring representation. *American Journal of Political Science* 22 (3): 475–510.

———. 1983. Toward theories of data: The state of political methodology. In *Political science: The state of the discipline*, ed. Ada W. Finifter, 69–93. Washington, DC: American Political Science Association.

———. 1986. *The statistical analysis of quasi-experiments*. Berkeley and Los Angeles: University of California Press.

Adams, Greg D. 1997. Abortion: Evidence of an issue evolution. *American Journal of Political Science* 41 (3): 718-37.

Adorno, Theodor W., Else Frenkel-Brunswik, Daniel J. Levinson, and R. Nevitt Sanford. 1950. *The authoritarian personality*. New York: Harper and Row.

Alesina, Alberto, and Edward L. Glaeser. 2004. *Fighting poverty in the US and Europe: A world of difference*. Oxford: Oxford University Press.

Alesina, Alberto, John Londregan, and Howard Rosenthal. 1993. A model of the political economy of the United States. *American Political Science Review* 87 (1): 12–33.

Alford, John, Carolyn Funk, and John R. Hibbing. 2005. Are political orientations genetically transmitted? *American Political Science Review* 99 (2): 164–67.

Allport, Gordon W. 1935. Attitudes. In *Handbook of social psychology*, ed. Carl Murchison, 798–844. Worcester, MA: Clark University Press.

———. 1954. *The nature of prejudice*. Cambridge, MA: Addison-Wesley.

Almond, Gabriel A., and Sidney Verba. 1963. *The civic culture: Political attitudes and democracy in five nations*. Princeton, NJ: Princeton University Press.

Altemeyer, Bob. 1981. *Right-wing authoritarianism*. Winnipeg: University of Manitoba Press.

———. 1988. *Enemies of freedom: Understanding right-wing authoritarianism*. San Francisco: Jossey-Bass.

———. 1996. *The authoritarian specter*. Cambridge, MA: Harvard University Press.

Althaus, Scott L. 2005. How exceptional was turnout in 2004? *Political communication report of the International Communication Association and American Political Science Association* 15 (1): Available at http://www.unr.edu/organizations/pcr/1501_2005_winter/commentary.htm.

Alvarez, R. Michael, and John Brehm. 2002. *Hard choices, easy answers: Values, information, and American public opinion*. Princeton, NJ: Princeton University Press.

Alwin, D. F. 1984. Trends in parental socialization values: Detroit, 1958–1983. *American Journal of Sociology* 90:359–82.

———. 1988. From obedience to autonomy: Changes in traits desired in children, 1924–1978. *Public Opinion Quarterly* 52:33–52.

Anderson, J. R. 1983. A spreading activation theory of memory. *Journal of Verbal Learning and Verbal Behavior* 22:261–95.

Ansolabehere, Stephen, and Charles Stewart III. 2005. Truth in numbers: Moral values and the gay-marriage backlash did not help Bush. *Boston Review* (February/March).

Arterton, F. Christopher. 1993. Campaign '92: Strategies and tactics of the candidates. In *The election of 1992*, ed. Gerald M. Pomper, F. Christopher Arterton, Ross K. Baker, Walter Dean Burnham, Kathleen A. Frankovic, Marjorie Randon Hershey, and Wilson Carey McWilliams, 74–109. Chatham, NJ: Chatham House.

Asch, Solomon E. 1951. Effects of group pressure upon the modification and distortion of judgment. In *Groups, leadership, and men*, ed. H. Guetzkow, 177–90. Pittsburgh: Carnegie Press.

———. 1952. *Social psychology*. New York: Prentice-Hall.

Atkinson, R. C., and R. M. Shiffrin. 1968. Human memory: A proposed system and its control processes. In *The psychology of learning and motivation*, vol. 8, ed. K. W. Spence and J. T. Spence, 89–195. London: Academic Press.

Ayres, Ian. 2001. *Pervasive prejudice? Unconventional evidence of race and gender discrimination*. Chicago: University of Chicago Press.

Bandura, A. 1969. *Principles of behavioral modification*. New York: Holt, Rinehart, and Winston.

Bargh, John A. 1999. The cognitive monster: The case against the controllability of automatic stereotype effects. In *Dual-process theories in social psychology*, ed. Shelly Chaiken and Yaacov Trope, 361–82. New York: Guilford Press.

Bartels, Larry M. 1988. *Presidential primaries and the dynamics of public choice*. Princeton, NJ: Princeton University Press.

———. 1991a. Constituency opinion and congressional policy making: The Reagan defense buildup. *American Political Science Review* 85 (2): 457–74.

———. 1991b. Instrumental and "quasi-instrumental" variables. *American Journal of Political Science* 35 (3): 777–800.

———. 2000. Partisanship and voting behavior, 1952–1996. *American Journal of Political Science* 44 (1): 35–50.

———. 2006. Three virtues of panel data for the analysis of campaign effects. In *Capturing campaign effects*, ed. Henry E. Brady, and Richard Johnston, 134–63. Ann Arbor: University of Michigan Press.

———. 2008. *Unequal democracy: The political economy of the new gilded age*. Princeton, NJ: Princeton University Press and Russell Sage Foundation.

Bates, Robert H., ed. 1988. *Toward a political economy of development: A rational choice perspective*. Berkeley and Los Angeles: University of California Press.

Baumgartner, Frank R., and Bryan D. Jones. 1993. *Agendas and instability in American politics*. Chicago: University of Chicago Press.

Bell, Daniel. 1955. Interpretations of American politics. In *The new American*, rev. ed., ed. Daniel Bell, 3–32. New York: Criterion Books.

Berelson, Bernard. 1952. Democratic theory and public opinion. *Public Opinion Quarterly* 16 (3): 313–30.

Berelson, Bernard R., Paul F. Lazarsfeld, and William N. McPhee. 1954. *Voting: A study of opinion formation in a presidential campaign*. Chicago: University of Chicago Press.

Berinsky, Adam J. 2004. *Silent voices: Public opinion and political participation in America*. Princeton, NJ: Princeton University Press.

Billig, Michael, and Henri Tajfel. 1973. Social categorization and similarity in intergroup behavior. *European Journal of Social Psychology* 3:27–52.

Black, Earl, and Merle Black. 1987. *Politics and society in the south*. Cambridge, MA: Harvard University Press.

Blake, Robert R., and Jane S. Mouton. 1962. Overevaluation of own group's product in intergroup competition. *Journal of Abnormal and Social Psychology* 64:237–38.

———. 1979. Intergroup problem solving in organizations. In *The social psychology of intergroup relations*, ed. William G. Austin, and Stephen Worchel, 19–32. Monterey, CA: Brooks/Cole.

Blalock, Hubert M., Jr. 1967. *Toward a theory of minority-group relations*. New York: Wiley.

Blumer, Herbert. 1958. Race prejudice as a sense of group position. *Pacific Sociological Review* 1:3–7.

Bobo, Lawrence. 1988. Group conflict, prejudice, and the paradox of contemporary racial attitudes. In *Eliminating racism: Profiles in controversy*, ed. Phyllis A. Katz and Dalmas A. Taylor, 85–116. New York: Plenum Press.

———. 1999. Prejudice as group position: Microfoundations of a sociological approach to racism and race relations. *Journal of Social Issues* 55:455–72.

Bobo, Lawrence, and Vincent L. Hutchings. 1996. Perceptions of racial group competition: Extending Blumer's theory of group position to a multiracial social context. *American Sociological Review* 61:951–72.

Bobo, Lawrence, Mary Jackman, James Kluegel, John Shelton Reed, Howard Schuman, and A. Wade Smith. 1988. General Social Surveys Module on Inter-Group Relations, 1990. Chicago: NORC.

Bobo, Lawrence, and Frederick C. Licari. 1989. Education and political tolerance: Testing the effects of cognitive sophistication and target group affect. *Public Opinion Quarterly* 53 (3): 285–308.

Bobo, Lawrence, and Ryan A. Smith. 1998. From Jim Crow racism to laissez-faire racism: The transformation of racial attitudes. In *Beyond pluralism: The conception of groups and group identities in America*, ed. Wendy F. Katkin, Ned Landsman, and Andrea Tyree. Urbana: University of Illinois Press.

Bobo, Lawrence D., and Mia Tuan. 2006. *Prejudice and politics: Group position, public opinion, and the Wisconsin treaty rights dispute.* Cambridge, MA: Harvard University Press.

Bollen, Kenneth A. 1989. *Structural equations with latent variables.* New York: Wiley.

Bonacich, Edna. 1972. A theory of ethnic antagonism: The split labor market. *American Sociological Review* 37 (5): 547–59.

———. 1973. A theory of middleman minorities. *American Sociological Review* 38 (5): 583–94.

Borjas, George J., and Richard B. Freeman, eds. 1992. *Immigration and the work force: Economic consequences for the United States and source areas.* Chicago: University of Chicago.

Bouchard, T. J., and J. C. Loehlin. 2001. Genes, evolution, and personality. *Behavior Genetics* 31 (3): 243–73.

Bouchard, T. J., D. T. Lykken, M. McGue, N. L. Segal, and A. Tellegen. 1990. Sources of human psychological differences: The Minnesota study of twins reared apart. *Science* 250 (October): 223–28.

Boyd, Robert, and Peter J. Richerson. 1985. *Culture and the evolutionary process.* Chicago: University of Chicago.

———. 2005. *The origin and evolution of cultures.* Chicago: University of Chicago.

Brewer, Marilynn B. 1979. Intergroup bias in a minimal intergroup situation: A cognitive-motivational analysis. *Psychological Bulletin* 86:307–24.

———. 1988. A dual process model of impression formation. In *Advances in social cognition*, vol. 1, ed. T. K. Srull and R. S. Wyer, 1–36. Hillsdale, NJ: Erlbaum.

———. 1999. The psychology of prejudice: Ingroup love or outgroup hate? *Journal of Social Issues* 55 (3): 429–44.

———. 2007. The importance of being *we*: Human nature and intergroup relations. *American Psychologist* 62 (8): 728–38.

Brewer, Marilynn B., and Rupert J. Brown. 1998. Intergroup relations. In *Handbook of social psychology*, 4th ed., ed. Daniel Gilbert, Susan T. Fiske, and Gardner Lindzey, 554–94. Boston: McGraw-Hill.

Brewer, Marilynn B., and Donald T. Campbell. 1976. *Ethnocentrism and intergroup attitudes.* New York: Wiley.

Brewer, Marilynn B., Ying-Yi Hong, and Qiong Li. 2004. Dynamic entitativity. In *The psychology of group perception: Perceived variability, entitativity, and essentialism*, ed. Vincent Yzerbyt, Charles M. Judd, and Olivier Corneille, 25–38. Philadelphia: Psychology Press.

Brewer, Marilynn B., and Kramer, R. M. 1985. The psychology of intergroup attitudes and behavior. *Annual Review of Psychology* 36:219–43.

Brewer, Marilynn B., and M. Silver. 1978. Ingroup bias as a function of task characteristics. *European Journal of Social Psychology* 8:393–400.

Brimelow, Peter. 1995. *Alien nation: Common sense about America's immigration disaster.* New York: Random House.

Broadbent, D. 1958. *Perception and communication.* London: Pergamon Press.

———. 1971. *Decision and stress.* New York: Academic Press.

———. 1982. Task combination and the selective intake of information. *Acta Psychologica* 50:253–90.

Brody, Leslie R., and Judith A. Hall. 2000. Gender, emotion, and expression. In *Handbook of emotions,* 2nd ed., ed. Michael Lewis and Jeannette M. Haviland-Jones, 338–49. New York: Guilford Press.

Brody, Richard A. 1991. *Assessing the president: The media, elite opinion, and public support.* Stanford, CA: Stanford University Press.

———. 1994. Crisis, war, and public opinion: The media and public support for the president. In *Taken by storm: The media, public opinion, and U.S. foreign policy in the Gulf War,* ed. W. Lance Bennett, and David L. Paletz, 210–27. Chicago: University of Chicago Press.

Brown, Roger. 1965. *Social psychology.* New York: Free Press.

———. 1986. *Social psychology.* 2nd ed. New York: Free Press.

Burden, Barry C. 2004. An alternative account of the 2004 presidential election. *The Forum* 2 (4): Article 2.

Burnham, Walter Dean. 1974. The United States: The politics of heterogeneity. In *Electoral behavior,* ed. Richard Rose, 635–725. New York: Free Press.

Burstein, Paul. 1985. *Discrimination, jobs, and politics.* Chicago: University of Chicago Press.

Burtless, Gary. 1994. Public spending on the poor: Historical trends and economic limits. In *Confronting poverty: Prescriptions for change,* ed. Sheldon H. Danziger, Gary D. Sandefur, and Daniel H. Weinberg, 51–84. Cambridge, MA: Harvard University Press.

Buss, D. M., and D. Kenrick. 1998. Evolutionary social psychology. In *The handbook of social psychology,* 4th ed., vol. 2, ed. Daniel T. Gilbert, Susan T. Fiske, and Gardner Lindzey, 982–1026. Boston: McGraw-Hill.

Button, James W., Barbara A. Rienzo, and Kenneth D. Wald. 2000. The politics of gay rights at the state and local level. In *The politics of gay rights,* ed. Craig A. Rimmerman, Kenneth D. Wald, and Clyde Wilcox, 269–89. Chicago: University of Chicago Press.

Cacioppo, J. T., and R. E. Petty. 1979. Effects of message repetition and position on cognitive response, recall, and persuasion. *Journal of Personality and Social Psychology* 37:97–109.

Cameron, J. A., J. M. Alvarez, D. N. Ruble, and A. J. Fuligni. 2001. Children's lay theories about ingroups and outgroups: Reconceptualizing research on prejudice. *Personality and Social Psychology Review* 5:118–28.

Campbell, Angus. 1981. *The sense of well-being in America.* New York: McGraw-Hill.

Campbell, Angus, Philip E. Converse, Warren E. Miller, and Donald E. Stokes. [1960] 1980. *The American voter,* unabridged ed. Chicago: Midway Reprint.

Campbell, Angus, Philip E. Converse, and Willard L. Rodgers. 1976. *The quality of American life: Perceptions, evaluations, and satisfactions.* New York: Russell Sage Foundation.

Campbell, Angus, Gerald Gurin, and Warren E. Miller. 1954. *The voter decides.* Evanston, IL: Row, Peterson.

Campbell, David E., and J. Quin Monson. 2005. The religion card: Gay marriage and the 2004 presidential election. Paper presented at the annual meetings of the American Political Science Association, Washington, DC.

Campbell, Donald T. 1947. "The generality of a social attitude." PhD diss., University of California, Berkeley.

———. 1965. Variation and selective retention in socio-cultural evolution. In *Social change in developing areas*, ed. Herbert R. Barringer, George I. Blanksten, and Raymond W. Mack, 19–49. Cambridge, MA: Schenkman.

———. 1967. Stereotypes and the perception of group differences. *American Psychologist* 22:817–29.

———. 1975. On the conflicts between biological and social evaluation and between psychology and moral tradition. *American Psychologist* 30 (12): 1103–26.

Campbell, Donald T., and Robert A. LeVine. 1961. A proposal for cooperative cross-cultural research on ethnocentrism. *Journal of Conflict Resolution* 5:82–108.

Campbell, Donald T., and Boyd R. McCandless. 1951. Ethnocentrism, xenophobia, and personality. *Human Relations* 4:185–92.

Campbell, Donald T., C. R. Siegman, and M. B. Rees. 1967. Direction-of-wording effects in the relationships between scales. *Psychological Bulletin* 68:293–303.

Cappella, Joseph N., and Kathleen Hall Jamieson. 1997. *Spiral of cynicism: The press and the public good.* New York: Oxford University Press.

Carbonell, Jaime G. 1981. *Subjective understanding: Computer models of belief systems.* Ann Arbor: University of Michigan Press.

Carmines, Edward G., and Richard A. Zeller. 1979. *Reliability and validity assessment.* Beverly Hills, CA: Sage.

Carroll, Susan J. 1985. *Women as candidates in American politics.* Bloomington: Indiana University Press.

Caspi, Avshalom, Brent W. Roberts, and Rebecca L. Shiner. 2005. Personality development. *Annual Reviews of Psychology* 56:453–84.

Centers, Richard. 1949. *The psychology of social classes.* Princeton, NJ: Princeton University Press.

Centers for Disease Control and Prevention. 2006a. Epidemiology of HIV/AIDS—United States, 1981–2005. *Morbidity and Mortality Weekly Report* 55 (21): 589–92.

———. 2006b. The global HIV/AIDS pandemic. *Morbidity and Mortality Weekly Report* 55 (31): 841–44.

———. 2006c. Twenty-five years of HIV/AIDS—United States, 1981–2006. *Morbidity and Mortality Weekly Report* 55 (21): 585–89.

———. 2008. Estimates of new HIV infections in the United States. *CDC HIV/AIDS Facts* (August). http://www.cdc.gov/hiv/topics/surveillance/resources/factsheets/pdf/incidence.pdf

Cheah, Pheng, and Bruce Robbins. 1998. *Cosmopolitics: Thinking and feeling beyond the nation.* Minneapolis: University of Minnesota Press.

Chhibber, Pradeep, and Ken Kollman. 1998. Party aggregation and the number of parties in India and the United States. *American Political Science Review* 92 (2): 329–42.

Chiozza, Giacomo. 2007. Disaggregating anti-Americanism: An analysis of individual attitudes towards the United States. In *Anti-Americanism in world politics*, ed. Peter J. Katzenstein and Robert O. Keohane, 93–126. Ithaca, NY: Cornell University Press.

Chong, Dennis, and Jamie N. Druckman. 2007. Framing public opinion in competitive democracies. *American Political Science Review* 101:637–55.

Christie, Richard. 1954. Authoritarianism re-examined. In *Studies in the scope and method of The Authoritarian Personality*, ed. Richard Christie and Marie Jahoda, 123–96. New York: Free Press.

Christie, Richard, Joan Havel, and Bernard Seidenberg. 1958. Is the F scale irreversible? *Journal of Abnormal and Social Psychology* 56:143–59.

Christie, Richard, and Marie Jahoda, eds. 1954. *Studies in the scope and method of* The Authoritarian Personality. New York: Free Press.

Citrin, Jack, Donald P. Green, Christopher Muste, and Cara Wong. 1997. Public opinion toward immigration reform: The role of economic motivations. *Journal of Politics* 59 (3): 858–81.

Citrin, Jack, Beth Reingold, Evelyn Walters, and Donald P. Green. 1990. The "Official English" movement and the symbolic politics of language in the United States. *Western Political Quarterly* 43 (3): 535–59.

Clodfelter, Micheal. 1992. *Warfare and armed conflicts: A statistical reference to casualty and other figures, 1618–1991.* Jefferson, NC: McFarland.

Clotfelter, Charles T. 2004. *After Brown: The rise and retreat of school desegregation.* Princeton, NJ: Princeton University Press.

Cohen, Cathy. 1999. *The boundaries of blackness: AIDS and the breakdown of black politics.* Chicago: University of Chicago Press.

Conover, Pamela. 1984. The influence of group identifications on political perception and evaluation. *Journal of Politics* 46 (3): 760–85.

———. 1988. The role of social groups in political thinking. *British Journal of Political Science* 18 (1): 51–76.

Conover, Pamela, and Stanley Feldman. 1981. The origins and meaning of liberal/conservative self-identification. *American Journal of Political Science* 25 (4): 617–45.

———. 1986a. Emotional reactions to the economy: I'm mad as hell and I'm not going to take it anymore. *American Journal of Political Science* 30 (1): 50–78.

———. 1986b. Morality items on the 1985 pilot study. ANES Pilot Study Report No. nes002251. Available at ftp://ftp.electionstudies.org/ftp/nes/bibliography/documents/nes002251.pdf.

Conover, Pamela Johnston, and Virginia Sapiro. 1993. Gender, feminist consciousness, and war. *American Journal of Political Science* 37 (4): 1079–99.

Converse, Philip E. 1958. The shifting role of class in political attitudes and behavior. In *Readings in social psychology*, 3rd ed., ed. Eleanor E. Maccoby, Theodore M. Newcomb, and Eugene L. Hartley, 388–99. New York: Holt, Rinehart, and Winston.

———. 1964. The nature of belief systems in mass publics. In *Ideology and discontent*, ed. David E. Apter, 206–61. New York: Free Press.

———. 1966. Information flow and the stability of partisan attitudes. In *Elections and the political order*, ed. Angus Campbell, Philip E. Converse, Donald Stokes, and Warren E. Miller, 136–57. New York: Wiley.

———. 1970. Attitudes and non-attitudes: Continuation of a dialogue. In *The quantitative analysis of social problems*, ed. Edward R. Tufte, 168–89. Reading, MA: Addison-Wesley.

———. 1975. Public opinion and voting behavior. In *Handbook of political science*, vol. 4, ed. Fred I. Greenstein and Nelson W. Polsby, 75–169. Reading, MA: Addison-Wesley.

———. 2000. Assessing the capacity of mass electorates. *Annual Review of Political Science* 3:331–53.

Converse, Philip E., and Gregory B. Markus. 1979. Plus ça change . . . The new CPS election study panel. *American Political Science Review* 73 (1): 32–49.

Converse, Philip E., and Roy Pierce. 1986. *Political representation in France.* Cambridge, MA: Belknap-Harvard University Press.

Cook, Fay Lomax, and Edith J. Barrett. 1992. *Support for the American welfare state*. New York: Columbia University Press.

Cook, T. E., and D. C. Colby. 1992. The mass-mediated epidemic. In *AIDS: The making of a chronic disease*, ed. Elizabeth Fee, and Daniel M. Fox, 84–122. Berkeley and Los Angeles: University of California Press.

Coser, Lewis A. 1956. *The functions of social conflict*. Glencoe, IL: Free Press.

Couch, Arthur, and Kenneth Kenniston. 1960. Yeasayers and naysayers: Agreeing response set as a personality variable. *Journal of Abnormal and Social Psychology* 24 (August): 349–54.

Crelia, R. A., and A. Tesser. 1996. Attitude heritability and attitude reinforcement: A replication. *Personality and Individual Differences* 21:803–8.

Cronbach, Lee J. 1946. Response sets and test validity. *Educational and Psychological Measurement* 6:475–94.

Dahl, Robert A. 1961. *Who governs? Democracy and power in an American city*. New Haven, CT: Yale University Press.

———. 1989. *Democracy and its critics*. New Haven, CT: Yale University Press.

Dahrendorf, Ralf. 1964. *Class and class conflict*. Stanford, CA: Stanford University Press.

D'Amico, Francine. 2000. Sexuality and military service. In *The politics of gay rights*, ed. Craig A. Rimmerman, Kenneth D. Wald, and Clyde Wilcox, 249–65. Chicago: University of Chicago Press.

Dao, James. 2004. Same-sex marriage key to some GOP races. *New York Times*, November 4.

Darwin, Charles. 1871. *The descent of man*. New York: Appleton. Available at http://books. google.com/books?id=ZvsHAAAAIAAJ.

Davies, G., and M. Derthick. 1997. Race and social welfare policy: The Social Security Act of 1935. *Political Science Quarterly* 112 (2): 217–35.

Dawson, Michael C. 1994. *Behind the mule: Race and class in African-American politics*. Princeton, NJ: Princeton University Press.

de Figueiredo, Rui J. P., Jr., and Zachary Elkins. 2003. Are patriots bigots? An inquiry into the vices of in-group pride. *American Journal of Political Science* 47 (1): 171–88.

Delli Carpini, Michael X., and Scott Keeter. 1996. *What Americans know about politics and why it matters*. New Haven, CT: Yale University Press.

D'Emilio, John. 2007. Will the courts set us free? Reflections on the campaign for same-sex marriage. In *The politics of same-sex marriage*, ed. Craig A. Rimmerman and Clyde Wilcox, 39–64. Chicago: University of Chicago Press.

Derthick, Martha. 1979. *Policymaking for Social Security*. Washington, DC: Brookings Institution.

Devine, Patricia G. 1989. Stereotypes and prejudice: Their automatic and controlled components. *Journal of Personality and Social Psychology* 56 (1): 5–18.

Devos, T., and M. R. Banaji. 2005. American = white? *Journal of Personality and Social Psychology* 88:447–66.

Diamond, Alexis, and Jasjeet S. Sekhon. 2005. Genetic matching for estimating causal effects: A general multivariate matching method for achieving balance in observational studies. Working paper. Available at http://sekhon.berkeley.edu/papers/GenMatch.pdf.

Dobzhansky, Theodosius. 1964. *Heredity and the nature of man*. New York: Harcourt, Brace, and World.

Donovan, Todd, Jim Wenzel, and Shaun Bowler. 2000. Direct democracy and gay rights initiatives after *Romer*. In *The politics of gay rights*, ed. Craig A. Rimmerman, Kenneth D. Wald, and Clyde Wilcox, 161–89. Chicago: University of Chicago Press.

Downs, Anthony. 1957. *An economic theory of democracy.* New York: Harper.

Druckman, James N. 2001. On the limits of framing effects: Who can frame? *Journal of Politics* 63 (4): 1041–66.

———. 2004. Political preference formation: Competition, deliberation, and the (ir)relevance of framing effects. *American Political Science Review* 98 (4): 671–86.

Druckman, James N., and Kjersten R. Nelson. 2003. Framing and deliberation: How citizens' conversations limit elite influence. *American Journal of Political Science* 47 (4): 729–45.

Dubin, Jeffrey A., and Douglas Rivers. 1989. Selection bias in linear regression, logit, and probit models. *Sociological Methods and Research* 18 (2) & (3): 360–90.

Du Bois, W. E. B. [1903] 1907. *The souls of black folk.* Chicago: A. C. McClurg.

Eaves, L. J., and H. Eysenck. 1974. Genetics and the development of social attitudes. *Nature* 249 (5454): 288–89.

Eaves, L. J., H. J. Eysenck, and N. G. Martin. 1989. *Genes, culture, and personality: An empirical approach.* New York: Academic Press.

Eaves, Lindon, Andrew Heath, Nicholas Martin, Hermine Maes, Michael Neale, Kenneth Kendler, Katherine Kirk, and Linda Corey. 1999. Comparing the biological and cultural inheritance of personality and social attitudes in the Virginia 30,000 study of twins and their relatives. *Twin Research* 2:62–80.

Edmonston, Barry, and Jeffrey S. Passel. 1994. The future immigrant population of the United States. In *Immigration and ethnicity: The integration of America's newest arrivals,* ed. Barry Edmonston and Jeffrey S. Passel, 317–52. Washington, DC: Urban Institute Press.

Edwards, Kari, and Edward E. Smith. 1996. A disconfirmation bias in the evaluation of arguments. *Journal of Personality and Social Psychology* 71:5–24.

Eley, Geoff, and Ronald Grigor Suny. 1996. *Becoming national: A reader.* New York: Oxford University Press.

Ellis, Margaret E. 2005. Gay rights: Lifestyle or immorality? In *Moral controversies in American politics,* 3rd ed., ed. Raymond Tatalovich and Byron W. Daynes, 121–44. Armonk, NY: Sharpe.

Ellwood, David. 1988. *Poor support: Poverty in the American family.* New York: Basic Books.

Elster, Jon. 1989. *Nuts and bolts for the social sciences.* New York: Cambridge University Press.

Emerson, Ralph Waldo. 1841. *Essays.* London: James Fraser.

Enloe, Cynthia. 1972. *Ethnic conflict.* Boston: Little, Brown.

Erikson, Robert S. 1978. Constituency opinion and congressional behavior: A reexamination of the Miller-Stokes representation data. *American Journal of Political Science* 22 (August): 511–35.

Espenshade, Thomas J. 1995. Unauthorized immigration to the United States. *Annual Review of Sociology* 21:195–216.

Espenshade, Thomas J., and Charles A. Calhoun. 1993. An analysis of public opinion toward undocumented immigration. *Population Research and Policy Review* 12:189–224.

Fan, David P. 1988. *Predictions of public opinion from the mass media: Computer content analysis and mathematical modeling.* Westport, CT: Greenwood Press.

Farley, Reynolds, and Walter R. Allen. 1987. *The color line and the quality of life in America.* New York: Russell Sage.

Farnham, S. D., A. G. Greenwald, and M. R. Banaji. 1999. Implicit self-esteem. In *Social identity and social cognition,* ed. Dominic Abrams and Michael A. Hogg, 230–48. Oxford: Blackwell.

Fazio, Russell H., and B. C. Dunton. 1997. Categorization by race: The impact of automatic and controlled components of racial prejudice. *Journal of Experimental Social Psychology* 33:451–70.

Feldman, Stanley. 1988. Structure and consistency in public opinion: The role of core beliefs and values. *American Journal of Political Science* 32 (2): 416–40.

———. 2003. Values, ideology, and the structure of political attitudes. In *Oxford handbook of political psychology*, ed. David O. Sears, Leonie Huddy, and Robert Jervis, 477–508. New York: Oxford University Press.

Feldman, Stanley, and Karen Stenner. 1997. Perceived threat and authoritarianism. *Political Psychology* 18 (4): 741–70.

Feldman, Stanley, and John R. Zaller. 1992. The political culture of ambivalence. *American Journal of Political Science* 36 (1): 268–307.

Fenno, Richard F., Jr. 1978. *Home style: House members in their districts.* New York: Harper-Collins.

Feshbach, S. 1994. Nationalism, patriotism, and aggression: A clarification of functional differences. In *Aggressive behavior: Current perspectives*, ed. L. Rowell Huesmann, 275–91. New York: Putnam.

Festinger, Leon. 1954. A theory of social comparison processes. *Human Relations* 7:117–40.

Finegold, Kenneth. 1988. Agriculture and the politics of U.S. social provision: Social insurance and food stamps. In *The politics of social policy in the United States*, ed. Margaret Weir, Ann Shola Orloff, and Theda Skocpol, 199–234. Princeton, NJ: Princeton University Press.

Fiorina, Morris. 1974. *Representatives, roll calls, and constituencies.* Lexington, MA: Lexington Books.

———. 2004. "Holy war" over moral values or contempt for opinion? *San Francisco Chronicle*, November 21.

Fisher, R. A. 1918. The correlation between relatives on the supposition of Mendelian inheritance. *Transactions of the Royal Society of Edinburgh* 52:339–433.

Fiske, Susan T. 1998. Stereotyping, prejudice, and discrimination. In *Handbook of social psychology*, 4th ed., ed. Daniel Gilbert, Susan T. Fiske, and Gardner Lindzey, 357–411. Boston: McGraw-Hill.

Fiske, Susan T., and Donald R. Kinder. 1981. Involvement, expertise, and schema use: Evidence from political cognition. In *Personality, cognition, and social interaction*, ed. Nancy Cantor and John F. Kihlstrom, 171–90. Hillsdale, NJ: Erlbaum.

Fiske, Susan T., Richard R. Lau, and Richard A. Smith. 1990. On the varieties and utilities of political expertise. *Social Cognition* 8 (1): 31–48.

Fix, Michael, and Jeffrey S. Passel. 1994. *Immigration and immigrants: Setting the record straight.* Washington, DC: The Urban Institute.

Fowler, James H., and Cindy D. Kam. 2007. Beyond the self: Social identity, altruism, and political participation. *Journal of Politics* 69 (3): 813–27.

Fox, John. 1997. *Applied regression analysis, linear models, and related methods.* Thousand Oaks, CA: Sage.

Fraley, C., and B. W. Roberts. 2005. Patterns of continuity: A dynamic model for conceptualizing the stability of individual differences in psychological constructs across the life course. *Psychological Review* 112:60–74.

Frankovic, Kathleen A. 1993. Public opinion in the 1992 campaign. In *The election of 1992*, ed. Gerald M. Pomper, F. Christopher Arterton, Ross K. Baker, Walter Dean Burnham,

Kathleen A. Frankovic, Marjorie Randon Hershey, and Wilson Carey McWilliams, 110–31. Chatham, NJ: Chatham House.

Fredrickson, George M. 2002. *Racism: A short history.* Princeton, NJ: Princeton University Press.

Free, Lloyd A., and Hadley Cantril. 1967. *The political beliefs of Americans: A study of public opinion.* New Brunswick, NJ: Rutgers University Press.

Freeman, Jo. 1975. *The politics of women's liberation: A case study of an emerging social movement and its relation to the policy process.* New York: Longman.

Freese, Jeremy L., J. C. A. Li, and L. D. Wade. 2003. The potential relevances of biology to social inquiry. *Annual Review of Sociology* 29:233–56.

Funkhouser, G. R. 1973. The issues of the sixties: An exploratory study in the dynamics of public opinion. *Public Opinion Quarterly* 37 (1): 62–75.

Futuyma, D. J. 1998. *Evolutionary biology.* Sunderland, MA: Sinauer.

Gaertner, Samuel L., and John F. Dovidio. 2000. *Reducing intergroup bias: The common ingroup identity model.* Philadelphia: Psychology Press.

Gamble, Barbara. 1997. Putting civil rights to a popular vote. *American Journal of Political Science* 41:245–69.

Geertz, Clifford. 1973. Ideology as a cultural system. In *The interpretation of cultures: selected essays,* 193–233. New York: Basic Books.

Gelman, Susan A. 2003. *The essential child.* New York: Oxford.

Gelman, Susan A., and Hirschfeld, L. A. 1999. How biological is essentialism? In *Folk biology,* ed. S. Atran and D. Medin. Cambridge, MA: MIT Press.

Gibson, Campbell J., and Emily Lennon. 1999. *Historical census statistics on the foreign-born population of the United States, 1850–1990.* Population Division, U.S. Bureau of the Census, Washington, DC. Available at http://www.census.gov/population/www/documentation/twps0029/tab01.html.

Gibson, James L., and Amanda Gouws. 2000. Social identities and political intolerance: Linkages within the South African mass public. *American Journal of Political Science* 44 (2): 272–86.

Gil-White, Francisco. 2001. Are ethnic groups biological "species" to the human brain? Essentialism in our cognition of some social categories. *Current Anthropology* 42 (4): 515–54.

Gilens, Martin. 1999. *Why Americans hate welfare.* Chicago: University of Chicago Press.

———. 2001. Political ignorance and collective policy preferences. *American Political Science Review* 95 (2): 379–96.

Giles, Micheal W., and Arthur Evans. 1986. The power approach to intergroup hostility. *Journal of Conflict Resolution* 30 (3): 469–86.

Giles, Micheal W., and Kaenan Hertz. 1994. Racial threat and partisan identification. *American Political Science Review* 88 (2): 317–26.

Gilovich, Thomas, Dale Griffin, and Daniel Kahneman, eds. 2002. *Heuristics and biases.* New York: Cambridge University Press.

Glaser, James M. 1994. Back to the black belt: Racial environment and white racial attitudes in the south. *Journal of Politics* 56 (1): 21–41.

Glick, P., and S. T. Fiske. 1996. The ambivalent sexism inventory: Differentiating hostile and benevolent sexism. *Journal of Personality and Social Psychology* 70:491–512.

———. 1997. Hostile and benevolent sexism: Measuring ambivalent sexist attitudes toward women. *Psychology of Women Quarterly* 20:119–35.

Gonzeles v. Carhart. 2007. Supreme Court of the United States. 550 U.S. 124.

Goffman, Erving. 1977. The arrangement between the sexes. *Theory and Society* 4 (3): 301–31.

Goodridge v. Department of Public Health. 2003. Supreme Judicial Court of Massachusetts. 440 Mass. 309.

Gourevitch, Philip. 1998. *We wish to inform you that tomorrow we will be killed with our families: Stories from Rwanda.* New York: Farrar, Straus, and Giroux.

Government Printing Office. 2007. Historical tables, budget of the United States Government, fiscal year 2007. http://frwebgate1.access.gpo.gov/cgi-bin/TEXTgate.cgi?WAISdocI D=225872210315+3+1+0&WAISaction=retrieve.

Green, Donald P., Bradley Palmquist, and Eric Schickler. 2002. *Partisan hearts and minds.* New Haven, CT: Yale University Press.

Greeno, J. G. 1977. Processes of understanding in problem solving. In *Cognitive theory,* ed. N. J. Castellan, D. B. Pisoni, and G. R. Potts, 43–48. Hillsdale, NJ: Erlbaum.

Gurin, Patricia, Shirley Hatchett, and James S. Jackson. 1989. *Hope and independence.* New York: Russell Sage.

Gusfield, Joseph R. 1963. *Symbolic crusade: Status politics and the American temperance movement.* Urbana: University of Illinois Press.

Haider-Markel, Donald P., and Kenneth J. Meier. 1996. The politics of gay and lesbian rights: Expanding the scope of conflict. *Journal of Politics* 58 (2): 332–49.

Haldane, J. B. S. 1932. The time of action of genes and its bearing on some evolutionary problems. *American Naturalist* 66 (702): 5–24.

Hamilton, W. D. 1964. The genetical evolution of social behaviour. *Journal of Theoretical Biology* 7:1–52.

———. 1970. Selfish and spiteful behavior in an evolutionary model. *Nature* 228:1218–20.

———. 1971a. Geometry for the selfish herd. *Journal of Theoretical Biology* 31:295–311.

———. 1971b. Selection of selfish and altruistic behaviour in some extreme models. In *Man and beast: Comparative social behavior,* ed. J. F. Eisenberg, and Wilton. S. Dillon, 57–91. Washington, DC: Smithsonian.

———. 1972. Altruism and related phenomena, mainly in social insects. *Annual Review of Ecological Systems* 3:193–232.

Hartz, Louis. 1955. *The liberal tradition in America.* New York: Harcourt Brace.

Harwood, E. 1986. American public opinion and U.S. immigration policy. In *Annals of the American academy of political and social science,* vol. 487, ed. R. J. Simon, 201–12. Beverly Hills, CA: Sage.

Hasenfeld, Yeheskel, and Jane A. Rafferty. 1989. The determinants of public attitudes toward the welfare state. *Social Forces* 67 (4): 1027–49.

Hayes, J. R., and H. A. Simon. 1977. Psychological differences among problem isomorphs. In *Cognitive theory,* vol. 2, ed. N. J. Castellan, D. B. Pisoni, and G. R. Potts, 21–41. Hillsdale, NJ: Erlbaum.

Heard, A. 1952. *A two-party South?* Chapel Hill: University of North Carolina Press.

Heckman, James J. 1979. Sample selection bias as a specification error. *Econometrica* 47 (1): 153–61.

Heider, F. 1944. Social perception and phenomenal causality. *Psychological Review* 51:358–74.

———. 1946. Attitudes and cognitive organization. *Journal of Psychology* 21:107–12.

———. 1958. *The psychology of interpersonal relations.* New York: Wiley.

Heine, S. J., D. R. Lehman, H. R. Markus, and S. Kitayama. 1999. Is there a universal need for positive self-regard? *Psychological Review* 106:766–94.

Heise, David R. 1969. Separating reliability and stability in test-retest correlation. *American Sociological Review* 34:93–101.

Held, David. 2000. Regulating globalization: The reinvention of politics. *International Sociology* 15 (2): 394–408.

Henry, P. J., and David O. Sears. 2002. The symbolic racism 2000 scale. *Political Psychology* 23 (2): 253–83.

Herek, Gregory M. 1988. Heterosexuals' attitudes toward lesbians and gay men: Correlates and gender differences. *Journal of Sex Research* 25:451–77.

———. 2002. Gender gaps in public opinion about lesbians and gay men. *Public Opinion Quarterly* 66 (1): 40–66.

Herek, Gregory M., Jared B. Jobe, and Ralph M. Carney, eds. 1996. *Out in force: Sexual orientation and the military.* Chicago: University of Chicago Press.

Herrnstein, Richard J., and Charles Murray. 1994. *The bell curve: Intelligence and class structure in American life.* New York: Free Press.

Hewstone, M., M. Rubin, and H. Willis. 2002. Intergroup bias. *Annual Review of Psychology* 53:575–604.

Higham, John. 1955 [1988]. *Strangers in the land: Patterns of American nativism, 1860–1925.* 2nd ed. New Brunswick, NJ: Rutgers University Press.

Hillygus, D. Sunshine, and Todd G. Shields. 2005. Moral issues and voter decision making in the 2004 presidential election. *PS: Political Science and Politics* 38 (2): 201–9.

Hirschfeld, Lawrence A. 1996. *Race in the making.* Cambridge, MA: MIT Press.

Ho, Daniel H., Kosuke Imai, Gary King, and Elizabeth Stuart. 2007. Matching as nonparametric preprocessing for reducing model dependence in parametric causal inference. *Political Analysis* 15 (3): 199–236.

Hofstadter, Richard. [1944] 1959. *Social Darwinism in American thought.* Rev. ed. New York: Braziller.

———. 1948. *The American political tradition and the men who made it.* New York: Knopf.

———. 1955. *The age of reform.* New York: Knopf.

Hogg, Michael A., and Dominic Abrams. 1988. *Social identifications: A social psychology of intergroup relations and processes.* London: Routledge.

Holsti, Ole R. 1996. *Public opinion and American foreign policy.* Ann Arbor: University of Michigan Press.

Horowitz, Donald L. 1985. *Ethnic groups in conflict.* Berkeley and Los Angeles: University of California Press.

Hout, Michael, Clem Brooks, and Jeff Manza. 1993. The persistence of classes in post-industrial societies. *International Sociology* 8:259–77.

———. 1995. The democratic class struggle in the United States. *American Sociological Review* 60:805–28.

———. 1999. Classes, unions, and the realignment of U.S. presidential voting: 1952–1992. In *The end of class politics? Class voting in comparative context,* ed. Geoffrey Evans, 83–95. Oxford: Oxford University Press.

Huddy, Leonie. 2003. Group identity and political cohesion. In *Oxford handbook of political psychology,* ed. David O. Sears, Leonie Huddy, and Robert Jervis, 511–58. New York: Oxford University Press.

Huddy, Leonie, Stanley Feldman, Charles Taber, and Gallya Lahav. 2005. Threat, anxiety, and support of antiterrorism policies. *American Journal of Political Science* 49 (3): 593–608.

Huddy, Leonie, and Nadia Khatib. 2007. American patriotism, national identity, and political involvement. *American Journal of Political Science* 51 (1): 63–77.

Huntington, Samuel P. 1976. The democratic distemper. In *The American commonwealth—
1976*, ed. Nathan Glazer, and Irving Kristol, 9–38. New York: Basic Books.

———. 2004. *Who are we? The challenges to American's national identity.* New York: Simon
and Schuster.

Hyman, Herbert, and Paul B. Sheatsley. 1954. *The Authoritarian Personality*—A methodological critique. In *Studies in the scope and method of* The Authoritarian Personality, ed.
Richard Christie and Marie Jahoda, 50–122. New York: Free Press.

Iyengar, Shanto. 1990. Shortcuts to political knowledge: The role of selective attention and
accessibility. In *Information and democratic processes*, ed. John A. Ferejohn and James H.
Kuklinski, 160–85. Urbana: University of Illinois Press.

Iyengar, Shanto, and Donald R. Kinder. 1987. *News that matters: Television and American
opinion.* Chicago: University of Chicago Press.

Jackman, Mary R. 1994. *The velvet glove: Paternalism and conflict in gender, class, and race
relations.* Berkeley and Los Angeles: University of California Press.

Jackson, John E. 1974. *Constituencies and leaders in Congress.* Cambridge, MA: Harvard
University Press.

Jackson, John E., and David King. 1989. Public goods, private interests, and representation.
American Political Science Review 83 (4): 1143–64.

Jacoby, William G. 2000. Issue framing and public opinion on government spending. *American Journal of Political Science* 44 (4): 750–67.

Jamieson, Kathleen Hall, and Paul Waldman. 2002. *The press effect: Politicians, journalists,
and the stories that shape the political world.* New York: Oxford University Press.

Jaynes, Gerald David, and Robin M. Williams Jr. 1989. *A common destiny: Blacks and American society.* Washington, DC: National Academy Press.

Jencks, Christopher. 1992. *Rethinking social policy: Race, poverty, and the underclass.* Cambridge, MA: Harvard University Press.

———. 2002. Does inequality matter? *Daedalus* (Winter): 49–65.

Jennings, M. Kent, and Gregory B. Markus. 1984. Partisan orientations over the long haul:
Results from the three-wave political socialization panel study. *American Political Science
Review* 78:1000–1018.

Jennings, M. Kent, and Richard G. Niemi. 1974. *The political character of adolescence.* Princeton, NJ: Princeton University Press.

———. 1981. *Generations and politics.* Princeton, NJ: Princeton University Press.

Jennings, M. Kent, and Laura Stoker. 1999. The persistence of the past: The class of 1965 turns 50.
Paper presented at the annual meeting of the Midwest Political Science Association, Chicago.

Jones, Bryan D. 1994. *Reconceiving decision-making in democratic politics: Attention, choice,
and public policy.* Chicago: University of Chicago Press.

Jones, Maldwyn Allen. 1992. *American immigration.* Chicago: University of Chicago Press.

Jones-Correa, Michael. 1998. *Between two nations: The political predicament of Latinos in New
York City.* Ithaca, NY: Cornell University Press.

Jöreskog, K. G. 1969. A general approach to confirmatory maximum likelihood factor analysis. *Psychometrika* 34:183–202.

Jost, J. T. 2001. Outgroup favoritism and the theory of system justification: An experimental
paradigm for investigating the effects of socio-economic success on stereotype content.

In *Cognitive social psychology: The Princeton symposium on the legacy and future of social cognition*, ed. G. Moskowitz, 89–102. Mahwah, NJ: Erlbaum.

Jost, J. T., M. R. Banaji, and B. A. Nosek. 2004. A decade of system justification theory: Accumulated evidence of conscious and unconscious bolstering of the status quo. *Political Psychology* 25:881–919.

Kagan, Jerome, and Nancy Snidman. 2004. *The long shadow of temperament*. Cambridge, MA: Harvard University Press.

Kahneman, Daniel, and S. Frederick. 2002. Representativeness revisited: Attribute substitution in intuitive judgment. In *Heuristics and biases*, ed. Thomas Gilovich, Dale Griffin, and Daniel Kahneman, 49–81. New York: Cambridge University Press.

Kahneman, Daniel, Paul Slovic, and Amos Tversky, eds. 1982. *Judgment under uncertainty: Heuristics and biases*. New York: Cambridge University Press.

Kahneman, Daniel, and Amos Tversky. 1979. Prospect theory: An analysis of decision under risk. *Econometrica* 47:263–91.

———, eds. 2000. *Choices, values, and frames*. New York: Cambridge University Press and the Russell Sage Foundation.

Kam, Cindy D., and Robert J. Franzese, Jr. 2007. *Modeling and interpreting interactive hypotheses in regression analysis*. Ann Arbor: University of Michigan Press.

Kam, Cindy D., and Donald R. Kinder. 2007. Terror and ethnocentrism: Foundations of American support for the War on Terrorism. *Journal of Politics* 69 (2): 318–36.

Kam, Cindy D., and Carl L. Palmer. 2008. Reconsidering the effects of education on participation. *Journal of Politics* 70 (3): 612–31.

Kam, Cindy D., and Jennifer M. Ramos. 2008. Joining and leaving the rally: Understanding the surge and decline in presidential approval following 9/11. *Public Opinion Quarterly* 72 (4): 619–50.

Katz, Michael B. 1986. *In the shadow of the poorhouse: A social history of welfare in America*. New York: Basic Books.

Katzenstein, Peter J., and Robert O. Keohane, eds. 2007. *Anti-Americanism in world politics*. Ithaca, NY: Cornell University Press.

Keele, Luke, and David K. Park. 2004. Difficult choices: An evaluation of heterogeneous choice models. Paper presented at the annual meeting of the American Political Science Association, Chicago.

Kellstedt, Paul M. 2003. *The mass media and the dynamics of American racial attitudes*. New York: Cambridge University Press.

Kennan, George F. 1946. *The Charge in Soviet Union to the Secretary of State: 861.00/2-2246 [The "Long Telegram"]*. Available at http://www.trumanlibrary.org/whistlestop/study_collections/coldwar/documents/index.php?documentdate=1946-02-22anddocumentid=6-6andstudycollectionid=andpagenumber=1.

Kernell, Samuel. 1978. Explaining presidential popularity: How ad hoc theorizing, misplaced emphasis, and insufficient care in measuring one's variables refuted common sense and led conventional wisdom down the path of anomalies. *American Political Science Review* 72 (2): 506–22.

Key, V. O., Jr. 1949. *Southern politics in state and nation*. New York: Knopf.

———. 1961. *Public opinion and American democracy*. New York: Knopf.

Kinder, Donald R. 1981. Presidents, prosperity, and public opinion. *Public Opinion Quarterly* 45 (1): 1–21.

————. 1982. Enough already about ideology. Paper presented at the annual meeting of the American Political Science Association, Denver, CO.

————. 1983. Diversity and complexity in American public opinion. In *Political science: The state of the discipline*, ed. Ada W. Finifter, 389–425. Washington, DC: American Political Science Association.

————. 1998. Opinion and action in the realm of politics. In *The handbook of social psychology*, 4th ed., vol. 1, ed. Daniel T. Gilbert, Susan T. Fiske, and Gardner Lindzey, 778–867. Boston: McGraw-Hill.

————. 2003. Communication and politics in the age of information. In *Handbook of political psychology*, ed. David O. Sears, Leonie Huddy, and Robert L. Jervis, 357–93. New York: Oxford University Press.

————. 2006. Belief systems today. *Critical review* 18 (1–3): 197–216.

————. 2007. Curmudgeonly advice. *Journal of Communication* 57 (1): 155–62.

————. 2009. Myrdal's prediction: Principles versus prejudice in American political life. Department of Political Science, University of Michigan.

Kinder, Donald R., and Claudia Deane. 1997. Closing the golden door? Exploring the foundations of American opposition to immigration. Paper presented at the annual meeting of the Midwest Political Science Association, Chicago.

Kinder, Donald R., and D. Roderick Kiewiet. 1981. Sociotropic politics: The American case. *British Journal of Political Science* 11 (2): 129–61.

Kinder, Donald R., and Corinne M. McConnaughy. 2006. Military triumph, racial transcendence, and Colin Powell. *Public Opinion Quarterly* 70 (2): 139–65.

Kinder, Donald R., and Lynn M. Sanders. 1990. Mimicking political debate. *Social Cognition* 8 (1): 73–103.

————. 1996. *Divided by color*. Chicago: University of Chicago Press.

Kinder, Donald R., and Janet A. Weiss. 1978. In lieu of rationality: Psychological perspectives on foreign policy decision making. *Journal of Conflict Resolution* 22 (4): 707–35.

Kinder, Donald R., and Nicholas Winter. 2001. Exploring the racial divide: Whites, blacks, and opinion on national policy. *American Journal of Political Science* 45 (2): 439–56.

King, Gary, James Honaker, Anne Joseph, and Kenneth Scheve. 2001. Analyzing incomplete political science data: An alternative algorithm for multiple imputation. *American Political Science Review* 95 (1): 49–69.

King, Gary, Michael Tomz, and Jason Wittenberg. 2000. Making the most of statistical analyses: Improving interpretation and presentation. *American Journal of Political Science* 44 (2): 347–62.

Kingdon, John W. 1973. *Congressmen's voting decisions*. Ann Arbor: University of Michigan Press.

Klinkner, Philip A., and Rogers M. Smith. 1999. *The unsteady march: The rise and decline of racial equality in America*. Chicago: University of Chicago Press.

Kluegel, James R., and Elliot R. Smith. 1986. *Beliefs about inequality: Americans' views of what is and what ought to be*. Hawthorne, NY: Aldine de Gruyter.

Kochhar, Rakesh, Roberto Suro, and Sonya Tafoya. 2005. *The new Latino South: The context and consequences of rapid population growth*. Pew Hispanic Center Report (July 26).

Kohn, Melvin L. 1977. *Class and conformity: A study in values*. Chicago: University of Chicago Press.

Kousser, J. Morgan. 1974. *The shaping of southern politics*. New Haven, CT: Yale University Press.

Krosnick, Jon A., Arthur Lupia, Matthew DeBell, and Darrell Donakowski. 2008. *Problems with ANES questions measuring political knowledge.* http://www.electionstudies.org/announce/newsltr/20080324PoliticalKnowledgeMemo.pdf.

Krosnick, Jon A., and Michael A. Milburn. 1990. Psychological determinants of political opinionation. *Social Cognition* 8 (1): 49–72.

Krueger, J., M. Rothbart, and N. Sriram. 1989. Category learning and change: Differences in sensitivity to information that enhances or reduces intercategory distinctions. *Journal of Personality and Social Psychology* 56:866–75.

Kunda, Ziva. 1990. The case for motivated reasoning. *Psychological Bulletin* 108 (3): 480–98.

Kunda, Ziva, and Katherine C. Oleson. 1995. Maintaining stereotypes in the face of disconfirmation: Constructing grounds for subtyping deviants. *Journal of Personality and Social Psychology* 55:187–95.

———. 1997. When exceptions prove the rule: How extremity of deviance determines deviants' impact on stereotypes. *Journal of Personality and Social Psychology* 72: 965–79.

Lakoff, George. 1996. *Moral politics: How liberals and conservatives think.* Chicago: University of Chicago Press.

Lane, Robert E. 1959. *Political life: Why people get involved in politics.* Glencoe, IL: Free Press.

———. 1962. *Political ideology.* New York: Free Press.

Lapinski, John S., Pia Peltola, Greg Shaw, and Alan Yang. 1997. Trends: Immigrants and immigration. *Public Opinion Quarterly* 61 (2): 356–83.

Lasswell, Harold, and Abraham Kaplan. 1950. *Power and society: A framework for political inquiry.* New Haven, CT: Yale University Press.

Lau, Richard R., and David P. Redlawsk. 2001. Advantages and disadvantages of cognitive heuristics in political decision making. *American Journal of Political Science* 45 (4): 951–71.

Lawrence v. Texas. 2003. Supreme Court of the United States. 539 U.S. 558.

Leach, Colin Wayne, Naomi Ellemers, and Manuela Barreto. 2007. Group virtue: The importance of morality (vs. competence and sociability) in the positive evaluation of in-groups. *Journal of Personality and Social Psychology* 93 (2): 234–49.

LeVine, Robert A. 2001. Ethnocentrism. In *International encyclopedia of the social and behavioral sciences,* 4852–54.

Levinson, Daniel J. 1949. An approach to the theory and measurement of ethnocentric ideology. *The Journal of Psychology* 28:19–39.

Lévi-Strauss, Claude. 1961. *Race et histoire.* Paris: Gonthier.

———. 1983. Race and history. In *Structural anthropology,* vol. 2, ed. Claude Lévi-Strauss, 323–63. Chicago: University of Chicago Press.

Levitan, Sar, and Robert Taggart. 1976. *The promise of greatness.* Cambridge, MA: Harvard University Press.

Levitin, Teresa E., and Warren E. Miller. 1979. Ideological interpretations of presidential elections. *American Political Science Review* 73:751–71.

Lewis, Gregory B. 2005. Same-sex marriage and the 2004 presidential election. *PS: Political Science and Politics* 38 (2): 195–99.

Lewis, Gregory B., and Jonathan L. Edelson. 2000. DOMA and ENDA: Congress votes on gay rights. In *The politics of gay rights,* ed. Craig A. Rimmerman, Kenneth D. Wald, and Clyde Wilcox, 193–216. Chicago: University of Chicago Press.

Lieberman, R. C. 1998. *Shifting the color line: Race and the American welfare state.* Cambridge, MA: Harvard University Press.

Lijphart, Arend. 1999. *Patterns of democracy: Government forms and performance in thirty-six countries.* New Haven, CT: Yale University Press.

Likert, Rensis. 1932. A technique for the measurement of attitudes. *Archives of psychology* 140:1–55.

Lippmann, Walter. [1922] 1997. *Public opinion.* New York: Free Press Paperbacks.

Lipset, Seymour Martin. 1959. *Political man: The social bases of politics.* Baltimore: Johns Hopkins University Press.

Lipset, Seymour Martin, and Stein Rokkan. 1967. *Party systems and voter alignments: Cross-national perspectives.* New York: Free Press.

Locksley, A., V. Ortiz, and C. Hepburn. 1980. Social categorization and discriminatory behavior: Extinguishing the minimal intergroup discrimination effect. *Journal of Personality and Social Psychology* 39:773–83.

Loehlin, J. C. 1992. *Genes and environment in personality development.* Newbury Park, CA: Sage.

Loftus, Jeni. 2001. America's liberalization in attitudes toward homosexuality, 1973 to 1998. *American Sociological Review* 66 (5): 762–82.

Long, J. Scott. 1997. *Regression models for categorical and limited dependent variables.* Thousand Oaks, CA: Sage.

Lord, Charles, M. Ross, and Mark Lepper. 1979. Biased assimilation and attitude polarization: The effects of prior theories on subsequently considered evidence. *Journal of Personality and Social Psychology* 27:2098–109.

Luker, Kristin. 1984. *Abortion and the politics of motherhood.* Berkeley and Los Angeles: University of California Press.

Lumsden, Charles J., and Edward O. Wilson. 1981. *Genes, mind, and culture: The coevolutionary process.* Cambridge, MA: Harvard University Press.

Lush, Jay L. 1940. Intra-sire correlations or regressions of offspring on dam as a method of estimating heritability of characteristics. *Proceedings of the American Society of Animal Production* 33:293–301.

———. 1949. *Animal breeding plans.* 3rd ed. Ames: Iowa State College Press.

Luskin, Robert. 1987. Measuring political sophistication. *American Journal of Political Science* 31 (4): 856–99.

Lynch, Michael, and Bruce Walsh. 1998. *Genetics and analysis of quantitative traits.* Sunderland, MA: Sinauer.

Maccoby, Eleanor. 2000. Parenting and its effects on children: On reading and misreading behavior genetics. *Annual Review of Psychology* 51:1–27.

MacKuen, Michael B. 1981. Social communication and the mass policy agenda. In *More than news: Media power in public affairs,* ed. Michael B. MacKuen and Steven L. Coombs, 19–144. Beverly Hills, CA: Sage.

———. 1983. Political drama, economic conditions, and the dynamics of presidential popularity. *American Journal of Political Science* 27 (2): 165–92.

Malone, Nolan, Kaari F. Baluja, Joseph M. Costanzo, and Cynthia J. Davis. 2003. *The foreign-born population: 2000: Census 2000 brief.* Washington, DC: U.S. Census Bureau. Available at http://www.census.gov/prod/2003pubs/c2kbr-34.pdf.

Mansbridge, Jane J. 1986. *Why we lost the ERA.* Chicago: University of Chicago Press.

March, James G., and Johan P. Olsen. 1989. *Rediscovering institutions: The organizational basis of politics.* New York: Free Press.

Marcus, George E., John Sullivan, Elizabeth Theiss-Morse, and Sandra Wood. 1995. *With malice toward some.* Cambridge: Cambridge University Press.

Markovits, Andrei S. 2007. *Uncouth nation: Why Europe dislikes America.* Princeton, NJ: Princeton University Press.

Markus, Gregory B. 1993. American individualism reconsidered. Unpublished manuscript, University of Michigan.

———. 2001. American individualism reconsidered. In *Citizens and politics: Perspectives from political psychology,* ed. James H. Kuklinski, 401–32. New York: Cambridge University Press.

Martin, N. G., L. J. Eaves, A. C. Heath, Rosemary Jardine, Lynn M. Feingold, and H. J. Eysenck. 1986. Transmission of social attitudes. *Proceedings of the National Academy of Sciences* 83 (12): 4364–68.

Massey, Douglas S., Joaquin Arango, Graeme Hugo, Ali Kouaouci, Adela Pellegrino, and J. Edward Taylor. 1993. Theories of international migration: A review and appraisal. *Population and Development Review* 19 (3): 431–66.

———. 1994. An evaluation of international migration theory: The North American case. *Population and Development Review* 20 (4): 699–751.

Massey, Douglas S., and Nancy A. Denton. 1993. *American apartheid: Segregation and the making of the underclass.* Cambridge, MA: Harvard University Press.

Massey, Douglas S., and Kristin E. Espinosa. 1997. What's driving Mexico–U.S. migration? A theoretical, empirical, and policy analysis. *American Journal of Sociology* 102 (4): 939–99.

Matthews, Donald R., and James W. Prothro. 1963. Social and economic factors and Negro voter registration in the South. *American Political Science Review* 57 (1): 24–44.

Mayer, Jane, and Jill Abramson. 1994. *Strange justice: The selling of Clarence Thomas.* Boston: Houghton Mifflin.

Mayer, Nonna. 1993. Ethnocentrism, racism, and intolerance. In *The French voter decides,* ed. Daniel Boy and Nonna Mayer, 21–44. Ann Arbor: University of Michigan Press.

Mayr, Ernst. 2001. The philosophical foundations of Darwinism. *Proceedings of the American Philosophical Society* 145 (4): 488–95.

McCauley, C., C. L. Stitt, and M. Segal. 1980. Stereotyping: From prejudice to prediction. *Psychological Bulletin* 87:195–208.

McClearn, G. E., and J. C. DeFries. 1973. *Introduction to behavior genetics.* San Francisco: Freeman.

McClosky, Herbert, and Alida Brill. 1983. *Dimensions of tolerance: What Americans think about civil liberties.* New York: Russell Sage.

McClosky, Herbert M., and John Zaller. 1984. *The American ethos: Public attitudes toward capitalism and democracy.* Cambridge, MA: Harvard University Press.

McCombs, M., and D. L. Shaw. 1972. The agenda-setting function of mass media. *Public Opinion Quarterly* 36:176–87.

McConahay, John B. 1982. Self-interest versus racial attitudes as correlates of anti-busing attitudes in Louisville. *Journal of Politics* 44:692–720.

———. 1986. Modern racism, ambivalence, and the modern racism scale. In *Prejudice, discrimination, and racism: Theory and research,* ed. John F. Dovidio and Samuel L. Gaertner. New York: Academic Press.

McCourt, K., T. J. Bouchard Jr., D. T. Lykken, A. Tellegen, and M. Keyes. 1999. Authoritarianism revisited: Genetic and environmental influence examined in twins reared apart and together. *Personality and Individual Differences* 27:985–1014.

McDonald, Michael P. 2004. Up, up, and away! Voter participation in the 2004 presidential election. *The Forum* 2 (1): Article 4.

McFarland, Sam G., Vladimir S. Ageyev, and Marina A. Abalikina. 1993. The authoritarian personality in the United States and former Soviet Union: Comparative studies. In *Strengths and weaknesses: The authoritarian personality today*, ed. William F. Stone, Gerda Lederer, and Richard Christie, 199–228. New York: Springer-Verlag.

McFarland, Sam G., Vladimir S. Ageyev, and Marina A. Abalikina-Paap. 1990. Authoritarianism in the former Soviet Union. *Journal of Personality and Social Psychology* 63 (6): 1004–10.

McGuire, William J. 1985. Attitudes and attitude change. In *Handbook of social psychology*, 3rd ed., vol. 2, ed. Elliot Aronson, and Gardner Lindzey, 233–346. New York: Random House.

McKelvey, R. D., and W. Zavoina. 1976. A statistical model for the analysis of ordinal level dependent variables. *Journal of Mathematical Sociology* 4:103–20.

McNeil, B. J., S. G. Pauker, H. C. Sox Jr., and A. Tversky. 1982. On the elicitation of preferences for alternative therapies. *New England Journal of Medicine* 306 (21): 1259–62.

Meloen, Jos D. 1993. The F-scale as a predictor of fascism: An overview of 40 years of authoritarianism research. In *Strengths and weaknesses: The authoritarian personality today*, ed. William F. Stone, Gerda Lederer, and Richard Christie, 47–69. New York: Springer-Verlag.

Melvern, Linda. 2000. *A people betrayed: The role of the West in Rwanda's genocide*. New York: St. Martin's Press.

Mendelberg, Tali. 2001. *The race card*. Princeton, NJ: Princeton University Press.

Merton, Robert K. 1957. Continuities in the theory of reference groups and social structure. In *Social theory and social structure*, 2nd ed., ed. Robert K. Merton, 281–386. New York: Free Press.

Merton, Robert K., and Alice S. Rossi. 1957. Contributions to the theory of reference group behavior. In *Social theory and social structure*, 2nd ed., ed. Robert K. Merton, 225–80. New York: Free Press.

Messick, D. M., and D. M. Mackie. 1989. Intergroup relations. *Annual Review of Psychology* 40:45–81.

Milgram, Stanley. 1974. *Obedience to authority: An experimental view*. New York: Harper and Row.

Mill, John Stuart. [1869] 1998. On the subjection of women. In *On liberty and other essays*, ed. John Gray, 1–128. Oxford: Oxford University Press.

Miller, G. A. 1957. The magic number seven, plus or minus two: Some limits on our capacity for processing information. *Psychological Review* 63:81–93.

Miller, Warren E., and Donald E. Stokes. 1963. Constituency influence in Congress. *American Political Science Review* 57 (1): 45–56.

Mills, Nicolaus, ed. 1994. Introduction to *Arguing immigration*, 11–27. New York: Simon and Schuster.

Molden, D. C., and E. T. Higgins. 2005. Motivated thinking. In *The Cambridge handbook of thinking and reasoning*, ed. K. Holyoak, and R. Morrison, 295–320. New York: Cambridge University Press.

Mondak, Jeffery J. 1999. Reconsidering the measurement of political knowledge. *Political Analysis* 8 (1): 57–82.

————. 2001. Developing valid knowledge scales. *American Journal of Political Science* 45 (1): 224–38.

Monroe, Kristen Renwick. 1998. *The heart of altruism.* Princeton, NJ: Princeton University Press.

Mueller, Carol M. 1987. Collective consciousness, identity transformation, and the rise of women in public office in the United States. In *The women's movement of the United States and Western Europe,* ed. Mary F. Katzenstein and Carol M. Mueller, 89–108. Philadelphia: Temple University Press.

Mueller, John. 1973. *War, presidents, and public opinion.* New York: Wiley.

————. 1994. *Policy and opinion in the Gulf War.* Chicago: University of Chicago Press.

Mullen, B., R. Brown, and C. Smith. 1992. Ingroup bias as a function of salience, relevance, and status: An integration. *European Journal of Social Psychology* 22:103–22.

Myrdal, Gunnar. 1944. *An American dilemma: The Negro problem and modern democracy.* New York: Harper and Row.

Nagourney, Adam. 2004. "Moral values" carried Bush, Rove says. *New York Times,* November 10.

————. 2007. For G.O.P., first stop on '08 trail is hotbed of immigration politics. *New York Times,* March 20.

National Commission on Terrorist Attacks. 2004. *The 9/11 commission report: The final report of the National Commission on Terrorist Attacks upon the United States.* Authorized ed. New York: Norton.

Nelson, Thomas E., Rosalee A. Clawson, and Zoe M. Oxley. 1997. Media framing of a civil liberties conflict and its effect on tolerance. *American Political Science Review* 91 (3): 567–83.

Neuman, W. Russell. 1990. The threshold of public attention. *Public Opinion Quarterly* 54:156–76.

Newell, Allen, and Herbert A. Simon. 1972. *Human problem solving.* Englewood Cliffs, NJ: Prentice-Hall.

Nie, Norman H., Jane Junn, and Kenneth Stehlik-Barry. 1996. *Education and democratic citizenship in America.* Chicago: University of Chicago Press.

North, Douglas C. 1990. *Institutions, institutional change, and economic performance.* Cambridge: Cambridge University Press.

Novick, L. R., and M. Bassock. 2005. Problem solving. In *The Cambridge handbook of thinking and reasoning,* ed. Keith J. Holyoak, and Robert G. Morrison, 321–49. New York: Cambridge University Press.

Nunn, Clyde Z., Harry J. Crockett Jr., and J. Allen Williams Jr. 1978. *Tolerance for nonconformity.* San Francisco: Jossey-Bass.

Nussbaum, Martha C. 1996. Patriotism and cosmopolitanism. In *For love of country: Debating the limits of patriotism,* ed. Joshua Cohen, 2–18. Boston: Beacon Press.

————. 2001. *Upheavals of thought: The intelligence of emotions.* Cambridge: Cambridge University Press.

————. 2008. Toward a globally sensitive patriotism. *Daedalus* 137:78–93.

Olzak, Susan. 1992. *The dynamics of ethnic competition and conflict.* Palo Alto, CA: Stanford University Press.

Olzak, Susan, and Joanne Nagel, eds. 1986. *Competitive ethnic relations.* Orlando: Academic Press.

Ordeshook, Peter, and Olga Shvetsova. 1994. Ethnic heterogeneity, district magnitude, and the number of parties. *American Journal of Political Science* 38 (1): 100–123.

Orloff, Ann Shola. 1988. The political origins of America's belated welfare state. In *The politics of social policy in the United States*, ed. Margaret Weir, Ann Shola Orloff, and Theda Skocpol, 37–80. Princeton, NJ: Princeton University Press.

Otten, S., and G. B. Moskowitz. 2000. Evidence for implicit evaluative ingroup bias: Affect-biased spontaneous trait inference in a minimal group paradigm. *Journal of Experimental Social Psychology* 36:77–89.

Otten, S., and D. Wentura. 1999. About the impact of automaticity in the minimal group paradigm: Evidence from an affective priming task. *European Journal of Social Psychology* 29:1049–71.

Page, Benjamin I., and Robert Y. Shapiro. 1992. *The rational public.* Chicago: University of Chicago Press.

Palmquist, Bradley, and Donald P. Green. 1992. Estimation of models with correlated measurement errors from panel data. *Sociological Methodology* 22:119–46.

Park, Bernadette, and Myron Rothbart. 1982. Perception of out-group homogeneity and levels of social categorization: Memory for the subordinate attributes of in-group and out-group members. *Journal of Personality and Social Psychology* 42:1051–68.

Patterson, James T. 1981. *America's struggle against poverty: 1900–1980.* Cambridge, MA: Harvard University Press.

———. 1996. *Grand expectations: The United States, 1945–1974.* New York: Oxford University Press.

Payne, J. W. 1982. Contingent decision behavior. *Psychology Bulletin* 92:382–402.

Peffley, Mark, Jon Hurwitz, and Paul Sniderman. 1997. Racial stereotypes and whites' political views of blacks in the context of welfare and crime. *American Journal of Political Science* 41 (1): 30–60.

Perdue, Charles W., John F. Dovidio, Michael B. Gurtman, and Richard B. Tyler. 1990. Us and them: social categorization and the process of intergroup bias. *Journal of Personality and Social Psychology* 59 (3): 475–86.

Perreault, S., and R. Y. Bourhis. 1999. Ethnocentrism, social identification, and discrimination. *Personality and Social Psychology Bulletin* 25:92–103.

Pettigrew, Thomas F. 1959. Regional differences in anti-Negro prejudice. *Journal of Abnormal and Social Psychology* 49:28–36.

———. 1982. Prejudice. In *Prejudice*, ed. Thomas F. Pettigrew, George M. Frederickson, Dale Knobel, Nathan Glazer, and Reed Ueda, 1–29. Cambridge, MA: Harvard University Press.

Philips, Charles, and Alan Axelrod. 2005. *Encyclopedia of wars.* New York: Facts on File.

Pitkin, Hanna F. 1967. *The concept of representation.* Berkeley and Los Angeles: University of California Press.

Pomerantz, Eva M., Shelly Chaiken, and Rosalind S. Tordesillas. 1995. Attitude strength and resistance processes. *Journal of Personality and Social Psychology* 69:408–19.

Pomper, Gerald M. 1993. The presidential election. In *The election of 1992*, ed. Gerald M. Pomper, F. Christopher Arterton, Ross K. Baker, Walter Dean Burnham, Kathleen A. Frankovic, Marjorie Randon Hershey, and Wilson Carey McWilliams, 132–56. Chatham, NJ: Chatham House.

Portes, Alejandro, and Cynthia Truelove. 1987. Making sense of diversity: Recent research on Hispanic minorities in the United States. *Annual Review of Sociology* 13:359–85.

Posner, Daniel N. 2004. Measuring ethnic fractionalization in Africa. *American Journal of Political Science* 48 (4): 849–63.

———. 2005. *Institutions and ethnic politics in Africa.* Cambridge: Cambridge University Press.

Power, Samantha. 2002. *A problem from hell: America and the age of genocide.* New York: Basic Books.

Price, Vincent. 1989. Social identification and public opinion: Effects of communicating group conflict. *Public Opinion Quarterly* 53 (2): 197–224.

Price, Vincent, and John Zaller. 1993. Who gets the news? Alternative measures of news reception and their implications for research. *Public Opinion Quarterly* 57 (2): 133–64.

Protess, David L., Fay Lomax Cook, Jack C. Doppelt, James S. Etterma, Margaret T. Gordon, Donna R. Leff, and Peter Miller. 1991. *The journalism of outrage: Investigative reporting and agenda building in America.* New York: Guilford Press.

Prothro, E. Terry. 1950. Ethnocentrism and anti-Negro attitudes in the deep South. *Journal of Abnormal and Social Psychology* 47:105–8.

Putnam, Hilary. 1970. Is semantics possible? In *Contemporary philosophical thought.* Vol. 1 of *Languages, belief, and metaphysics,* ed. Howard E. Kiefer, and Milton K. Munitz, 50–63. Albany: State University of New York Press.

Putnam, Robert D. 1993. *Making democracy work.* Princeton, NJ: Princeton University Press.

———. 1995. Tuning in, tuning out: The strange disappearance of social capital in America. *PS: Political Science and Politics* 28 (4): 664–83.

———. 2000. *Bowling alone: The collapse and revival of American community.* New York: Simon and Schuster.

Quadagno, Jill. 1988. *The transformation of old age security.* Chicago: University of Chicago Press.

———. 1994. *The color of welfare: How racism undermined the War on Poverty.* New York: Oxford University Press.

Quillian, Lincoln. 1995. Prejudice as a response to perceived group threat: Population composition and anti-immigrant and racial prejudice in Europe. *American Sociological Review* 60:586–611.

Quine, W. V. O. 1977. Natural kinds. In *Naming, necessity, and natural kinds,* ed. Stephen P. Schwartz, 13–41. Ithaca, NY: Cornell University Press.

Rawls, John. 1971. *A theory of justice.* Cambridge, MA: Belknap Press of Harvard University Press.

Rhode, Deborah L. 2004. *Access to justice.* New York: Oxford University Press.

Rhum, Michael. 1997. Ethnocentrism. In *The dictionary of anthropology,* ed. Thomas Barfield, 155. Oxford: Blackwell.

Richerson, Peter J., and Robert Boyd. 2005. *Not by genes alone: How culture transformed human evolution.* Chicago: University of Chicago Press.

Rimmerman, Craig A., Kenneth D. Wald, and Clyde Wilcox, eds. 2000. *Politics of gay rights.* Chicago: University of Chicago Press.

Rimmerman, Craig A., and Clyde Wilcox, eds. 2007. *The politics of same-sex marriage.* Chicago: University of Chicago Press.

Roberts, B. W., and W. F. DelVecchio. 2000. The rank-order consistency of personality from childhood to old age: A quantitative review of longitudinal studies. *Psychological Bulletin* 26:3–25.

Roe v. Wade. 1973. Supreme Court of the United States. 410 U.S. 113.

Roediger, David R. 1999. *The wages of whiteness: Race and the making of the American working class*. Rev. ed. New York: Verso.

Roemer, John E., Woojin Lee, and Karine Van der Straeten. 2007. *Racism, xenophobia, and redistribution: Multi-issue politics in advanced democracies*. Cambridge, MA: Harvard University Press.

Rom, Mark Carl. 2000. Gays and AIDS: Democratizing disease? In *The politics of gay rights*, ed. Craig A. Rimmerman, Kenneth D. Wald, and Clyde Wilcox, 409–23. Chicago: University of Chicago Press.

Rosenbaum, Paul R., and Donald B. Rubin. 1985. Constructing a control group using multivariate matched sampling methods that incorporate the propensity score. *The American Statistician* 39 (1): 33–38.

Rosenberg, Milton J., and Robert P. Abelson. 1960. An analysis of cognitive balancing. In *Attitude, organization, and change: An analysis of consistency among attitude components*, ed. M. J. Rosenberg, C. I. Hovland, W. J. McGuire, R. P. Abelson, and J. W. Brehm, 112–63. New Haven, CT: Yale University Press.

Rosenstone, Steven J. 1983. *Forecasting presidential elections*. New Haven, CT: Yale University Press.

Rosenstone, Steven J., and John Mark Hansen. 1993. *Mobilization, participation, and democracy in America*. New York: Macmillan.

Rosenstone, Steven J., John Mark Hansen, and Donald R. Kinder. 1986. Measuring change in personal economic well-being. *Public Opinion Quarterly* 50:176–92.

Rosenstone, Steven J., Margaret Petrella, and Donald R. Kinder. 1993. Excessive reliance on telephone interviews and short-form questionnaires in the 1992 National Election Study: Assessing the consequences for data quality. NES Technical Report # nes010161. Available at ftp://ftp.electionstudies.org/ftp/nes/bibliography/documents/nes010161a.pdf.

Ross, Steven L., and John Yinger. 2002. *The color of credit*. Cambridge, MA: MIT Press.

Rothbart, Myron, and Bernadette Park. 2004. The mental representation of social categories: Category boundaries, entitativity, and stereotype change. In *The psychology of group perception: Perceived variability, entitativity, and essentialism*, ed. Vincent Yzerbyt, Charles Judd, and Olivier Corneille, 79–100. Philadelphia: Psychology Press.

Rothbart, Myron, and Marjorie Taylor. 1992. Category labels and social reality: Do we view social categories as natural kinds? In *Language, interaction, and social cognition*, ed. Gün R. Semin, and Klaus Fiedler, 11–36. London: Sage.

Romer v. Evans. 1996. Supreme Court of the United States. 517 U.S. 620.

Rubin, Donald B. 1974. Estimating causal effects of treatments in randomized and nonrandomized studies. *Journal of Educational Psychology* 66 (5): 688–701.

Sachdev, I., and R. Y. Bourhis. 1991. Power and status differentials in minority and majority group relations. *European Journal of Social Psychology* 21:1–24.

Scarr, S., and R. A. Weinberg. 1981. The transmission of authoritarianism in families: Genetic resemblance in social-political attitudes. In *Race, social class, and individual differences in IQ*, ed. Sandra Scarr, 399–430. Hillsdale, NJ: Erlbaum.

Schank, Roger, and Robert Abelson. 1976. *Scripts, plans, goals, and understanding*. Hillsdale, NJ: Erlbaum.

Scheve, Kenneth J., and Matthew J. Slaughter. 2001. Labor-market competition and individual preferences over immigration policy. *Review of Economics and Statistics* 83:133–45.

Schildkraut, Deborah. 2005. *Press "one" for English: Language policy, public opinion, and American identity*. Princeton, NJ: Princeton University Press.

Schlesinger, Arthur M., Jr. 1992. *The disuniting of America*. New York: Norton.

Schlozman, Kay Lehman, and Sidney Verba. 1979. *Insult to injury: Unemployment, class, and political response*. Cambridge, MA: Harvard University Press.

Schuman, Howard, and Stanley Presser. 1981. *Questions and answers in attitude surveys: Experiments on question form, wording, and context*. New York: Academic Press.

Schuman, Howard, Charlotte Steeh, Lawrence Bobo, and Maria Krysan. 1997. *Racial attitudes in America: Trends and interpretations*. Cambridge, MA: Harvard University Press.

Schwartz, Shalom H. 1992. Universals in the content and structure of values. *Advances in experimental social psychology* 25:1–65.

Sears, David O. 1975. Political socialization. In *Handbook of political science*, vol. 2, ed. Fred Greenstein and Nelson Polsby, 93–153. Reading, MA: Addison-Wesley.

———. 1988. Symbolic racism. In *Eliminating racism: Profiles in controversy*, ed. Phylis Katz and Dalmas A. Taylor. New York: Plenum.

Sears, David O., P. J. Henry, and Rick Kosterman. 2000. Egalitarian values and contemporary racial politics. In *Racialized politics*, ed. David O. Sears, Jim Sidanius, and Lawrence Bobo, 75–117. Chicago: University of Chicago Press.

Sears, David O., Jim Sidanius, and Lawrence Bobo, eds. 2000. *Racialized politics: The debate about racism in America*. Chicago: University of Chicago Press.

Sears, David O., and R. E. Whitney. 1973. *Political persuasion*. Morristown, NJ: General Learning Press.

Seelye, Katherine Q. 2004. Moral values cited as a defining issue of the election. *New York Times*, November 4.

Sekhon, Jasjeet S. 2004. The varying role of voter information across democratic societies. Paper presented at the annual meeting of the Society for Political Methodology, Palo Alto, CA.

———. 2007. Multivariate and propensity score matching software with automated balance optimization: The matching package for R. Available at http://sekhon.polisci.berkeley. edu/matching/.

Selznick, Gertrude J., and Stephen Steinberg. 1969. *Anti-Semitism in contemporary America*. New York: Harper and Row.

Semetko, Holli A. 2007. Political communication. In *The Oxford handbook of political behavior*, ed. Russell J. Dalton and Hans-Dieter Klingemann, 123–43. Oxford: Oxford University Press.

Shapiro, Robert Y., and Harpreet Mahajan. 1986. Gender differences in policy preferences: A summary of trends from the 1960s to the 1980s. *Public Opinion Quarterly* 50 (1): 42–61.

Sherif, Muzafer, O. J. Harvey, B. Jack White, William R. Hood, and Carolyn W. Sherif. 1961. *Intergroup conflict and cooperation: The Robbers Cave experiment*. Norman, OK: University Book Exchange.

Sherif, Muzafer, and Carolyn W. Sherif. [1953] 1966. *Groups in harmony and tension*. New York: Octagon Books.

Shilts, Randy 1987. *And the band played on: Politics, people, and the AIDS epidemic*. New York: Penguin Books.

Sidanius, Jim, and R. Kurzban. 2003. Evolutionary approaches to political psychology. In *Oxford handbook of political psychology*, ed. David O. Sears, Leonie Huddy, and Robert Jervis, 146–81. New York: Oxford University Press.

Sigelman, Lee, and Susan Welch. 1991. *Black Americans' views of racial inequality: The dream deferred*. New York: Cambridge University Press.

Simmel, Georg. [1923] 1955. *Conflict and the web of group-affiliations.* Trans. Kurt H. Wolff and Reinhard Bendix. Glencoe, IL: Free Press.

Simon, Dan, and Keith J. Holyoak. 2002. Structural dynamics of cognition: From consistency theories to constraint satisfaction. *Personality and Social Psychology Review* 6:283–94.

Simon, Herbert A. 1955. A behavioral model of rational choice. *Quarterly Journal of Economics* 69 (February): 99–118.

———. 1967. Motivation and emotional controls of cognition. *Psychological Review* 74:29–39.

———. 1978. Rationality as process and as product of thought. *American Economic Review* 68:1–16.

———. 1979. Information processing models of cognition. *Annual Review of Psychology* 30:364–96.

———. 1979. *Models of thought.* New Haven, CT: Yale University Press.

———. 1983. *Reason in human affairs.* Palo Alto, CA: Stanford University Press.

———. 1985. Human nature in politics: The dialogue of psychology with political science. *American Political Science Review* 79 (2): 293–304.

Simon, Herbert A., and J. R. Hayes. 1976. The understanding process: Problem isomorphs. *Cognitive Psychology* 8:165–90.

Simon, Rita J., and Susan H. Alexander. 1993. *The ambivalent welcome: Print media, public opinion, and immigration.* Westport, CT: Praeger.

Singer, E., T. F. Rogers, and M. Corcoran. 1987. Poll report: AIDS. *Public Opinion Quarterly* 51:580–95.

Skocpol, Theda. 1992. *Protecting soldiers and mothers: The political origins of social policy in the United States.* Cambridge, MA: Harvard University Press.

Smith, Adam. [1759] 1817. *The theory of moral sentiments.* Philadelphia: Anthony Finley. Available at http://books.google.com/books?id=z1sAAAAAMAAJ.

Smith, Rogers M. 1997. *Civic ideas.* New Haven, CT: Yale University Press.

———. 2008. Paths to a more cosmopolitan human condition. *Daedalus* 137:39–49.

Smith, Tom W. 1987. That which we call welfare by any other name would smell sweeter. *Public Opinion Quarterly* 51:75–83.

Sniderman, Paul, Richard A. Brody, and Phillip Tetlock, eds. 1991. *Reasoning and choice.* Cambridge, MA: Cambridge University Press.

Sniderman, Paul M., Pierangelo Peri, Rui J. P. de Figueiredo Jr., and Thomas Piazza. 2000. *The outsider: Prejudice and politics in Italy.* Princeton, NJ: Princeton University Press.

Sniderman, Paul M., and Sean M. Theriault. 2004. The dynamics of political argument and the logic of issue framing. In *Studies in public opinion: Gauging attitudes, nonattitudes, measurement error, and change,* ed. William E. Saris and Paul M. Sniderman, 133–65. Princeton, NJ: Princeton University Press.

Sober, Elliott, and David Sloan Wilson. 1998. *Unto others: The evolution and psychology of unselfish behavior.* Cambridge, MA: Harvard University Press.

Social Security Administration. 2007. *Statistical supplement to the Social Security bulletin, 2006.* http://www.ssa.gov/policy/docs/statcomps/supplement/2006/supplement06.pdf.

Stangor, Charles, and James E. Lange. 1994. Mental representations on social groups: Advances in understanding stereotypes and stereotyping. *Advances in experimental social psychology* 26:357–416.

Steeh, Charlotte, and Maria Krysan. 1996. The polls—trends: Affirmative action and the public, 1970–95. *Public Opinion Quarterly* 60:128–58.

Stein, Arthur A. 1976. Conflict and cohesion. *Journal of Conflict Resolution* 20 (1): 143–72.

Stenner, Karen. 2005. *The authoritarian dynamic.* Cambridge: Cambridge University Press.

Stimson, James A. 2004. *Tides of consent: How public opinion shapes American politics.* Cambridge: Cambridge University Press.

Stimson, James A., Michael B. MacKuen, and Robert S. Erikson. 1995. Dynamic representation. *American Political Science Review* 89 (3): 543–65.

Stoker, Laura. 1987. Morality and politics: Conduct and control. A report on new items in the 1987 National Election Pilot Study. ANES Pilot Study Report No. nes002273. Available at ftp://ftp.electionstudies.org/ftp/nes/bibliography/documents/nes002273.pdf.

———. 1992. Interests and ethics in politics. *American Political Science Review* 86 (2): 369–80.

Stokes, Donald E. 1966. Party loyalty and the likelihood of deviating elections. In *Elections and the political order,* ed. Angus Campbell, Philip E. Converse, Warren E. Miller, and Donald E. Stokes, 125–35. New York: Wiley.

Stouffer, Samuel. 1955. *Communism, conformity, and civil liberties.* New York: Doubleday.

Sturgis, Patrick, Nick Allum, and Patten Smith. 2008. An experiment on the measurement of political knowledge in surveys. *Public Opinion Quarterly* 72 (1): 90–102.

Sullivan, John L., James E. Piereson, and George E. Marcus. 1982. *Political tolerance and American democracy.* Chicago: University of Chicago Press.

Sumner, William Graham. [1906] 2002. *Folkways: A study of mores, manners, customs, and morals.* Mineola, NY: Dover Publications.

Sumner, William Graham, Albert G. Keller, and M. R. Davie. 1927. *The science of society.* New Haven, CT: Yale University Press.

Taber, Charles S., and Milton Lodge. 2006. Motivated skepticism in the evaluation of political beliefs. *American Journal of Political Science* 50 (3): 755–69.

Tajfel, Henri. 1981. *Human groups and social categories.* Cambridge: Cambridge University Press.

———. 1982. *Social identity and intergroup relations.* Cambridge: Cambridge University Press.

Tajfel, Henri, Michael G. Billig, Robert P. Bundy, and Claude Flament. 1971. Social categorization and intergroup behavior. *European Journal of Social Psychology* 1 (2): 149–78.

Tajfel, Henri, and John C. Turner. 1979. An integrative theory of intergroup conflict. In *The social psychology of intergroup relations,* ed. William G. Austin and Stephen Worchel, 33–48. Monterey, CA: Brooks/Cole.

Takaki, Ronald T. 1989. *Strangers from a different shore.* Boston: Little, Brown.

Tate, Katherine. 1993. *From protest to politics: The new black voters in American elections.* Cambridge, MA: Harvard University Press.

Taylor, Shelly E., Susan T. Fiske, Nancy L. Etcoff, and Audrey J. Ruderman. 1978. Categorical bases of person memory and stereotyping. *Journal of Personality and Social Psychology* 36:778–93.

Tesser, Abraham. 1993. The importance of heritability in psychological research: The case of attitudes. *Psychological Review* 100:129–42.

Tetlock, Phillip E. 1998. Close-call counterfactuals and belief system defenses: I was not almost wrong but I was almost right. *Journal of Personality and Social Psychology* 75:639–52.

Thernstrom, Stephan, and Abigail Thernstrom. 1997. *America in black and white: One nation indivisible: Race in modern America.* New York: Simon and Schuster.

Thompson, Leonard Monteath. 2001. *A history of South Africa*. New Haven, CT: Yale University Press.

Tilly, Charles. 1978. *From mobilization to revolution*. Reading, MA: Addison-Wesley.

———. 1998. *Durable inequality*. Berkeley and Los Angeles: University of California Press.

Times Mirror Center for the People and the Press. 1995. *Energized Democrats backing Clinton*. Washington, DC: Pew Research Center for the People and the Press. Available at http://people-press.org/report/?pageid=422.

Tocqueville, Alexis de. [1848] 1994. *Democracy in America*. New York: Knopf.

Tufte, Edward R. 1978. *Political control of the economy*. Princeton, NJ: Princeton University Press.

Turner, John C., and Katherine J. Reynolds. 2003. The social identity perspective. In *Blackwell handbook of social psychology: Intergroup processes*, ed. Rupert Brown and Sam Gaertner, 133–52. Oxford: Blackwell.

Tversky, Amos, and Daniel Kahneman. 1974. Judgment under uncertainty: Heuristics and biases. *Science* 185:1124–31.

———. 1981. The framing of decisions and the psychology of choice. *Science* 211 (4481): 453–58.

U.S. Census Bureau. 2005. *Cumulative estimates of the components of population change for the United States and states: April 1, 2000 to July 1, 2005* (NST-EST2005-04) (table 4). Available at http://www.census.gov/popest/states/tables/NST-EST2005-04.xls.

———. 2007. Statistical abstract of the United States. Available at http://www.census.gov/compendia/statab/2007/2007edition.html.

van den Berghe, Pierre. 1978. *Man in society: A biosocial view*. New York: Elsevier.

———. 1981. *The ethnic phenomenon*. New York: Elsevier.

———. 1995. Does race matter? In *Ethnicity*, ed. John Hutchinson and Anthony D. Smith, 57–63. Oxford: Oxford University Press.

Varshney, Ashutosh. 2002. *Ethnic conflict and civic life: Hindus and Muslims in India*. New Haven, CT: Yale University Press.

Verba, Sidney, Kay Lehman Schlozman, and Henry E. Brady. 1995. *Voice and equality: Civic voluntarism in American politics*. Cambridge, MA: Harvard University Press.

Wald, Kenneth D. 2000. The context of gay politics. In *The politics of gay rights*, ed. Craig A. Rimmerman, Kenneth D. Wald, and Clyde Wilcox, 1–28. Chicago: University of Chicago Press.

Wald, Kenneth D., James W. Button, and Barbara A. Rienzo. 1996. The politics of gay rights in American communities: Explaining anti-discrimination ordinances and policies. *American Journal of Political Science* 40:1152–78.

Wald, Kenneth D., and Graham B. Glover. 2007. Theological perspectives on gay unions: The uneasy marriage of religion and politics. In *The politics of same-sex marriage*, ed. Craig A. Rimmerman and Clyde Wilcox, 105–30. Chicago: University of Chicago Press.

Weingast, Barry R. 1998. Political stability and civil war: Institutions, commitment, and American democracy. In *Analytical narratives*, ed. Robert H. Bates, Avner Greif, Margaret Levy, Jean-Laurent Rosenthal, and Barry R. Weingast, 148–93. Princeton, NJ: Princeton University Press.

Weir, Margaret, Ann Shola Orloff, and Theda Skocpol, eds. 1988. *The politics of social policy in the United States*. Princeton, NJ: Princeton University Press.

Weissberg, Robert. 1978. Collective versus dyadic representation in Congress. *American Political Science Review* 72:535–47.

Wilcox, Clyde, Linda Merolla, and David Beer. 2006. Saving marriage by banning marriage: The Christian Right finds a new issue in 2004. In *The values campaign? The Christian Right in the 2004 elections*, ed. John C. Green, Mark J. Rozell, and Clyde Wilcox, 56–78. Washington, DC: Georgetown University Press.

Wilcox, Clyde, and Barbara Norrander. 2002. Of moods and morals: The dynamics of opinion on abortion and gay rights. In *Understanding public opinion*, 2nd ed., ed. Barbara Norrander and Clyde Wilcox, 121–48. Washington, DC: CQ Press.

Wilcox, Clyde, and Robin Wolpert. 1996. President Clinton, public opinion, and gays in the military. In *Gay rights, military wrongs: Political perspectives on lesbians and gays in the military*, ed. Craig A. Rimmerman, 127–45. New York: Garland.

———. 2000. Gay rights in the public sphere: Public opinion on gay and lesbian equality. In *The politics of gay rights*, ed. Craig A. Rimmerman, Kenneth D. Wald, and Clyde Wilcox, 409–32. Chicago: University of Chicago Press.

Wiley, David E., and James A. Wiley. 1970. The estimation of measurement error in panel data. *American Sociological Review* 35 (1): 112–17.

Wiley, James A., and Mary Glenn Wiley. 1974. A note on correlated errors in repeated measurements. *Sociological Methods and Research* 3:172–88.

Wilson, David Sloan, and Edward O. Wilson. 2007. Rethinking the theoretical foundation of sociobiology. *Quarterly Review of Biology* 82 (4): 327–48.

Wilson, Edward O. 1975. *Sociobiology: The new synthesis.* Cambridge, MA: Harvard University Press.

———. 1978. *On human nature.* Cambridge, MA: Harvard University Press.

———. 1998. *Consilience: The unity of knowledge.* New York: Knopf.

Wilson, Glenn D., ed. 1973. *The psychology of conservatism.* London: Academic Press.

Wilson, Pete. 1993. An open letter to the President of the United States on behalf of California. *New York Times*, August 10.

Wilson, William Julius. 1973. *Power, racism, and privilege: Race relations in theoretical and sociohistorical perspective.* New York: Free Press.

———. 1987. *The truly disadvantaged: The inner city, the underclass, and public policy.* Chicago: University of Chicago Press.

Winter, Nicholas. 2006. Beyond welfare: Framing and the racialization of white opinion on social security. *American Journal of Political Science* 50 (2): 400–20.

Winter, Nicholas, and Adam J. Berinsky. 1999. What's your temperature? Thermometer ratings and political analysis. Paper presented at the annual meeting of the American Political Science Association, Atlanta.

Wolbrecht, Christina L. 2000. *The politics of women's rights: Parties, positions, and change.* Princeton, NJ: Princeton University Press.

Wright, Gerald C., Jr. 1976. Community structure and voting in the south. *Public Opinion Quarterly* 40:201–15.

———. 1977. Contextual models of electoral behavior: The southern Wallace vote. *American Political Science Review* 71:497–508.

Wright, Sewall. 1921. Correlation and causation. *Journal of Agricultural Research* 20 (January): 557–85.

Zajonc, Robert B. 1968. Cognitive theories in social psychology. In *The handbook of social psychology*, 2nd ed., ed. Gardner Lindzey and Elliot Aronson, 1:320–411. Reading, MA: Addison-Wesley.

———. 1980. Feeling and thinking: Preferences need no inferences. *American Psychologist* 35:151–75.

———. 1981. On the primacy of affect. *American Psychologist* 36:102–3.

Zaller, John R. 1986. *Analysis of information items in the 1985 NES Pilot Study: A Report to the Board of Overseers for the National Election Studies.* NES Pilot Study Report No. nes002261. Ann Arbor, MI: National Election Studies.

———. 1989. Bringing Converse back in: Modeling information flow in political campaigns. *Political Analysis* 1:181–234.

———. 1990. Political awareness, elite opinion leadership, and the mass survey response. *Social Cognition* 8 (1): 125–53.

———. 1991. Information, values, and opinion. *American Political Science Review* 85 (4): 1215–37.

———. 1992. *The nature and origins of mass opinion.* Cambridge: Cambridge University Press.

———. 1994. Elite leadership of mass opinion: New evidence from the Gulf War. In *Taken by storm: The media, public opinion, and U.S. foreign policy in the Gulf War,* ed. W. Lance Bennett and David L. Paletz, 186–209. Chicago: University of Chicago Press.

Zaller, John R., and Mark Hunt. 1994. The rise and fall of candidate Perot: Unmediated versus mediated politics—Part I. *Political Communication* 11:357–90.

———. 1995. The rise and fall of candidate Perot: Unmediated versus mediated politics—Part II. *Political Communication* 12:97–123.

Index

Abelson, Robert P., 39, 257n15
abortion, ethnocentrism and opinion on, 173–76
Abrams, Dominic, 21
acquiescence response set, 15–16, 248n18, 249n22
activation, of ethnocentrism. *See* ethnocentrism, activation
Adorno, Theodor. See *The Authoritarian Personality* (Adorno, et al.)
affirmative action: African American support for, and ethnocentrism, 205; white American opposition to, and ethnocentrism, 206, 207; and women, 177, 302n10
Afghanistan, war in, 80
African Americans: concern about AIDS, 299nn20, 22; ethnocentrism and authoritarianism, 268n51; ethnocentrism and group identification, 204–6; ethnocentrism and opposition to policies targeting Hispanic and Asian Americans, 204; ethnocentrism and support for government spending on AIDS, 164, 165; ethnocentrism and support for South African sanctions, 113; ethnocentrism in the realm of race, 202–6, 215–16, 217; in-group attachment, 200–201; lack of effect of ethnocentrism on attitudes toward welfare programs, 185, 199; limited in-group favoritism, 50, 51, 68; support for Head Start, 306n16
age, and attitudes toward Social Security, 198
agenda-setting: news media and public opinion, 39, 258n16; role of emotion in, 256n13

aggression, 252n42
AIDS, 151, 180; African American concern about, 299nn20, 22; African American support for government spending on, and ethnocentrism, 164, 165; American public's loss of interest in, 235; Clinton initiatives, 158; opposition to government spending on, and religiosity, 154; support for political responses to, and ethnocentrism, 159–60, 163
Aid to Families with Dependent Children (AFDC). *See* means-tested income transfers; welfare system
Alliance for Marriage, 153
Allport, Gordon, 3, 21–22, 28–29, 44
Almond, Gabriel A., 60
al-Qaeda, 75
Altemeyer, Bob, 248n18, 249n21
altruism: genetic theory of, 26, 252n45; and universalism, 313n15
ambivalence, 26–27, 117–18
The American Voter (Campbell, Converse, Miller, and Stokes), 312n9
anti-Americanism, 229–30
antidemocratic belief: and ethnocentrism, 232; and psychodynamic theory, 12, 14
anti-Semitism, 52, 91, 229
anti-Semitism scale, 12–13, 15, 248n12
apartheid: American opinion on, 112–13; in South Africa, 110–12
Asch, Solomon, 22
Asian Americans: ethnocentrism and attitudes toward immigration, 292–94n39; general in-group favoritism, 50
Atta, Mohamed, 74

authoritarianism: differences from ethno-centrism, 225–27; and ethnocentrism, 13–18, 34, 64–65, 87–88, 268n51; and op-position to immigration, 137; and political intolerance, 17–18; studies of, 11–16; and support for war on terrorism, 88–89; and tension between personal autonomy and social cohesion, 17, 34, 64, 137, 225, 255n11; theories of origins of, 248n16, 255n6; threat as key trigger for, 226
The Authoritarian Personality (Adorno et al.), 7, 11–16, 23, 29, 36, 52, 57, 85, 87, 91, 248n16, 260n8

Baumgartner, Frank R., 258n17
behavioral economics, 256n12
behavioral genetics, 253n46
Bell, Daniel, 170
Billig, Michael, 250n27
Bin Ladin, Osama, 74
Blake, Robert R., 246n6
bounded rationality: and activation of eth-nocentrism, 38; and political opinions, 37–38
Brewer, Marilynn: *Ethnocentrism and Inter-group Attitudes* (with Donald Campbell), 48–49, 51, 251nn35–36; and in-group at-tachment, 55, 61; minimal group experi-ment, 250n28; theory of social identity, 21–22
Brown, Roger, 13, 247n9, 251n29
Bryant, Anita, 154
Buchanan, Pat, 145
Bundy, Robert P., 250n27
Burke, Edmund, 314n26
Burnham, Walter Dean, 32
Burroughs, Charles, 182
Bush, George H. W., 128, 177; and Desert Storm, 91–93, 101; and Saddam Hussein, 100; supported by ethnocentric Ameri-cans, 99, 119
Bush, George W.: response to 9/11, 74–75, 77, 275n17; supported by ethnocentric Ameri-cans, 84; support for constitutional ban on gay marriage, 166

California, Proposition 187, 145
Campbell, Donald: *Ethnocentrism and Inter-group Attitudes* (with Marilynn Brewer),

48–49, 51, 251n35; study of ethnocentrism in multiple cultural settings, 48; and xe-nophobia, 246n4
Carter, Jimmy, 115
child care, 177
Christian Coalition, 152
Christian Right: campaigns against same-sex marriage, 153; opposition to gay rights movement, 152, 154, 166, 180
Christie, Richard, 248n17
Churchill, Winston, 122
Civil Rights Act of 1964, 176
Clinton, Bill: and AIDS initiatives, 158; and Family Leave and Medical Act, 178; and gays in the military, 152; and 1992 election campaign, 128; prohibition of discrimina-tion based on sexual orientation in fed-eral agencies, 154; and Rwandan genocide, 105, 280n2
Cold War, and ethnocentrism, 89–91
communism, goal of preventing spread of, and ethnocentrism, 91
compassion, cognitive underpinnings of, 123
Comprehensive Anti-Apartheid Act, 112
Conover, Pamela Johnston, 296n7
conservatism, 254n51; distinct from ethno-centrism, 58, 61, 87; genetic components of, 29
containment, doctrine of, 89, 90
Converse, Philip, 232
Coser, Lewis A.: *The Functions of Social Con-flict*, 9–10
cosmopolitanism, and ethnocentrism, 227–28
Cross-Cultural Study of Ethnocentrism, 251n35
Cuban exiles, American opposition to refu-gee status for, 129

Dade County, Florida, persecution of gays and lesbians, 154
Dahl, Robert, 39
Dahrendorf, Ralf, 9
Darfur, genocide in, 235
Darwin, Charles: *The Descent of Man*, 25–26; *On the Origin of Species by Means of Natu-ral Selection*, 24
Delli Carpini, Michael X., 225

Democrats: attitudes toward spending on welfare and Social Security, 198; attitudes toward war on terrorism, 84

Department of Homeland Security, 76, 80

Desert Storm, 74, 93, 99; emotional reactions to, 119–20; ethnocentrism and support for war in 1990, 1991, and 1992, 91–93, 99–103

Dirksen, Everett, 123

"Don't Ask, Don't Tell," 153

Downs, Anthony: *An Economic Theory of Democracy*, 36–37

Du Bois, W. E. B.: *The Souls of Black Folk*, 217

education: higher, effect on ethnocentrism, 65–66, 268n55; higher, effect on ethnocentrism before and after propensity score matching, 270n55; and tolerance, 34–35

Ellwood, David, 184

El Salvador, 115

Elster, Jon: *Nuts and Bolts for the Social Sciences*, 35–36, 230

Emerson, Ralph Waldo, 182

emotion: responses to Desert Storm, 93, 119–20; role in agenda setting, 256n13

Enloe, Cynthia, 49

environmental issues, and ethnocentrism, 221

Equal Employment Opportunity Commission (EEOC), 177

equal rights amendment (ERA), 172

Erikson, Robert S., 235

ethnic hatred, 253n49

ethnocentrism: and antidemocratic sentiments, 33, 232; causal relation to prejudice, 208–15; and commanding attention, 38–39; consequences of, 35–41; contrasted with intolerance, 246n4; and cosmopolitanism, 227–28; defined, 7–8; distinguished from authoritarianism, 225–27; distribution of based on group sentiment, 58; distribution of based on racial stereotypes, 56; division of world into in-groups and out-groups, 8, 42, 47, 85–89, 173, 219; durability, 66–68, 220, 228; and education, 65–66, 268n55, 270n55; foundational element of public opinion, 220; and framing, 39–41; as general predisposition, 8; and group attachment, 217, 246n4; ignored in empirical studies of American public

opinion, 2, 245n3; and intolerance, 17–18; and knowledge, 222–25; and multiple party systems, 231; and nativism, 246n4; nature of, 31–32; outside the U.S., 229–31; as prejudice, broadly conceived, 11, 42, 52–55, 85, 104, 139, 142; primacy of race in American, 230; and race prejudice, 217; as readiness to act, 36; relation of parental and offspring, 63–64, 267nn48–49; sources of evidence, 42–44; Sumner's view of, 1–2; surveys, variables, and coding, 237–39; and tendency to view groups as natural kinds, 162

ethnocentrism, ACTIVATION OF, 36, 96–103; effect on voter turnout in 2004 in states with and without same-sex ballot initiatives, 169–70, 300n28; and opposition to foreign aid before and after 9/11, 121–22; and opposition to gay rights in 2004 in states with and without same-sex ballot initiatives, 166–70, 300nn26–27; and opposition to immigration conditional upon increase in state's foreign-born population, 147–49; and opposition to immigration under conditions of low and high salience, 146–47; and opposition to same-sex marriage by exposure to antigay marriage campaigns, 168–69; and support for Desert Storm in 1990, 1991, and 1992, 99–103, 279n39, 280n40; and support for war on terrorism immediately after 9/11, 97; and support for war on terrorism in 2000 NES and 2002 NES, 97–99, 100, 279n37

ethnocentrism, AND AMERICAN ATTITUDES TOWARD FOREIGN AID: attitudes toward aid before and after 9/11, 121–22; attitudes toward aid for countries of Eastern Europe, 109–10, 111, 281n8; attitudes toward aid for countries of former Soviet Union, 110, 111; attitudes toward aid in general, 107–9, 122, 281n5; attitudes toward aid in particular, 109–18, 122

ethnocentrism, AND AMERICAN ATTITUDES TOWARD GAY RIGHTS: and belief in immorality of sexual practices, 161–62; and beliefs about nature of homosexuality, 162–63; and opposition to gay rights, 154–57, 297n9; and opposition to

ethnocentrism, AND AMERICAN ATTI-
TUDES TOWARD GAY RIGHTS (*cont.*)
gay rights in 2004 in states with and
without same-sex ballot initiatives,
166–70; and opposition to same-sex marriage by exposure to antigay marriage
campaigns, 168–69; and support for political responses to AIDS, 159–60, 163,
165

ethnocentrism, AND AMERICAN ATTI-
TUDES TOWARD IMMIGRATION, 129–36;
effects among Hispanic Americans, 142–
44; increasing effects as immigrant population becomes less familiar, 138–39; and
in-group pride and out-group hostility,
139–42; and opposition to immigration,
132, 136–37; and opposition to immigration conditional upon increase in state's
foreign-born population, 147–49; and opposition to immigration controlling for
attitudes toward Hispanics and Asians,
141; and opposition to immigration under
conditions of low and high salience, 146–
47; and view of consequences of immigration, 132–36. *See also* immigration to U.S.,
American opposition to

ethnocentrism, AND AMERICAN ATTI-
TUDES TOWARD PROBLEMS OF OTHER
NATIONS, 105–6; ambivalence toward
Nicaraguan contras, 117–18; attitudes toward sanctions against South Africa, 1990,
113–15, 281n10, 282nn11–13; indifference to
casualties of war, 119–20; indifference to
suffering of others, 113, 123–24

ethnocentrism, AND AMERICAN ATTI-
TUDES TOWARD WAR AND CONFRON-
TATION, 2, 3–4, 35; and approval of
George H. W. Bush's performance, 93,
101–2; and approval of George W. Bush's
performance, 83, 95, 98; and the Cold
War, 89–91; and favoring of military intervention over diplomacy, 93; and opposition to Soviet Union, 90–91; and support for Desert Storm, 91–93; and support
for Desert Storm in 1990, 1991, and 1992,
99–103; and support for military action to
remove Saddam Hussein, 94, 95; and support for tougher dealings with Russia, 95,
116; and support for war on terrorism,

78–89, 94, 97; support for war on terrorism
in 2000 NES and 2002 NES, 97–99,
100

ethnocentrism, AND AMERICAN ATTI-
TUDES TOWARD WOMEN'S RIGHTS: and
abortion rights, 173–76; and sexual harassment, 179–80; and "women's issues,"
176–78

ethnocentrism, AND WHITE AMERICANS'
ATTITUDES TOWARD THE WELFARE
STATE, 185–99; and in-group pride, out-
group hostility, and support for social
insurance programs, 189; and opinion
on human capital programs, 190–91; and
opinion on human capital programs targeted either on poor Americans or on
black Americans, 194–98; and opposition
to Head Start, 191, 193; and opposition to
means-tested welfare, 186, 306n19; and racialization of programs, 199; and support
for social insurance, 186–89

ethnocentrism, CORRELATES OF, 58–61;
egalitarian principles, 60; ideological
identification, 60, 87; limited government,
59–60; partisanship, 59; social trust, 60–61

ethnocentrism, IN REALM OF RACE AMONG
AFRICAN AMERICANS, 202–6; and opinions on policies designed to help blacks,
215–16; and opinions on policies targeting black, Hispanic, and Asian Americans,
203–4; and support for liberal racial policy, 202; and support for race policy with
or without controlling for sense of common fate, 205–6

ethnocentrism, IN REALM OF RACE AMONG
WHITE AMERICANS, 206–15; and opinions on policies designed to help blacks,
215–16; and opinions on policies targeting black, Hispanic, and Asian Americans, 208–9; and opinions on policy with
and without controlling for prejudice,
212–14; and opposition to race policy, 206,
207; and opposition to race policy with
or without controlling for race prejudice,
210–12; and prejudice, 206, 208–15

ethnocentrism, MEASURING, 44–48; commonly expressed through stereotypes, 44,
45; primary measure of using stereotypes,
55–57; secondary measure using thermom-

eter scale, 57–58, 84–85; using nonracial criteria, 313n16

ethnocentrism, ORIGINS OF: consolidation and stability in adulthood, 35; early readiness, 33; education, 34–35, 65–66; genetic transmission and social learning, 33–34, 62; parents, 61–64; personality, 11–18, 34, 64–65. *See also* ethnocentrism, theories of

ethnocentrism, POLITICAL IMPLICATIONS, 231–36; as an imperfect solution for ideological innocence, 232–33; and general political participation, 233–34; and policy, 234–36

ethnocentrism, THEORIES OF: as consequence of realistic group conflict, 9–11; as expression of social identity, 18–24; as outcome of natural selection, 24–29; as outgrowth of authoritarian personality, 11–18

ethnocentrism scale, 13, 15, 248n14

Euripedes, 2

Europe, and anti-immigrant prejudice, 229

Family Leave and Medical Leave Act, 177–78

Family Research Council, 153

Feldman, Stanley, 17, 88, 137, 225, 226, 296n7; measure of authoritarianism, 250n22

Festinger, Leon, 251n31

Fisher, R. A., 27

Flament, Claude, 250n27

Focus on the Family, 152, 153

folkways, 1

food stamps. *See* means-tested income transfers; welfare system

Ford, Gerald, 188

foreign aid: American support for versus support for other government programs, 1973–2004, 106–7. *See also* ethnocentrism, and American attitudes toward foreign aid

framing effects, 258n18, 258n20; command of citizens' attention and how they think, 40–41; and ethnocentrism, 39–41

Frenkel-Brunswik, Else, 11–16, 248n16

friendliness, ethnocentric attitudes about among all ethnic groups, 51

F scale (fascism scale), 13, 15, 247n14, 249n21

gay marriage. *See* gay rights; same-sex marriage, and state ballot initiatives

gay rights, 180; Christian Right opposition to, 152, 154, 166, 180; public opinion on, 151, 152–57; religiosity, and opposition to, 154. *See also* ethnocentrism, and American attitudes toward gay rights; same-sex marriage, and state ballot initiatives

gays in the military, 152, 153, 294n3

Geertz, Clifford, 7

gender, and ethnocentrism, 297n7

General Social Surveys (GSS), 43–44, 237; measure of ethnocentrism in terms of stereotypes, 45; social groups defined by race, 46; surveys, variables, and coding, 238; variable codes, 243

genocide, and U.S. inaction, 105, 123–24, 235, 280n2

glasnost, 109

Goodridge v. Department of Public Health, 165–66

Gorbachev, Mikhail, 90, 109

Great Society, 125

group, psychological defining point, 32

group conflict theory, 289n23. *See also* realistic group conflict theory

group identification: and ethnocentrism among African Americans, 204–6; and ethnocentrism among Hispanic Americans, 291n34

group selection theory, and ethnocentrism as an adaptation, 26–27, 252n44

group stereotypes: held by whites, 54; held by whites, blacks, Hispanics, and Asians, 49–51; measures of, 43

Gulf War. *See* Desert Storm

Haldane, J. B., 27

Hamilton, William, 252n45

Head Start, 183; activation of ethnocentrism and racialization of, 191, 194; African American support for, 306n16; ethnocentrism and white opposition to, 191, 193, 194

Heider, F., 257n15

Higham, John: *Strangers in the Land*, 2, 206, 208, 246n2, 246n4

higher education: effect on ethnocentrism, 65–66, 268n55; effect on ethnocentrism before and after propensity score matching, 270n55

Hill, Anita, 177

Hispanic Americans: ethnocentrism and support for immigration, 131–32, 136, 142–44, 149, 289n24; group identification, 291n34; lack of effect of ethnocentrism on attitudes toward welfare programs, 185, 199; limited in-group favoritism, 50, 51, 68
HIV (human immunodeficiency virus), 158. *See also* AIDS
Hofstadter, Richard, 170
Hogg, Michael A., 21
Horowitz, Donald, 23
Huddy, Leonie, 275n19
human behavioral genetics, 27–29; and heritability of social attitudes, 28–29; "natural experiments," 28
human capital programs: ethnocentrism and white opinion on, 190–91, 193; favorably viewed by most Americans, 184–85; Head Start, 183, 191, 193, 194, 306n16; Job Corps, 183; Job Training Partnership Act, 183
Hussein, Saddam, 74, 75, 77, 100, 119
Hyman, Herbert, 248n17

identity: as psychological matter, 20. *See also* social identity theory
Illegal Immigration Reform and Immigrant Responsibility Act, 126, 146
immigrants: first-generation, and ethnocentrism, 127–28; illegal, 125, 126; increase in between 1990 and 2000, 285n4; from Latin America and Asia, 125; patterns of settlement, 292n36; of 1980s and 1990s, 125, 145; share of U.S. population, 1900–2005, 126. *See also* immigration to U.S., American opposition to
Immigration and Nationality Act Amendments, 125
Immigration Reform and Control Act of 1986, 126
Immigration Restriction Act of 1924, 125
immigration to U.S., American opposition to, 126–29, 132, 138, 290n29; and economic pessimism, 130; and in-group pride and out-group hostility, 139–42; and moral traditionalism, 130; and parochialism, 129; and partisanship, 130; and perception of threat, 129–30; and political principles, 130; and scapegoating, 129. *See also* ethno-centrism, and American attitudes toward immigration
independent variables, surveys, variables, and coding, 239–43
inequalities, durable, 200; race as, 217–18
in-group solidarity, 48–52; African Americans, 50, 51, 68, 200–201; Asian Americans, 50; and conflict, 10; defined by attraction and identification, 32; expressed through sentiment, 52, 68; expressed through stereotypes, 49–50, 68; Hispanic Americans, 50, 51, 68; limited connection with out-group prejudice, 55; and minimal group experiments, 19–20; moderated by sense of fairness, 21; testing for using stereotypes, 49–51; testing for using thermometer scale, 51–52; white Americans, 50, 51
intolerance, and ethnocentrism, 17–18, 246n4
Iran-contra affair, 116, 117
Iraq, invasion of Kuwait by, 91

Jahoda, Marie, 248n17
Jencks, Christopher, 177
Jennings, M. Kent, 62, 63, 66, 237, 265n39, 266n44, 268n55
Jewish exiles, American opposition to opening U.S. borders to, 129
Job Corps, 183
Job Training Partnership Act, 183
Johnson, Lyndon: Executive Order 11246, 176–77; Great Society, 125; War on Poverty, 183, 191
Jones, Bryan D., 258n17
Jones-Correa, Michael, 127

Kahneman, Daniel, 37, 40, 53, 256n12
Keeter, Scott, 225
Kennan, George, doctrine of containment, 89, 90
Kerry, John, 166
Key, V. O.: *Public Opinion and American Democracy*, 231, 289n23; *Southern Politics in State and Nation*, 11, 35, 247n7
Kinder, Donald R., 37, 201
Kurds, indifference to plight of, and ethnocentrism, 119–20
Kuwait, 91

Lane, Robert, 60
LePen, Jean, French voters' support for, 229
LeVine, Robert, 48, 246n2, 251n35
Levinson, Daniel: and meaning and mea-
    surement of ethnocentrism, 57, 247n10;
    and origins of authoritarianism, 248n16.
    See also *The Authoritarian Personality*
    (Adorno et al.)
Lévi-Strauss, Claude, 219, 246n2
Likert method, 15
Lippmann, Walter: *Public Opinion*, 259n3; on
    public political interest, 38
Lipset, Seymour Martin: *Party Systems and
    Voter Alignments* (with Rokkan), 254n2;
    on social class, 296n7
low-status groups, evaluation of high-status
    groups, 51
Luker, Kristin, 174

MacKuen, Michael B., 235
Marcus, George E., 255n8
Markovits, Andrei S., 229
Marshall, George C., 122
Marshall Plan, 122–23
Martin, N. G., 29
Marx, Karl, 9
Massachusetts Colony, 1700 law denying en-
    try to sick or physically disabled immi-
    grants, 129
Mayr, Ernst, 24
McCain, John, 147, 291n36
McCarthy hearings, 34
McGuire, William, 253n49
means-tested income transfers, 182–83; Aid
    to Families with Dependent Children
    (AFDC), 182, 184; ethnocentrism and op-
    position to among white Americans, 186,
    192, 193; food stamps, 182, 184; Medicaid,
    182; offensive to Americans, 183–84, 303n7,
    305n14
Medicaid, 182
Medicare, 183, 236
Mendel, Gregor, law of single-gene inheri-
    tance, 27
Milgram, Stanley, 22
Mill, John Stuart, 181
minimal group experiments, 18–23, 250n27,
    251n37

Minnesota Study of Twins Reared Apart
    (MISTRA), 253n48
Monroe, Kristen, 313n15
Mouton, Jane S., 246n6
Mueller, John, 99–100
Multi-City Study of Urban Inequality
    (MCSUI), 50–51, 203–4, 208, 237, 261n16,
    292n39; surveys, variables, and coding,
    238–39; variable codes, 243
multiple party systems, and ethnocentrism,
    231

National Black Election Study (NBES),
    204–5, 237; surveys, variables, and coding,
    239; variable codes, 243
National Election Studies (NES), 43–44, 60,
    64, 116, 237; "feeling thermometer" scale,
    47–48; lack of questions about Africa over
    last twenty-five years, 122; social groups
    defined by race, 46; surveys, variables, and
    coding, 237–38; variable codes, 242
National Front, 229, 231
National Organization of Women, 177
nativism, and ethnocentrism, 206, 208, 246n4
"natural experiments," 28, 96
natural kind categories, 255n3
natural selection, ethnocentrism as outcome
    of, 24–29
nepotism, 252n45
New Deal, 183, 198
Newell, Allen, 257n15
news media, and agenda setting, 39, 258n16
Newsom, Gavin, 166
Nicaraguan contras, 115–16
North, Oliver, 116
Nussbaum, Martha, 123, 227–28, 313n15

Obama, Barak, 217
out-group animosity: and conflict, 10; gener-
    ality and consistency of, 16; limits on con-
    nection to in-group loyalty, 22, 55
out-groups: defined by condescension and
    opposition, 32; stereotyping of, 45

parents and children, relation of ethnocen-
    trism, 63–64, 267nn48–49
parochialism, and opposition to immigra-
    tion, 129

partial-birth abortion, 174
partisanship: and opposition to immigration, 130; and political awareness, 275n18; relation to ethnocentrism, 59; roughly equal influence with ethnocentrism, 220–21; and support for war on terrorism, 79, 84
Patriot Act, 75, 80
perception of threat, and opposition to immigration, 129–30
perestroika, 109
Persian Gulf War. See Desert Storm
personality: heritability of, 28, 254n52; and origins of ethnocentrism, 11–18, 34, 64–65. See also authoritarianism
Pettigrew, Thomas, 246n2, 246n4
Piereson, James E., 255n8
Pitkin, Hanna, 314n26
political engagement, measure of, 222–23, 312n9
political institutions, and expression of ethnocentrism in politics, 230
political knowledge, and effect of ethnocentrism on opinion, 223–24, 311–12n7
political opinion. See public opinion
Political Socialization Study, 237; surveys, variables, and coding, 239
political tolerance, 34
Posner, Daniel, 46
Power, Samantha, 123–24
prejudice: causal relation of ethnocentrism to, 208–15; contrasted with ethnocentrism, 8, 206, 208; and ethnocentrism, 217; and ethnocentrism among white Americans, 206, 208–15, 310nn19–20; ethnocentrism as, broadly conceived, 11, 42, 85, 104, 139, 142; white American opposition to affirmative action and ethnocentrism, controlling for, 210–12, 217. See also race prejudice
pro-life movement, 173–74
Proposition 187, California, 145
psychodynamic theory, and antidemocratic belief, 12, 14
public opinion: agenda-setting and news media, 39, 258n16; and bounded rationality, 37–38; defined, 35; effect on government policy, 235; ethnocentrism as foundational element of, 220; and media

agenda-setting, 39, 258n16; models of formation, 257n15
Putnam, Robert, 60

race: as central theme of American political life, 200; as durable inequality, 217–18; folk theory of, 46
race segregation, as central organizing principle of American social life, 217–18
racial code, 199
racial divide, 201
racism: contrasted with ethnocentrism, 246n4. See also prejudice
rational choice theory, 36–37, 40
Reagan, Ronald, 90, 109, 112; and immigration, 126; silence on AIDS epidemic, 158; support for Nicaraguan contras, 115
realistic group conflict theory, 10–11, 18, 19, 129, 247nn5, 8
reference group theory, 254n1
religiosity: and opposition to gay rights, 154; and opposition to government spending on AIDS, 154
representative democracy, 234–35, 314n26
Republicans: attitudes toward immigration, 130; attitudes toward spending on welfare and Social Security, 198; support for war on terrorism, 79, 84
Rhum, Michael, 246n2
Roe v. Wade, 172, 173
Rokkan, Stein: Party Systems and Voter Alignments (with Lipset), 254n2
Romer v. Evans, 154
Roosevelt, Franklin D., 188, 198
Rosenberg, Milton J., 39, 257n15
Rwandan genocide, and U.S. inaction, 105, 123, 235, 280n2
Ryan White Comprehensive AIDS Resources Emergency Act, 158

same-sex marriage, and state ballot initiatives, 153, 164–70, 180, 234, 294n11; effect on voter turnout in 2004 in states with and without same-sex ballot initiatives, 169–70; opposition to by exposure to antigay marriage campaigns, 168–69
Sanders, Lynn M., 201
Sandinistas, 115

Sanford, Neville, study of authoritarian personality, 11–16, 248n16

Scalia, Anton, 164–65, 299n23

scapegoating, and opposition to immigration, 129

Schroeder, Patricia, 177

September 11, 2001, 39, 74–76; Bush response to, 74–75, 77, 275n17; ethnocentrism, and attitudes toward foreign aid before and after, 121–22; ethnocentrism, and support for war on terrorism immediately after, 97; and stability of ethnocentrism before and after, 67–68

sexual harassment, 177; ethnocentrism and attitudes toward, 179–80

Sheatsley, Paul B., 248n17

Sherif, Muzafer, and Robbers Cave study, 10, 18, 247n6, 251n37

Silver, M., 250n28

Simmel, Georg, 9, 246n5

Simon, Herbert, 37, 256nn12–13, 257n15, 258n19

slavery, 200

Smith, Adam, 113; The Theory of Moral Sentiments, 105–6

Smith, Rogers, 227

Sniderman, Paul, 229, 230

Sober, Elliott, 26

social attitudes, heritability of, 28–29

social categorization, and identity, 20–21

social identity theory, 18–24, 251n31, 262n19, 271n58

social insurance programs: ethnocentrism and support for among white Americans, 186–89, 192; favorably viewed by most Americans, 184; in-group pride, out-group hostility, and white support for, 189; Medicare, 183; Social Security, 183; unemployment insurance, 183

social learning theory: and ethnocentrism, 33–34; and parents, 61, 63

social psychology, European perspective on, 18

Social Security, 183, 235; age and attitudes toward, 198; Republican and Democratic attitudes toward spending on, 198; symbolic association with whiteness, 188

social trust, measurement of, 265nn36–37

Sorel, Elliott, 9

South Africa: apartheid, 110–12; ethnocentrism, and American attitudes toward sanctions against, 1990, 113–15, 281n10, 282nn11–13; Nationalist Party, 110

southern black belt, and reactionary politics, 11, 247n7

South Vietnamese, American opposition to assisting evacuation of, 129

Soviet Union: dissolution of, 89, 109; opposition to, and ethnocentrism, 90–91

Stenner, Karen, 225–26; The Authoritarian Dynamic, 17–18, 64, 88, 137; authoritarianism as universal predisposition, 255n6; relevance of authoritarianism when social cohesion is threatened, 255n11

stereotypes, 259n3; ethnocentrism expressed through, 44, 45, 56; grounded in ordinary cognitive processes, 44–45; group, 43, 54; in-group solidarity expressed through, 49–50, 68; permeated by affect, 45; portrayal of out-group members, 45

Stimson, James A., 235

Stoker, Laura, 237

Stokes, Donald, 220

"Stonewall Riots," 151

Stouffer, Samuel, 34, 65

subjective rationality, 257n15

Sullivan, John L., 255n8

Sumner, William Graham, 7, 9, 29, 254n1; definition of ethnocentrism, 1–2; on ethnocentrism and conflict, 73; on ethnocentrism as universal condition, 36, 48, 51; Folkways (A Study of the Sociological Importance of Usages, Manners, Customs, Mores, and Morals), 1, 9, 48; linking of in-group solidarity with out-group prejudice, 55; political pursuits, 245n1; The Science of Society (with Keller and Davie), 9, 48

Tajfel, Henri, 7, 30; ethnocentrism as one-way street, 51; minimal group experiment, 18–20, 22–23, 36, 250n27; and social comparison processes, 251n31; social identity theory, 18–20, 251n31, 262n19, 271n58

Takaki, Ronald, 125, 285n4

Taliban, 75

Thomas, Clarence, 177

threat, perceptions of likely terrorist attack, 79–80
Tilly, Charles, 200, 217
Tocqueville, Alexis de, 60
Tower Commission, 116
Truman, Harry S., 122
Tversky, Amos, 37, 40, 53, 256n12
twin studies, in human behavioral genetics, 28–29

unemployment insurance, 183, 198
U.S. military, policy of exclusion of gays, 153

Van den Berghe, Pierre, 252n45
Verba, Sidney, 60
Voice and Equality (Verba, Schlozman, and Brady), 312n9
The Voter Decides (Campbell, Gurin, and Miller), 312n9

War on Poverty, 183, 191
war on terrorism, support for, 39, 76–78; and authoritarianism, 88–89; and education, 79; and ethnocentrism, 79–80, 81, 82–83, 84, 94, 97–99, 100, 272n4, 313n13; and in-group pride and out-group hostility, 86–87; and partisanship, 79, 84; and perception of threat, 79–80, 313n13
Weiss, Janet A., 37
welfare system: Democratic attitudes toward spending on, 198; human capital programs, 183; means-tested income transfers, 182–83; public opinion of, 184–85; social insurance, 183. See also ethnocentrism, and white Americans' attitudes toward the welfare state

White, Ryan, 158
white Americans: ethnocentrism and attitudes toward the welfare state, 185–93; ethnocentrism and opposition to immigration, 136; ethnocentrism and prejudice among, 206, 208–15, 310nn19–20; ethnocentrism and social trust, 265n37; ethnocentrism in realm of race, 206–15, 306n18; general in-group favoritism, 50, 51; race prejudice, ethnocentrism, opposition to affirmative action, 210–12; support for social insurance programs and ethnocentrism, 186–89, 192
Wiley, D., 66, 270n56, 271n58
Wiley, J., 66, 270n56, 271n58
Wilson, David Sloan, 26
Wilson, Edward O., 7, 27, 29, 30; approach to activation, 36; Consilience, 24; Genes, Mind, and Culture, 24; on genetic differences in human behavior, 62; On Human Nature, 24; on relation of ethnocentrism and aggression, 103–4, 252n42; Sociobiology: The New Synthesis, 24, 252n40
Wilson, William J.: Power, Racism, and Privilege, 246n4
Winter, Nicholas, 188
women's rights, 172–73; and abortion rights, 173–76; and affirmative action, 177, 302n10; ethnocentrism and attitudes toward, 176–78, 180–81, 221, 302n10
Wright, S., 27

xenophobia, 246n4

Zajong, Robert, 258n15
Zaller, John, 35, 222–23, 311nn4–5

DATE DUE

BRODART, CO.   Cat. No. 23-221